With a Foreword by J. Carter Brown, Director,
National Gallery of Art

Selected Photography by Richard Cheek

Alfred A. Knopf 🐎 New York 1980

In Praise of America

American Decorative Arts, 1650-1830 / Fifty Years of Discovery Since the 1929 Girl Scouts Loan Exhibition

Wendy A. Cooper

For the late Charles F. Montgomery
whose scholarly drive and enthusiastic delight
in objects continues to be an inspiration to
both his students and colleagues alike

This is a Borzoi Book
Published by Alfred A. Knopf, Inc.

Copyright © 1980 by Girl Scouts of the United States of America.
All rights reserved under International and Pan-American
Copyright Conventions. Published in the United States by
Alfred A. Knopf, Inc., New York, and simultaneously in
Canada by Random House of Canada Limited, Toronto.
Distributed by Random House, Inc., New York.

Girls Scouts of the U.S.A. expresses its sincere gratitude to the
following corporations and foundations whose generous support
contributed to the development of this book.

Ford Motor Company Fund
and
Barra Foundation, Inc.
Candid Productions, Inc.
DABCO/Frank Foundation, Inc.
D.A.B. Industries, Inc.
Hennage Creative Printers, Inc.
Kennedy Galleries
Israel Sack, Inc.
Sack Foundation
Wunsch Americana Foundation

Library of Congress Cataloging in Publication Data
Cooper, Wendy A.   In praise of America.
Includes index.
1. Art industries and trade, Early American.
2. Art industries and trade—United States—History—19th
century. 3. Antiques—United States. I. Title.
NK806.C63 1980   745'.0974   79-3477
ISBN 0-394-50994-3

Manufactured in the United States of America
First American Edition

Cover Photograph by Richard Cheek:
Center Table, New York, 1810–15,
from the Collection of Mr. and Mrs. Stuart P. Feld.
Cover Design by Janet Odgis.
Cover Calligraphy by Gun Larsen.

Graphic Credits
The text of this book was set in a film version of Palatino that
has been redrawn from the face created by the noted German
typographer Herman Zapf. Named after Giovanbattista Pala-
tino, a writing master of Renaissance Italy, Palatino is beauti-
fully balanced and exceedingly readable. This book was
photo-composed in film by New England Typographic Service,
Inc., Bloomfield, Connecticut. The black-and-white reproduc-
tions were scanned by Alithochrome Corporation, Hauppauge,
New York. The color separations were produced by Offset
Separations, New York, New York, and Turin, Italy. The
book was printed by Rae Publishing Co., Inc., Cedar Grove,
New Jersey, and bound by American Book–Stratford Press,
Inc., Saddle Brook, New Jersey. Production and manufacturing
were directed by Carole Frankel. Manuscript and proofs were
supervised by John Woodside. Graphics were directed by
R. D. Scudellari. Art direction and design by Janet Odgis.

Contents

Sponsor's Foreword

In Praise of America: 1650–1830 is more than a celebration of the fiftieth anniversary of the now historic Girl Scouts Loan Exhibition. It also commemorates the foresight of our predecessors in the Girl Scouts movement, and it reaffirms our belief that American youth should be encouraged to acquire an appreciation of the beauty of superior craftsmanship.

In undertaking this project, Girl Scouts of the United States of America has been privileged to have the counsel of a remarkable group of people—curators, collectors, and other connoisseurs whose dedication to our American heritage is unsurpassed. For their support and unflagging pursuit of excellence we are especially indebted to the members of the advisory committee whose names appear at right and to Wendy A. Cooper, guest curator, for the outstanding scholarship which has enriched this publication.

We also express appreciation to J. Carter Brown and his talented staff at the National Gallery of Art for their collaboration in this fiftieth anniversary celebration, to numerous museums for making research sources available, and to those private and institutional collectors who generously permitted us to reproduce the illustrations which appear throughout the pages of this work.

Finally, on behalf of Girl Scouts everywhere, we acknowledge with sincere gratitude our great debt to Mrs. Harold L. Frank, member of our board of directors and chairman of the advisory committee, who originally conceived the project and carried it forward with unparalleled enthusiasm and skill.

MRS. ORVILLE L. FREEMAN, NATIONAL PRESIDENT, GIRL SCOUTS OF THE U.S.A.

ADVISORY COMMITTEE

MRS. HAROLD L. FRANK, CHAIRMAN

MRS. ROBERT L. McNEIL, JR., CO-CHAIRMA

MR. ERIC M. WUNSCH, CO-CHAIRMAN

MR. CLEMENT E. CONGER

MR. LAWRENCE FLEISCHMAN

MR. WENDELL D. GARRETT

MR. JOSEPH H. HENNAGE

MR. GRAHAM S. HOOD

MR. CHARLES F. HUMMEL

MISS JULIE KAMMERER

PROFESSOR CHARLES F. MONTGOMERY

PROFESSOR JULES D. PROWN

MR. HAROLD SACK

MR. BERRY TRACY

*A*rt exhibitions serve scholarship in a variety of ways. They provide an impetus to survey our current knowledge and bring together in print the advances made in our understanding of the past. They help chart the unanswered questions and point the way to future study. They put the research that underlies an exhibition, which is necessarily temporary, into a lasting form. And by juxtaposing objects in their physical reality, they kindle fresh awareness, and allow us to assess the significance of our visual legacy.

One of the most influential exhibitions in the field of American art was the one held in 1929, at the American Art Association's galleries in New York, and organized as a benefit for Girl Scouts of the United States of America. It inspired a generation of collectors, scholars, and connoisseurs. As the fiftieth anniversary of that exhibition approached, the Girl Scouts commissioned Wendy A. Cooper, a talented curator at the Museum of Fine Arts, Boston, to begin research on an exhibition in the same field, to be entitled "In Praise of America."

The survey of the field undertaken by Ms. Cooper, and the scholarly documentation of the objects investigated in that project, have resulted in this book.

After plans for a very large anniversary exhibition in New York proved to be impractical the National Gallery offered to find space in an already crowded exhibition schedule to present a distillation of that material. This has allowed us to combine the best of two worlds. The scholarly publication could be expanded, surveying fifty years of discovery since the 1929 show, while the gallery could mount a rigorously selected anthology in its new East Building, drawing attention to the aesthetic quality of the material. This is the first time a show at the gallery has focused solely on American decorative arts, isolating individual objects as works of art in their own right. Meanwhile the simultaneous publication of this book puts those objects into the broader context of contemporary scholarship.

It is therefore with pride that the National Gallery of Art heralds the publication of this handsome volume in conjunction with the exhibition of the same name. It is time that we count among our country's artistic achievements the contributions of an earlier skilled and sophisticated society of artisans. Geographically standing at the center of the original colonies, the capital is a most appropriate place for this tribute to those who have helped shape our national cultural heritage.

J. CARTER BROWN, DIRECTOR, NATIONAL GALLERY OF ART

Author's Note

All measurements in the book have been taken
to the nearest eighth of an inch, and represent
overall dimensions. In the case of seating furniture, however, the measurement of the overall
depth was taken at the seat. Those illustrations
marked with a ■ are objects shown in the exhibition "In Praise of America, 1650–1830," at
the National Gallery of Art, Washington,
D.C., from February 17 through July 6, 1980.

In Praise of America

Introduction

On September 25, 1929, the Girl Scouts Loan Exhibition opened in New York City at the American Art Association's galleries on the corner of Madison Avenue and Fifty-Seventh Street, the forerunner of Sotheby Parke Bernet. Although the exhibition lasted only two weeks, closing on October 9, the New York *Sun* praised it as "the finest display of early American furniture ever got together in one place at one time." Malcolm Vaughan, of the New York *Herald Tribune,* reflected with tremendous pride that "the great collectors of New York have consented to lend their American antiques for public exhibition" and that "most of these rarities have never before been seen in public and probably never will be again on view in this generation." Perhaps the most interesting comment was in the *Herald Tribune* of September 22, 1929, where Vaughan noted:

America today is a nation of collectors more cosmopolitan than any the world has ever known. Yet in the midst of cosmopolitanism our collectors remain finely national. The most widespread love among them is for the relics of our ancestors. The majority of our collectors want to surround themselves—especially in their country houses, where they have the most leisure—with the furniture of our forebears, the portraits of our early Americans and the china, glass and precious bric-a-brac of those who gave our nation to us. This Americana passion is so widespread at present as to be an epidemic rage.

Undoubtedly, the high point of the exhibition was the superb furniture, over three hundred pieces made between about 1650 and 1830. This vast quantity of furniture was grouped according to chronological style and then carefully placed in charming room settings, complete with glorious bouquets of flowers arranged by Mrs. Giles Whiting, a lender and noted early collector (figs. 1 and 2). Thirty-four American oil paintings, primarily portraits (see pls. 1 and 2), were hung throughout the rooms in places compatible with the dates of the furniture. In addition to the furniture and oils, the exhibition contained twenty-eight watercolors, about seventy-five pieces of English lustreware from the collection of Andrew Varick Stout, twenty-five pieces of what was then termed "Sino-Lowestof," and approximately five hundred pieces of American glass from the collection of George S. McKearin. These smaller, more delicate items were displayed in glass cases lining the hallways of the American Art Association Building (figs. 3 and 4). The intent of this large, important exhibition was to present objects of supreme beauty and aesthetic excellence in both design and craftsmanship. From the viewpoint of scholars today, these objects clearly reflect, in addition, the collecting tastes and antiquarianism of the 1920s, according to which objects associated with historical figures were especially revered.

The moving force behind the show was Louis Guerineau Myers, a collector and informal dealer who served as treasurer of the Rockefeller Foundation from 1913 until his death in 1932. Through his association with the Rockefeller family, he was responsible for acquiring many objects for the restoration of Colonial Williamsburg, begun in 1926 by John D. Rockefeller, Jr. Myers's connection with the Girl Scouts was a personal one; his wife was on the National Board of Directors. The show seems to have had its genesis sometime before April of 1929 when Mrs. Myers spoke of it at a National Board Meeting:

When Mrs. Brady [sister of the collector Francis P. Garvan] had her wonderful exhibit of primitives for the benefit of the Clara Club, it occurred to me that if she could do that there was no reason why we couldn't have an exhibition of Americana. I talked it over with her and she wanted to know what I thought about the possibility so we wished it on my husband. He went to the managers of the American Art Gallery, because he said if the thing is done at all it must be done with a Girl Scout standard, which was the best that could be done, and that the only place we could show the type of furniture we wanted to show was in a very large place, that the American Art Galleries stood for the development of just such exhibitions and was the best known place in the country for us to have it.[1]

In the next five months Louis G. Myers assembled one of the most extraordinary American art exhibitions of the first three decades of the twentieth century. He also produced a sizable and almost fully illustrated catalogue that has become an important resource for the students and collectors who followed. This was not accomplished single-handedly, for Myers had a committee of sponsors composed of the most prominent and knowledgeable collectors and scholars of his day. The preference of Myers and his fellow sponsors for the high-style, sophisticated, urban production of our early craftsmen may be seen in the abundance of furniture in the Queen Anne and Chippendale styles as well as that in the style of Duncan Phyfe's work. The visitors to the

1. The Federal room in the 1929 exhibition in New York. *The focal piece of furniture in this section of the room was Mr. Henry Francis du Pont's Baltimore cylinder-top desk and bookcase, now in the Winterthur Museum.*

2. Outside the Federal room.
This view of the 1929 exhibition installation indicates the expanse of the galleries and the vastness of the show. Just outside the Federal room are two pairs of Philadelphia Queen Anne side chairs owned by Henry Francis du Pont and Mr. and Mrs. Allan B. A. Bradley. The burl-veneered William and Mary high chest of drawers was lent by Mrs. Francis P. Garvan, and the William and Mary dressing table by Mr. du Pont. Over the dressing table is a John Singleton Copley pastel of Mrs. Gawen Brown (now in the Bayou Bend Collection, the Museum of Fine Arts, Houston), and a James Peale portrait of George Washington is over the chairs; both were lent by Mr. and Mrs. Luke Vincent Lockwood.

3. Glass pieces lining the corridors.
The large quantity of glass in the exhibition lined the corridors, with windsor chairs between the cases. The brace-back side chair in figure 254 can be seen on the left with its mate, lent by Mrs. Francis P. Garvan.

4. Furniture in the hallways.
Some of the more elegant Philadelphia furniture was placed in the hallways along with ceramics and prints. The large upholstered armchair in the left rear corner is the Williamsburg-made governor's chair illustrated in figure 121.

5. Chippendale room. *This is a view of the impressive Chippendale room. The Philadelphia settee on the far right was Mr. du Pont's (see fig. 71), along with the unusual Newport block and shell bureau under the Gilbert Stuart portrait of Ann Penn Allen (see pl. 1). Mr. and Mrs. John D. Rockefeller, Jr., lent the Edward Duffield tall case clock and the Philadelphia upholstered armchair with Marlborough legs, both of which are now in the collections of Colonial Williamsburg along with the Massachusetts corner chair. The Massachusetts blockfront desk and bookcase with hairy paw feet was owned by George A. Cluett, and the Philadelphia piecrust tea table was Mrs. Charles Hallam Keep's and is now privately owned.*

6. Philadelphia side chair.
This Philadelphia side chair, 1760–75, bears the label of James Gillingham (1736–81) and is currently in the White House Collection, Washington, D.C. It is almost identical to a side chair in the 1929 exhibition (no. 641 in original catalogue and seen in fig. 5.), and may well have been the labeled chair referred to in the 1929 publication.

6

show seemed to show the same preference as unquestionably the greatest attraction there seemed to be the Queen Anne and Chippendale room (figs. 5 and 7). Mrs. Myers had already outlined the importance of this room when she had spoken to the board at the April 1929 meeting:

> If you don't speak of this, I will tell you some of the advance ideas. Do you know the American Galleries at all? The rooms are enormous. As you go in, there is Room A. I think you all know how difficult it is to get Chippendale furniture. Queen Anne comes first and Chippendale second. That first great big room will be purely a Chippendale drawing room. That has never been done before. We will have everything in it in the way of ornaments and portraits that will go in Chippendale surroundings.[2]

The impressive group of sponsors, many of whom were also lenders, deserves a closer examination. Among the committee members were the most important authors, collectors, scholars, and curators of the early twentieth century. Through this exhibition they exerted a substantial impact on the tastes and collecting preferences of numerous others. In addition, their personal collections set standards of excellence still difficult to surpass today. These men and women, the second generation of collectors of American objects, were spawned by the eccentric antiquarians of the latter half of the nineteenth century and were nurtured on the early publications of their colleagues, Irving W. Lyon (*The Colonial Furniture of New England*, 1891), Esther Singleton (*Furniture of Our Forefathers*, 1901), and Luke Vincent Lockwood (*Colonial Furniture in America*, 1902). In many instances, their collections were given to major museums, and in two specific cases, the collections of Henry F. du Pont and Francis P. Garvan, they became institutions in themselves.

Henry Francis du Pont was the largest single lender to the exhibition, a remarkable achievement since in 1929 he had only been collecting American objects for about three or four years. However, he had bought exuberantly in those few years, and when the show was being planned, many of his purchases were still in storage in New York, awaiting eventual installation in his Delaware home, Winterthur. Looking through the photographs of the 1929 installation, one recognizes many important pieces of furniture that today can be viewed at Winterthur in the over one hundred rooms now open to the public, such as the finely inlaid Baltimore cylinder-top desk and bookcase (in fig. 1), the highly figured, veneered William and Mary dressing table (in fig. 2), the unusual Philadelphia upholstered settee (figs. 5 and 71), and the outstanding eight-legged New York Federal sideboard (in fig. 9). One might assume that Mr. du Pont was one of Myers's close friends judging from the prominence of his collection in the exhibition, but that does not seem to have been the situation. Though he was undoubtedly aware of du Pont's interest in American arts, the fact that Myers hardly knew du Pont is apparent in their correspondence just prior to the show. However, when it came time for the installation, Mr. du Pont must have offered to accompany his objects to the gallery and to help with the final installation. In Mrs. Myers's report to the 1929 meeting of the National Board, it was clear that Mr. du Pont actually played an active role in the installation. Apparently he had arrived with his objects and, as if a matter of course, shed his hat and coat and begun hanging pictures and arranging furniture. Although there were others there to do the heavy work, Mr. du Pont was remembered as having worked as hard as anyone else. This information helps to explain why the 1929 exhibition so closely resembled the rooms at Winterthur today. The importance of the du Pont objects in the exhibition, his integral role in the installation, and ultimately his impact on the acquisition habits of the collectors of the 1960s and 1970s cannot be overemphasized.

Francis P. Garvan was another major lender. His wife was listed as a sponsor and his sister, Mrs. Nicholas F. Brady, was chairman of the National Board of Girl Scouts. He was one of the most important collectors of his day and could not possibly have refused to lend to the exhibition. Garvan had been actively collecting since about 1912 and had amassed an impressive collection that included not only furniture but also notable paintings and some of the most important pieces of American silver as well. In 1930 Garvan began to give his collection to Yale University, a gift that would ultimately include over ten thousand pieces of American craftsmanship. Much like du Pont's resolution that Winterthur become part of a teaching institution, Garvan's initial intent was that this gift should "educate America, and become a moving part in a great

7. Another view of the Chippendale room. *If looked at from the opposite direction (see fig. 5), the view is equally impressive. The "Lansdowne" portrait of* George Washington *by Gilbert Stuart, lent by Mr. and Mrs. Walter B. Jennings, surveys this portion of the exhibition with a monumental aura of authority.*

8. Federal dining room. *The Federal dining room was elegantly installed, with Mrs. Garvan's towering Philadelphia desk and bookcase dominating one wall.*

9. Another Federal dining room. *A second Federal dining room was almost more impressive than the one in figure 8. Mr. du Pont's sideboard, the Peale double portrait, Mr. Louis Guerineau Myers's Baltimore marbletop side table, and Mr. and Mrs. Allan B. A. Bradley's desk and bookcase neatly surround the walls, looking out on the handsome Baltimore dining table (anonymous loan) and Mrs. J. Amory Haskell's magnificent set of New York shieldback chairs.*
Figure 9 is on page 3.

panorama of American arts and crafts which, under the leadership of Yale University, shall be made to pass over the years before every man, woman and child in our country."[3]

Garvan's loans to the 1929 exhibition displayed the broad range of styles in his collection including two early carved chests (a Hadley-type and a so-called Sunflower-type from Wethersfield, Connecticut), an exceptional William and Mary high chest of drawers (in fig. 2), a grand Newport six-shell desk and bookcase (originally owned by John Brown of Providence), and a rare Federal bookcase from Philadelphia (in fig. 8).

Other sponsors and lenders to the exhibition who eventually donated their collections to public or private institutions included Mrs. Harry Horton Benkard, Mrs. J. Insley Blair, Mrs. J. Amory Haskell, and Mr. Andrew Varick Stout. In 1934 Mrs. Benkard gave a complete room including many important furnishings to the Museum of the City of New York in memory of her husband. Mrs. J. Insley Blair presented many outstanding objects to the Metropolitan Museum of Art, including the turned seventeenth-century "Great chair," or "Brewster" chair, that is discussed in Chapter 4 (see fig. 140). Both Mr. Stout and Mrs. Haskell were also generous to the Metropolitan, while the latter was perhaps the most ambitious and prolific of her collecting peers. A fascinating comment illustrating Mrs. Haskell's inveterate collecting instincts came to light recently in a letter from one of her granddaughters:

■ Plate 1. Portrait of *Ann Penn Allen.*
*(Mrs. John Greenleaf, 1769–1851.) Gil-
bert Stuart (1755–1828). Painted in Philadelphia in 1795 and lent to the exhibition
by Richard D. Brixey. Later acquired by
the Metropolitan Museum of Art, it is
now appropriately in the Allentown Art
Museum Collection.*

Plate 2. Portrait of *Benjamin and Eleanor
Ridgely Laming (1788). Charles Willson
Peale's stunning double portrait remains
even today one of his most accomplished
and supreme compositions. In 1929 it was
lent by Mr. and Mrs. Luke Vincent Lockwood; today, it is owned by the National
Gallery of Art, the gift of Morris Schapiro.
Plates 1 and 2 are on pages 10 and 11.*

> I well remember her house—absolutely jammed with furniture, chairs two deep along a huge long
> entrance hall that almost ran the width of the house.... Her front parlor and living room were like-
> wise—like the inside of a used furniture store. I know she left everyday in a chauffeur-driven limousine
> for points unknown to me—all to do with her collection.[4]

The Monmouth County Historical Association in New Jersey received Mrs. Haskell's
bequest including nearly six hundred pieces of furniture. Parke Bernet dispersed the
remainder of her collection in a series of six auction sales in 1944 and 1945, following
her death.

George A. Cluett, another lender, was a native of Troy, New York, who summered in
Williamstown, Massachusetts. His children have lent a portion of his collection and
given a number of objects to the Historic Deerfield Foundation. A number of other
pieces of furniture from his collection are on loan to the Sterling and Francine Clark Art
Institute in Williamstown, including the outstanding hairy-paw-foot Massachusetts
blockfront desk and bookcase (fig. 5) and the Massachusetts blockfront chest-on-chest
(fig. 7).

Luke Vincent Lockwood and R. T. Haines Halsey were two of the foremost collec-
tors-scholars and authors in this field in the early years of this century. Lockwood, a
practicing attorney, devoted all of his leisure time to the study and acquisition of
American furniture, paintings, and silver. His early work, *Colonial Furniture in America*
(1901), had second and third editions in 1913 and 1926 and has recently been reprinted
because of its continuing significance for scholars, students, and collectors.

With Halsey, Lockwood had played a key role in the selection and catalogue preparation of the first great American decorative arts exhibition of this century, the 1909
Hudson-Fulton Exhibition held at the Metropolitan Museum. After that event, he
turned his allegiance to the Brooklyn Museum where he became a governor in 1914.
That same year a department of "Colonial and Early American Furniture" was established at Brooklyn, and in 1915 the museum acquired the woodwork for its first American period room.[5] During the next decade or so, Lockwood was chiefly responsible for
the acquisition of eleven more period rooms, and finally in December 1929 the museum's first group of twelve period rooms was opened to the public. While Lockwood is
most remembered today as a pioneer furniture collector, he also owned some superb
American paintings. Perhaps the most impressive canvas in the 1929 exhibition was
his—a huge double portrait of Benjamin and Eleanor Ridgely Laming painted by Charles
Willson Peale in 1788 (pl. 2). In 1929 it had a position of prominence over Mr. du Pont's
New York sideboard (in fig. 9), not far from Mr. Myers's (and now Winterthur's)
marble-top Baltimore pier table. While Lockwood gave much of his collection away
during his lifetime, portions of it were dispersed shortly after his death in 1951 in a
Parke Bernet sale and more recently in a 1978 sale by a local Connecticut auctioneer.[6]

R. T. Haines Halsey, like Lockwood, had an avocational interest in the American arts
that ultimately eclipsed his professional business interests. Elected to the Board of
Governors of the New York Stock Exchange in 1899, he became a trustee of the Metropolitan in 1914 and within nine years had sold his seat on the Stock Exchange in order to
assume curatorial functions in preparation for the opening of the museum's new American Wing in 1924.[7] During these years, and until his death in 1942, he wrote prolifically
and must certainly be counted among the most devoted and important early American
art scholars.

Three other important scholars of American arts, Fiske Kimball, Charles Over Cornelius, and John Hill Morgan, served on the committee. Fiske Kimball, then director of
the Philadelphia Museum of Art, is best remembered for his publications on *Domestic
Architecture of the American Colonies and of the Early Republic* (1922), *Mr. Samuel McIntire,
Carver, the Architect of Salem* (1940), and *The Creation of the Rococo* (1943). Charles Over
Cornelius was with the Metropolitan Museum of Art from 1917 to 1925 and was
responsible for the first major exhibition and publication of the production of the
workshop of Duncan Phyfe. The exhibition at the Metropolitan in 1922 heightened
admiration for furniture in the ever-popular "Phyfe style." The prominence and abundance of early nineteenth-century New York furniture shown in the 1929 exhibition
(fig. 10) reflected the great popularity of the style among collectors and scholars, a fact
that itself may have contributed to the creation of the "Phyfe myth." Finally, the chief
paintings scholar on the committee was John Hill Morgan, not only a great collector of

PL. 1

paintings and miniatures (many of which are now at Yale) but also the author of *Early American Painters* (1921), *The Life Portraits of Washington and Their Replicas* (with Mantle Fielding in 1931), and *Gilbert Stuart and His Pupils* (1945).

These early collectors focused their primary attention on the aesthetic quality and connoisseurship of objects, yet at the same time they were part of a generation that embraced a cultural and historical perspective of American decorative arts. Their cultural approach, the desire to actually show "how it was," developed from the nineteenth-century antiquarian fever begun even before the 1876 centennial celebrations. The 1880s and 1890s witnessed the first generation of collectors like Cummings Davis of Concord, Massachusetts; Ben: Perley Poore of West Newbury, Massachusetts; George Sheldon of Deerfield; and Henry Davis Sleeper of Gloucester, Massachusetts.[8] Many of these early collectors acquired objects not so much for aesthetic reasons, but rather primarily for cultural or historical ones. Typical of this attitude was George Sheldon's "Note to Visitors" prefacing his *Catalogue of the Collection of Relics in Memorial Hall.*

Not a single article is here preserved on account of its artistic qualities. The Collection is founded on purely historical lines and is the direct memorial of the inhabitants of this valley, both Indian and Puritan. . . . Many articles may seem trivial in themselves, but as a part of the whole broad scheme of the projectors the most humble belong here as much as the most notable.[9]

In order to compare the purposes of the 1929 exhibition with those of this survey, and of the 1980 show, it is important to look briefly at the development of major museum collections of American decorative arts in the first three decades of this century. The first major collection of high-style American furniture to be given to a public institution was bequeathed to the Museum of Art, Rhode Island School of Design, by Charles L. Pendleton in 1904, with the specific provision that a structure be built in the Georgian style to house it. Then, in 1909, the Metropolitan Museum's Hudson-Fulton Exhibition provided the arena for experimenting with the concept of displaying American decora-

PL. 2

10

tive arts in a fine arts museum. The exhibition was very popular, and that same year Mr. Russell Sage gave the Metropolitan funds to purchase from Eugene Bolles his entire American collection of over six hundred pieces of furniture, many of which had been exhibited in the 1909 show. Shortly after this major purchase, the museum began to acquire whole rooms of architectural woodwork, as it had been decided that the most sympathetic and appropriate environment in which to display American decorative arts would be in period room settings. Undoubtedly George Francis Dow's 1907 installation of period rooms at the Essex Institute in Salem, Massachusetts, had some influence on H. W. Kent, Halsey, and Robert W. de Forest, then secretary of the museum. As the Metropolitan continued to purchase and assemble rooms for eventual installation, so did other museums, including the Brooklyn Museum; the Museum of Fine Arts, Boston; the Philadelphia Museum of Art; the Baltimore Museum of Art; and the St. Louis Museum of Art. Finally in 1922 the de Forests announced their gift of an American wing to the Metropolitan Museum, and two years later it was opened to the public. By 1928 Boston and Philadelphia had opened their rooms, and in 1929, 1930, and 1931 Brooklyn, Baltimore, and St. Louis, respectively, could boast period room installations. Concurrently collecting rooms, or whole houses, were private collectors like Henry Ford, Henry Davis Sleeper, John D. Rockefeller, Jr., and Henry Francis du Pont. By the end of the 1920s collecting American decorative arts had achieved a dual approach: (1) the purely aesthetic one based on established, twentieth-century taste and current principles of connoisseurship,[10] and (2) the cultural perspective, in which a context was designed in order to display the original functions of objects within the society that created them. In 1929 Myers made no attempt to create such period settings for the objects, but he did recognize the advantage of grouping the pieces according to style in order to have visually compatible rooms.

In 1980, after more than fifty years of museums' acquiring and exhibiting, collectors' collecting, and scholars' writing, there still exists a similar duality in the attitudes, both public and professional, toward American decorative arts. On the one hand there are those who wish to view objects purely aesthetically, outside of their societal context, examining them as works of art or pieces of sculpture. On the other hand, many students and scholars find it difficult to isolate the object from the society that created it for a specific function. This "total cultural" approach leads scholars to reexamine regional areas within a specific time frame, taking notice anew of all aspects of everyday life that might have affected both crafts production and client preference. For example, seventeenth-century New England is currently the subject of a major investigation being undertaken jointly by the Museum of Fine Arts, Boston, and Boston University, Department of American and New England Studies. The research involves all aspects of the culture including primary (contemporary) documents, as well as the reevaluation of numerous objects. It is hoped that our knowledge of the total seventeenth-century culture—including its aesthetics—can be more completely delineated.[11]

In much the same way that scholars in New England are reexamining our first century of settlement, many institutions are also reevaluating their period room installations to determine if they are valid, accurate interpretations of specific economic, regional, and chronological situations. The entire methodology of museum interpretation is continually being questioned, reevaluated, and altered as knowledge grows with new generations of scholars and collectors. Nonetheless, even with the new scholarship and advanced technological tools, one is often amazed to realize how much our predecessors knew in the early years of this century and grateful for the firm foundation of knowledge they provided for today.

In addition to celebrating the contributions of our early scholars, the publication of this book not only recognizes the fiftieth anniversary of the landmark 1929 Girl Scouts Loan Exhibition but also attempts to combine both aesthetic and cultural approaches in an effort to bridge the now-classic dichotomy in American decorative arts. Following the guidelines of the 1929 show, objects have been included to represent the finest and most beautiful creations of American craftsmen. Also, and equally important, they demonstrate the development of knowledge in the field of American decorative arts over the past fifty years, utilizing and highlighting the most current scholarship as well as the classical investigations of the decades immediately following the 1929 exhibition.

Unlike the 1929 show, only American-made objects are included. Thus, while there are fewer ceramics and pieces of glass, those selected represent the most sophisticated production of this country between 1650 and 1830 and illustrate an area of particularly productive recent research. The 1929 show did not contain American pewter or any other types of metals. This is surprising since Myers had a large pewter collection himself, and Mrs. Myers had stated at the Board Meeting in April 1929, "There will probably be a pewter room. That has been by request, too, with the fine American pieces." Rather surprising also is the fact that no silver was exhibited, for Halsey had a major collection and had been a pioneering author in that area since 1906 when he wrote the catalogue introduction for the first major exhibition of American silver held at the Museum of Fine Arts, Boston. In the two decades after 1906 there were a number of important silver exhibitions and several major publications. For example, Judge Alfonso T. Clearwater began lending his American silver collection to the Metropolitan in 1910, and Francis Hill Bigelow, in 1917, wrote the famous book *Historic Silver of the Colonies and Its Makers.* Consequently, it would be a serious shortcoming if silver were excluded in 1980, and since there is an increasing interest in other American metalwork, a small sampling of iron, brass, and pewter has been included to show the new directions in knowledge and scholarship of American metalsmiths.

There has been no attempt in this presentation to be wholly representative of forms or regional distributions. Perhaps an entirely different selection of objects would have been equally justified and illustrative. In presenting new knowledge or "discoveries," aesthetic considerations occasionally have had to take a rear seat. It would have been enticing to have boasted, as Vaughan did in 1929, that most of the objects had never before been seen in public, but today, considering the limited number of truly great objects, such a claim is unreasonable if the highest quality is to be maintained. Because it is not possible to be definitive, it is hoped the text may raise questions and arouse the curiosity of students, scholars, and collectors in areas still needing exploration.

Unlike the 1929 presentation, the organization here does not follow a strictly stylistic formula. While the discussions directly reflect the didactic and introspective scholarly attitudes of the 1970s, the organization cuts across the confines of time and medium in an effort to be visually appealing and intellectually meaningful. The material that follows examines a variety of topics including European origins, domestic cultural patterns, economic concerns, client preferences, and the abilities and specialties of various craftsmen. The final chapter is the only one that echoes the organization of the original show, for it discusses an entire stylistic period, the neoclassical, in a variety of different materials. The intent of this varied organization is to break away from the stylistic and chronological confines in order to raise questions about thematic concerns that integrate whole groups of objects.

Finally, although the text covers a vast amount of scholarship, it cannot be entirely inclusive. On the contrary, the hope is that with various footnotes and bibliographical references, the interest of both the amateur and the scholar will be spurred on to new areas of reading, research, and knowledge, in much the same way that the impact of the 1929 exhibition has driven scholars over the past fifty years to unearth the knowledge that we now possess.

Chapter 1

Search and Re-Search

The Documented Object

One of the most significant phenomena to occur during this century in American art research is scholars' and collectors' avid interest in the "documented" object. This means any object whose maker, place of origin, and/or date of manufacture is known either by some direct mark of identification on the object itself or by some accompanying source of documentation such as a bill of sale, ledger account, inventory notation, or other written substantiation. This compelling desire to know the makers of old and revered American objects has been strongest with regard to furniture, owing no doubt to the fact that so little American furniture was ever marked or identified by the early makers. (In contrast is American silver, which was customarily marked and which consequently will not be considered in this chapter.) There are also smaller three-dimensional objects that were not always marked, and many of these present as great a challenge to students today as the more weighty, sizable pieces of furniture. Base metals like copper, brass, and iron present some of the broadest unknown areas, and glass and ceramics also are currently undergoing close scrutiny with regard to dates and sources of manufacture. The numerous discoveries of signed or otherwise documented objects over the past five decades have established important benchmarks upon which larger bodies of information are currently being built. As will be discussed in later chapters, whole regional schools of craftsmen are currently being identified through the association of undocumented objects with two or three pieces by known craftsmen.

A puzzling question arises when we ask why more talented American craftsmen did not often mark or label their products. Even in eighteenth-century records we find evidence that some craftsmen's names held sufficient significance to cause an inventory recorder to make special note of the maker of certain objects. For instance, in 1788 when the inventory of Jonathan Deming of Colchester, Connecticut, was made, it was noted that his "chest of drawers" (see fig. 250), along with thirty-five other pieces of furniture, was the work of Samuel Loomis.[1] When the belongings of James Bowdoin were inventoried in Boston in 1774, just as the British were about to occupy the city, many of his silver pieces were listed with a notation as to the makers. Clearly, if an object was outstanding for some reason, for instance either finely wrought or of great value, contemporary recognition of the craftsman who had done the work was sometimes given even if he had not marked the work itself, as in the case of Mr. Deming's fine chest of drawers.

The pioneering scholars of American furniture were extremely academic and surprisingly astute in their knowledge and citations of early documents and inventories, yet even their earliest works refer to only a few documented pieces of furniture. The first comprehensive book on American furniture was Irving W. Lyon's *The Colonial Furniture of New England* (1891), in which the author mentioned a few pieces of furniture whose makers were then known. In one instance he illustrated a piece that actually bore a signature and a date, and in another case he cited a bill of sale that had remained in the same family along with the piece of furniture. The signed example was the important slant-top desk (pl. 3) made by Benjamin Burnham of Colchester, Connecticut, and inscribed on the bottom, "This desk was maid in the / year 1769 Buy Benjⁿ Burnam that sarvfed his time in Felledlfay [Philadelphia]." Lyon clearly felt a certain degree of confidence in this inscription since he noted that it had "all the appearances of age and genuineness."[2] This statement belies the fact that he was both scholar and skeptic to scrutinize the aspect of the inscription and recognize the possibility that in some cases signatures are not always contemporary with the manufacture of the piece. In 1890 this desk was owned by Walter Hosmer of Wethersfield, Connecticut, who had purchased it from an estate in Hartford. After Hosmer's death the desk was acquired by the well-known Hartford collector, George S. Palmer, much of whose collection was acquired by the Metropolitan Museum in 1918. While there had been considerable confusion in ascertaining the precise identity of the Benjamin Burnham who signed this piece,[3] it has nevertheless become the cornerstone for the attribution of a whole school of Colchester, Connecticut, cabinetmaking. In addition, the extremely close relationship of this desk to another desk originally owned by Eliphalet Bulkeley of Colchester has extended the current knowledge of Colchester cabinetmakers. Through an admirable study of New London County furniture that resulted in an exhibition at the Lyman Allyn Museum in 1974, Minor Myers, Jr., discovered the inscription "Lomis" on a drawer of the desk

Plate 3. Slantfront desk, 1769, Colchester, Connecticut. *Benjamin Burnham (ca. 1730–73). Cherry, white pine, yellow pine, poplar, rosewood or ebony; inscribed on the bottom: "This desk was maid in the / year 1769 Buy Benjⁿ Burnam/ that sarvfed his time in Felledlfay." H. 49¾ in., W. 44¼ in., D. 24¼ in. The Metropolitan Museum of Art. John Stewart Kennedy Fund, 1918. Plate 3 is on page 15.*

11. Pier table, 1804–10, New York. *Charles-Honoré Lannuier (1779–1819). Mahogany veneer, ebony and satinwood inlay, white pine and brass moldings; labeled on center back of skirt: "Honore Lannuier/ Cabinet Maker/ (From Paris) at his Ware-House and Manufactory/ And Cabinet Ware of the Newest Fashion/ At 60 Broad St."; repeated in French. H. 37 in., W. 49 in., D. 24 in. The Henry Francis du Pont Winterthur Museum.*

■ **12. Pier table, ca. 1803–5, New York.** *Charles-Honoré Lannuier (1779–1819). Mahogany and mahogany veneer, ormolu mounts, marble top; bears same label as figure 11. H. 37 in., W. 40¼ in., D. 18¼ in. Mrs. Maria Martin Jones.*

13. *Collection des Meubles et Objets de Goût, plate 50, published 1803, Paris. Pierre La Mésangère (1761–1831). Joseph Downs Manuscript Collection. The Henry Francis du Pont Winterthur Museum.*

owned by Bulkeley. This discovery led to the conclusion that quite possibly Samuel Loomis (the maker of the Deming chest-on-chest in figure 250) was apprenticed to Benjamin Burnham and perhaps they had made the second desk together. Furthermore, through a detailed study of specific construction features, Myers was able to distinguish the workmanship of several different makers. It is through this process of reexamination of previously known documents that scholars today come to valuable insight, advanced knowledge, and significant new conclusions.

The second example of a firmly documented object that Lyon presented was a sideboard with its accompanying bill of sale from Aaron Chapin of Hartford, dated November 22, 1804.[4] Lyon stated that "the original bill is preserved by the family," and he again felt confident that his documentation was not subject to question. The bill referred quite specifically to the purchaser, "Mr. Frederic Robbins," and it also gave a brief description of the object: "1 Mahogany fashioned 8 leg Sideboard . . . $68.00." Thus, in this instance there was little room for confusion with another object.

Admittedly one is subject to a range of pitfalls in the pursuit of documented objects. First of all, the "age and genuineness" of any label or mark must be ascertained, just as Lyon did in his judgment of the Burnham desk. When examining an object with some type of label, signature, brand, or bill, one has to ask some specific questions based on rigid standards previously established. Has the label always been on the object, is the coloration around the label proper, is the label actually old, or, in the instance of a signature, is it contemporary with the fabrication of the object? Even after a judgment has been made and accepted for many years, these matters are still open to reexamination. For instance, in 1923, the noted American furniture scholar Luke Vincent Lockwood published a recent discovery in both the *Bulletin of the Metropolitan Museum* and *Antiques* magazine. He had acquired a seventeenth-century carved chest-over-drawers with the incised inscription "Mary ALLyns Chistt Cutte and/ joyned by Nich. Disbrowe" on the back of one of the drawers. For many years the inscription was accepted as genuine, and much was attributed to Disbrowe on the strength of that one chest. However, even though this perfectly authentic seventeenth-century chest is now in a major public collection, the authenticity of its inscription has been challenged by contemporary scholars, who believe it the work of a much later, and less scrupulous, hand.[5]

A second hazard of documenting an object through an associated bill or account is the possibility that perhaps there might be other similar objects in the same family, and thus it is difficult to assign a direct correspondence with absolute certainty. However, the most common pitfall of all is the wholesale attribution (often by an overenthusiastic scholar) of a large body of work to one maker, thus creating an entire myth on the basis of one or two documented pieces. However, even in the early 1920s students and scholars were aware of this problem as is illustrated by the comment of Homer Eaton Keyes, editor of *Antiques* magazine, about the Metropolitan Museum's current exhibition of the furniture of Duncan Phyfe: "On the one hand, a good many persons will become reasonably expert in differentiating between the work of Phyfe and that of his contemporaries; on the other hand, a great deal of material will be attributed to the Fulton Street master which never passed the portals of his shop."[6] Even with such a straightforward warning, Mr. Keyes's worst suspicions were bound to materialize in the years that followed with the grand exploitation of the "Phyfe myth."

The quest for documented objects quickened its pace not long after 1900. Duncan Phyfe's work actually led the parade, while William Savery's and John Goddard's were not far behind. In May 1922, Walter A. Dyer wrote a pioneering article on John Goddard for *Antiques*, and he prefaced his research with these comments:

> Duncan Phyfe of New York, and his work, have been known for a bare ten years. Within a year or two we had our first adequate glimpse of William Savery of Philadelphia. John Goddard, perhaps the greatest of them all, remains almost a myth.
>
> Luke Vincent Lockwood, the most thorough, perhaps, of all our students of American furniture, ran across Goddard's trail some years since. You will find a passing mention of him in *Colonial Furniture in America.*[7]

Certainly in the past sixty or seventy years our recognition and knowledge of numerous American craftsmen and artists has grown tremendously, even with the myths and mistakes. Much has been gained through the examination and exploration of particular

Plate 4. Pier table, 1810–15, Philadelphia. *Joseph Barry (1757[?]–1839) and Son. Mahogany and burl-elm veneers on mahogany, with ormolu and brass; labeled "Joseph B. Barry & Son/ Cabinet Maker & Upholsterer / N 132 Tenth Second Street Philadelphia." H. 38¾ in., W. 53⅞ in., D. 23⅞ in. The Metropolitan Museum of Art. Purchase, 1976.*

cornerstones in American art, while new discoveries have been made to substantiate or refute previous conclusions about whole bodies of material objects.

The purpose of the material that follows is to provide perspectives on both past and future research. The documented objects presented here represent some cornerstones upon which our knowledge has been built as well as some of the more recent discoveries in this growing body of data. They cover a broad chronological range as well as different physical media. The objects have been selected for their quality of workmanship as well as their significance in the history of knowledge about certain makers and schools of workmanship.

During the early years of this century when there was newfound fascination with labels, brands, and signatures on art objects, Mrs. Louis Guerineau Myers told the National Board of Directors in April 1929, as the first Girl Scouts Loan Exhibition was being planned, that:

> There will be one room that will be devoted to what we call labeled pieces. You know some of our furniture has the label of the original cabinet-maker on it. They are so valuable that you can't get them except for a thing of this kind. People won't let them go out of their houses. We can only get them because of the collector's interest, and I think they have been awfully good about the fact that they are doing it for Girl Scouts.[8]

However, apparently Mr. Myers must have decided against a separate section on documented objects, for the show was simply organized according to stylistic periods in different rooms. Possibly since there was only a handful of labeled pieces in the show, Myers just decided it was too small a number to warrant a separate grouping.

One of the best-known objects in that first exhibition (no. 709) was an unusually large and stately pier table (fig. 11) that bore the label of the French emigré cabinetmaker, Charles-Honoré Lannuier. At the time of the exhibition the table was owned by Mr. Myers, but in 1931 Henry Francis du Pont purchased it for his home and eventual museum, Winterthur. While this table reflects a strong reliance on English sources and tradition, it does have very marked French characteristics, such as the sheet brass strips that outline the edges of the top and the cross stretchers. Along with the many "Duncan Phyfe" pieces of furniture that were included in the 1929 show, this table brought to the forefront the existence of other fine cabinetmakers working in New York, as well as the important influence of French emigré craftsmen. Not too many years after the exhibition, Thomas Hamilton Ormsbee published several articles in *Antiques* (vol. 23, nos. 5–6) featuring the work of Lannuier.

While the pier table in figure 11 must have been made by Lannuier within the first few years that he was in this country, another more recently discovered pier table by the same maker (fig. 12) exhibits a distinctly different interpretation, yet possibly was made around the same time. Although the pier table bears the same label as the preceding one, it directly copies French designs of the first decade of the nineteenth century. In fact, this more rigidly classical table with reeded tapered columns surmounted with gilt figural busts derives directly from plate 50 of *Collection des Meubles et Objets de Goût* (fig. 13) published in Paris by Pierre La Mésangère in 1803. Lannuier is supposed to have arrived in America some time in 1803, and he may even have brought with him the recently published plates from La Mésangère. However, because Lannuier worked at No. 60 Broad Street until he died in 1819, it is possible that he may have made this table later in the 1810s, even though it would have seemed a bit out of fashion by that date.[9]

As early as 1935, William MacPherson Hornor, in his celebrated *Blue Book of Philadelphia Furniture*, recognized the significance of the outstanding pier table made in Philadelphia between about 1810 and 1815 and labeled by the firm of Joseph Barry and Son (pl. 4). The provenance and documentation of this table is as flawless as is the quality of workmanship, aesthetic proportion, and diversity of both materials used and decorative techniques employed. The label (not unlike that of William Whitehead, fig. 17), composed of images from Thomas Sheraton's 1802 *Appendix* to *The Cabinet-Maker and Upholsterer's Drawing-Book*, has to date from about 1810, as Barry's son joined him in business in that year. Since Barry went to London and Paris in 1811–12, this table may have been inspired by his viewing the latest fashions abroad. Clearly many of the design motifs derive from a number of plates from Pierre La Mésangère's *Collection des Meubles et Objets de Goût*, published in Paris from 1796 to 1830.[10] Finally, the provenance of the

14

15

table shows a clear line of descent from Louis Clapier, a Philadelphia victualler, directly to his great-great-great-grandson, Thomas Wistar Brown III, from whose family the table was purchased in recent years by the Metropolitan Museum of Art.

As already noted, the work of Duncan Phyfe became well-known and exploited by collectors and scholars by the end of the first quarter of this century. By 1922 the Metropolitan's show and Charles Over Cornelius's *Furniture Masterpieces of Duncan Phyfe* (Garden City, New York: Doubleday, Page and Co. for the Metropolitan Museum of Art, 1922) established Phyfe in a position of prominence. Another exhibition at the Metropolitan in 1934 and its catalogue, *New York State Furniture*, focused more attention on Phyfe, and by 1939 Nancy McClelland published her major work on the great master, *Duncan Phyfe and the English Regency, 1795–1830*.

While a great deal of furniture is associated with Phyfe's workshop through surviving bills and other documents, only a small number of labeled pieces actually are known today. The unusual desk and bookcase with scrolled pediment in figure 14 was exhibited in the 1934 exhibition and bears two labels, each reading: "D. PHYFE'S / CABINET WAREHOUSE, / No. 170 Fulton-street, / NEW-YORK. / N.B. CURLED HAIR MATRASSES, CHAIR AND / SOFA CUSHIONS. / AUGUST 1820." Surprisingly delicate and diminutive, this desk and bookcase was originally owned by Thomas Lattimer Bowie of Philadelphia and remained in the hands of his descendants until 1973. Phyfe's use of beautifully figured mahogany veneer, combined with a delightfully imaginative (yet seemingly *retarditaire*) broken scroll pediment, makes this desk and bookcase one of the more important documented pieces from the famous master's workshop.

Like many fine American craftsmen, Phyfe made a number of objects for the use and enjoyment of his own family, and today some of these survive in public and private collections. Perhaps one of the most beautiful and extraordinary of these objects is the large, four-post bed he made for his daughter Elizabeth's wedding prior to 1820. In 1939 Nancy McClelland illustrated this bed (p. 133), but in her book it was difficult to see the veneers and carving. Shown here without its tester frame or hangings (fig. 15), the four magnificent posts can be fully appreciated. The complexity and unity of design of the posts is outstanding, and the use of carved paw feet on the foot posts is unusual. Almost every element of Phyfe's ornamental vocabulary was used, including the veneered and ormolu-capped columns flanking the footboard. The lighter veneered panels of the footboard are another very special detail, and the unusual solid "plumb pudding" mahogany headboard was also a mark of the highest quality. This bed remained in the hands of Phyfe descendants until its sale just a few years ago.

In surprising contrast to the research on Phyfe, extensive study and knowledge of New York furniture before the time of Duncan Phyfe has gone relatively unplumbed. Over the past few years several students and scholars have studied one or two individual cabinetmakers, and more recently there has been a study of the seventeenth-century and William and Mary style in New York,[11] but no published study has carefully

16

examined the rise of neoclassicism in New York and the cabinetmakers and other allied craftsmen who were involved in the production of objects such as the exciting and visually striking sideboard in figure 16. The overall sweeping design of this sideboard combined with a superior choice of veneers to accent the surface pattern of circles and ovals are ample criteria to term it an outstanding example from the period. (Certainly this sideboard is as fine as the more well-known eight-legged New York sideboard that Mr. du Pont lent to the first Girl Scouts Exhibition. See fig. 9.) In addition, the survival of two identical labels on the inside surface of the central compartment doors makes this an important discovery that has already led to the documentation of a similar sideboard bearing fragments of the same label.[12] The label (see fig. 17), which depicts five pieces of furniture all derived from plates in Thomas Sheraton's *The Cabinet-Maker and Upholsterer's Drawing-Book* (London, 1793), was engraved and printed by John Scoles and reads: "William Whitehead/CABINET & CHAIR MAKER/No. 75/Pearl Street/New York." To date, this sideboard, the related one with fragmentary label, and a pair of accompanying knife boxes are the only documented examples of Whitehead's work. Little is known about Whitehead at this time, but he does appear in the New York directory at the 75 Pearl Street address between 1794 and 1799. Apparently he was working in New York by 1792, for he was listed at 43 Beekman in that year, and at 6 Nassau in 1793. After 1799 virtually nothing else is known of Mr. Whitehead.[13]

Mr. du Pont exhibited a fine and handsomely made Boston tambour desk in the 1929 Exhibition (no. 710), and less than a year after the close of the show he was the fortunate purchaser of another strikingly similar desk. However, the tambour desk (fig. 18) that he acquired from the Philip Flayderman collection[14] had the distinction of bearing the label of John Seymour and Son of Boston on the underside of the bottom drawer. This desk was the first of two known labeled objects made by the Seymours to become well publicized in this century. Subsequently, on the basis of this tambour desk and another desk owned later by George A. Cluett of Troy, New York, a large body of cabinetry has been zealously attributed to the Seymours. Starting in 1805, Thomas Seymour had a cabinet warehouse in Boston where he displayed and stored the work presumably supplied him by other cabinetmakers along with items produced by his own shop. In addition to the two early desks with the John Seymour and Son label on them, there are a number of labeled pieces along with several bills that document specific work to Thomas Seymour's manufactory, if not specifically to his hand.[15] In much the same way that Duncan Phyfe became a myth from the 1920s onward, even to this day the Seymours are the focal point of yet another myth and wholesale attribution.

Until just a few years ago only two pieces of furniture were known that bore the label of the shop of John and Thomas Seymour. Yet perhaps hundreds of other similar, and some not so similar, objects have been associated with that famous team. In the past few years, another piece with the same label (fig. 19) has been noted and adds a new dimension to the repertoire of forms known. The delicate half-round card table in figure 20 is related through several elements of its design and decorative motifs to the labeled

17

tambour desks, yet it does not bear any of the notable lunette inlay work that is usually associated with the Seymour shop. The bell-flower swags that ornament the skirt of the table are similar to those that appear on the tambour doors of the Flayderman–du Pont labeled desk, and the cuffed spade feet appear on several other attributed examples but are different from those on the labeled desk in the Cluett collection. The dot and leaf inlay that circles the top edge of the card table does appear on the Cluett desk, but it is not a common feature on other pieces attributed to the Seymours. However, that same inlay is found on another half-round card table that bears the label of Thomas Foster, a Boston cabinetmaker about whom little is known.[16] The above fact focuses on the ultimate problem: the hazard of attributing objects on the basis of inlays. Inlays were both imported into this country as well as made here by specialized craftsmen. In 1795 the following advertisement appeared in the *Columbian Centinel:* "To the Cabinet Makers/ An invoice of Sundries for/ Inlaying, to be disposed of very Cheap No. 5 Butler's Row." Furthermore, by 1809 a listing appeared in the Boston Directory for a John Dewhurst, who called himself a "banding and stringing maker" and lived on Salem Street in the North End. We must therefore conclude that no one cabinetmaker or shop had a monopoly on any one inlay and several different cabinet shops could have used the same inlay as ornamentation. Hence, it is risky to depend too heavily on related or identical inlay for definitive attribution.

In the nineteenth century it was frequent practice to stencil information about the cabinetmaker or manufactory inside a drawer or on a backboard or bottomboard. Such is the case with the classical and neatly restrained dressing table (fig. 21) made and marked by the manufactory of "ISAAC VOSE & SON/CABINET, CHAIR &/FURNI-TURE WAREHOUSE/WASHINGTON STREET/BOSTON." This table, originally owned by the Coolidge family of Boston, is one of a growing body of documented examples of Boston cabinetry made in the Empire style, from about 1800 through 1830–40. (See also fig. 284.) Just within this past decade scholars and collectors have begun to define and recognize the "Boston school" of this period. Heretofore Phyfe and Lannuier were the principals usually sharing the limelight on the Empire stage. Now, however, names like Isaac Vose, Joshua Coates, Thomas Emmons, George Archibald, and Timothy Hunt are becoming well known and associated with specific objects and clients. It is interesting, too, that in 1824 Isaac Vose and Son advertised that "Their Cabinet Manufactory is under the direction of Mr. Thomas Seymour, and all orders for furniture will receive as good attention as heretofore. . . ."[17] Clearly the Boston makers were as aware of foreign sources as those in New York and Philadelphia, yet they do not seem to have copied them as directly as other makers. The Vose dressing table is a good example of this point because it borrows elements from several of La Mésangère's plates

17. Detail of label on sideboard in figure 16.

18. Tambour desk, 1794–1804, Boston. *John Seymour (1738–1818) and Thomas Seymour (1771–1848). Mahogany inlaid with light wood, white pine; label under bottom drawer reads "JOHN SEY-MOUR & SON,/ CABINET MAKERS,/ CREEK SQUARE,/BOS-TON."—along with chalk initials on back of upper section reading "CS" or "SS." H. 41⅝ in., W. 37¾ in., D. 18½ in. The Henry Francis du Pont Winterthur Museum.*

19. Detail of label on card table in figure 20. *Same as label on tambour desk in figure 18.*

■ **20. Card table, 1794–1804, Boston.** *John Seymour (1738–1818) and Thomas Seymour (1771–1848). Mahogany with curly maple or satinwood panels, white pine; label as illustrated in figure 19. H. 28¾ in., W. 36 in., D. 18 in. Mr. and Mrs. George M. Kaufman.*

21. Dressing table with looking glass, 1819–25, Boston. *Isaac Vose (1767–1823) and Isaac Vose, Jr. (1794–1872). Rosewood and mahogany veneers, baywood, chestnut, stamped brass beading, ormolu mounts; stenciled label, "ISAAC VOSE & SON/ CABINET, CHAIR &/ FURNITURE WAREHOUSE/ WASHINGTON STREET/ BOS-TON." H. 64½ in., W. 42 in., D. 21⅝ in. The St. Louis Art Museum. Purchase and Decorative Art Funds.*

18

19

20

21

(especially pl. 442, dated 1817), but it does not seem to be a close copy of any specific published design. The most exciting and revolutionary fact about the discovery of documented Boston Empire furniture is that there was a highly sophisticated and superbly crafted body of objects made there that could in many instances rival the work of Phyfe, Lannuier, and Barry.

The existence of a distinct Newport, Rhode Island, school of cabinetmaking, featuring blocked fronts, frequently surmounted with gloriously carved shells, was noted as early as 1901 when Luke Vincent Lockwood published his first edition of *Colonial Furniture in America*. At that time Lockwood illustrated the superb nine-shell desk and bookcase originally owned by Joseph Brown of Providence (see pl. 29). In the first issue of *Antiques* magazine in January 1922, another nine-shell Newport piece, also supposedly owned by Joseph Brown, was published as the frontispiece. By May of that same year, with Walter A. Dyer's article "John Goddard and His Block-Fronts," widespread attribution of block and shell Newport furniture to the shops of the Goddards and Townsends had begun. However, among the numerous pieces that Dyer discussed, the only document he presented was a bill from Goddard for ten mahogany chairs.[18]

Today there exists a sizable body of objects known to have been made by the various members of the Goddard and Townsend families. Some are labeled, others signed, and several documented by bills of sale. In some instances the dates of fabrication are recorded on the labels and bills. The discovery of the slant front desk in figure 22 not long ago added to this group the first labeled desk of this type. The label (fig. 23) inside the top drawer boldly states in handwritten script "Made by/John Townsend/Rhode Island/1765." This desk is closely related to a bureau, or chest of drawers, owned by the Metropolitan Museum of Art, for that piece has an almost identical label bearing the same date. Only a few other block and shell slant front desks are known, and one is illustrated in figure 47 of Ralph Carpenter's well-known volume *The Arts and Crafts of Newport, Rhode Island, 1640–1820* (1954).

While each new documenting of a Newport object adds to our knowledge, the one factor that remains a puzzle is that even today we know little about the overall composition of the Goddard and Townsend shops. Only one account or ledger seems to exist, that of Job Townsend, Jr., and it provides little evidence about the size and composition of his shop. Were several family members working together, or did they all have separate establishments? Judging from the wide variety of carving evidenced in the shells and on the knees of tea tables, card tables, dressing tables, and high chests of drawers, there must have been a number of different craftsmen employed for just carving. The "Newport school" might at first glance appear to be a well-known and

22

22. Slantfront desk, 1765, Newport. *John Townsend (1732–1809). Mahogany, secondary woods unexamined; labeled inside top drawer: "Made by/ John Townsend/ Rhode Island/ 1765." H. 42 in., W. 42 in., D. 23 in. Mr. and Mrs. Stanley P. Sax.*

23. Detail of label in slantfront desk in figure 22.

23

■ **24. Card table, 1762, Newport.**
John Townsend (1732–1809). Mahogany,
maple, chestnut, white pine; signed in
script on back gate, "John Townsend/
Newport/ 1762," and again on bottom of
center support, "John Townsend/1762."
H. 27⅛ in., W. 25¼ in., D. 18¼ in.
Peter W. Eliot.

25. High chest of drawers, 1760–90,
Newport. *Benjamin Baker (d. 1822).*
Mahogany with pine; chalk inscription
above leg on back reads: "Benjamin
Baker." H. 81¾ in., W. 39¼ in., D. 21
in. Newport Restoration Foundation.

24

25

documented area of craftsmanship, but there still remains much to be discovered with regard to specific primary documentation.

A recent discovery and heretofore unpublished example of the work of John Townsend is the bold and skillfully executed card table in figure 24. Dating it 1762 and placing his name on it twice, once on the back of the gate and again on the bottom of the center support, the craftsman clearly intended to sign his work; this is not a case of his simply having marked some lumber before deciding upon its use. This table is similar to several other known Newport card tables, including one now owned by the Redwood Library, a gift of Miss Ellen Townsend, granddaughter of John Townsend who presumably made it.[19] Some of the distinct Newport characteristics seen in this table include the very square, hard-edged legs, the pronounced, knuckled talons grasping high almost elongated balls, and the flowing, incised carving on the knees and knee brackets. Closely related to this carving is that found on the high chest of drawers by Benjamin Baker (fig. 25) and the Newport tea table (fig. 215).

To date, very little Newport furniture made between 1730 and 1790 has been definitely identified as from the hand of cabinetmakers other than Goddards and Townsends. Although some names of other makers working in Newport during that period are known, little of their work has been specifically identified. In 1971 the high chest of drawers in figure 25 sold at auction for a record price,[20] yet it was not until after its removal from the auction gallery and a closer examination once on loan to the Metropolitan Museum that the name of Benjamin Baker was discovered on the backboard. Since this writing appears upside down above the right rear leg, there is some question whether it was intended to be an identifying mark for the high chest itself or simply for that piece of wood, before fabrication. At any rate, one can safely assume that Baker had some hand in making this piece of furniture, whether in his own shop or one run by another cabinetmaker. Little research has been done on Baker, though he is recorded as a Newport joiner. Supposedly the accounts books (in the Newport Historical Society) of William Langley and Dr. William Hunter both mention Baker as a "joyner," and in 1884 George Mason Champlin wrote that: "David Huntington and Benjamin Baker found their market for furniture in New York and the West Indies."[21] Tradition records that this high chest was made for Lyman Hazard of Peacedale, Rhode Island.

It is a rare and happy situation when an actual bill of sale or receipt remains with the particular purchase throughout its life. Such has been the association between the simple, graceful Newport marbletop side table in figure 26 and the receipt (fig. 27) for the thirty pounds that Captain Anthony Low paid to John Goddard in September of 1755 for a "Mahogany Table Frame."[22] Apparently Captain Low purchased the gray and white marble elsewhere, since there is no charge for that noted on the receipt. This documentation has another significance, for it makes this "table frame" one of the earliest dated pieces of furniture specifically known to have been made by John Goddard. Another early Goddard piece of simple form, a slant front desk, bears a paper label which includes the date 1745.[23] The importance of the table's documentation was noted as early as 1933 when it appeared in *Antiques* magazine (July). The article stated that Goddard had made "an attempt to achieve something more or less in the French manner," and two other unusual pieces of Newport furniture that have appeared since then also suggest a strong French influence. The marbletop commode now owned by the Metropolitan Museum[24] is French in feeling and design with similar rounded, canted corners and short cabriole legs. Another related commode form, but with different proportions and having a solid mahogany top, has recently been exhibited at the Museum of Fine Arts, Boston. This piece is known to have been made for a Frenchman named Pierre Simon of Newport. What was the source of the French influence on Newport furniture, and could there have been Huguenot craftsmen in Rhode Island before the American Revolution? Certainly the search for the precise source of French influence on Newport designs is worth further research and study.[25]

An outstanding example of John Townsend's work in the neoclassical style can be seen in the side chair in plate 5, one of a set of at least four.[26] Like the desk cited above that bears a handwritten and dated label, inside the rear seat rail of this chair is a handwritten label that reads: *"Made by John Townsend/Newport 1800"* (fig. 28). This extremely sophisticated side chair is not typical of other known Rhode Island chairs of this period but instead is closely related to side chairs that were being made in New York at the same time. In fact, the 1929 exhibition included two armchairs, attributed to New York, that had similar shield-shaped backs, one with carved motifs and the other with an inlaid medallion. However, the legs on those two chairs did not have the graceful flare at the bottom but instead were straight and tapered. A handsome New York armchair of similar style with the same graceful legs, but with an inlaid medallion instead of the carved rosette below the peak of the crest, is in the Winterthur Museum collection.[27]

Another newly discovered documentation of the neoclassical style in Rhode Island is a pair of side chairs that bear the label of John Carlile and Sons of Providence (figs. 29 and 30). While the name of Carlile was mentioned early in the 1920s in an article by L. Earle Rowe in *Antiques* magazine (vol. 6, no. 6), not many pieces of furniture have been identified as coming from his shop. More important, though, is the direct association to a Providence shop of a chair with the typical and frequently seen shieldback with carved kylix urn. A chair of almost identical form and detailing, which appeared in the 1929 exhibition (no. 736), was attributed to Rhode Island, with the additional comment:

■ **26. Side table, 1755, Newport.** *John Goddard (1723–85). Mahogany, chestnut, maple, and marble. H. 27 in., W. 45¼ in., D. 21⅞ in. Mr. and Mrs. Joseph K. Ott.*

27. Receipt for the purchase of the marbletop side table in figure 26. *Anthony Low paid John Goddard thirty pounds for the frame in 1755. Mr. and Mrs. Joseph K. Ott.*

28. Detail of label on side chair in plate 5.

29. Side chair, 1790–1800, Providence, Rhode Island. *John Carlile (1730–96) and John Carlile Jr. (1762–1832). Mahogany with maple; bears label on inside of rear seat rail as seen in figure 30. H. 39 in., W. 21¼ in., D. 18½ in. Mr. and Mrs. Joseph K. Ott.*

30. Detail of label on side chair in figure 29.

31. Card table, 1765–75, Philadelphia. *Benjamin Randolph (1721–91). Mahogany with white oak and tulip poplar; label on rear inside of gate, partially worn away, reads: "All Sorts of /CABINET-/ and/ CHAIR-WORK/ MADE and SOLD BY/ BENJ.ᴺ RANDOLPH./ At the Sign of the Golden Eagle/ Chestnut-Street, PHILADELPHIA." H. 28¾ in., W. 33¼ in., D. 16 in. The Henry Francis du Pont Winterthur Museum.*

26

28

31

29

30

"Some have been traced to the Goddard family and may well have been made by John's sons, Stephen and Thomas, who were in partnership, as recently discovered records tell us." However, some chairs of this general form have been associated with a sketch by Samuel McIntire of Salem, and another side chair has the inscription "Benjᵃ Frothingham" (of Charlestown, Masachusetts) inside the rear seat rail.[28] While it is probably true that this style of chair was made from Salem to Providence, and perhaps also in Newport, this labeled example provides important evidence to support a specific regional identity. Another interesting note about an almost identical chair in the Winterthur Collection recalls that the chair was once upholstered with an old piece of cloth signed: "Chas. Burling Stevenson/Stephens & Satler Co./Providence 1810."[29]

Undeniably some of the most ornate and exuberant furniture made in eighteenth-century America in the rococo or Chippendale style was produced in Philadelphia. Examples like the lavishly carved gilt looking glass (fig. 153), the unsurpassed "Pompadour" high chest of drawers (pl. 30), and the Cadwalader family marbletop table (fig. 157) attest to this well-known fact. Much of this fine furniture came from the shops of cabinetmakers like Benjamin Randolph and Thomas Affleck, who must have employed numerous craftsmen to perform specialized functions such as carving and gilding. However, not everything from these notable shops was necessarily of the most ornate order, for much depended upon the pocketbook of the client, and the variations of the shop's repertoire were usually a function of how much he was willing to spend.[30] Benjamin Randolph worked on Chestnut Street at the "Sign of the Golden Eagle," where he produced some of his finest pieces for the Cadwalader family. Yet the simpler, more restrained card table in figure 31, which bears his label, indicates the variety of work produced by his large establishment. While the overall form of this table with its rounded corners is English in derivation, a distinct purity and simplicity can be seen in this example. And, although this table assuredly cost less than the one owned by the Vaux family of Philadelphia (fig. 213), the quality of the carving found on the two front legs is as fine and as sculptural as on any piece of Philadelphia workmanship. Randolph probably did not execute the carving himself. It is known that he did employ at least two carvers, Hercules Courtenay and John Pollard, both of whom were trained in London and were associated with Randolph by 1765 and 1766. Pollard may have continued to work for Randolph after 1773, by which time he had formed a partnership with Richard Butts, presumably a joiner, and carried on his business at the "Sign of the Chinese Shield."[31]

An interesting contrast to the richly carved rococo furniture of Philadelphia is a fascinating Virginia-made armchair with dolphin feet. Certainly the rarest piece of stamped furniture to be discovered in the past few years, this ambitious Grand Master's chair was made by Benjamin Bucktrout in Williamsburg, Virginia between 1767 and 1770 (fig. 32). This chair was a cornerstone of a recent study of eastern Virginia furniture[32] and is especially noteworthy because of its direct derivation from several plates in Thomas Chippendale's 1755 edition of *The Gentleman and Cabinet-maker's Director*.[33] Bucktrout was a London-trained cabinetmaker who emigrated to America and first advertised in the *Virginia Gazette* on July 25, 1766:

> **B. Bucktrout, CABINET MAKER, from London, on the main street near the Capitol in Williamsburg, makes all sorts of cabinet-work, plain or ornamental, in satisfaction to all Gentlemen who shall please to favour him with their commands. N.B. Where likewise may be hade the mathematical GOUTY CHAIR.**

By 1767 Bucktrout had established himself, for about that time he purchased the cabinetmaking business of Anthony Hay, one of Williamsburg's well-known early makers. Whether this chair was originally made for the Williamsburg Lodge, of which Bucktrout became a member in 1774, or for the nearby Norfolk Lodge, is still uncertain. However, in 1778 it was given to the Unanimity Lodge No. 7 in Edenton, North Carolina, where it has remained ever since. On the back of the carved Corinthian capital is the stamp "BENIMAN/BUCKTROUT."

For many years Boston has been acknowledged as the only colonial style center to produce the distinctive bombé form, at least as early as 1753.[34] The names of Benjamin Frothingham and John Cogswell have long been associated with the finest interpretation of this form, and many pieces have wantonly been attributed to the latter without more than a strand of evidence. For many years the great Boston collector, Maxim Karolik,

32. Masonic armchair, 1767–70, Williamsburg, Virginia. *Benjamin Bucktrout (w. 1766–79, d. 1813). Mahogany with black walnut; branded on the back of column capital: "BENIMAN/ BUCKTROUT." H. 65½ in., W. 31¼ in., D. 29½ in. Unanimity Lodge No. 7, A.F.&A.M., W. P. Goodwin, Secretary.*

32

knew of the existence of the bombé chest-on-chest in figure 33, yet he was never successful in purchasing it from the descendants of Elias Hasket Derby, for whom it was traditionally said to have been made. Mr. Karolik's tremendous desire to own this piece stemmed not only from its fine architectural proportions, well-articulated carving, and beautifully grained mahogany but also, and more importantly, from the fact that on the top board of the bottom case it is signed in bold script "Made by John/Cogswell in middle Street/Boston 1782" (fig. 34). To date, this is the only known piece of furniture signed by John Cogswell, and thus it is the keystone for the attribution of other related specimens.

Closely related in a number of ways to the Cogswell chest-on-chest is a recently "rediscovered" bureau, or chest of drawers, probably made in Salem, Massachusetts (fig. 35). Featuring a serpentine front and canted corners ornamented with carved fretwork and punched decoration, this form is more reminiscent of Philadelphia preferences. Only one other Massachusetts chest of this type is known, and it is in the Karolik Collection.[35] Owned for many years by the collector George A. Cluett, this chest was recently purchased and when reexamined, revealed some writing on the bottom board. Subsequent infrared photography disclosed the initials "TN" and the date "1783" (fig. 36). Further research in the archives of the Essex Institute, Salem, Massachusetts, turned up a bill from the cabinetmaker Thomas Needham of Salem to Elias Hasket Derby in 1783. While there is no certain connection between this chest and the bill, comparison of the script initials "TN" reveals a strikingly close similarity and this bureau probably came from the shop of Thomas Needham.[36] While little is known about Needham and the makeup of his shop, according to contemporary records and documents, he was the son of a cabinetmaker who was born and worked in Boston. In 1776 the family moved to Salem, where in 1780 Thomas had a son who also followed him in the same trade. Apparently by 1796 the family was back in Boston. Clearly Needham was apprenticed to his father and learned his craft in the style of Boston cabinetmakers. But did he actually execute the carving of the knees, feet, and central pendant? Or could there have been a Boston carver working also for Cogswell, who executed this finely done work for Needham? This discovery is but one more instance of new information opening a new door with a new set of questions and puzzles.

Another distinct group of furniture, often stamped or branded by its makers, and currently receiving much attention, is windsor chairs. While not all windsors are marked, the ones that are provide us with important touchstones for establishing regional groups. Though the production of Francis Trumble of Philadelphia may not seem like the most exciting, he is the earliest documented maker working in Philadelphia, and his "sack-back" armchairs are typical of a form popular throughout that city (fig. 37). In

■ **33. Chest-on-chest, 1782, Boston.**
John Cogswell (1738–1818). Mahogany with white pine; signed and dated on top of lower section as seen in figure 34. H. 97 in., W. 44¼ in., D. 23½ in. Museum of Fine Arts, Boston. William Francis Warden Fund.

34. Detail of signature on chest-on-chest in figure 33.

■ **35. Chest of drawers, 1783, probably Salem, Massachusetts.** *Attributed to Thomas Needham (1755–87). Mahogany and white pine; initialed and dated on bottom board as seen in figure 36. H. 36½ in., W. 44¼ in., D. 24¼ in. Private collection.*

36. Detail of signature on bottom of chest of drawers in figure 35.

34

33

36

35

37. Sack-back windsor armchair, ca. 1774, Philadelphia. *Francis Trumble (w. early 1740s–98). Tulip, soft maple, walnut, hickory and oak; stamped "F TRUMBLE" on underside of seat. H. 37⅛ in., W. 23 in., D. 16¼ in. Independence National Historic Park Collection, Philadelphia.*

38. Windsor armchair, 1790–1810, New York. *Walter MacBride (w. ca. 1785–1810). Painted woods—soft maple, tulip poplar, white oak; stamped on bottom of seat as in figure 39. H. 37¾ in., W. 25½ in., D. 21¾ in. The Henry Francis du Pont Winterthur Museum.*

39. Detail of stamp or brand on underside of windsor armchair in figure 38.

37

38

39

the 1770s he supplied Independence Hall with large orders of chairs, so it may be assumed that he was certainly among the better-known makers.[37]

Windsor chairs were made in New York by the end of the eighteenth century. Walter MacBride was one of the more prolific makers working on Pearl Street between 1792 and 1796, along with other makers such as Thomas and William Ash and John DeWitt (see figs. 91 and 92). The continuous arm brace-back chair in figure 38 is a fine example of a form typical of production in New York at this time. On the underside of the seat is the stamp "W. MACBRIDE/N=YORK" (fig. 39). Occasionally one finds windsor chairs with not only the mark of the maker on the underside but also the brand of the owner. In situations like these, confusion between owner and maker can lead to misinterpretations. Chairs similar to this one by MacBride were made in Connecticut by craftsmen like Ebenezer Tracy, and also in Rhode Island. However, each geographical region exhibited differences in the turnings, spindles, and the sweep and contour of the continuous bowback. Although this particular chair has always been painted a solid color, MacBride did advertise in 1795 that he made "chairs japanned any colour and neatly flowered."[38]

The mechanisms of American timepieces are frequently documented by a signature on the face of the clock, yet we are rarely enlightened about the maker of the case. However, occasionally the case itself will bear a label, as in the instance of the Newport tall clock owned by the Metropolitan Museum of Art and bearing the label of John Townsend, with the date of 1769 (or 1789) on the label. An exceedingly rare instance occurs when both the maker of the works and of the case appear on the dial of the clock, as is currently believed to be the situation with the fine specimen in plate 41. There is no question that Thomas Harland made the works, for his name appears prominently on the face, but the precise role of Abishai Woodward is still subject to slight question. Sometimes the original owner's name is inscribed on the face along with that of the maker,[39] but in this instance we know that Woodward was also a cabinetmaker and that the clock was not originally owned by him, but rather by Elias Brown. Hence, the names of both fabricators of this superb masterpiece seem to be those right on the face of the timepiece.

Certainly the Willard family of clockmakers from Grafton, Roxbury, and Boston, Massachusetts, are among the most well-known names in early American clockmaking innovations. Simon, older brother of Aaron, was the leading master and in 1802 patented his new mechanism for the so-called banjo clock. However, shortly after he obtained his patent, other makers, including his brother Aaron, began to adopt his innovations. The handsome Aaron Willard banjo clock in plate 6 is notable in several respects. Its most unusual visual feature is the trailing vine and leaf motif of composition ornament flanking the throat of the clock, in contrast to the simple brass supports found on most banjo clocks. Second, the brass works of the clock are stamped "A. WILLARD/BOSTON/1808." Third, the finely painted rectangular bottom glass depicting Atlas raising the globe upon his shoulders is signed on its reverse by Aaron Willard, Jr., and Spencer Nolen, indicating that the painted glasses were executed by that partnership of ornamental painters working in Boston between 1805 and 1809. Thus, with both a stamp and a signature, we know almost everything about the fabrication of this clock with the exception of the maker of the case and the composition ornament.[40]

While it is known that cabinetmaker John Townsend of Newport made clock cases, the question of who made cases for the Newport clockmaker James Wady still remains unanswered. Two of Wady's clocks have almost identical cases (fig. 40), and these masterpieces are among the finest pre-Revolutionary American tall clocks. With double arched bonnets, delicately scrolled and pierced fretwork, and unusual gilt, mushroom-shaped finial, these cases were certainly "top of the line" in both price and quality of craftsmanship. While one may guess that these cases came from the shop of a Goddard or a Townsend, future research could unearth contrary evidence. Wady, whose work is relatively rare, was probably trained by the Newport clockmaker William Claggett, since in 1736 Wady married Mary Claggett, daughter of the elder clockmaker.

The quest for documented or marked American metals is not an easy one. And once a mark is noted, sometimes the task of identifying the place of origin and the exact maker is even more arduous. Due to the dearth of marked metals extant today, the contemporary scholar-collector tends to forget how widespread production by American ironmasters, coppersmiths, braziers, and brass founders was throughout the seventeenth, eighteenth, and early nineteenth centuries. The romantic inclination of the nineteenth century has left us with several impressions of the proverbial smithy, not only in Henry Wadsworth Longfellow's time-honored poem "The Village Blacksmith," but also in the considerably earlier painting by John Neagle of *Pat Lyon at the Forge* (fig. 41), painted in 1826 and sold to the Boston Athenaeum shortly thereafter for $400. This powerful and fiery painting not only presents the image of one of Philadelphia's best-known and respected mechanical geniuses (being a locksmith, blacksmith, and maker of fire engines), but it also carefully delineates the interior of the smith's forge and some of his tools. Apparently Neagle was so concerned with doing an admirable job for his client that he took great care to be as precise as possible in his visual description. Reportedly Lyon gave him the following ultimatum when he ordered the painting: "Do it at full length, do it your own way; take your own time, and charge your own price; paint me as a blacksmith. I don't want to be represented as what I am not—a gentleman."[41] When this picture was commissioned, Lyon had become a well-to-do mechanic, with both position and stature in Philadelphia. However, the earlier part of his career had been marred by a brief unjustified imprisonment in 1798 in connection with a robbery at the Bank of Pennsylvania. Just a few months after his incarceration, the real guilty parties were discovered and he was released. Later, Lyon brought suit against the directors of the Bank and won a settlement of $9,000, which may have been the beginning of his soon-to-be established small fortune.

There are vast quantities of unmarked iron implements, from fireplace and cooking equipment to farming, woodworking, and even smithing tools, that assuredly were produced in this country during the time span being considered. Occasionally one will happen across an article like a toaster, or a waffle iron, or even a tipping kettle with initials or a full name stamped or incised into it. With such a small clue, it is often impossible to isolate the geographic origin or identity of the maker. However, the systematic recording of many marked objects is beginning to establish related groups. Already scholars have begun to identify regions and specific makers' work using characteristic techniques and design motifs, just as has happened in the area of furniture scholarship.[42] The signed wrought iron pipe tongs in figure 42 are a prime example of a finely made and sculpted utilitarian product curiously signed and dated, presumably by the blacksmith who wrought them. On one side of the tongs at the juncture where the curved spike or nail pins the two parts together is incised "JOSEPH CHAPIN," and on the opposite side is the date "SEPTE 29 = 1740" (fig. 43). Little is known about this ellusive maker, who may have been the noted gunsmith and mechanic Joseph Chapin who was born in 1718 in Long Meadow, Massachusetts, and who died in 1803 in Wethersfield, Vermont. The only other recorded pair of marked pipe tongs is a pair marked with the stamp of "I. AUSTIN," possibly for Josiah Austin of Charlestown, Massachusetts, a noted goldsmith.[43]

The iron and brass cross-arm candlestand in figure 44 is another example of work-

40. Tall clock, 1745–55, Newport. *James Wady (w. 1740–55). Walnut, ash, poplar, and brass; brass dial inscribed "JAMES WADY NEWPORT." H. 98¼ in., W. 17 in., D. 10 in. The Henry Francis du Pont Winterthur Museum.*

41. *Pat Lyon at the Forge*, 1826–27, Philadelphia. *John Neagle (1796–1865). Oil on canvas. H. 93 in., W. 68 in. Museum of Fine Arts, Boston. Herman and Zoe Oliver Sherman Fund.*

41

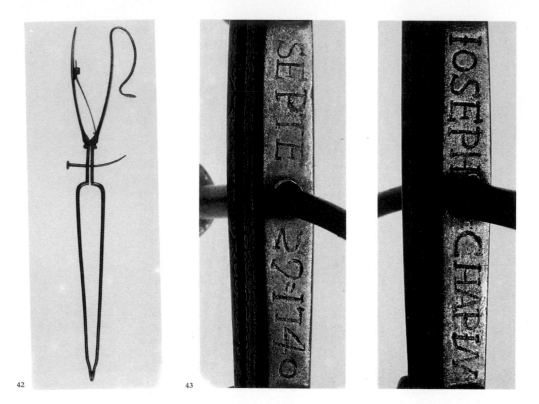

42

43

■ 42. Pipe tongs, 1740, probably Massachusetts. *Joseph Chapin (1718–1803). Wrought iron; marked as shown in figure 43. L. 22 in., W. 4⅛ in. The Henry Francis du Pont Winterthur Museum.*

43. Detail of the incised marks on the iron pipe tongs in figure 42.

■ 44. Candlestand, 1736, probably Boston area. *Benjamin Gerrish (ca. 1686–1750). Wrought iron and brass; signed in script at the bottom of the shaft: "B*Gerrish" and dated on the other side "1736." H. 49¼ in., Dia. of base, 15¼ in. Museum of Fine Arts, Boston. Gift of Hollis French.*

■ 45. Fireback, ca. 1770, Marlboro Furnace, Frederick County, Virginia. *Isaac Zane (d. 1795). Cast iron; bears arms of the Fairfax family and "ZANE MARLBRO" cast at bottom. H. 34½ in., W. 31 in. Fort Belvoir Officer's Club, Fort Belvoir, Virginia.*

manship from the shop of either a smith or a brazier. This is one of only two known marked American candlestands of this form, and both bear the name of "Gerrish" on them. Acquired by the Museum of Fine Arts, Boston, in 1940, it is signed in script near the bottom of the shaft "B*Gerrish" and dated on the opposite side "1736." The second candlestand is signed only "Gerrish" and is in the collection of the Metropolitan Museum of Art. The B. Gerrish who made these stands appears to have been a gunsmith, brazier, and shopkeeper of Cambridge, Boston, and Charlestown during the first half of the eighteenth century.[44] But since more than one B. Gerrish is known, this is a classic example of the difficulty one sometimes faces in determining which B. Gerrish really made the piece and where he was living. However, as further research continues and more illustrations are gathered and grouped according to style, provenance, and so on, the body of information about these objects and their makers is certain to increase.[45]

The establishment of blast furnaces for smelting iron ore occurred very shortly after settlement in America in the seventeenth century. By the mid-eighteenth century there were numerous furnaces in each colony, with Pennsylvania being a known center for iron production. While historians of the nineteenth century collected data and wrote about these ventures, the first interested scholar of the twentieth century to systematically undertake the study of the American manufacture of iron and the tools of colonial society in a truly ethnological manner was Henry Chapman Mercer. In 1914 he published his major work, *The Bible in Iron,* and not long after that in 1919 Wallace Nutting followed with his *Early American Ironwork.* As Mercer recognized in his great work on cast iron stove plates, some of the most aesthetically interesting articles produced by these American furnaces, namely stove plates and firebacks, were also utilitarian.

Among the many furnaces in Virginia was the Marlboro Furnace in Frederick County along Cedar Creek. Begun in 1763, by the early 1770s it was under the direction and ownership of the ironmaster General Isaac Zane, Jr., a Quaker from Philadelphia who served in the Virginia militia during the Revolution and later became a general. The boldly sculptural cast iron fireback in figure 45 was a product of this noted furnace. Especially important is the fact that through his brother-in-law, John Pemberton of Philadelphia, Zane obtained a carved pattern for this fireback from the noted carvers Nicholas Bernard and Martin Jugiez. In Pemberton's receipt book there is a notation that he paid Bernard and Jugiez "Eight pounds for the Carving the Arms of the Earl of Fairfax for a Pattern for the Back of Chimney sent Isaac Zane, Jr."[46] This impressive piece of

45

44

ironwork is visual testimony to the quality of production of many furnaces during colonial times. Unfortunately, documented examples from the everyday production of these furnaces is limited. However, there is little doubt that these furnaces were prosperous, as the comments of a young tutor, Philip Vickers Fithian, in 1775, bear witness to the great fortunes made by many colonial ironmasters:

Before Dinner, Col. Isaac Zane, Burgess for this County, came to the Store with Miss Betsey McFarland, his kept and confessed Mistress, and their young Son and Heir—Mr. Zane is a man of the first Rank here, both in Property and Office—He posses the noted Malbrow Iron-Works, six Miles from this Town—he has many Slaves, & several valuable Plantations. He is, with regard to Politicks, in his own Language, a "Quaker for the Times."—Of an open, willing, ready Conversation; talks much; and talks sensibly on the present Commotions—He is a Patriot of a Fiery Temper—In Dunmore County he is Col: of the Militia—One of the Burgesses in this—But he scorns to have a Wife!"[47]

Primary documents from the first half of the eighteenth century yield a good sampling of newspaper advertisements for braziers. In Boston in 1740 Thomas Russell, brazier, near the Drawbridge, advertised that he "Makes, Mends, and New-Tins, all sorts of Braziery ware, viz. Kettles, Skillets, Frying-Pans, Kettle-Pots, Sauce Pans, Tea Kettles, Warming Pans . . . and buys old Brass, Copper, Pewter, Lead and Iron."[48] There was even a place for women in the business, such as Mary Jackson of Boston who advertised in 1750: "N.B., Said Mary makes and sells Tea-Kettles, and Coffee Pots, Copper Drinking Pots, Brass and Copper Sauce-Pans, Stew-Pans, and Baking-Pans, Kettle-Pots and Fish-Kettles."[49] According to many contemporary ads, braziers or smiths frequently worked in a number of different media including copper, tin, brass, and iron. Sometimes they were even shopkeepers, and certainly much of their work must have involved repairing old and broken pieces.

Few early marked and dated examples of American braziers' work are known today, but even earlier than the marked Gerrish candlestand is the bell metal (a combination of copper and tin) posnet made in Newport, Rhode Island in 1730 and marked on its handle "LANGWORTHY 1730" (figs. 46 and 47). This heavy, footed pan with deep tapering sides is typical of an English form that was a popular utilitarian item in America during the eighteenth century. Other later marked American posnets are known, but this one made by Lawrence Langworthy appears to be among the earliest. Langworthy was a native Englishman, born in Ashburton, Devon, and the earliest manuscript record of his residence in Newport is a court record of September 1731. In the forthcoming decades presumably more attention will be paid to some of the craftsmen whose prod-

46. **Posnet, 1730, Newport.**
Lawrence Langworthy (1692–1739). Bell metal; top surface of handle marked as in figure 47. H. 9¼ in., Dia. of pan, 9⅞ in. The Henry Francis du Pont Winterthur Museum.

47. **Detail of mark on handle of posnet in figure 46.**

48. **Surveying compass (in original wooden case), 1813–30, New York.**
*Richard Patten (1792–1865). Brass, glass, wooden traveling case; marked on face of dial, "R**ᴰ PATTEN, N.YORK." L. 15⅜ in., H. 9¼ in. Eric M. Wunsch.*

49. **Account with John Bailey, 1792, New York.** *Joseph Downs Manuscript Collection. The Henry Francis du Pont Winterthur Museum.*

50. **Pair of andirons, 1795–1810, New York.** *Richard Wittingham (d. 1821). Brass and iron; marked on back of each plinth as seen in figure 51. H. 19¾ in., L. 20⅞ in., W. 10¼ in. The Henry Francis du Pont Winterthur Museum.*

51. **Detail of mark on andirons in figure 50.**

52. **Pair of andirons, 1760–90, Philadelphia.** *Attributed to Daniel King (1731–1806). Brass and iron. H. 28 in., W. 13 in., D. 22 in. The Dietrich Fine Arts Collections, Philadelphia.*

ucts were so much an integral part of our colonial society's daily life. Other types of items that were frequently produced by braziers included sundials and mathematical, surveying, and navigational instruments.

The compass shown in figure 48 is typical of the kind made by a number of instrument makers throughout the major American cities in the early nineteenth century. However, this particular one is exceptional because of the quality of engraving on the brass face. Little is known about most of these instrument makers—where they learned their craft, whether or not they imported some of their wares, and how long they were in business. Usually the best source of information on them can be found in the city directories that list the professions of all inhabitants, their business addresses, and sometimes their home addresses. If a piece bears a label with an address on it, then with the aid of directories one should be able to determine between what dates an object was made. For example, Richard Patten of New York does not appear in any directories until the year 1813, at which time he is listed at 350 Water Street. In 1814 it appears that he moved from 350 Water to 184 Water Street, where he remained until 1820 when he moved to 180 Water, the corner of Burling-slip. In *Mercein's City Directory, New-York Register and Almanac . . .* published in June 1820, Patten placed a two-page advertisement with elaborate engravings of telescopes and other instruments. He called himself a "Manufacturer of/ MATHEMATICAL INSTRUMENTS" and said he would "guarantee every article made, equal to any in the city of London." It seems clear that Patten was not importing any of his wares but was actually making them himself. Whether or not he was doing the fancy engraving himself is a question that is more difficult to answer. According to *Longworth's Directory* through 1830–31, Patten was still working at 180 Water Street at that date.

Perhaps because so little American brass is marked, scholars have failed to recognize the extensive number of brass-founders working in this country by the end of the eighteenth and in the early nineteenth century. While it cannot be denied that significant amounts of brass, copper, and iron were imported from England, much was made on this side of the Atlantic. Occasionally a tradesman or craftsman would even separate his listings of what was imported and what he was actually making, as in the case of William Zane when he advertised in the *Pennsylvania Gazette* in October 1792. He specifically stated that he imported a great and general assortment of ironmongery, cutlery, and saddlery, including "brass head and iron shovel and tongs." However, in a smaller section at the end of the ad entitled "American Manufactory" he listed "a great variety of brass andirons, brass head and common iron ditto." Perhaps one of the earliest indications of American-made andirons is a notation in the 1721 inventory of the New York braziers William Taylor. This extensive listing of his stock included not only "Andirons, Tongs and shovels" but also "New iron and some unfinished andirons" along with "4 pr second-hand Andirons."[50] Another early advertisement of American manufacture of andirons was noted in the *Virginia Gazette* in 1751 when David and William Geddy of Williamsburg advertised that they were making "curious Brass fenders and Firedogs." Daniel King, probably Philadelphia's best-known brass-founder, advertised in the *Pennsylvania Chronicle and Universal Advertiser* in 1767 that he made andirons as well as door knockers, bells, and chandeliers. And from a bill to John Cadwalader from King, dated September 4, 1770, it can be ascertained that Daniel King made at least six different types of andirons at six different prices.[51] John Bailey, a New York craftsman, advertised right on his billhead (fig. 49) that he was able to work in a variety of metals, calling himself a "Brass Founder, Cooper Smith and Ironmonger."

The majority of documented American andirons were made between 1790 and 1840, with most examples produced by makers like William C. Hunneman, John Clark, James Davis, and John Molineaux in Boston; John Bailey, Robert Carr, and Richard Wittingham in New York; and Daniel King and John Steel in Philadelphia.[52] The andirons in figure 50 are marked on the back of the plinth "R. WITTINGHAM/N. YORK" (fig. 51) and were probably made between 1795 and 1810. Richard Wittingham, Sr., was born in 1747/8 in England and was trained as a brass-founder in Birmingham before coming to Philadelphia with his wife and family in 1791. By 1795 he had left Philadelphia and relocated in New York City where he first appeared in the New York directory as a brass-founder on Henry Street. The delicate engraving on the fronts and sides of the plinths of the andirons in figure 50 as well as a number of other pairs by Wittingham might well have been executed by William Rollinson, a New York engraver whose daughter married Richard Wittingham, Jr., in 1805. While little is known about Rollinson and his work, it is this type of interrelationship between various craftsmen that must be pursued and documented to shed new light on the shop practices of many significant and highly productive craftsmen.[53]

The andirons in figure 52 are among the handsomest that have come to be associated with the name of Daniel King of Philadelphia, though they are not marked, and to date only one marked pair of King andirons is known. The marked pair of King andirons is in the Winterthur collection, and the pieces are marked in a rather uncommon manner that suggests they may have been marked later than the date of their fabrication. On the top of their capitals are engraved the words "DANIEL KING FECIT," certainly an extravagant and ostentatious way of denoting the maker. While the Winterthur andirons have no particular history of ownership, the ones in figure 52 were originally owned by the Loockerman family of Dover, Delaware. If Loockerman did in fact buy these andirons from King, they might have cost him as much as the "one Pare of the Best Rote [Wrought] fier Dogs with Crinthen [Corinthian] Coloms" that John Cadwalader purchased from King for £ 25.00.00 in 1770.[54]

Aside from the numerous marked copper water kettles that were made in America, very few other copper forms marked by American coppersmiths are known today. As is illustrated in the elaborately engraved tradecard (fig. 53) of the well-known Philadelphia coppersmith, Benjamin Harbeson (1728–1809), his production included a variety of objects, and certainly the manufacture of copper stills must have been chief among them. Since some of his work is not unlike that of other metalsmiths, it is possible that he may have bought imported parts from someone like Harmon Hendricks of New York.[55] Harbeson ultimately specialized in copper, but like many other smiths he must have begun working in a variety of metals because when he advertised in 1755 in the *Pennsylvania Gazette* he stated the following: "Tinplate worker . . . continues to make and sell all sorts of tinware wholesale and retail, and all sorts of best London pewter, copper tea kettles, coffee pots and saucepots, brass kettles, sorted iron and brass wire and sundry other goods cheap."[56]

By 1764, when his tradecard was engraved, he was working "At the Golden Tea Kettle" and probably specializing in copper. It is likely that by then he was making coffee pots like the one in figure 54, which bears his crescent mark with serrated edge, for illustrated in the upper-right hand corner of his tradecard is a seemingly identical pot. The graceful, sweeping lines of this pot make it one of the most handsome pieces of American copper to come to light within the past few years. The form is essentially English and can be found in both copper and brass on the other side of the Atlantic.[57] The quality of workmanship evident in the execution of this superb coffee pot shows that Harbeson was a highly skilled craftsman. That he had attained a position of great respect and stature among his contemporaries is suggested by the fact that in 1788 he led the coppersmiths in Philadelphia's Federal Procession to celebrate the Independence of the country on July 4.

53. Tradecard of Benjamin Harbeson, ca. 1764, Philadelphia. *Engraved by Henry Dawkins (w. ca. 1753–86); engraving and etching on laid paper, 13¼ in. by 8¼ in. Historical Society of Pennsylvania, Philadelphia.*

■ **54. Coffee pot, 1755–1809, Philadelphia.** *Benjamin Harbeson (1728–1809). Copper, brass, wooden handle; marked directly below handle "BHARBESON" in serrated crescent. H. 9⅛ in., Dia. 6¾ in. Philadelphia Museum of Art. Purchased: Joseph E. Temple, J. Stogdell Stokes, John T. Morris Funds.*

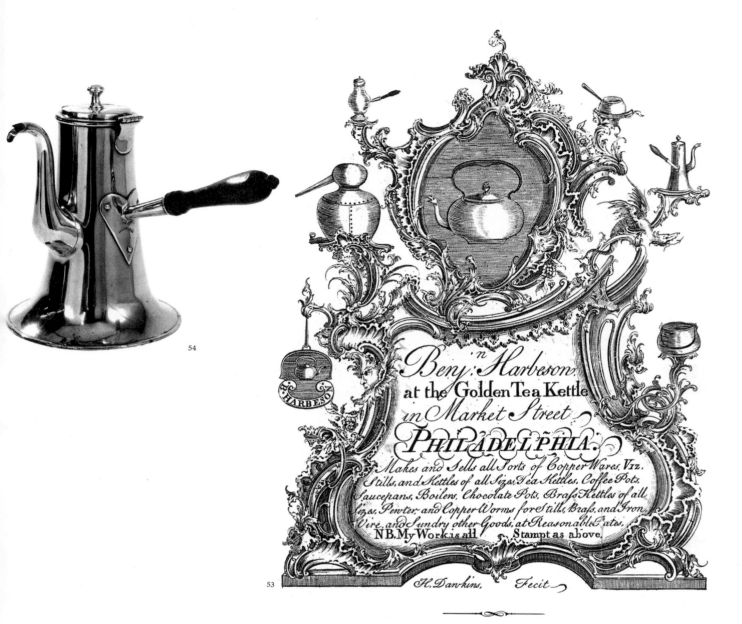

The large amount of glass on view in the 1929 exhibition demonstrated the enthusiasm for collecting American glass of those early years, but little eighteenth-century glass had been firmly documented by 1929. Consequently, many pieces had been attributed to factories without a firmly established basis of attribution, necessitating the reexamination and reattribution of many examples today. For instance, the earliest successful eighteenth-century American glasshouse was begun by a German immigrant named Caspar Wistar (1696–1752), who arrived in Philadelphia in 1717 and shortly began an enterprising manufactory of brass buttons. Recent extensive research into the success of the Wistarburgh Glass Manufactory in Salem County, New Jersey, has both added greatly to our knowledge of American glassmaking and brought to light certain key documented objects on the basis of which we can firmly attribute others.[58] With the assistance of a number of German glassblowers who had recently arrived in America, Wistar began his glass production in 1739. Obviously, since Wistar had no expertise in glassmaking, it was the German workmen whom he employed, and perhaps even recruited from Germany, who were largely responsible for the widespread use of the German techniques and styles that distinguished American glass at that time.

While it had been thought that Caspar Wistar, and his son Richard (1727–81) who succeeded him in ownership of the manufactory, made mostly common window glass, it is now known that they made a variety of hollowwares also. But it must not be overlooked that at the same time the Wistars were making their own glass, they were also importing finer wares from England to meet the great demands of many of their more affluent clients. The remarkably well preserved wine bottle (fig. 55) with seal marked "RW," presumably for Richard Wistar, which has descended through the Wistar family, is one of very few seal bottles that can be definitely attributed to an American manufactory. While there are several other closely related ones known, including one now owned by the Philadelphia Museum of Art and marked and dated for William Savery, the Philadelphia cabinetmaker, this bottle is an important touchstone for future attributions. In addition, contemporary manuscripts tell us that the prominent Philadelphian James Logan of Stenton also ordered his bottles from Wistar, for on July 17, 1747, he wrote to Wistar:

> As I drink nothing but Malt Liquors, of any kind of Beer, and scarce any of my family do the same, if thou wilt be pleased to furnish me with half a gross of Pint Bottles I will willingly pay ye as much as any others do for full quarts the first time thy furnace begins to work again, and thou wilt very much oblige herein.[59]

Extensive archaeology at the site of the Wistarburgh works has revealed a wide variety in both forms and colors of bottles that were made over the years.

Green glass similar to that seen in the "RW" bottle has been most frequently associated with Wistar's products, and it is interesting to note that some of the more unusual productions of the factory were the green glass tubes that Wistar made in the 1740s and 1750s for the electrical experiments of his close friend and neighbor Benjamin Franklin. Closely related to the bottle in both color and chemical composition is an impressive covered sugar bowl in the collection of the Newark Museum (fig. 56). Originally owned by Anne Morgan Hopkins of Gloucester County, New Jersey, this bowl establishes the use of parts/molds at the Wistarburgh factory, for both the body and the lid were patterned in a twenty-rib mold.[60]

In addition to its production of colorless and green glass, the Wistarburgh manufactory is now known to have used a brilliant shade of blue glass for certain objects. Not only is this color startling, but also several of the well-documented objects that have descended directly through various branches of the Wistar family introduce some surprisingly rare American forms. The diminutive blue glass taperstick in plate 7 is of a form quite unknown elsewhere in American glass production. It was originally owned by Elizabeth Clifford Morris (1813–92), the granddaughter of Rebecca Morris, Caspar's daughter. Sometime in the latter part of the nineteenth century Elizabeth catalogued her family treasures and noted that her taperstick had been blown at her great-grandfather's glasshouse.

A second unusual form also blown in blue glass is the charming little basket or bucket in figure 57, which may have been intended to hold sweetmeats or perhaps to be a cream pail, as found in eighteenth-century silver forms. Still owned in the Wistar family, this little bucket has a base that bears an old faded label, probably written by Richard Wistar Davids (1825–63), that reads "Blown at a Wistars glass about 1797 [1747] RWD." In combination with the two tapersticks, and also a similar blue glass bucket in the New Orleans Museum of Art, these new discoveries document another aspect of America's first successful eighteenth-century glasshouse. Primarily due to the Revolutionary War and attendant problems at his manufactory, Richard Wistar had ceased production at Wistarburgh by the end of 1777. However, the remarkable length of time that this singular manufactory was in profitable operation certainly established a worthy precedent for other ventures into American glass manufacturing.

After the Revolution and into the early nineteenth century, New England glasshouses began to take over the market from the English in their production of utilitarian tableware. Glass scholars today are just beginning to separate the production of various factories and reattribute numerous objects. In addition to New England production, the factory of John Frederick Amelung near Frederick County, Maryland, was among the successful manufactories outside the Northeast.[61] (The production of this manufactory will be discussed in subsequent chapters.) As has been demonstrated with regard to Wistar products, one respected way to identify the production of a certain factory is through the objects that have remained in the hands of descendants of the original owners. This is the case in the instance of two pieces of superb, free blown, colorless glass (fig. 58 and fig. 59), one from the South Boston Flint Glass Works and the other from Thomas Cains's Phoenix Glass Works (1819–65). Cains was born in England and trained at the Phoenix Glass Works in Bristol, England. In 1812 he came to Boston and by the end of that year had joined the South Boston Flint Glass Works, a subsidiary of the Boston Glass Manufactory. He remained in that establishment until 1819 or 1820

55. **Wine bottle, 1739–77, Wistarburgh Glassworks, Salem County, New Jersey.** *Caspar Wistar (1696–1752) and Richard Wistar (1727–81). Green blown glass; marked with "RW" seal for Richard Wistar, the original owner. H. 9³⁄₁₆ in., Dia. 4⁷⁄₁₆ in. Private collection.*

■ 56. **Covered sugar bowl, 1739–77, attributed to Wistarburgh Glassworks, Salem County, New Jersey.** *Caspar Wistar (1696–1752) and Richard Wistar (1727–81). Green blown glass. H. 10¼ in., Dia. 4¼ in. The Newark Museum.*

57. **Bucket, 1739–77, Wistarburgh Glassworks, Salem County, New Jersey.** *Caspar Wistar (1696–1752) and Richard Wistar (1727–81). Blue blown glass. H. 4⁵⁄₈ in. Private collection.*

when he set up his own glasshouse across the street.[62] Just as Wistar's German workmen established the style of eighteenth-century New Jersey–made glass, so Cains, with his English training, introduced the style characteristic of English flint glass into New England glassmaking by the early nineteenth century.

The heavy flint glass covered sugar bowl in figure 58 must be dated 1813 or thereafter, since the hollow knops of the stem and cover contain tenpence Irish bank tokens dated 1813. The large footed mug in figure 59 has an 1821 Columbian quarter in the knop of its stem and therefore must have been made shortly after Cains had begun his own Phoenix glassworks. The great technical achievement of these two pieces, combined with their fine aesthetic quality, makes them important touchstones for many other attributions on the basis of form, decoration, technique, and style of workmanship. It is hoped that with the advent of more serious research into American glass manufactories we will see more positive identification of pieces made by the many glassblowers from New Hampshire out into the Midwest.

This discussion of eighteenth-century American glasshouses would not be complete without mention of Baron von Stiegel's famous glassworks at Manheim, Pennsylvania. Though Stiegel's manufactory lasted only eleven years, from 1763 to 1774, many objects today are enthusiastically attributed to this venture. However, in recent years glass scholars have questioned the veracity of many of these Stiegel attributions, and currently research is being done to expand our knowledge of this glassworks' production. The serious difficulty with the Stiegel problem is precisely summarized as follows:

> Although there is considerable written documentation concerning Stiegel's eleven-year adventure in glassmaking, no objects have been assigned with any degree of certainty to any of his glasshouses. . . . If Stiegel did indeed develop a lead glass technology . . . it may well be impossible to distinguish Pennsylvania glass from the quantities of low-grade English glasswares exported to America during that period.[63]

55   56   57

44

PL. 7

58

59

58. Covered sugar bowl, ca. 1813, South Boston Flint Glass Works. *Thomas Cains (1779–1865). Colorless blown glass. H. 9½ in. The Corning Museum of Glass.*

59. Footed mug, ca. 1825, Phoenix Glass Works, Boston. *Thomas Cains (1779–1865). Colorless blown glass. H. 9⅜ in., Dia. at rim, 6 in. William L. Johnston.*

Hence, the question must be posed: Will there ever be a firmly documented body of Stiegel glass?

Curiously, while there were large amounts of American glass shown at the 1929 exhibition, the ceramic pieces were limited to foreign ones made for the American market. Certainly this was not a choice made because little was known of American ceramics. As early as 1893 Edwin Atlee Barber had written a major work, *The Pottery and Porcelain of the United States,* that chronicled the history of ceramics manufacture in America and included valuable information about marks on known pieces. Even today Barber's work is the starting point for many interested collectors and scholars as they explore a complex and fascinating field. His 1904 publication of *Marks of American Potters* provides reference material that is still unsurpassed. Why, then, did Mr. Myers and his colleagues choose "Sino-Lowestoft" and English "lustrewares" over American productions? Perhaps because the overall focus of the exhibition was high-style, and perhaps because at that time they did not recognize the American competition to sophisticated imported English and Continental wares.

In the past few decades increased interest in historical archaeology has led to numerous investigations of pottery sites. Combining documentary evidence with actual physical remains, ceramics scholars have shed new light on a number of the American efforts to compete with the handsome Chinese, Dutch, and English wares so widely imported into this country during the seventeenth and eighteenth centuries and the first half of the nineteenth century. Probably the most exciting early ceramics discovery made in recent years at an archaeological site is the decorated and dated (1631) piece of slipware exhumed at an early colonial town near Williamsburg in 1977 (fig 60). In a major archaeological effort funded by the *National Geographic,* a 1619 settlement called Wolstenholme was discovered, yielding evidence of a seventeenth-century American lifestyle heretofore unknown. The pieces of pottery appear to have been made by people of extraordinary talent, probably English-trained, but because they lacked good materials and equipment, their production was of inferior quality and limited number.

One of the earliest documented attempts to produce porcelain in this country occurred in Savannah, Georgia, through the efforts of a stoneware potter, Andrew Duché, originally from Philadelphia.[64] From surviving documents it appears that Duché, working in Savannah by 1737, did succeed in producing "two kilns of handsome Ware" including "a small Teacup of which . . . when held against the Light, was very near transparency. . . .[65] However, by 1743, when he finally traveled to London to secure a patent for the production of these wares, he admitted that his efforts "were unsuccessful and profitless." Whether or not Duché's wares were of hard-paste or soft-paste porcelain remains unknown, though judging from the limit of his knowledge and skills, they were more likely of soft-paste. There is no positive evidence that following his return to America in 1744 he had anything to do with the manufacture of porcelain at the Bow Factory in England or that he was at all involved in the later Bonnin and Morris venture

60

in Philadelphia by the early 1770s. Although no specimens of Duche's work are known today, nevertheless his experimentation in ceramics production both in America and England is important and must be recognized.

Another southern venture that should not go unrecognized revolved around an Englishman named John Bartlam who arrived in Charleston in 1765. On September 28, 1765, the *South Carolina Gazette* of that city noted that he had "set up a Pottery about 9 miles from this, has met with so good Clay for his purpose, that he scarce doubts of his ware's exceeding that of Delft: He proposes to make every kind of Earthen Ware that is usually imported from England, and as it will be sold cheaper, he cannot fail to meet with encouragement."

Apparently Bartlam suffered some hardships, including illness, during the next four years, but by 1769 and 1770 he had recovered and by October of 1770 advertised that "He already makes what is called QUEEN'S WARE, equal to any imported: and, if he meets with suitable Encouragement, makes no Doubt of being able to supply the Demands of the whole Province."[66] While Bartlam had his manufactory in Charleston in 1770, by 1774 he was apparently producing his wares in Camden, South Carolina, for in April of that year he announced: "Some samples of Queen's and other Earthen Ware have been lately brought to Town, from CAMDEN in this Province, where it was made, and there is a considerable Quantity on Hand, which is equal in Quality and Appearance, and can be afforded as cheap, as any imported from England."[67]

To date there have been no pieces positively identified as the work of Bartlam's enterprise, although recent years have produced more research and some archaeological excavations at the Camden site. It is known that one of the English potters whom Bartlam employed for a time, William Ellis of Hanley, eventually left South Carolina and made his way to Salem, North Carolina, where he worked with the Moravian potter Gottfried Aust and was responsible for introducing English styles and techniques into the manufacture of earthenwares at Bethabara.

The first soft-paste porcelain manufactory in America, from which there are actual specimens surviving today, was that enterprise begun in 1770 in Philadelphia by Gousse Bonnin (1741–80) and George Anthony Morris (1742/45–73). Though this venture lasted less than two years, it must be recognized for its importance as a great experiment as well as for the actual wares produced. While Edwin Atlee Barber and several of his colleagues and students in the early part of this century reported on the existence of this enterprise and cited the one example attributed to the factory (a reticulated fruit basket similar to the one shown in figure 61, given to the Franklin Institute in 1841), it was not until extensive research and archaeological work at the site of the manufactory was done between 1965 and 1970 that the whole saga of Bonnin and Morris was revealed. The diminutive but finely researched volume published by Graham Hood in 1972, *Bonnin and Morris of Philadelphia: The First American Porcelain Manufactory, 1770–72*, tells the entire story.

The first announcement of the factory on January 1, 1770, in the *Pennsylvania Chronicle*

60. Virginia-made dish fragment.
The slip decoration reveals that the dish was made in 1631, and it is the earliest known dated example of American pottery. It was found in 1977 on a site in Martin's Hundred (now Carter's Grove Plantation) during archaeological excavations conducted by Colonial Williamsburg's archaeology department under a grant from the National Geographic Society.

61. Basket, 1770–72, Philadelphia.
Gousse Bonnin (1741–80) and George Anthony Morris (1742[5]–73). Soft-paste porcelain marked "Z" on bottom in underglaze blue. Dia. 6⅞ in. Museum of Fine Arts, Boston. Frederic Brown Fund.

62. Sweetmeat dish, 1770–72, Philadelphia. *Gousse Bonnin (1741–80) and George Anthony Morris (1742[5]–73). Soft-paste porcelain with underglaze blue decoration; marked "P" on bottom in underglaze blue. H. 5¼ in., Dia. 7¼ in. The Brooklyn Museum. Dick S. Ramsey Fund.*

■ **63. Covered openwork dish, 1770–72, Philadelphia.** *Gousse Bonnin (1741–80) and George Anthony Morris (1742[5]–73). Soft-paste porcelain with underglaze blue decoration; marked "P" on interior of cover and on bottom in underglaze blue. H. 3¾ in., Dia. 4⅛ in. Colonial Williamsburg Foundation.*

61

62

63

was most ambitious and full of grand pretensions claiming that the proprietors "have proved to a certainty, that the clays of America are productive of as good porcelain as any heretofore manufactured at the famous factory in Bow, near London . . ."[68] But this appears to have been a provocative statement intended to raise the enthusiasm of the American public. As is clear from other advertisements, the factory did not see its first production of porcelain until December 24, 1770. Establishing any kind of a manufactory in America took a good deal of capital, and this was no small venture, boasting, as it did, "three kilns, two furnaces, two mills, two clay vaults, cisterns, engines, and treading room" and a staff of nine workers whom Bonnin had recruited from England.[69] Existing documents show a viable manufacturing operation for a little more than a year during which Bonnin was constantly in need of money and having difficulty meeting his orders. Finally in September 1772, troubled by the high cost of labor and the incredible competition from much more cheaply priced (but equally good if not better) imported porcelains, the China Manufactory ceased production. Unfortunate as it might seem, there was no way an aristocratic Philadelphian was going to pay seven shillings and sixpence for a Bonnin and Morris teapot when he could have a Worcester one for between one shilling threepence and two shillings sixpence!

Bonnin and Morris advertised they made "compleat sets for dining and tea table together, or dining singly," yet none of these appear to have survived intact or at least to have been identified as such to date. A wide variety of forms have been identified (fig. 61 through 63), but the characteristic Bow or Worcester style of pierced fruit basket (fig. 61) is the type most generally associated with this Philadelphia venture. A bill to Thomas Wharton dated May 1771 enumerates some other forms that have yet to surface, including plain cups, handled cups, quilted cups, sugar dishes, cream ewers, and teapots, and archaeological work done on the site has yielded fragments of several forms and patterns including some of the quilted pattern. Like the fruit baskets, the two known sweetmeat dishes (one of which is shown in fig. 62) are also copies of wares that were being produced in England at the Bow and Worcester factories. As are almost all of the Bonnin and Morris porcelain pieces identified to date, this sweetmeat dish is marked on the bottom with a "P" in underglaze blue. The covered openwork dish (fig. 63) is also a great rarity, though there is another one known today, surviving without its cover.

In striking contrast to the refinement and sophistication of the preceding porcelain is the large, boldly decorated stoneware punch bowl in figure 64. Although this bowl, with its incised inscription "Elizabeth Crane, May 22, 1811, C. Crane," has been attributed to New Jersey,[70] its early date and thinly potted body suggest that it might well be the product of a New York City manufactory that was marketing wares both in the city and in New Jersey.[71] While there were many stoneware potters working in the New York–

64. Punch bowl, 1811, New York area. *Stoneware with cobalt-blue incised decoration and overall salt-glaze; incised inscription at top of rim "Elizabeth Crane, May 22, 1811, C. Crane." H. 7¾ in., Dia. 15½ in. Barry Cohen.*

New Jersey area in the early nineteenth century, most of their production known to date is confined to coarser, more mundane, utilitarian objects like storage jars and other large vessels, and some pitchers. The form of this bowl and its applied, straight foot-rim suggest an eastern precedent, while the flowing, incised decoration accented with cobalt glaze and the simple fish motif inside the bowl suggest a Dutch source of inspiration. Will the recognition of stoneware of this quality and sophistication at this relatively early date awaken the interest and scholarly pursuits of students and collectors to explore further this little-known realm of production?

Just as New York harbored a liberal number of potters in the early nineteenth century, Philadelphia spawned perhaps even more native potters who were trying both to meet the demands of the rapidly increasing population and to match the competition from imported earthenware and stoneware.[72] Between 1800 and 1825 a number of potteries flourished, including the Columbia Pottery of Alexander Trotter and the Washington Pottery Company owned by John Mullowny. While David G. Sexias made an imitation to compete with English Liverpool wares, the Franklin Institute cited the work of Abraham Miller in its 1824 competition:

> The few articles that were exhibited were from the manufactory of Abraham Miller, Zane st. Philadelphia, consisting of red and black glazed teapots, coffee pots, and other articles of the same description. Also a sample of platinated or lustre pitchers, with a specimen of porcelain and white ware, all of which exhibited a growing improvement in the manufacture both in quality and form of the articles.[73]

Though the competition was stiff, both from local production and imported wares, a young man named William Ellis Tucker became fascinated with the idea of china production and the challenge of creating the right formula for a fine American porcelain. Having worked in his father's china store from 1816 to 1823, and even having decorated and refired plain imported porcelain, Tucker soon began to experiment with various clays and formulas with the encouragement, both financial and otherwise, of his father Benjamin. His first experiments in 1826 were attempts at making Queensware, but on October 10, 1826, he recorded his first experiment for making porcelain. In 1827 he received the pottery and porcelain silver medal from the Franklin Institute for

> the best specimen of porcelain to be made in Pennsylvania, either plain white or gilt. This is a manufacturer of great importance to the country, as most of the capital extended is for the labor, the materials being taken from our soil, in great abundance and purity. The biggest credit is due to Mr. Wm. E. Tucker, for the degree of perfection to which he has brought this valuable and difficult art.[74]

Just as with the Bonnin and Morris venture over fifty years before, one of the principal concerns of the Tucker manufactory was money. However, this problem was solved by taking in partners, creating a series of several short-lived partnerships. One of those associations was with John Hulme, and thus the signature on the bottom of the pitcher in figure 65: "Tucker & Hulme/China/Manufacturers/Philadelphia/1828." Because the partnership was especially brief, lasting only from the early part of April 1828 until early June, this handsome example of some of the earliest American-made porcelain can be precisely dated to a span of two months. The form of this particular pitcher was simply called "vase-shaped" by Tucker in his design books, and of all the various pitcher forms he made, it was most distinctively his own creation, for all the others followed English or French precedents. In 1828 Tucker's brother Thomas joined him in the business and took charge of the decorating and gilding aspects. That same year he received another award from the Franklin Institute "For the best Porcelain made in the U.S. gilt, painted, and plain . . ."

In 1831 Tucker took on another partner, Joseph Hemphill, who bought the partnership for his son Alexander Wills. The next year William Ellis Tucker died at the age of thirty-three, and the Hemphills continued on in production until October of 1837 when they leased the factory to Thomas Tucker who then continued it for another year. Until 1841 Thomas operated a china store and sold mostly imported English and French wares, after which time he left the ceramics trade in favor of the cotton business.

A recent reexamination of the wealth of Tucker manuscript material at the Philadelphia Museum of Art has resulted in an informative and exhaustive study.[75] The numerous account books, pattern books, daybooks, and manuscripts have provided much evidence to support the attribution of pieces that have been unearthed over the past twenty-three years, since the first major exhibition of Tucker ware was held in 1957.

65   66

Even the secret code that was devised by William Ellis Tucker to conceal the formula for his "true" porcelain has been cracked. Tucker created this code and gave it to his brother in 1830 in order to keep the secret from his workmen lest some of them steal it, leave his employ, and start their own factories. Now, with increased data and a broader field of identified pieces, scholars have begun to use ultraviolet light to help distinguish between a true Tucker and a masquerading piece of English or French porcelain.

At precisely the same time that Tucker and Hulme were at work in Philadelphia, a potter named Jabez Vowdrey was working in Pittsburgh. The charming and curiously freehand decorated pitcher in figure 66 represents the only attributed example of Vowdrey's work to date. Made in 1828 as a presentation piece to William Price, owner of the Fort Pitt Glass Works, from his colleagues, the pitcher is decorated with images of Price's Round House, a glass furnace in full blast, a cannon, and articles made at a brass foundry Price owned.[76] Inscribed under the spout is "Friendships Gift/to/W$^{\underline{m}}$ Price/1828." Recent research has established the close relationship between Price and Vowdrey, who is thought to have moved to Louisville, Kentucky, about 1829, and then in 1839 to Troy, Indiana. Tradition has recorded that Price was responsible for bringing from England in 1827 both Vowdrey and his wife Sarah, herself a decorator of pottery. Current research and the transcription of the diary of Vowdrey and a fellow potter, William Frost, will, it is hoped, unearth more information about this important group of early nineteenth-century potters.[77]

Another important American manufactory was established in Jersey City, New Jersey, by David Henderson about 1825, on the site of the defunct Jersey Porcelain and Earthenware Company. This enterprise was the first to introduce an English style of pottery that could be produced at lesser expense and thus sold to the masses in direct competition with imported wares, at lower prices! Furthermore, the quality of Henderson's production was not inferior at all, as the *Niles Register* reported August 1, 1829:

> The manufacture of a very superior ware called "flint stone ware" is extensively carried on by Mr. Henderson at Jersey City, opposite New York. It is equal to the best English and Scotch stoneware, and will be supplied in quantities at 33 1/3 pc less than like foreign articles will cost, if imported. We have a pair of very handsome and much admired pitchers from this factory; at which a considerable variety of articles is made.[78]

The English-inspired Toby jug in figure 67 was listed in a lengthy advertisement enumerating various forms produced by Henderson in 1830. Actually a price list of "Fine Flint Ware Embossed and Plain," the advertisement states that this "Toby Philipot" sold for seventy-five cents at that time. Also included in the 1830 list were coffee pots, teapots, mugs, tea tubs, water coolers, ink stands, and assorted toys. This particular jug, exhibited at the Newark Museum in 1915, is marked on the base "D & J/Henderson/Jersey City" and on the small pitcher in Toby's hands "Uncle Toby/1829."

In 1929 English lustrewares were enjoying great popularity, for there were over seventy-five pieces exhibited. Since the latter years of the nineteenth century a small group of collectors have enthusiastically sought out "old china" and coveted various

67

68

65. Pitcher, 1828, Philadelphia.
William Ellis Tucker (1800–32) and John Hulme (n.d.). Porcelain with glaze and painted polychrome decoration and gilt; marked on bottom "Tucker & Hulme/ China/ Manufacturers/ Philadelphia/ 1828." H. 9½ in., Dia. 7½ in. New Jersey State Museum. Cybis Collection of American Porcelain.

66. Pitcher, 1828, probably Pittsburgh.
Jabez Vowdrey (1795–1860). Yellow earthenware with freehand painted decoration under the glaze; inscribed under the spout "Friendships Gift/ to/ Wᵐ Price/ 1828." H. 7 in. The Historical Society of Western Pennsylvania.

67. Toby jug, 1829, Jersey City, New Jersey. *David Henderson (d. 1845). Stoneware with brown and cream colored glaze; raised mark in a circle on the base, "D & J Henderson/ Jersey City," and incised on the small pitcher in Toby's hand, "Uncle Toby/1829." H. 9¾ in., Dia. 4½ in. The Brooklyn Museum. Dick S. Ramsey Fund.*

68. Teapot, ca. 1830, Rahway, New Jersey. *John Mann (n.d.). Earthenware with metallic lustrous glaze; raised mark on bottom, "John Mann/ Rahway." H. 6½ in., W. 10¾ in. Wadsworth Atheneum. Gift of Mrs. Albert Hastings Pitkin.*

specimens of "blue and white" and lustreware. However, as yet few American ceramics collectors have taken notice of the simulated, high-style lustrewares that were being produced on this side of the Atlantic. On September 29, 1818, the *Cleveland Gazette* advertised "Wedgwood Ware, or Black China" produced by Messrs. Ogden and Ludlow, potters, of Cincinnati and concluded by saying: "These gentlemen, I have also the satisfaction to inform you, have undertaken the manufacture of Lustreware, and will shortly be able to exhibit to public a specimen of it."[79]

As mentioned earlier, in 1824 Abraham Miller presented to the Franklin Institute "a sample of platinated or lustre pitchers." To an extent, the wares produced by Thomas Haig, a Scottish-trained potter who worked in Philadelphia, might fall into this category of "lustrewares." In 1825 he received an honorable mention from the Franklin Institute "for his very excellent specimens of red and black earthenware (if sent in time would have won)"—and in 1826 he was awarded the bronze medal for "the makers of the best red earthenware."[80]

Another example of this highly metallic lustrous glaze can be seen on the molded earthenware teapot in figure 68. With a medallion on one side that reads "BOLIVAR," this pot must be dated around 1830, contemporaneous with the death of the well-known South American hero. Obviously a very high-style piece, and probably produced in quantity to sell cheaply, this pot has a raised signature on its bottom that reads "John Mann/Rahway." To date little is known about Mann or about any sizable production in Rahway, but in J. W. Barber and H. Howe's *Historical Collections of The State of New Jersey* (1844), it is stated that "earthenware and stoneware" were being manufactured in Rahway.[81] Another marked John Mann teapot in the collection of the Brooklyn Museum exhibits a slightly different form but has the same glaze. The only other known signed piece of this sort is a teapot in the Yale University Art Gallery, related closely to both of the above, with the raised mark on the bottom, "JOHN GRIFFITH/ . . .OWN/N.J." Again, virtually nothing is known about the mysterious Mr. Griffith. Certainly a thorough inquiry into the production of "pseudolustrewares" made in America in the early nineteenth century is in order.

It is hoped that the objects that have been discussed and presented above have given some insight into the exhilaration that a collector or a scholar feels upon discovering a "documented object," as well as the frustration encountered in the exacting search to learn more about its makers. While frequently priding ourselves on the advanced state of our knowledge as it grows with every discovery, all too often we seem to forget the numerous questions still awaiting answers. The chapters that follow will raise even more searching and probing questions.

Chapter 2

Form and Fabric

PL. 8

The Art of the Upholstered Object

Advertisement

Rich? Kip Jun?

UPHOLSTERER,

at the State Bed

N.º 47 Smith Street

NEW YORK

Makes all sorts of Festoon Canopy Field and
Tent Bed Curtains, Drapery Window Curtains,
also Stuffs Sofas, Settees, Couches, Easy Chairs,
French Chairs, Back Stools, & Cushion Seats,
Likewise Matrasses, puts up Papier Maché
Ornaments, Silk Tapstery Velvet India &
Paper Hangings, with Neatness & Dispatch

I. Hutt Sculp. New. York — 1771

Orders from y.º Country & from beyond Sea Carefully Executed

69

I n this chapter on upholstered furniture, not only will the form or overall shape be examined, but there will also be a close consideration of objects still retaining their original upholstery. Several different points of view, or perspectives, will be dealt with in this discussion: (1) the aesthetic tastes and preferences established by early twentieth-century collectors, (2) the taste of the eighteenth-century upholsterer and his client, and (3) the viewpoint of the connoisseur and scholar of the 1970s, desirous of achieving what might have been the original look. Today we judge the merits of upholstered furniture by various standards that were probably neither of primary importance to the client who originally ordered the object nor even within his control. The epitome of quality today is sometimes seen in the vigorous sweep of the crest on a camelback sofa, sometimes in the proportions of a fine Philadelphia easy chair with generously shaped wings and arms that gently roll horizontally outward to gradually form a characteristic "C-scroll" that vertically joins the side seat rail. Or, on the other hand, to some collectors and museum curators, the finest quality upholstered objects can be distinguished by their carved or turned maple, walnut, or mahogany elements. A finely executed cabriole leg terminating in a strong, well-carved claw-and-ball foot, a meticulously cut Chinese or Gothic fret on a Marlborough leg, or a boldly turned medial stretcher on an early New England armchair will frequently be the difference between an object's being considered good, or great.

However, when we approach the subject of upholstered furniture from the point of view of the eighteenth-century client, we might find a very different awareness. For example, a rich and commodiously stuffed easy chair was usually more expensive than other pieces of furniture owing to the high cost of imported textiles. The consumer purchased such a piece of furniture from an upholsterer rather than a cabinetmaker. Until recent years, most American scholars have tended to overlook the fact that "during the eighteenth century the upholstery trade was deemed the most lucrative and prestigious craft profession."[1]

The upholsterer's business was multifaceted, and today we might consider him a general contractor of sorts. By eighteenth-century definition, the term upholsterer was actually a corruption of the word "upholder," and it referred to someone "who upholds; an undertaker, one who provided for funerals; one who makes beds and furniture for rooms, an upholsterer."[2] In 1794 N. Bailey in *An Universal Etymological English Dictionary* defined an upholsterer as "a maker of bolsters" or "a tradesman dealing in chamber furniture." Hence, we can understand how someone who made bolsters and cushions might have come to be called an upholder, since bolsters and cushions were in a sense a means of support, though more important and more prevalent in past centuries than today.

A fuller description that gives significant insight into the varied skills of the upholsterer in the eighteenth century can be found in *The London Tradesman,* a wonderful compendium written by Robert Campbell and published in London in 1747:

> I have just finished my House, and must now think of furnishing it with fashionable Furniture. The Upholder is chief Agent in this Case: He is the Man upon whose Judgment I rely in the Choice of Goods; and I suppose he has not only Judgment in Materials, but Taste in the Fashions, and Skill in the Workmanship. This Tradesman's Genius must be universal in every Branch of Furniture; though his proper Craft is to fit up Beds, Window-Curtains, Hangings, and to cover Chairs that have stuffed Bottoms: He was originally a Species of the Taylor; but, by degrees, has crept over his Head, and set up as a Connoisseur in every Article that belongs to a House. He employs Journeymen in his own proper Calling, Cabinet-makers, Glass-Grinders, Looking-Glass Frame-Carvers, Carvers for Chairs, Testers, and Posts of Bed, the Woolen Draper, the Mercer, the Linen-Draper, several Species of smiths, and a vast many Tradesmen of the other mechanic Branches.[3]

While upholsterers in colonial America probably did not exercise quite as full a range of duties as they did in England and continental Europe, they nevertheless did engage in a multitude of jobs including putting up and taking down beds, making bed hangings and curtains, paperhanging, and importing both textiles and other small items of luxury and necessity (fig. 69).

While only a small amount of American seating furniture has survived with the original upholstery, these examples merit serious examination and discussion. In addition to studying original outer coverings, scholars are beginning to take careful note of construction of the furniture frames, as well as of the materials and execution of the

■ **Plate 8. Sofa, 1763–71, Philadelphia.** *Attributed to the shop of Thomas Affleck (1740–95). Mahogany with oak and tulip poplar. H. 39⅞ in., L. 90⅜ in., D. 31½ in. Collection of Samuel Chew. Courtesy of the National Trust for Historic Preservation.*
Plate 8 is on page 52.

69. Advertisement of Richard Kip, Upholsterer, ca. 1771, New York. *Rare Book Division, The New York Public Library. Astor, Lenox and Tilden Foundations. Figure 69 is on page 53.*

under-upholstery. Detailed upholsterers' bills, existing examples of original "stuff," and contemporary paintings and prints all contribute in this fascinating search for a more detailed understanding of the original appearance of upholstered American furniture.

In the 1929 exhibition several of the most extraordinary and remarkable examples of American upholstered furniture were shown. The Philadelphia Museum of Art lent their superbly carved easy chair (fig. 70), which is now attributed without doubt to the workshop of Benjamin Randolph, with the carving probably executed by Hercules Courtenay. This chair descended directly through the family of Randolph's second wife and was owned by the noted Philadelphia collector Howard Reifsnyder in 1924 when it was exhibited at the Philadelphia Museum of Art. Just prior to the 1929 exhibition, it had been sold in the famous Reifsnyder Sale in April of that same year.[4] Even today, this chair remains unsurpassed both in creation of form and in quality of carving. The hairy paw feet, shaped rear legs, mask-carved front seat rail, and carved arms seem exceedingly English in derivation, yet this must be expected since Randolph employed a number of the London-trained carvers including Hercules Courtenay and John Pollard. Furthermore, it was a most prestigious advertisement if a craftsman could claim to execute work in "the best London fashion."

Another exemplary piece of furniture that was lent to the exhibition in 1929 by Henry Francis du Pont was the Philadelphia settee (figs. 5 and 71). With upholstered back and slip seat and open upholstered arms, this is a singular example of a form not widely produced in any region of the colonies. Settees were far more popular in England than in America, and today only a small group in the mid-eighteenth century rococo style survive.[5] This settee was supposedly first owned by Captain John Potts of Philadelphia and was purchased on North Twenty-First Street by A. J. Sussel around 1925. Just prior to Mr. du Pont's purchase of the settee, it was offered to George A. Cluett, the prominent Troy, New York, collector, who also lent a number of objects to the 1929 exhibition.

Even today, after a half-century of advancement in the state of knowledge and scholarship in American decorative arts, there remain persistent questions regarding the national origin of certain pieces of upholstered furniture. In the 1929 exhibition there were several objects that raised this same question, and even today museum curators, dealers, and collectors are puzzled over the true origin of the handsomely carved cabriole leg sofa (fig. 72), originally owned by James Prince of Newburyport, Massachusetts.[6] The critical factors on which to base·a conclusion include its manner of construction, style of carving, overall form, and secondary woods employed. In 1929 Louis Guerineau Myers wrote of this sofa that "the frame beneath the upholstery is maple and pine, confirmatory evidence of its New England derivation."[7] But is this sofa American, or does the recognized presence of beech in its frame pronounce it English?

Another debate raging in 1929 centered around a Philadelphia easy chair owned by Mrs. Charles Hallam Keep and exhibited in the first Girl Scouts Loan Exhibition (no. 630). The November issue of *Antiques* magazine commented on the controversy surrounding this piece of furniture. Homer Eaton Keyes, editor of the magazine, called the chair "one of the most arresting pieces of furniture displayed" at the exhibition, and he felt that it could "reasonably be attributed to the shop of William Savery." However, as Keyes noted, "one obdurate critic insisted that the chair was English in style and in origin, and consequently *hors concours* for collectors of things American." He went on to say that Mrs. Keep "had the courage to accept a contrary verdict. Her reward for following her convictions is the ownership of a probably unique specimen of furniture, whose special merits are likely to win a constantly increasing recognition. In this individual experience there probably lurks some profound moral for collectors in general; but it is an illusive one."[8] Whatever this illusive moral was, even today this same kind of struggle over English versus American origin is still occurring, perhaps with even greater frequency as scholars try to sort out the interpretation from the source. While today's scientific techniques offer some aids, wood analysis and metals analysis are not the ultimate detector, though they are an excellent source of additional information.

If surviving examples are considered, it seems Philadelphia upholsterers and cabinetmakers produced more rococo or Chippendale style sofas than craftsmen in other colonial regions. In terms of our aesthetic taste today, the degree of their success was

PL. 9   PL. 10

also greater than that of others producing the same products, and perhaps the finest expression of an outstanding Philadelphia sofa that survives today is the Marlborough leg sofa that was owned by Benjamin Chew of Philadelphia (pl. 8). This sofa and a large set of upholstered back stools (nine are extant and there were originally perhaps twelve) also owned by Chew have been attributed to the shop of the Scottish émigré cabinet-maker Thomas Affleck (1740–95), who is known to have made furniture for Governor John Penn and other affluent Philadelphia citizens. Family tradition in the form of a typescript letter by Mrs. Samuel Chew written about 1915 states that these pieces were "originally bought from John Penn by Chief Justice Chew carried to Hermit Lodge with the other furniture . . ." There was a sale in 1788 of Governor Penn's estate, but to date no record among Chew documents can be found to substantiate this attribution, and there was no mahogany sofa listed in that Penn sale.[9] Regardless of who the original owner or maker was, this sofa combines the quintessence of superior proportions and complementary cabinetry and ornamentation, along with a luxurious use of expensive fabric, the whole of which is outlined with highly polished brass-headed nails. The broad and graceful sweep of the back, with its two extra peaks flanking the central rise, is seen against the massive front rail that is lightened with its applied Gothic tracery and fine carved gadrooning. The substantial Marlborough legs add another element of weight, though again their surface is lightened with carved Gothic and Chinoiserie ornament.

The extensive yardage of fabric that originally covered this sofa made it an extremely costly item. The sofa was recently recovered in a vibrant yellow silk damask based on the discovery of a small piece of similarly colored silk that was found under an old tack. The survival of this fragment supported the family's statements that the sofa and curtains in the parlor were of yellow silk "en suite" at the turn of this century. The manner in which this sofa was reupholstered and tacked is documented through a number of visual sources. Several paintings by such prominent painters of members of the Philadelphia and Boston elite as Charles Willson Peale and John Singleton Copley portray their sitters reclining upon pillows on sofas with tightly upholstered seats that were then piled with puffy cushions. In 1787 and 1789, respectively, Peale painted *Mrs. Thomas McKean and her Daughter* and *Mrs. Richard Tilghman and her Sons* on similarly upholstered and pillowed sofas; Copley's most illustrative portrayal is that of an unknown New York subject (formerly known as *Mrs. Thrale*) lolling upon a sofa with at least three pillows "upholding" her in recumbent splendor. Dorothy Quincy (fig. 73), later to become Mrs. John Hancock, assumed a more formal pose, but Copley nevertheless, embellished the picture with the suggestion of a rich and expensive piece of seating furniture. Certainly in these deep-seated sofas pillows were essential, though their use and positioning was apparently quite flexible. In the third edition of *The Gentleman and Cabinet-maker's Director* (London, 1762), Thomas Chippendale noted about plate 31 that

Plate 9. Sofa, 1790–1800, Boston or Salem. *Mahogany with birch. H. 40½ in., L. 80½ in., D. 28 in. Museum of Fine Arts, Boston. M. and M. Karolik Collection.*

Plate 10. Upholstered armchair, 1795–1805, Boston or Salem. *Mahogany with maple. H. 38 in., W. 22⅛ in., D. 19½ in. Museum of Fine Arts, Boston. M. and M. Karolik Collection.*

"The Pillows and Cushions must not be ommited, though they are not in the Design." In the early 1790s Thomas Sheraton was flexible about the use of pillows and such in *The Cabinet-Maker and Upholsterer's Drawing-Book:*

> . . . Those loose cushions at the back are generally made to fill the whole length, which would have taken four; but I could not make the design so striking with four, because they would not have been distinguished from the back of the sofa by a common observer. These cushions serve at times for bolsters, being placed against the arms to loll against. The seat is stuffed up in front about three inches high above the rail, denoted by the figure of the sprig running longways; all above that is a squab, which may be taken off occasionally.[10]

While Philadelphia excelled in the artistry of rococo sofas, certainly the area of Boston and Salem in the latter part of the eighteenth century excelled in the design and execution of early Federal or neoclassical style sofas. Similar in overall form to the Chew sofa is the magnificent sofa that has descended through the family of the wealthy Salem merchant Elias Hasket Derby, who died in 1799 (pl. 9). While the form of the arms and the sweep of the back of both sofas are quite similar, the carved mahogany portions on the Derby sofa change the whole feeling of the piece. The languid sweep of the back crest, echoed in the serpentine of the front seat rail, is outlined with a carved mahogany band of alternating flutes and rosettes and is surmounted in the center with two delicately carved interlocking cornucopias joined with a wavy, flowing ribbon. (George Hepplewhite illustrated a sofa of similar form in plate 22 of his *The Cabinet-Maker and Upholsterer's Guide* [London, 1789] and a similar type of cresting ornament on the sofa in plate 24.) The forward sweep of the arms is faced with mahogany that sports a large rosette topping a cascade of grape leaves and vines. The front faces of the square, tapered legs are ornamented with bowknots and trailing grape vines, again reinforcing the overall light and airy feeling of this early neoclassical statement. While the craftsmen who framed, carved, and upholstered this great sofa are not known, these same motifs are found on a number of other pieces of Boston or Salem furniture that have descended through the family of Elias Hasket Derby and other Derbys. Although it has often been suggested that these pieces were probably from the Salem shop of Samuel McIntire, Derby looked to the Boston area for many of his more elegant furnishings and stylish accompaniments, so it is wholly possible that this sofa and a pair of similarly carved card tables (see fig. 147) might have come from the shop of a craftsman such as Stephen Badlam of Lower Dorchester Mills or John and Thomas Seymour of Boston.

A very different yet equally successful and neoclassical interpretation of the sofa form was produced in Baltimore. Figure 74 is among America's purest interpretations of Hepplewhite's plate 24, and it is a form that was most avidly embraced by Baltimore patrons and craftsmen. The graceful, continuous curve of the arms that sweep around to form the back of the sofa creates an unbroken tight and continuous unit. Instead of using carving, as seen on the Boston-Salem example above, the Baltimore cabinetmakers frequently lightened the surfaces of their square, tapered legs with bellflower inlay encircled with a light outline of string inlay. The deep brass casters were not only a practical feature but also added an element of ornamentation in the shiny brass cuff that neatly completed the taper of the leg. When this sofa was exhibited in the 1947 Baltimore Furniture Exhibition, it appeared with only three legs across the rear. Recently, a close examination just prior to reupholstering revealed that the sofa originally had four legs across the back, and so it has been correctly restored in that manner.

Upholstered back stools were inventoried in this country as early as the mid-seventeenth century; however, a widespread adoption of the upholstered back stool with open arms did not become popular in America until around the 1730s. This form was most popular in New York, and several early examples from Newport are also known.[11] During the second half of the eighteenth century the form became more popular, and soon the term "lolling chair" was fashionable. In 1765 the Reverend Thomas Dyche defined the verb "loll" in *A New General English Dictionary:* "to lean, or lie here or there in an idle, careless, or lazy manner or posture."

The original exhibition displayed two similar examples of this form, both with cabriole legs, and one with claw-and-ball feet and the other with pad feet, probably made in the 1760s—both were then owned by Henry Francis du Pont (cat. nos. 605 and 577). In contrast to the two in the first show, in 1923 an even finer chair had been given to the

70

71

72

Museum of Fine Arts, Boston, as a gift from Martha C. Codman, who later became the wife of collector Maxim Karolik (fig. 75). Miss Codman was a great-granddaughter of Elias Hasket Derby, and family tradition related that this chair, and another one acquired by the Museum in 1939, were originally owned by Derby. The overall proportions, shaping of the arms and arm supports, and outstanding quality of carving both on the knees and the claw-and-ball feet, as well as on the arms whose ends are carved eagles' heads (fig. 76), make this chair and its mate two of the most distinguished examples of this form known.

A Newport version of the same form can be seen in figure 77. This particular chair has lost a small amount of height from its base; nevertheless it was originally intended as a "lowe" chair and may have been used in a bedroom as a lady's dressing chair. Just exactly why certain chairs were made with a lower seat height has never been properly ascertained, but it has been thought that they may have been used in bedrooms for dressing and putting on one's shoes or "slippers" and thus sometimes are called slipper chairs today, but the eighteenth-century name seems to have been "lowe chair." The arms of this chair are exceedingly well shaped and vigorous and are reminiscent of arms found on earlier William and Mary chairs like those in figure 78 and figure 79. This Newport chair might well have been made ten or twenty years earlier than the Boston one; this is supported by the broad, flattened cabriole legs and the more unusual, earlier shell carving on the knees. The block and vase turned stretchers are also an earlier form than the plain, rectangular stretchers found on the Derby family chair.

Another singularly beautiful example of Boston chair-making and carving can be seen in a pair of armchairs that again were given to the Museum of Fine Arts in 1923 by Martha C. Codman (pl. 10). These chairs have no parallels in Boston furniture of this style, either in overall form or in quality and execution of carving. The workmanship of the front legs, however, is closely related to the legs on a superb oval wine cooler that was originally owned by E. H. Derby, and it may have come from the same shop as these chairs.[12] Thomas Sheraton would have called these chairs "fauteuils," the French term for a closed-back armchair. In his 1791–93 *Drawing-Book*, plate 32 shows "A View of the

70. Easy chair, 1767–77, Philadelphia.
Attributed to Benjamin Randolph (1721–91) and Hercules Courtenay (1744[?]–84). Mahogany with white oak. H. 45¼ in., W. 28 in., D. 24⅜ in. Philadelphia Museum of Art. Purchased: Museum Fund.

■ **71. Settee, 1765–75, Philadelphia.**
Mahogany and yellow pine. H. 38¾ in., L. 66¼ in., D. 30 in. The Henry Francis du Pont Winterthur Museum.

72. Sofa, 1755–70, probably England.
Mahogany with European beech. H. 47⅜ in., L. 84 in., D. 36 in. Colonial Williamsburg Foundation.

73. *Dorothy Quincy* **(Mrs. John Hancock, 1747–1830), ca. 1772, Boston.** *John Singleton Copley (1738–1818). Oil on canvas. H. 50 in., W. 39 in. Museum of Fine Arts, Boston. Charles H. Bayley Fund and partial gift of Anne B. Loring.*

73

Prince of Wales's Chinese Drawing Room" in which there are four armchairs similar to the Derby ones lining the walls of the room. In *The Cabinet Dictionary* (London, 1803), Sheraton shows six chairs in plate 8, and describes No. 2 as follows: "... a fauteuil, having a moulded top-rail and arm, and turned stumps, which are either gilt or painted, But this pattern will suit best to be gilt, on account of the legs, which have heads."[13] While Derby's chairs were not gilt and certainly not as lavishly carved with figural heads, they were probably derived from this French inspired form and undoubtedly must have been in the "newest fashion" when they were made.

During the past five to ten years American and English students and collectors alike have come to regard the fascinating study of original upholstery coverings as necessary to the total understanding of both individual objects and the cultural and social framework against which the objects are seen.[14] The extremely high value placed on textiles in both England and America from the seventeenth century onward gives us great insight into economics, wealth, social status, and prestige that we are unable to ascertain in any other manner. One fact stands out: in almost every inventory where there is a bed cited with all its "furniture," or hangings, it is usually the most highly valued item in the whole listing. All too frequently we believe that life was not very opulent in the struggling American colonies during the seventeenth and eighteenth centuries, but specific documentation of rich furniture and fabrics often dispels this myth. We are increasingly aware that objects were not as simple and somber as some people would assume. In the eighteenth century the bed, with all its accompanying hangings, was the forte of the upholsterers' craft. When we read that the Philadelphia upholsterer Plunket Fleeson used fifty-six yards of "fine red and white Copper plate Cotton" for making "a plestoon [festoon] bed full trimd, with plumes, laces, & hed board, fringed," for John Cadwalader's new house on Second Street in 1770, we begin to comprehend the richness and wealth enjoyed by the elite classes in colonial America.[15]

One of the most interesting early textile survivals still *in situ* on a piece of seventeenth-century American seating furniture is the "turkey work" found on the Boston

74

couch in plate 11. Although this is one of only two known seventeenth-century American upholstered couches (the other one is in the Winterthur collection), inventories indicate that while it was not a common form on this side of the Atlantic there were others made in New England. The American form was derived from an English antecedent, but the English ones were usually found in the homes of nobles and at court, while in France the form was more common during the sixteenth and early seventeenth centuries. The most notable English example from the early seventeenth century still survives at the great house Knole Park, in Kent, "covered with cramoisie crimson velvet, fastened to the beech framework by gilt nails and trimmed with a crimson fringe; the ends let down on a steel ratchet."[16] In England, the later Cromwellian couches were less luxurious and more likely covered in leather with little padding.[17] Similar English couches had side wings that came out from the upper portion of the back and were hinged to fold downward to form a bedlike arrangement, and it is therefore possible that the Essex Institute's couch also had such wings. While the turkey work on this American couch is quite worn and at this time in its life not visually appealing, one can imagine how striking it must have been when new. Brilliant shades of red, blue, and yellow wool yarn were skillfully woven on a very coarse canvas in a geometric pattern to imitate hand-knotted, Turkish-made carpets. Small fragments of a fringe that ornamented the lower edge of the seat rail still survive. While very little original American turkey work is known, there are two other examples still extant on side chairs that are closely related to this couch.[18] Also of interest is the original girt webbing still in place on the couch and the original inner stuffing of spike grass *(Disticilis spicata)*, portions of which can be seen through worn sections of the turkey work.

This couch is not only a rare survival, but it also has an exceedingly interesting nineteenth-century history. It was purchased in 1819 by William Bentley of Salem, and on May 18 of that year he recorded in his diary:

> **This day I was at a Vendue where I received from the family of Appleton a settle which was formerly in the family of Dr. Appleton. Dr. Holyoke, now living aet.91, & son of President Holyoke, near neighbor to Dr. Appleton at Cambridge, recollects the settle for 80 years, & it is an antient part of the furniture of the family at Ipswich. . . . I was not a little pleased with the possession & I found no rival claims. All were willing honourably to dispose of to a friend of the family what they feared to destroy & dared not disgrace.[19]**

As early as 1871 the couch was in the collections of the Essex Institute and was described as on display in a seventeenth-century Friends Meeting House that was moved to the grounds of the Institute in 1865. Recent research regarding the original owner of this precious item has resulted in a possible resolution of its line of descent to the Appleton

74. **Sofa, 1790–1805, Baltimore.**
Mahogany with chestnut and tulip poplar.
H. 38¼ in., L. 78¼ in., D. 26½ in. The
Maryland Historical Society, Baltimore.

■ 75. **Armchair, or lolling chair, 1760–**
90, Boston or Salem. *Mahogany with*
maple. H. 41¼ in., W. 24½ in., D. 19
in. Museum of Fine Arts, Boston.
M. and M. Karolik Collection.

76. **Detail of arm on chair in figure 75.**

77. **Armchair, or "lowe" chair, 1730–50,**
Newport. *Mahogany with maple. H. 43*
in., W. 25½ in., D. 19½ in. Mr. and
Mrs. Joseph K. Ott.

75　　　　　　　77

family, to Bentley, and then to the Essex Institute.[20] If all presumptions in the current theory put forth by Robert F. Trent are true, the "Turkey Work for a Couch 16/," along with two dozen turkey work chairs that were recorded in the inventory of Captain Thomas Berry, descended through his widow to John Leverett (1662–1724) and then to Leverett's nephew, Nathaniel Appleton, may well be the "work" on the Essex Institute couch. If only the turkey work existed in 1697, then it could be assumed that shortly thereafter Leverett had the couch made. This seems a late date for a couch of this presumably earlier fashion, but is it? We can hope for an answer to this as further research is carried out on seventeenth-century documents and sources.[21]

The turnings seen on the exposed maple members of this couch relate to a number of other pieces of Boston-made seating furniture and several seventeenth-century Boston dressing tables. One of the most recent and important discoveries of seventeenth-century furniture is the "great chayer" with its original Russia leather covering and upholstery seen in plate 12. While this chair was illustrated as early as 1895 in Thomas B. Wellman's *History of the Town of Lynnfield, Mass.,*[22] until the summer of 1977 it had gone unnoticed for many years in a little-known private Massachusetts collection. Although Wellman believed the chair to have originally been the property of Massachusetts governor John Endicott (1588–1665), it is now thought that the chair was originally purchased by the governor's son, Dr. Zerubbabel Endicott I (1633–83/4), in whose inventory upon his death there were listed "2 great chayers, 6 high Chayers."[23] While to date this chair is the only known surviving example of this particular form, it provides a firm indication that chairs of this stature and richness were made in the Boston area possibly as early as 1660. William Allen, who in 1633 was the earliest Boston uphol-

76

62

78

79

sterer recorded, may have arrived in that city a few years before and could have done the kind of work necessary on a great chair such as this one.[24] The large puffy cushion that rests on the leather seat of the chair is a modern addition; however, it reinforces the well documented fact that both in England and America this type of chair would have had additional cushioning in the form of one or possibly two pillows.

Leather coverings for chair seats were not only durable but also handsome and, when neatly fitted and tacked with a double row of shiny brass-headed nails, quite dazzling. From some of the earliest chairs made in this country through at least the early nineteenth century, this use of leather and brass nails for accent flourished. The Boston leather-backed armchair in figure 78 must have been the most expensive type of armchair one could have purchased in Boston (with the possible exception of a fabric-covered easy chair) between about 1700 and 1725.[25] The design and carving seen on the crest and front stretcher of this chair are of the finest sort and, together with the superbly shaped arms with their bold termination of scrolled knuckles, make this one of the best examples of chairs of this kind to survive with original upholstery today. This chair might well have been the type of work that was done by Thomas Fitch (1669–1736), upholsterer of Boston, who developed a highly successful and lucrative business that after his death was carried on by his apprentice, Samuel Grant (1705–84). On February 8, 1714/15 Fitch wrote to a Madam Hooglant to say: "Here enclosed is receipt for One Dozn of carved Russhia leather chairs . . . which are good & hope will suit you. I can't yet get the Elbow chairs. So soon as they are done, shall send them . . . The price of these is as usual 21/ps."[26] On May 4, 1720, Fitch sold to Isaac Lopez a similar form of chair and billed him for "12 Carv'd Russhia Leather chairs & 1 elbow £ 16:2:—."[27] These carved Russia leather elbow chairs that Fitch was obtaining from another craftsman, upholstering, and then marketing may well have been like the chair in figure 78. Brock W. Jobe has noted in his study of the accounts of these two upholsterers that the use of Russia leather in New England was popular up until about 1725.[28] Imported through

78. Armchair, 1700–1725, Boston.
Maple and oak with original Russia leather upholstery, stuffing, and brass tacks. H. 53⅛ in., W. 23 in., D. 17 in. The Henry Francis du Pont Winterthur Museum.

79. Armchair, 1700–1725, New York.
Maple with cherry and oak, original Russia leather upholstery, stuffing, and brass tacks. H. 47½ in., W. 23 in., D. 18 in. Museum of Fine Arts, Boston. Arthur Tracy Cabot Fund.

80. Side chair, 1720–50, Boston area.
Maple and oak with original leather upholstery, stuffing, and tacks. H. 44⅝ in., W. 18¾ in., D. 15 in. Private collection.

80

England, by about 1725 it became increasingly more difficult to obtain. In 1727 Fitch is noted as having written to Colonel Coddington in Massachusetts to break the sad news that he had "no Russhia leather Chairs nor other, nor Leather to make them of. Russhia Leather is so very high at home that It wont answer, If I had any they would Certainly be att Your Service. I think Mr Downs has New England red Leather, but there's no Russhia in Town."[29] One distinctive characteristic that even today is visible on eighteenth-century Russia leather is a tightly-spaced crosshatched pattern that was formed when the leather was consistently struck with a sharp implement. This was done to break the surface overall and release the natural oils in the hide, aiding in the tanning process and assuring greater longevity for the piece.

A New York counterpart to Winterthur's great leather-backed "elbow" chair can be seen in figure 79, which also retains its original Russia leather covering and upholstery. When first acquired by the Museum of Fine Arts, Boston, in 1973, this chair was thought to be of Boston or eastern Massachusetts origin. However, with the ever-advancing state of knowledge about this early period, it can now assuredly be cited as a New York City product.[30] With the exception of the two vertical iron rods that were inserted between the arms and the side seat rails sometime probably in the past century, the chair is in its original state—and only missing an inch or so off the bottom of its legs. Now recognized as the work of New York craftsmen are the distinctive leaf carvings on the arms at the juncture with the rear stiles as well as on the front scroll termination. The turned elements of this chair also exhibit characteristics that indicate its origin and that are in great contrast to those same parts on the Boston armchair in figure 78. Compare, for instance, the turnings on the arm supports of both chairs and note the symmetry of the double baluster and central ring turning on the New York example as opposed to the more slender baluster and ring-and-ball turning on the Boston chair. Notice also the similar contrast on the turnings of the front legs: the flattened ball on the New York chair and the more attenuated vase or baluster turning on the Boston chair. The complex group of turnings on the rear stiles of the New York chair are unusual and very different from the slender, tapered columns seen in the Boston example. The same configuration of turnings on the rear stiles is found on a small group of New York side chairs of similar form and date.[31] The plain, rectangular, double side and single rear stretchers all placed at the same level are also a New York characteristic that appears on related side chairs. To date, however, this is the only known New York armchair that is both of this quality and in original condition, and it must be recognized as perhaps the finest production of New York's still unexplored body of skilled craftsmen.[32] Now that this group has been identified, are there not more awaiting similar recognition?

In 1722/23 the account books of the Boston upholsterer Thomas Fitch began to note the manufacture and sale of "crook'd-back" leather chairs; on February 27 of that year Fitch sold Edmund Knight "1 doz. crook'd back chairs . . . £ 16:4:—."[33] Possibly this type of chair might refer to the form seen in figure 80, a style that remained popular throughout the 1730s and 1740s and seems to have been widely exported from Boston.[34] Fitch's successor, Samuel Grant, is known to have developed a sizable trade with local merchants and was selling them chairs that were then packed in crates and sent out on ships as export cargo.[35] After about 1730, with the diminished availability of Russia leather, New England leather was used by Grant. Apparently his practice was to purchase sealskins or goatskins and then sell them to a tanner, who finished them and cut them for chair seats and then sold them back to Grant. Worthy of note is the specific technique for finishing the leather upholstery of the seat around the rails; on all the chairs so far illustrated and discussed, regardless of regional origin, there is a separate applied strip of leather that surrounds the seat rail and covers the juncture of the leather where it is attached to the seat rail. This separate band of leather is then fastened in place with a row of brass-headed nails at top and bottom. This technique is probably what Fitch meant when he referred to the chairs he sold William Brooker on April 7, 1720, as "1 doz. carv'd chairs double nail'd 23/ . . . £ 13:16:—."[36] From the examination of chairs surviving with original coverings this appears to have been an absolutely standard manner of finishing.

The export of these chairs from Boston became so extensive in the eighteenth century that New York and Philadelphia upholsterers began to feel their business threatened, and they tried to compete with this wholesale importation. Plunket Fleeson of Philadelphia must have been feeling some competition when he advertised in the *Pennsylvania Gazette* on September 23, 1742:

> Made and to be sold by Plunkett Fleeson, at the easy Chair, in Chestnut-Street. Several Sorts of good Chair-frames, black and red leather Chairs, finished cheaper than any made here, or imported from Boston, and in Case of any defects, the Buyer shall have them made good; an Advantage not to be had in the buying Boston Chairs, besides the Damage they receive by the Sea . . . and all kinds of Upholsterers Work done after the best manner.[37]

These leather-backed chairs were also popular on the Eastern Shore of Maryland in Dorchester County before the mid-eighteenth century. Thomas Nevett, a well-to-do merchant, died in 1749, and his inventory recorded, "In the Hall Garrett . . . 43 New England Chairs at 2/ . . . . 4:6:00."[38] And in 1750 the inventory of John Scott, another Dorchester County resident, noted "1/2 Doz best N England flagg^d D^o [chairs] at 5/6."[39]

As far as we know, the fully upholstered easy chair appears to have been nonexistent (except perhaps by importation) in the American colonies before the eighteenth century. The earliest surviving examples of this form as interpreted by American craftsmen are a group of easy chairs closely related to the one in figure 81, but with the earliest ones having completely turned bases and not cabriole legs and Spanish feet. Unfortunately none of the earliest easy chairs in this group has survived with original covering and upholstery.

The one in figure 81 has been recovered in a French loomed flamestitch that is not incompatible with the chair but most likely would not have been the type of material used with this style by an American upholsterer. Samuel Grant's accounts for easy chairs indicate that "cheney" was the fabric most often used by him between 1729 and 1735, with diminishing amounts of harrateen, plush, and "burdt" also employed. While cheyney and harrateen refer to woolen fabrics, plush would have probably been a silk pile cut fabric and burdt perhaps a corruption of bourette, a fabric made of uneven silk yarns.[40] Of course, it is also possible in this period that an industrious lady of the household, or a professional needleworker, might have worked some canvas for her own easy chair and then had it applied by a competent upholsterer.

81

81. **Easy chair, 1725–35, Boston area.** *Maple, secondary woods unexamined; H. 50½ in., W. 29½ in., D. 22¼ in. New Hampshire Historical Society. Prentis Collection.*

82. **Mrs. Nicholas Salisbury (1704–92), 1789, Worcester.** *Christian Gullager (1759–1826). Oil on canvas. H. 35⅞ in., W. 28¾ in. Worcester Art Museum, Worcester, Massachusetts.*

■ 83. **Easy chair, 1758, Newport.** *Walnut and maple with original flamestitch needlework on front and sides, and crewel worked scene on back; inscribed "Gardner junr/ Newport May/ 1758" on back of crestrail. H. 46¾ in., W. 31½ in., D. 26 in. The Metropolitan Museum of Art. Gift of Mrs. J. Insley Blair, 1950.*

84. **Easy chair, 1765–75, Philadelphia.** *Mahogany with oak, poplar, and yellow pine, and original girt webbing, stuffing, and linen covering. H. 45½ in., W. 36⅜ in., D. 24½ in. Peter W. Eliot.*

82

83

84

The discovery of the Fitch and Grant accounts in 1975 by Brock W. Jobe has proved to be an important contribution to current knowledge about specific shop practices and upholstery techniques of eighteenth-century American "upholders."[41] In most cases the upholsterer supplied everything from the rough frame for the chair down to the binding and even materials for packing and shipping, if necessary. The following account between Grant and Jacob and John Wendell, Boston merchants, on July 10, 1731, provides interesting insight into the entire finishing of an "Easie" chair:[42]

Jacob and John Wendell Dr to Shop			
2 Easie Chair frames	a	36/6	3..15
Linnen 15/Tax 11/			1...6..
Girtweb 14/Curld hair	8P	21/4	1..15..4
34 Yd. binding			..17..
14 Yd. Chainy	a	7/	4..18..0
2 Yd. Print			....8..
6P feath 1 .. 1/Tick 9/			1..10
line & thd 2/makg 2 cha:70/			3..12
			18..01..4
11 Yd rusha Linnon to pack in			...9 ..2
Truckg			...2 ..
			18..12..6

Of course, Grant supplied the frames for the chairs, and whether or not the client had very much to say about the style of frame and the material of the frame is impossible to determine, though Grant does occasionally mention that an easy chair frame had a "Walnutt foot." The girtweb would be the first thing applied to the frame, then a layer of canvas (actually linen) before the actual stuffing or "Curld hair" was put in place, and then it would be covered overall with more canvas (linen). The "Chainy" in the Wendell account was the finish fabric, but Grant also used "2 Yd Print," which probably went under the seat cushion, to save expenses where finer fabric would not be seen. The six pounds of feathers were for the cushions, which were covered with ticking and then finally the finish fabric. Each chair (and cushion) was then finished with the "binding" that outlined and emphasized the curved contours of the frame. A fine image of this important detail of finishing the chair with cord or binding can be seen in Christian Gullager's painting of Mrs. Nicholas Salisbury, 1789 (fig. 82); although Mrs. Salisbury is seated in a chair of somewhat later date than those Grant was making, the effect and importance of the binding is still the same.

In the Queen Anne and Chippendale styles, there are a few American easy chairs that have survived to this day with either all of their original upholstery and outer covering intact, or with portions of their under-upholstery still extant. The Brooklyn Museum owns an important easy chair with all its original harrateen/moreen upholstery intact. This chair was recognized in the 1930s by Luke Vincent Lockwood, who wrote to Walter H. Crittenden, another Board Member, on February 1, 1932:

I saw on Saturday a piece of furniture that I wish to urge the Brooklyn Museum to purchase. It is a bandy legged cozy chair of about 1730 period New England and upholstered in its original material. It is the only piece of original American upholstery that I have seen in all the years I have collected and I feel that it is a piece that the Museum should own and is a fine record of the way things were done at the time the furniture was new.[43]

Unquestionably the most extraordinary and well-known Queen Anne–style easy chair of this type is the one owned by the Metropolitan Museum of Art (fig. 83). In terms of overall form, quality of cabinetry, proportion, and the remarkable workmanship and state of preservation of the canvas work covering, this chair exceeds all others of its period and kind surviving to date. In typical New England manner, the great arms on this Rhode Island chair are formed by vertical, tapered cones that provide flat horizontal surfaces for the sitter to rest his or her arms upon. The cushion appears to be quite puffy, perhaps a full three or four pounds of feathers, and the whole is outlined with a narrow cord or piping. The marvelously colorful diamond pattern worked on a fine canvas covers the whole chair, with the exception of the back panel. Apparently the woman who created this fine handiwork realized that the chair would most frequently sit out in the room, away from any walls, and thus the back would be readily seen, so she worked a fascinating landscape in crewel for the back of the chair. It would seem that

85. Side chair, 1735–65, Newport. *Walnut, maple seat frame, original leather upholstery. H. 40⅞ in., W. 20¼ in., D. 17 in. Society for the Preservation of New England Antiquities, Boston.*

86. Side chair, 1770–85, Massachusetts. *Mahogany, maple, and original girt webbing, stuffing, and leather covering with brass nails. H. 38¼ in., W. 22 in., D. 20 in. The Metropolitan Museum of Art. Purchase, The Wunsch Foundation, Inc., Gift, and Friends of the American Wing Fund, 1975.*

87. Detail of the underside of the side chair in figure 86, showing original girt webbing and linen.

88. Side chair, 1770–80, Williamsburg, Virginia. *Walnut, yellow pine, and original leather upholstery and stuffing. H. 37⅝ in., W. 21⅛ in., D. 17½ in. Colonial Williamsburg Foundation.*

perhaps it was customary at the time to place a contrasting textile on the back of a richly upholstered easy chair, for a related Massachusetts example has a lovely flamestitch canvas work on its front and sides, and an English harrateen or moreen covering the back with a rich pattern of birds and butterflies woven in it.[41]

When the upholstery was at one time removed from this superb Rhode Island easy chair, a signature was discovered on the back of the crestrail that read "Gardner junr/Newport May/1758." While to date virtually nothing is known of any craftsman named Gardner working in Newport at that time, it has been surmised that he was the upholsterer since a Caleb Gardner, upholsterer, advertised in the *Providence Gazette* on May 31, 1783.[45] Could the person working in 1758 have been the same upholsterer, or perhaps a father? Future research may tell us.

Frequently easy chairs are associated with the infirm or aged, and they are often thought of as having been used in bedchambers. There is a large amount of truth in this belief, which is supported by paintings of the elderly seated in such chairs, for example, Mrs. Salisbury, who was eighty-five years old when painted by Gullager. John Singleton Copley depicted Mrs. John Powell (1764) and Mrs. Anna Dummer (1764) in similar poses as older women seated in easy chairs. George Hepplewhite illustrated a gouty stool along with his easy chair in *The Cabinet-Maker and Upholsterer's Guide* (London, 1789) and stated that it "is particularly useful to the afflicted." In addition, one could have an easy chair fitted with a commode, as was a standard offer in *The Cabinet-makers' Philadelphia and London Book of Prices* (1796):[46]

EASY CHAIRS

An easy chair frame, plain feet, no low rails
If commode front,
If with close stool,
Frame seat, extra,
Loose seat plowing and tonguing the ends,
Clamping square ditto,
Lower rails to ditto,
If no lower back rail, deduct,
Other extras—See plain Bannister Chair.

However, it is not absolutely unheard of to find an easy chair in a front parlor or a dining room as well as in a chamber. And certainly they were purchased by young persons as well as the old and sick. Both John and Nicholas Brown of Providence, Rhode Island, were ordering easy chairs from Plunket Fleeson in Philadelphia in the early years of their marriages and again shortly after the births of their first children. Possibly this form was just as popular among nursing mothers as among aging grandparents!

The overall form of a Philadelphia easy chair is different from that of a Rhode Island or Massachusetts one as can be seen when comparing figure 83 with plate 13. The Philadelphia Queen Anne easy chair in plate 13 is not unlike the ones that the Browns of Providence were ordering from Fleeson in 1764, although the extremely fine quality of this chair can be noted in the balance and grace of the C-scroll arms and more particularly in the generous cant of the back as well as the rarity of the shaped rear legs. While the feature of the shaped rear legs does occur more on English chairs, a number of Philadelphia ones are also noted for this, including a pair now in the Winterthur collection. In overall contrast to the Rhode Island chair, the Philadelphia example most fully embodies a truly rococo spirit with its continuously curving outlines and aversion to any hint of stiffness and angularity. Certainly the original invoice for this chair must have read something like the one that Fleeson sent to John Brown via the merchant John Relfe in 1764:[47]

1764 April 13th	To Plunket Fleeson D[ebto]r	
To a Mahogany Easy Chair Frame		2:05:00
To Bottoming 6 Chairs @ 5/		1:10:10
To 11 Yds Harateen @ 4/		2:04:00
To 13 Yds Canvas for the Chair @1/6		19:00
To 8 lbs. Curled Hair @ 1/10		14:00
To girth & Tax		07:00
To 3½ of Feathers @ 3/		10:06
To 1½ Yds of Ticken @ 3/6		05:03
To 18 Yds Silk Lace @ 8d		12:00
To thread Silk & Cord		03:00
To a sett castors		08:00
To making the Easy Chair		1:15:00
		£ 11:13:11

Rarely do we get any hint of critical comments from customers during the eighteenth century, but apparently Brown was not pleased with one of the chairs that Fleeson sent him in July 1763. In his next order he specifically complained "Last you Sent us was Very Slightly made,"[48] and one's suspicion is that he is probably referring to the manner in which the chair was stuffed—probably not full enough for the corpulent frame of John Brown.

The Philadelphia easy chair in figure 84 is closely related in upholstered form to the previous one, but the legs and feet were executed in the Chippendale manner with substantial claw-and-ball feet and exquisitely carved leafage springing from the knee brackets and scrolling inward to trail down the knee almost to the base of the foot. One of the more fascinating aspects of this chair is that shortly after its recent acquisition it was discovered, as preparation was begun for its reupholstery, that underneath several

89. Side chair, 1760–80, Boston or Salem. *Mahogany, maple, and white pine, and original girt webbing, stuffing, and linen covering. H. 38¼ in., W. 23⅝ in., D. 17¾ in. Massachusetts Historical Society.*

90. *The Painter's Triumph*, 1838, New York. *William Sidney Mount (1807–68). Oil on canvas; signed lower left, "Wᵐ S. MOUNT / 1838." H. 19½ in., W. 23½ in. Pennsylvania Academy of the Fine Arts.*
Figure 90 is on pages 70 and 71.

89

layers of late nineteenth- and twentieth-century fabric, there still lurked the original eighteenth-century webbing, stuffing, and linen! Fortunately, the owner of the chair was sympathetic enough to the cause of scholarship to be persuaded to allow the chair to be studied and photographed in this half-stripped state before a new outer covering was placed on it for practical use. No obvious signs of the original finish fabric were immediately apparent when excess layers of fabric were slowly and cautiously peeled from the chair. However, as the job progressed, a small fragment of eighteenth-century crimson worsted fabric was found wedged against a vertical framing member. The final removal of all later fabric from the right-hand side of the chair revealed original linen, girt webbing, straw, and curled-hair stuffing. Furthermore, there was evidence of original brass tacks outlining the graceful curve of the wings and scrolled arms. With nineteenth-century padding removed, it was clear that the eighteenth-century upholsterer believed in a minimum of stuffing, placing it only for the client's comfort and providing a good definition of the overall form of the chair. One cannot but wonder how many other eighteenth-century easy chairs might also still possess remnants of original under-upholstery.

This chair probably was made in the late 1760s or the 1770s and could have come from any of several prosperous shops in Philadelphia at that time. Certainly the carving is of the quality attributed to men like Hercules Courtenay or John Pollard, but in the case of this chair the lack of any information prohibits us from trying to trace its genesis. We must also recognize that quite possibly a chair of quality could have been finished simply in canvas or linen and then fitted with a number of "cases" or slipcovers either to protect a perishable fabric that might have been secured to the frame, or simply to provide a change of color and pattern for the delight of the owner. John Cadwalader's accounts with Plunket Fleeson for the years 1770–71 indicate that he had a number of sofas and chairs as well as at least one easy chair "Stuff'd & finished in Canvis" and with a case made to accompany the chair.[49]

"Work'd bottom" chairs remained popular in pre-Revolutionary America, or at least until the advent of the neoclassical style in most geographical regions, and today there are a respectable number of surviving examples of these once colorful canvas work triumphs. The side chairs in plate 14 show how the Queen Anne style was interpreted in two quite different geographic areas and how two women chose to design and work a set of covers for the chairs. The left-hand one was presumably made in the town or area of Wethersfield, Connecticut, originally for Dr. Ezekiel Porter, who died in 1775. Five chairs from this set are known today and are still in museum collections at Brooklyn, Yale University, and Boston. Luke Vincent Lockwood, an original lender to the 1929 exhibition, played a large part in acquiring many objects for the American collections at the Brooklyn Museum, and in 1914 he negotiated the purchase of nine pieces of furniture including these chairs. Austere and unornamented, this chair indicates the quality of much Connecticut furniture of this mid-century style. Most notable among the unusual regional features are the tall, straight, almost shapeless back with its elongated vase-shaped splat, the distinctive and diminutive knee brackets, and rear legs that rake back just at the base. The slip seat cover is worked in a popular pattern frequently described as bargello or flamestitch.

In contrast to Dr. Porter's side chair is the very sophisticated New York interpretation of the same period. The principal difference between the chairs is in the use of the claw-and-ball feet, and it is a clue that a new style is approaching. While both of these chairs might well have been made within a few years of each other, Dr. Porter chose to have a fully Queen Anne chair, whether for reasons of style preference, lack of knowledge of another fashion, or for economic considerations. On the other hand, when Hannah Fayerweather married Henry Bromfield in 1749, it is presumed that her father ordered for her a set of chairs in the latest style from New York, as both he and Bromfield had numerous mercantile connections there.[50] The canvas work on these chairs is infinitely more imaginative and creative than that on the Porter chair. An overall and intricate floral pattern has been skillfully handled to create a fitting complement to the lusciousness of the crestrail's boldly carved shell flanked with delicate trailing vines and flowers and to the brilliant veneer of the splat. The broadly rounded shaping of the splat, the distinctive cupid's bow on the shoe at the base of the splat, the bold, round knee brackets, and the squarely shaped rear feet are all special characteristics of New York chairs of this time. This set may have contained a dozen chairs since the numbers incised in the seat rail fronts indicate at least ten chairs were made.

Stylistically the Newport, Rhode Island, chair in figure 85 presents a fitting contrast to its Connecticut and New York counterparts, although the original covering of the seat is leather and not a worked seat cover.[51] In 1929 an almost identical chair was exhibited, and even today these Newport chairs might well be considered by many collectors the most desirable Queen Anne style to acquire. The tall simple back with its gracious vertical curve and rounded rear stiles and crest, the finely carved shell, and the deeply shaped "compass" seat all contribute to make this a most handsome example. This chair, which is one of a pair, appears to be virtually identical to a set of chairs now owned by the Moses Brown School in Providence, Rhode Island, and originally ordered from John Goddard by Moses Brown in 1763. In a letter dated October 10, 1763, from Brown to Goddard, he stated: "The cherry Table and *Leather Chairs* I sent ye money for as I Wrote and should Gladly have sent it for ye others were they ready at that Time ..."[52] Presumably the extant set of chairs are the same ones that Moses wrote to Goddard about, and though they do have leather seats today, it is not the original leather. Apparently it was quite usual for expensive chairs of this form to have leather seats as the following recollection from George G. Channing's *Early Recollections of Newport, Rhode Island* (1868) indicates: "The most valuable chairs were of mahogany, with straight, varnished backs, consisting of a centre-piece supported by a narrow slab on each side. The seats, many of them, were of polished leather, stained black."[53]

Two other remarkable survivals of original leather seats are seen in figures 86 and 88. The Massachusetts side chair (fig. 86) is of extremely fine quality with a neatly carved and shaped crestrail, finely moulded front legs and stretchers, and chamfered rear legs. While this would have been a less expensive chair than its counterpart with cabriole legs and claw-and-ball feet, the craftsman who made it nevertheless carried out his job with skill and pride. Upholstered over the seat rails, in contrast to having a slip seat frame covered in leather (as in figure 85), this chair has the same double row of brass-headed nails found in chairs made much earlier in the eighteenth century. However, by this time the practice of finishing the rails with an extra strip of leather had been abandoned and the leather was simply and neatly cut across the bottom of the seat rail. An underside

view (fig. 87) of the chair shows the neat finish of the upholstery and the original girt webbing and canvas covering over which was placed the curled hair stuffing.

Leather was used in the South as well as the North during this same time, and the chair in figure 88 is a recently discovered and attributed product of a Williamsburg cabinetmaking shop. A simple chair with good proportions and fine quality of craftsmanship, this chair also retains its original leather covering over its yellow pine slip seat frame. Recently acquired by Colonial Williamsburg, the chair has a clear history of ownership in the Galt family of Williamsburg since its creation. Not only is the chair noteworthy for its simple quality and its original leather covering, but it is also important to the study of cabinetmakers and craftsmen working in eastern Virginia.[54]

As mentioned earlier in this discussion with regard to easy chairs, it is now believed that some chairs were never upholstered in a finished fabric but rather done neatly in canvas, and then a number of "cases" were prepared by an upholsterer.[55] Judging from visible evidence, it is quite possible that this superior example of Massachusetts chairmaking was never upholstered with a formal and final fabric (fig. 89). Certainly in Philadelphia slipcovers for chairs must have been quite acceptable, since Plunket Fleeson is recorded as having made quite a number of them for the chairs of John Cadwalader in 1770–71. One portion of his account with Cadwalader noted charges: "To making 6 chair cases red & white fringed thread & tape," and still again: "To 51 yds fine Saxon blue Fr Chk for Cases of 3 Sopha's & 76 Chair Cases / To 152 yds of blue & white fringe for Chair & Sopha Cases."[56] As can be seen in certain pictorial references to upholstered work as well as slipcovers (pl. 17), the use of fringe to ornament upholstery work in the eighteenth century was very much in fashion. Occasionally one of these rare slipcovers surfaces, but few have survived intact; a particularly exceptional survival is in the Winterthur Museum collection[57] and is made of English copperplate printed

91. Windsor armchair (part of a set of two armchairs and three side chairs), 1797, New York. *Made by John DeWitt (w. 1794–98) and upholstered by William W. Gallatian. n.d. Tulip, maple, oak, or hickory; label of John DeWitt glued to bottom of seat, with four tack holes where label of Gallatian once was. H. 35¼ in., W. 16¾ in., D. 17¼ in. Colonial Williamsburg Foundation.*

92. Detail of label on armchair in figure 91.

91

92

cotton that is documented by Robert Jones, Old Ford, 1762. This chair case has a deep
ruffle and narrow strings at the rear with which to fasten it to the rear stiles of the chair.
It may have been just this type of case that George Washington was referring to when he
wrote to his nephew Bushrod on September 22, 1783, requesting him to procure: "two
dozen strong neat and plain, but fashionable, Table chairs (I mean chairs for a dining
room) could be had; with strong canvas bottoms to receive a loose covering of check or
worsted, as I may hereafter choose."[58] It is possible that unlike the chair in figure 89,
what Washington may have meant as table chairs were straight-legged chairs since the
most expensive portion of a cabriole-legged, carved chair would have been hidden
beneath the table.

The use of shiny brass tacks and fringe when upholstering the seat of a chair or sofa
was not confined only to those high-style chairs made of fine walnut or mahogany but
might also be found on the more sturdy and humbler windsor chair, as depicted in
William Sidney Mount's vivid genre scene of *The Painter's Triumph* (1838) (fig. 90).
Unquestionably a chair of New York origin, the bowback windsor side chair in this
painting appears to be covered with a black striped fabric, possibly a durable haircloth,
and then finished around its lower edge with a fringe and a closely spaced row of
brass-headed tacks. When such a windsor chair was made specifically to receive upholstery, the seat of the chair was never completely shaped and finished as can be seen in
the continuous back New York armchair in figure 91. This armchair is one of a group of
two arm and three side chairs in which the side chairs quite closely resemble the one in
Mount's painting. These chairs were made in New York City by John DeWitt and
upholstered by William W. Gallatian. It is believed that they were originally made for
Killian Van Rensselaer and Margarita Sanders of Claverack, New York (1763–1845). All
the chairs in this set (which was probably originally larger) have either complete labels
or fragments of both DeWitt and Gallatian (fig. 92). The DeWitt label reads: "JOHN DE
WITT / Windsor Chair Maker / No. 47, Water-Street, near / Coenties Slip, New York."

74

PL. 11

PL. 12

**Plate 11. Couch, 1660–1700, probably
Boston.** *Maple with turkey work upholstery of wool on canvas. H. 46½ in., L. 60
in., D. 21 in. Essex Institute, Salem,
Massachusetts.*

■ **Plate 12. Armchair, or great chair,
1660–65, probably Boston.** *Oak, soft
maple, original Russia leather covering,
stuffing, and brass tacks. H. 38 in.,
W. 23⅝ in., D. 16⅜ in. Museum of Fine
Arts, Boston. Seth K. Sweetzer Fund.*

■ **Plate 13. Easy chair, 1740–50, Phila-
delphia.** *Walnut, hard pine and oak.
H. 46 in., W. 37 in., D. at seat, 21 in.
Private collection.*

**Plate 14. Side chair (left), 1735–65,
Wethersfield, Connecticut.** *Cherry
with pine slip seat frame, and original
needlework upholstered seat. H. 41⅛ in.,
W. 19⅝ in., D. 17½ in. Museum of Fine
Arts, Boston. By exchange with the Garvan Collection.* **Side chair (right), 1750–60,
New York.** *Walnut, walnut veneer, white
pine, maple seat frame, and original needlework upholstery. H. 38½ in., W. 22
in., D. 18⅜ in. Museum of Fine Arts,
Boston. Gift of Mrs. Jean Frederick Wag-
niere, in memory of her mother.*

PL. 13

PL. 14

According to New York directories of the period, DeWitt appears to have been working only at this specific location in 1796 and 1797. The Gallatian label, which was tacked over the DeWitt label in each instance, reads:

> WILLIAM W. GALLATIAN/Upholsterer and paper Hanger/No. 10, Wall Street, New York
> Informs his friends and the public in general, that he carries on the above BUSINESS in all its branches on the most reasonable terms: Those Ladies and Gentlemen who favor him with their employ, may depend Upon their work being done with neatness and dispatch—Vessels supplied with MATRASSES, and orders from the Country carefully attended to. . . . MAY 1797

The dual labels on these chairs are not only a rare document but are also important because they so specifically affix the date of manufacture and upholstery of the chairs to the year 1797. Perhaps Gallatian was buying the chairs from DeWitt, upholstering them himself, and then marketing them in his shop.

Within a few years of the time the DeWitt/Gallatian windsor chairs were made in New York, the armchair in figure 93, along with at least one other armchair and two side chairs, was purchased by Alexander Hamilton (fig. 94), probably when he was Treasurer of the United States and living in Philadelphia from 1790 to 1795. Because Hamilton was from New York, these pieces have always been thought to have been products of a New York cabinetmaker who was perhaps trained in France or inspired by French furniture already owned in New York.[59] However, within the past few years a number of other closely related chairs have been noted that either bear the label of Adam Hains of Philadelphia or are documented with an existing bill from Hains. The chair in figure 95, shown in its original under-upholstery, is from a set of six armchairs and two settees that descended in the Lyman and Sears families of Boston and have recently been reunited. Two of the chairs in this group bear the label: "ALL KINDS OF / CABINET AND CHAIRWORK / DONE BY / ADAM HAINS, / NO 135, NORTH THIRD-STREET / PHILADELPHIA." Since Hains was working at the 135 North Third Street address from 1793 to 1797, these chairs must have been completed before 1797. Two other armchairs, unfortunately without any firm documentation or provenance but with the same label inside the rear seat rail and also the chalk inscriptions "Girard" and "Lyceum," are presently owned by the Museum of Fine Arts, Boston. Finally, the Longfellow National Historic Site in Cambridge, Massachusetts, has a set of twelve very similar armchairs purchased by Andrew Craigie as original furnishings of the Longfellow-Craigie house and documented to the workshop of Hains with the existing bill dated 1793.[60]

These Philadelphia armchairs were very French in style, and they may have derived from existing French examples that various people had brought back from France or perhaps England. On the other hand, in *The Cabinet-Maker and Upholsterer's Drawing-Book* (London, 1791–93), Sheraton illustrated in plate 6 two "Drawing Room" chairs, one of which closely resembles the Hains examples, but was "intended to be finished in burnished gold, and the seat and back covered with printed silk." While it is not known what the chair in figure 95 was originally covered with, fragments of silk were found across the back of the covering under the back framing. In its present state one can see how the late eighteenth-century upholsterer stuffed and built up the under-upholstery so as to produce the very boxy look that was such an important and integral part of the overall form of these French-style chairs. When finally covered with the finish fabric, these chairs were then tacked all the way around the edges with a single row of brass-headed nails. In several ways, this later type of upholstery workmanship differed dramatically from what we have previously seen on the easy chairs and sofas of the Queen Anne and Chippendale styles in America.

As has been evident throughout the above discussion, the subject of American upholstered furniture is a vast and rapidly growing field of specialization. The technique of the eighteenth-century upholsterer, along with the chosen covering, meant everything as far as the finished, overall appearance was concerned. While it has just been in the past five years or so that our study in this area has intensified, a number of our forerunners were insightful enough to recognize the value of original upholstery and to preserve it, as Luke Vincent Lockwood did in 1932. Future generations will benefit as collectors and scholars perpetuate this interest and sensitivity while they continue to discover, preserve, and study these important documents.

93. Armchair, 1793–97, Philadelphia. *Probably by Adam Hains (1768–after 1820). Mahogany, secondary woods unexamined. H. 34³/₁₆ in., W. 23 in., D. 19½ in. Museum of the City of New York.*

94. *Alexander Hamilton*, 1792, New York. *John Trumbull (1756–1843). Oil on canvas. H. 85 in., W. 58 in. New York Chamber of Commerce and Industry.*

95. Armchair, 1793–97, Philadelphia. *Adam Hains (1768–after 1820). Mahogany and ash, with original under-upholstery and stuffing; note this chair does not bear the Hains label, but two of the six chairs in the set do have the label cited in the text on them. H. 33¾ in., W. 23⅛ in., D. 19½ in. Society for the Preservation of New England Antiquities, Boston.*

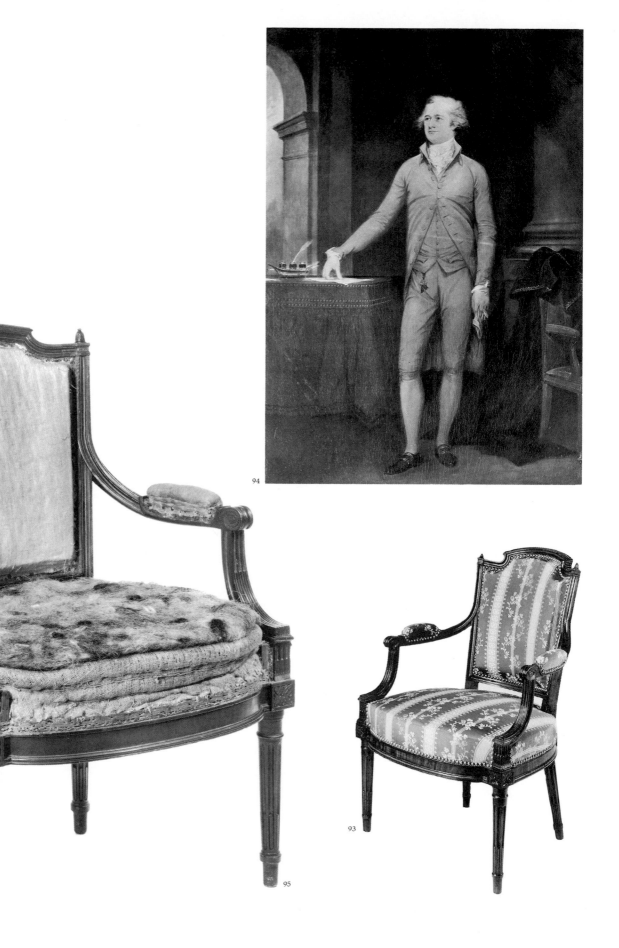

94

93

95

Chapter 3

American Patronage

Special Commissions

Plate 15. *Henry Pelham (Boy With a Squirrel)*, 1765, Boston. *John Singleton Copley (1738–1815). Oil on canvas. H. 30¼ in., W. 25 in. Museum of Fine Arts, Boston. Anonymous gift. Plate 15 is on page 79.*

Unlike her European and British predecessors, America did not develop a distinct patronage of the fine arts until well into the nineteenth century. For centuries, European countries had maintained a grand tradition, through their royalty and aristocracy, of cultivating and supporting painters, architects, sculptors, and craftsmen. But there was little time or place for such extravagance in colonial America. The demand for portrait artists in the colonies was as close as we came in the eighteenth century to what a foreigner might call "patronage of the arts." And even with a sufficiently large number of commissions constantly flowing in, the American-born artist John Singleton Copley complained in 1768 that painting was "no more than any other useful trade . . . like that of a Carpenter or shew maker."[1] Two years later Copley wrote to his friend Benjamin West in London saying, "You are sensable in this country the hands of an Artist is tied up, not having it in his power to prosicute any work of fancy for want of meterials. Than my time is so intirely engrosed in painting portraits as to make it very difficult for me to exhibit constantly."[2]

Although Copley had never traveled abroad, he was cognizant of the difference between the European or English use of the word "patronage" and the American. The incomparable wealth of the leisure classes on the other side of the Atlantic signified not only an economic difference but also a social difference. Affluence and extravagance did not fit into the repertoire of colonists, but the Americans did develop a certain style of patronage that was better suited to their new lifestyle and that called upon the talents of their native artists and craftsmen, even if it did not allow a great deal of artistic license or creativity. Colonial society had a distinct set of special needs, many of which were rooted, in one way or another, in the concept of social status. This American patronage can be observed in two sectors: private commissions requested by individuals for either personal use or as gifts to friends, and institutional commissions ordered either for presentation to honored persons or for use by the state, church, or a fraternal body.

The most important reason for taking a closer look at specially commissioned or personally selected objects is that here we find some of the finest and most extraordinary work of our native artists and craftsmen. Whether the client actually demanded the best or was merely willing to pay more for the latest fashion is often not known, yet exceptional quality was usually demonstrated in this kind of American-style patronage.

Almost all portraits in colonial America were specially commissioned; therefore, paintings will not be discussed in depth in this chapter, but several must be mentioned for specific points of interest and explanation. One of John Singleton Copley's best-known portraits is that of his young half brother, Henry Pelham (pl. 15). This painting deserves attention for the very reason that it was not a commission but rather was painted on the artist's own initiative for a particular purpose. By 1765 Copley was in great demand and quite successful in his native Boston, but he was well aware of the artistic climate on the Continent and in England, and he had a growing desire to know how his work might be judged among that of his English peers. Therefore, in 1765 he completed this delicate yet realistically rendered likeness and sent it to London for exhibition at the Royal Academy. He wrote to his good friend Captain R. G. Bruce who conveyed the painting to London for him: "I confess I am under some apprehension of its not being so much esteem'd as I could wish."[3] The painting was received with great praise and excitement. In a personal letter, Benjamin West recounted the applause of Copley's peers, while Captain Bruce reported that the noted master Joshua Reynolds had commented about him saying that " 'the advantages of the Example and Instruction which you could have in Europe' could make him 'one of the finest Painters in the World' provided he could receive these Aids 'before it is too late in Life, and before your Manner and Taste were corrupted or fixed byworking in your little way in Boston.' "[4] Although flattered by this reception, Copley decided to continue his work at home, where his fortunes were more secure.

Prior to Copley's journey to Italy in 1774 and his removal to England following that trip, he received numerous private commissions in America. Only rarely did he paint children, whether by choice or sheer happenstance; hence the three charming likenesses in figures 96, 97, and 98 are rare and unusual for Copley. They represent some of his earliest work, probably executed between 1755 and 1758; also, they may well have been posthumous portraits done shortly after the little Greenleaf children, Priscilla (b. 1746),

96

97

98

96. John Greenleaf (b. 1750),
ca. 1755–58, Boston. *John Singleton Co-*
pley (1738–1815). Oil on canvas. H. 21½
in., W. 17¾ in. Private collection.

97. Elizabeth Greenleaf (b. 1748), ca.
1755–58, Boston. *John Singleton Copley*
(1738–1815). Oil on canvas. H. 21½ in.,
W. 17¾ in. Private collection.

98. Priscilla Greenleaf (b. 1746), ca.
1755–58, Boston. *John Singleton Copley*
(1738–1815). Oil on canvas. H. 22⅜ in.,
W. 18⅛ in. Mrs. Everell M. LeBaron.

PL. 16

■ **Plate 16. Monteith, 1705–10, Boston.** *John Coney (1655[6]–1722[3]). Silver; marked three times with crowned "IC" over a coney (rabbit) in escutcheon; engraved with Livingston arms on the body and scrolled cipher "R A L" in rim above arms. H. 9⅛ in., Dia. 11⅝ in. Franklin Delano Roosevelt Library.*

Plate 17. *The Reverend Eleazar Wheelock* **(1711–79), ca. 1794–96, Hampton, Connecticut.** *Joseph Steward (1753–1822). Oil on canvas. H. 79 in., W. 70½ in. Dartmouth College Museum and Galleries, Hanover, New Hampshire.*

Elizabeth (b. 1748), and John (b. 1750), had died, purportedly poisoned by their nurse, as traditionally recounted in the family genealogy. Only within recent years has this unusual "triptych" been recognized in its entirety,[5] although the portraits of Elizabeth and John came to light in 1938. Possibly one of his most unusual early commissions, the portrait of John Greenleaf, which shows Copley's strong dependence on English mezzotint sources, is obviously contrived—which may also have had something to do with the absence of an actual sitter.[6]

Next to portraiture, the demand for and importance of silver commissions in colonial and post-Revolutionary America cannot be overemphasized. From the earliest Massachusetts silver coinage made by the mint-master John Hull to the magnificent pair of covered urns made by Thomas Fletcher and Sidney Gardiner for DeWitt Clinton (see fig. 134), there seemed always to be a need for something special in silver or gold. Sometimes these objects were simply gifts in appreciation of a personal favor, or a present upon a birth or marriage, or sometimes even a death as was the case with mourning rings and spoons. The superbly wrought rococo salver engraved with the Phillips arms in fig. 99 appears to have been a marriage present, for it is inscribed on the bottom "The Gift/ of William White/ to William Phillips/ 1760" (fig. 100). William White of Haverhill was the uncle of William Phillips, who married Margaret Wendell in Boston on June 12, 1760. Made by the noted goldsmith Paul Revere, this salver is his earliest dated piece of domestic silver known today. Closely related to it are two other salvers,[7] made and dated the following year by Revere and also given as marriage presents. The engraving on both the face and bottom of the early salver is exceptional, and it is interesting to speculate that perhaps in this instance the engraver Nathaniel Hurd might have assisted in the embellishing. The interrelationship of clients and craftsmen was vast at that time and can be illustrated by the fact that the goldsmith Daniel Henchman made a silver tankard with the engraved inscription "The Gift of Mr Wm White to Sarah Phillips Jany 1759." Sarah, the sister of William Phillips, married Nathaniel Taylor on January 15, 1759, and it is possible that Nathaniel Hurd, brother-in-law of Henchman, did execute this engraving.[8]

The tankard proved to be a popular form for gifts and presentations, especially to churches and for a variety of thanks for special functions performed by the recipients. A Boston tankard and a Philadelphia one are juxtaposed in figures 101 and 102. Both of

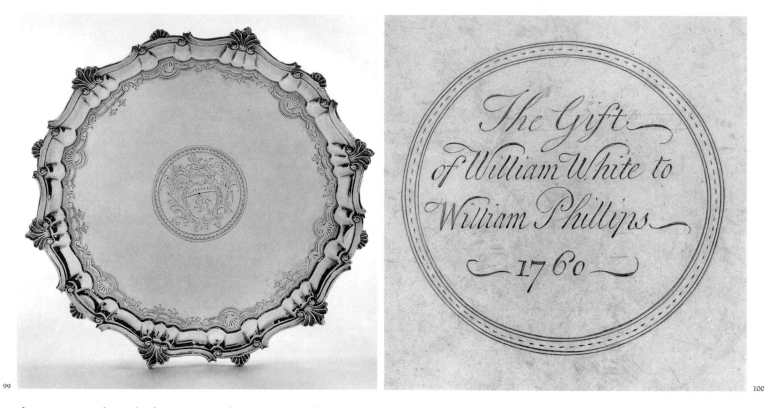

99

100

them were made in the late 1780s and were awarded to men in respectful gratitude for services rendered. The Boston domed-top tankard by Benjamin Burt was given to Richard Devens, Esqr., by the proprietors of the Charles River Bridge upon its completion in 1786. Devens had been a director of this project along with David Wood, and together they supervised the erection of the first bridge across the Charles River. This fine tankard provided Devens with a charming remembrance of his accomplishment, for engraved above the mid-band in bright-cut ovals on each side are an appropriate inscription and a view of the new span with its array of forty lights to illuminate it at night. David Wood, the other director, received a straight-sided oval teapot with the same view and inscription on opposite sides.[9]

The dramatically different, flat-topped Philadelphia tankard by Joseph Anthony, Jr., was also awarded in "Respectful Acknowledgement" of services rendered (fig. 103). However, unlike the full illustration of accomplishment on the Burt tankard, in this instance the precise services are not engraved. But nonetheless, lack of knowledge does not detract from the simple and well-proportioned lines of this piece and the delicate style of neoclassical engraving. Anthony moved to Philadelphia in 1782 from Newport, Rhode Island, and enjoyed patronage from the elite shortly after his arrival. By 1793 Anthony occupied a dwelling on Market Street near Third, where he kept his shop on the first floor and had a workshop and forge on the third floor of a three-story back building. An insurance survey of that year described the interior elegance of his shop with "flat panels and Mahogany Tops" as well as a "neat cornice" and in the entry "two setts of Fluted pilasters with arched soffets Cornice round and Washboards and Surbase." This is one of two identical tankards Anthony made for the Penn family to give to Gunning Bedford and Charles Jarvis. It has been supposed that the services rendered by Jarvis and Bedford involved the finalization of certain personal matters of the Penns just before they left Philadelphia after the loss of their proprietary interests.[10]

Perhaps one of the most elegant wedding presents that one could give a young bride in the first quarter of the nineteenth century was a "new-fashioned" bread or cake basket like the one wrought by Harvey Lewis of Philadelphia that Elizabeth Powel presented to her great-niece Anne Francis (fig. 104). Elizabeth Willing Powel was the widow of Samuel Powel, mayor of Philadelphia, and judging from her inventory of 1830, she patronized Lewis for other silver items in addition to the cake baskets that she sometimes gave as presents. Anne Francis was presumably the daughter of Thomas

99. Salver, 1760, Boston.
Paul Revere (1735–1818). Silver; marked on back "•REVERE" three times and also three times with "PR" mark in script; engraved with Phillips arms on front in a circular medallion, and in a similar medallion on the back the inscription seen in figure 100. Dia. 12⅞ in. Collection of The Paul Revere Life Insurance Company.

100. Detail of inscription on reverse of salver in figure 99.

101. Tankard, ca. 1786, Boston.
Benjamin Burt (1729–1805). Silver; marked "BENJAMIN/BURT" in cartouche on body at each side of the handle, and inscribed "ᴿDᴱ" on handle; engraved with a view of the Charles River Bridge on one side, and on the other this inscription: "Presented to/ Richard Devens, Esqʳ./ by the Proprietors of/ CHARLES RIVER BRIDGE,/ in Testimony of their entire Approbation/ of his faithful Services,/ as a special Director of that Work./ begun A. D. 1785,/ and perfected/ A.D. 1786." H. 9⅛ in., Dia. of base 5¼ in. Museum of Fine Arts, Boston. M. and M. Karolik Collection.

102. Tankard, ca. 1788, Philadelphia.
Joseph Anthony (1762–1814). Silver; marked twice inside cover: "J.Anthony" in script in a rectangle; engraved with the Penn coat of arms and inscription as seen in figure 103. H. 6⅞ in., Dia. of base 5 in. Wadsworth Atheneum. Philip H. Hammerslough Collection.

103. Detail of engraving on tankard in figure 102.

Willing Francis and Dorothy Willing Francis (cousins); she married James Asheton Bayard in 1823. The date of this union is perfectly appropriate for the manufacture of the basket, for its enigmatic combination of both neoclassical and rococo ornament place it stylistically in the period between 1820 and 1825. It is closely related to two other baskets also marked by Lewis with the same touch as he used on an 1822 presentation piece. While Lewis was listed as a silversmith as early as 1802 on a tax list, he advertised infrequently. In 1818 his ad in the *Philadelphia Gazette and Daily Advertiser* boasted that he sold a wide selection of rich Sheffield plated ware of "quite new and very superb patterns"; these might have provided inspiration for some of his own work. His most ambitious advertisement was in 1822 in Joshua Shaw's *United States Directory*.[11]

Rarely in the early nineteenth century were any sketches or preliminary designs made for either domestic silver commissions or special presentation pieces. However, with the increased interest in the nineteenth century over the past decade, a group of drawings have come to light at the Metropolitan Museum of Art that have been attributed to the Philadelphia entrepreneur/designer/silversmith Thomas Fletcher. The sketch for a coffee urn shown in figure 105 is clearly a preliminary illustration for the finished product in figure 106. Fashioned by the Philadelphia firm of Fletcher and Gardiner sometime between 1820 and 1825, this urn exhibits the same combination of neoclassical and rococo ornament seen in the cake basket by Harvey Lewis. Although a specific provenance for this urn is lacking, its monumental stature and the fact that a preliminary drawing was made suggest that it must have been a special commission. Closely related to it is another coffee urn made by Fletcher and Gardiner for Daniel Webster, which is inscribed with his name above the spout.[12]

As has just been illustrated with the coffee urn, occasionally a private patron would order something of extraordinary form, ornament, or cost simply for his own personal use. One of the rarest forms in pre-Revolutionary American silver is the monteith, a large scalloped-edged bowl that was used for rinsing wine glasses. The word monteith is derived from "Monteigh," the name of a Scotsman who lived in the latter part of the seventeenth century and who supposedly wore a cloak that was similarly scalloped along its lower edge.[13] To date only three of these unusual vessels are known to have been made in America before 1775. Surprisingly, two of them, each dramatically different from the other, were made by the Boston goldsmith John Coney. Supremely plain and void of any ornamentation except the elegant engraved arms of the Livingston family beneath the interlaced cipher for Robert and Alida Livingston, this monteith (pl. 16) with a once detachable rim is remarkably close in form to a recently discovered punch bowl made by Coney for the Riddell family and now owned by the Museum of Fine Arts, Boston. Yale University's famous Colman family monteith, also by Coney, with its high baroque gadrooning and cast ornament of cherubs' heads, stands in direct contrast to the Livingston monteith. While any accounts or records belonging to John Coney are unknown to date, the papers of Samuel Vetch, Robert Livingston's son-in-law, provides an interesting insight into the possible date and source of the Livingston monteith. On September 22, 1709, Vetch sent a letter from Boston to the Honorable Francis Nicholson, Esqr. (Commander of the expedition against Canada that was encamped at Wood Creek, New York), stating: "Conforme to your orders I have caused make a handsome montig & ladell for my ffather about the value you directed which will be delivered you at Road Island." Though Vetch does not mention any particular maker and we do not know if Nicholson was asking for this as a present to Livingston or simply serving as a middleman relaying a message, there is the strong possibility that this Coney monteith is the one mentioned, for there is no other Livingston monteith of this date known. If this does refer to the Coney monteith that exists today, one cannot but wonder what has become of the "ladell" ordered at the same time.[14]

In addition to the two Coney monteiths, the only other known American piece of this form was made in 1771 as a special gift to be presented to the Reverend Eleazar Wheelock, the first president of Dartmouth College, from Governor John Wentworth of New Hampshire, upon the first commencement of the college (see fig. 107). Of slightly different form from the monteith in plate 16, the rim on this piece is still detachable, as was the practice. Not only is the applied scrollwork around the top edge of this monteith particularly handsome, but also the finely engraved inscription adds an important element of design and ornamentation. Beneath the entire inscription is a delightfully incised dove holding a piece of olive branch in its mouth, and on one leaf of that branch is the note "N.H. scp." This clarifies the fact that while the Boston goldsmith Daniel Henchman fashioned the monteith, the goldsmith/engraver Nathaniel Hurd added the inscription and calligraphic decoration. It is a specific example of the kind of relationship between engravers and goldsmiths that must have occurred more frequently than ever noted. Of course, Henchman was married to Hurd's sister Elizabeth, the daughter of Jacob Hurd, one of Boston's most notable early eighteenth-century goldsmiths.

Eleazar Wheelock (1711–99), a graduate of Yale's class of 1733, was a fascinatingly liberal cleric who, upon settling as minister of the Second Society in Lebanon, Connecticut, soon began preparing both white and Indian scholars for college. In 1743 he began to instruct a Mohegan, Samson Occum, and ultimately conceived a plan for educating and converting the Indians. In 1765 he sent Nathaniel Whitaker and Samson Occum to England and Scotland where they raised £12,000. Desirous of establishing a college as well as a preparatory school by the end of the 1760s, Wheelock obtained a charter from Governor John Wentworth of New Hampshire on December 13, 1769, after having lost favor in New York with Sir William Johnson.[15]

When the trustees of Dartmouth commissioned Joseph Steward (Dartmouth, class of 1780) to paint full-length portraits of both Eleazar Wheelock (see pl. 17) and John Phillips in 1793, Steward must already have attained a substantial reputation. However, these are the earliest dated works by Steward known today. Though Steward studied for the ministry after graduation, by 1786 he was taken ill in Newport, Rhode Island, and by 1789 was back in Hampton, Connecticut, where he later married. Presumably sometime in the late 1780s he began painting, perhaps as an alternative to a more rigorous life as a cleric. The stiffness of this portrait might be in part attributed to the fact that it is a posthumous image, yet Steward would have remembered Wheelock from his undergraduate days at Dartmouth. The painting is a bold and literal statement of a man and his times and has many of the characteristic devices and the realistic style often found in the work of Ralph Earl, another Connecticut artist working in the 1790s. While the career of Earl is well-known, including his sojourn to study in England, it is interesting to speculate about the early career of Steward and the influence that resulted in his strong and distinctive style.

In direct contrast to the linear and provincial nature of the Wheelock portrait, is that of Edward Holyoke, president of Harvard College from 1737 until his death in 1769 (fig.

104. **Cake basket, ca. 1823, Philadelphia.** *Harvey Lewis (w. 1802–28, d. 1835). Silver; marked twice on bottom in rectangle, "HARVEY • LEWIS"; inscribed on one side of the base, "A Bridal gift, from Elizabeth Powel to her/ beloved Great niece Anne Francis with sin-/cere wishes that each succeeding year of/her Union, may add to her happiness." H. 5 in., L. 15⅜ in., D. 9¾ in. Private collection.*

■ 105. **Drawing for a Coffee Urn, 1820–25, Philadelphia.** *Probably by Thomas Fletcher (1787–1866). Pencil and paper. H. 16¼ in., W. 10⅜ in. The Metropolitan Museum of Art. The Elisha Whittelsey Collection, the Elisha Whittelsey Fund, 1953.*

■ 106. **Coffee urn, 1820–25, Philadelphia.** *Thomas Fletcher (1787–1866) and Sidney Gardiner (d. 1827). Silver; marked on bottom in circular seal mark, "FLETCHER & GARDINER PHILᴬ." H. 14 in., Dia. handle to handle 10 in. Private collection.*

■ 107. **Monteith, ca. 1771, Boston.** *Wrought by Daniel Henchman (1730–75). Engraved by Nathaniel Hurd (1729–77). Silver; marked "Henchman" in rectangle on bottom; engraved on side of body, "His Excellency John Wentworth Esqʳ/ Governor of the Province of New Hampshire/ And those Friends who accompanied him/ To Dartmouth College the first Commencement 1771./ In Testimony of their Gratitude and good Wishes/ Present this to the/ Revᵈ Eleazer Wheelock, D.D. President/ And to his Successors in that Office." H. 4⅝ in., Dia. 10 in. Dartmouth College Museum and Galleries, Hanover, New Hampshire.*

104

105

7

106

108

109

110

111

108. *Edward Holyoke (1689–1769), ca. 1759–61, Boston.* John Singleton Copley (1738–1815). Oil on canvas. H. 50½ in., W. 40½ in. Harvard University Portrait Collection.

109. High chest of drawers, 1710–20, Boston area. *Walnut, walnut veneers, and white pine. H. 69¾ in., W. 43⅛ in., D. 21 in. The Metropolitan Museum of Art. Gift of Clarence Dillon, 1975.*

110. Pair of candlesticks, 1724, Boston. *John Burt (1692[3]–1745[6]). Silver; marked on the foot of each stick: "I B" crowned, with pellet below, in a shield; inscribed on facet next to maker's mark, "Donum/ Pupillorum/ 1724." H. 7 in. Courtesy of the President and Fellows of Harvard College.*

■ **111. Two-handled covered cup, 1701, Boston.** *John Coney (1655[6]–1722[3]). Silver; marked "IC" above a fleur-de-lys, in a heart-shaped punch on side with inscription; engraved on one side with the Stoughton arms in foliate cartouche and on the other side inscribed, "The Gift of the Hon. William Stoughton, who died at Dorchester, July 7th, 1701." H. 10 in., Dia. at lip 7 in. Courtesy of the President and Fellows of Harvard College.*

108). John Singleton Copley's startling ability to capture the innermost qualities of his sitter's personality and manner of life comes through with great strength in this portrait. Born into the heritage of a staunch and stalwart seventeenth-century Massachusetts family, Holyoke received his education at Harvard, became a tutor and then a fellow of the Corporation, and by 1716 was ordained as pastor of the Second Congregational Church in Marblehead. Jules Prown, in his exhaustive study of Copley (1966), has dated this image in the late 1750s or very early 1760s, along with several other "vigorous portraits of old men that are among the strongest of Copley's artistic achievements." Given Copley's obvious use of specific devices symbolizing academia and authority—the President's chair of seventeenth-century origin, the robes, the book, the wig, and the college buildings in the background—one would assume that this portrait was a commission from the college, as was the case with the Wheelock portrait. But that information is not known, and even in Holyoke's personal diary there is no mention, ever so brief, of his having sat for his likeness.[16] The fact that Holyoke never felt it necessary to make any notation about his portrait was probably very much in keeping with his general character, for a contemporary described him thus: he had "fine commanding presence and united great dignity with great urbanity in his manners. In conversation, as well as in public discourse, he spoke with fluency and appropriateness, and yet without any appearance of ostentation. In the government of the college he was mild, but yet firm and efficient and in the whole admirably qualified to be its head."[17] Since Holyoke never mentioned sitting for Copley, one could not hope that he would ever so vainly mention his purchase of such an ostentatious piece of household furniture as the elaborately veneered high chest of drawers in figure 109. This elegant piece of early eighteenth-century Massachusetts case furniture actually belonged to Holyoke, though its maker and date of fabrication are unknown. Still retaining original brasses and fine patina, this particular high chest of drawers has a design that is enhanced by fluted pilasters flanking each side of the upper case and by a top cornice that conceals a narrow drawer below the elaborate moldings.[18] While Holyoke never noted purchases in his diary, he did mention his three marriages. The first one took place in 1717, and a year later, on December 19, 1718, he noted: "First dwelt in my own house." Possibly Holyoke acquired this piece upon or shortly after his first marriage or when he moved into his own house in Marblehead in 1718. However, since Holyoke married again in 1725 and in 1742, it is also probable that the high chest of drawers entered his household with one of these unions.

As president of Harvard College, Holyoke participated in the traditions of the early American educational system which was, of course, firmly rooted in that of the English. Among these, the practice of each entering class's being assigned a tutor for their remaining years of study was a circumstance of great benefit both for the students and the tutors. As a result of this system, many tutors became the fortunate recipients of handsome gifts of silver as each appreciative class graduated and deemed it appropriate to express thanks and gratitude to their beloved tutor. Henry Flynt and Nicholas Sever were two tutors much loved by students, and today a number of pieces of "tutorial plate" survive as heartfelt reminders of the bond that must have existed between tutor and student. In 1934 the Fogg Museum exhibited fourteen pieces of silver that had been owned by Sever, seven of which were tutorial gifts.[19] Included in that exhibition was this pair of exquisite hexagonal, baluster form candlesticks made by John Burt of Boston and presented to Sever in 1724, appropriately engraved "Donum Pupillorum" (fig. 110). Sever received gifts in 1724 and again in 1728, in which year he decided to make a complete inventory of his plate prior to his removal from the college. Inventories such as Sever's are rare, but when discovered they provide great insight into the lifestyles and manners of their owners. In addition to the candlesticks, a rare form in eighteenth-century American silver, Sever also received that same year a finely wrought pair of chafing dishes, also made by John Burt.[20]

Tutorial gifts have only rarely come back to rest in the institution through which they were originally generated, but as we have already seen in the case of the Dartmouth College monteith, occasionally a special piece of plate would be given specifically to the college or university. Harvard's most significant and ambitious piece of plate is the monumental two-handled covered cup made by John Coney and presented to the college in 1701 by Lieutenant-Governor William Stoughton, just before his death in July of that year (fig. 111). Characteristic of the baroque style popular in England during the late seventeenth century and the reign of King William and Queen Mary, the cast caryatid handles, raised bands of gadrooning and fluting, and finely engraved arms enveloped in acanthus mantling were all elements of design that Coney and his contemporaries employed on various other forms of silver. Jeremiah Dummer used the same fluting on a pair of church cups he made for Stoughton to present to the First Church of Dorchester. Just one week before Stoughton's death he had a visit from Judge Samuel Sewall who afterward recorded the following in his diary:

> Monday, June 30. Lt. Govr said would go to the Commencement once more in his life-time; so would adjourn the Court to Friday; and did so. But was very much pained going home. Mr. Nelsen, Secretary and I visit him on Thursday to dissuade him from going, lest some ill consequence should happen. He consented, and order'd us to present his Bowl. After Dinner and singing, I took it and had it fill'd up, and drunk to the president, saying that by reason of the absence of him who was the Firmament and Ornament of the Province, and that Society I presented that Grace-Cup *pro more Academarium in Anglia.*[21]

Stoughton died just seven days later, but his generosity and love for his alma mater (class of 1650) have long been remembered at Harvard. His image by an unknown American limner graces the halls of that time-honored institution to this day.

College presidents and wealthy benefactors are not the only esteemed citizens whose images were captured on canvas by notable artists, both native-born and émigré. Until just a few years ago when this portrait of Reverend Ebenezer Turell by John Smibert (1688–1751) was acquired by the Newark Museum, it hung in the First Parish Church of Medford, Massachusetts (fig. 112). While Henry Wilder Foote knew of and recorded this painting in his major work on Smibert published in 1950, it was not until the discovery and subsequent publication of Smibert's notebook in 1969 that it became known that Smibert had painted Turell's image in 1734. At that same time, during the month of October 1734, Smibert also did a half portrait of Turell's wife, the former Jane Colman (who died the next year), and her father, the Reverend Benjamin Colman, pastor of the church in Brattle Street and under whom Turell had studied in 1723. When Turell died in 1778, after three marriages that undoubtedly brought great revenue into his estate, his inventory totaled over £9300. in value. In his estate were eight portraits, including one of Turell, a wife, Benjamin Colman (these three must have been the Smiberts), Charles II, Oliver Cromwell, Judge Addington Davenport, and Judge Isaac Addington. After his death, Turell was spoken of by people who had known him as a "handsome, social, vivid, genial man who enjoyed society and contributed largely to its pleasure; yet no wise neglecting the duties of a devout, ernest and faithful minister."[22]

While Turell was not an exceedingly wealthy man, years before his death he saw fit to bequeath to his church a large handsome tankard by the Boston goldsmith Jeremiah Dummer, which was engraved "The Gift of the/ Revd Ebenezer Turell A.M./ to the first/ Church of Christ/ in Medford/ 1759." This tankard, fashioned many years before its gift to the church, bears the initials of its original owners "N^CE" on the handle, and it might well have come into Turell's possession through one of his marriages. The custom of giving or bequeathing to churches silver or money to purchase "plate" was widespread in America from the seventeenth through the nineteenth centuries. The churches of Massachusetts are especially rich in early silver by American goldsmiths, and this wide array of plate is ample testimony to the piety and respect for spiritual matters that our ancestors had. In addition to giving Harvard its outstanding "Grace-Cup," Lieutenant-Governor William Stoughton also bequeathed in his will of 1701 "To the Church of Dorchester . . . two pieces of Plate for ye Communion of £6 value each. allso £50 the yearly income to be for any such service of the Church as shall be most needful."[23] Still owned by the First Church of Dorchester, the two pieces of plate (fig. 113) are a pair of standing cups with gadrooned bases, baluster stems, and fluting around the lower part of their bowls that bear the same finely engraved Stoughton arms as the Coney grace cup at Harvard. An original inscription on each cup reads "Ex dono Hon^{bls} Guliel:Stoughton Armig^{ris} Anno 1701," while a later inscription was added in English: "The Gift of/ Gov. William Stoughton/ to the/ Church in Dorchester/ 1701." Whether Stoughton owned and used these cups personally before bequeathing them to the church is unknown, but this was a form made on a number of other occasions by Dummer and other goldsmiths, and similar standing cups are owned by numerous other New England churches.

112

113

114

112. *The Reverend Ebenezer Turell, 1734,* Boston. *John Smibert (1688–1751). Oil on canvas. H. 29½ in., W. 24½ in. The Newark Museum.*

113. Standing cup, one of a pair, 1701, Boston. *Jeremiah Dummer (1645–1718). Silver; marked "ID" in a heart over a fleur-de-lys on top of base; inscribed "Ex dono Hon*bls *Guliel:Stoughton Armig*ris *Anno 1701," with later inscription "The Gift of/ Gov. William Stoughton/ to the/ Church in Dorchester/ 1701." H. 8 in., Dia. at rim 4¼ in. The First Parish Church in Dorchester, Gathered 1630.*

114. Beaker, 1700–1710, New York. *Henricus Boelen (1697–1755). Silver; marked with a cojoined "HB." H. 6¾ in., Dia. at rim 4¼ in. The Brooklyn Museum. Gift of Timothy Ingraham Hubbard.*

115

While churches outside of New England are not as rich in early American silver, many of them were the recipients of fine pieces of plate that were used for various sacraments in the church. In the Dutch Reformed churches in the New York and New Jersey area, the most common objects given to churches were tall beakers with straight, flaring sides, applied bands or ornament around their bases, and engraved overall decoration. The beaker in figure 114, one of a pair, was originally made for the Dutch Reformed Church in Flatlands. Typical of much early New York silver is the applied, molded band around the base, the engraved strapwork band around the top, and the simply engraved, scrolled foliate ornament. The crude figures of Faith, Hope, and Charity are found on other New York beakers, and it is questionable whether the goldsmith Henricus Boelen, who fashioned this beaker, actually did the engraving also.

Many churches from Philadelphia southward were also given gifts of silver, but frequently these pieces were wrought by London goldsmiths because of closer ties in these regions with the mother country, and sometimes simply because of a dearth of competent craftsmen who could execute specially commissioned pieces. By the mid-eighteenth century though, Charleston, South Carolina, was an elite and fashionable metropolis, with every pretension of being the most sophisticated city in the New World. Alexander Petrie seems to have been one of Charleston's most talented goldsmiths, as a number of ambitious pieces of his workmanship bear witness to this fact today. In 1755 Henry Middleton, second president of the Continental Congress in 1774 and owner of the celebrated Middleton Place plantation just outside of Charleston, ordered an unusual scalloped dish (fig. 115) from Petrie and had the following inscription engraved on it: "The Gift of Henry Midelton Esq./ to St Georges Church in Dorchester/ 1755." Over a century later the following inscription was added below the first: "Presented to/St. Michaels Church/by/Henry A. Middleton Esqr./Charleston S.C./April 1871." Apparently when the St. George's congregation disbanded, the plate was transferred to St. Michael's Church, where it has remained to this date.

While the various Protestant and Catholic churches in the colonies had their assortment of ritualistic silver equipage such as communion cups, plates, baptismal basins, and patens, the Jews who settled in Newport, New York, Philadelphia, and Charleston before the Revolution also brought with them from their homelands religious customs that called for specific ritualistic accoutrements for ceremonies in the synagogues. Four categories of objects were often commissioned for use on the Torah: the crown of the Torah, the scroll bells or rimonim, the breastplate, and the pointer. In terms of the goldsmith's art, the scroll bells were probably the most difficult and challenging of all religious objects to fabricate (fig. 116). Although the design was derived from English precedents from the first half of the century, Myer Myers varied the traditional design in which the overall form was strictly pyramidal, making his vase-shaped or pyriform. The delicacy and skill with which he pierced and chased these religious objects seems to surpass most domestic production of other eighteenth-century goldsmiths.

Silver was not the only medium used to fashion objects for religious ritual; pewter and other base metals were popular in less affluent areas. In fact, religious objects made out of pewter could be equally (if not more) handsome and ambitious as their counter-

116

117

118

119

parts in silver. The singularly important pewter candlesticks (two of a set of four) in figure 117 are among the most elaborate Christian ceremonial articles made in America before the end of the Revolution. Though Catholic in form and symbolism, it is presumed that they were made for a Moravian church because they were found near Reading, Pennsylvania. Boldly marked "LANCASTER/ICH" (fig. 118) by their maker, Johann Christoph Heyne, they may have been modeled after the seventeenth-century German ones that could have been owned by someone in the surrounding area in Lancaster County. Born in Saxony, Germany, Heyne apparently learned his craft there and then went to Stockholm, Sweden, in 1735, to serve as a journeyman before finally coming to Philadelphia in 1742 with a group of Moravians. Heyne settled in Bethlehem with the group, where he proceeded to serve as a missionary and itinerant minister, even making a trip to Ireland in 1747–49. By 1750 he was living in Tulpehocken, the hometown of his wife's family, and by 1757 he was listed on the Lancaster tax rolls, though he must have been working between 1750 and 1757, for dated pieces of pewter from his hand survive from that period. Many pieces of great quality and skill came from Heyne's shop in Lancaster, and one must not forget that during Heyne's lifetime, Lancaster was the largest inland town in the colonies. This fact, along with its proximity to Philadelphia, accounts for the style and sophistication of the products of many of Lancaster's craftsmen.[24]

Another unusual form in American ecclesiastical pewter just recently came to light bearing the marks of Henry Will, pewterer of New York and Albany between 1761 and 1793. This deep, scalloped-edge baptismal basin (fig. 119) derives its form from European and English precedents, but unfortunately its provenance has been lost and nothing is known about the person who originally ordered it or the church that first owned it. However, the applied molding around the scalloped rim makes it one of the handsomest and most pleasing of known pewter basins of this type. Henry Will was born in Herborn, Germany, and came to New York with his parents and two brothers and sister soon after 1750. Henry's father John was also a noted pewterer of New York, though his two brothers, William and Philip, established themselves in Philadelphia. Between 1768 and 1772 Henry's shop in the Old Slip was advertised as "The Sign of the Block-tin Teapot." In 1775 he was listed as a lieutenant in the Albany Militia, and by the time the British occupied New York City in 1776, Henry removed his business to Albany until 1783 when he resumed work in New York. Ledlie Laughlin has called Henry Will "the most gifted of American pewterers," and he may well have been. In addition to the recent discovery of this bowl, an account book kept by Henry Will between 1763 and 1793 has come to the attention of pewter scholars[25] and might provide valuable insight into the relationship between the New York and Philadelphia Wills as well as into various exchanges and trade practices.

American ecclesiastical metalwork is not difficult to locate; more rare are pieces of furniture that were made for use in churches prior to 1800. Known to date are a number of important communion tables and several significant pieces of seating furniture. One of the most impressive items is the baptismal font made and given to Christ Church by Jonathan Gostelowe, a noted Philadelphia cabinetmaker, just three months before his marriage to Elizabeth Towers in April 1789 in the same church. This extraordinary octagonal mahogany font with cover (fig. 120) is very architectural in its overall form, proportion, and detailing. This is not surprising when one realizes that a number of well-known English Builder's Guides such as those by Batty Langley and William Pain published designs for pulpits, fonts, and various vases and pedestals. Many of these works were known and owned in Philadelphia, so Gostelowe may have been inspired by just such a book. The delicately carved moldings, central stop-fluted pedestal, and carved flame finial exhibit the finest aspects of Philadelphia cabinetwork. The ogee base and fluted pedestal are reminiscent of the massive canted corners and ogee bracket feet that appear on a number of documented Gostelowe chests of drawers.[26] Closely related in form and overall appearance to this font is a similar octagonal one in St. Paul's Church, Philadelphia (erected 1761), which may be Gostelowe's work also.[27] Gostelowe, a native Philadelphian, was apprenticed to George Claypoole, and after having served in the Revolution, he resumed his cabinetmaking activities in 1783 in a shop on Church Alley, right near Christ Church between Market and Arch, and Second and Third

120

121

122

120. Baptismal font, 1789, Philadelphia.
Jonathan Gostelowe (1744–95). Mahogany and pine; incised inscription inside top, "THE GIFT OF/ JONATHAN GOS-TELOWE/ CABINET MAKER PHI-LADEL / TO / CHRIST CHURCH JANUARY 1789." H. 59 in., Dia. of top 15 in. Christ Church, Philadelphia.

121. Armchair, 1750–60, Williamsburg, Virginia. *Attributed to the Anthony Hay shop; carving probably by James Wilson. Mahogany with beech. H. 49 in., W. 21½ in., D. 24½ in. Colonial Williamsburg Foundation.*

122. Masonic armchair, ca. 1775, probably Williamsburg. *Attributed to the Anthony Hay shop. Mahogany with walnut. H. 42½ in., W. 27½ in., W. 18⅞ in. Fredericksburg Lodge No. 4, A.F.&M., Fredericksburg, Virginia.*

123. Masonic armchair, 1765–90, Boston area. *Mahogany with maple, traces of gilt decoration, original webbing and hair-cloth under present covering; date "1792" in paint on back of splat. H. 50½ in., W. 25½ in., D. 19½ in. Mr. & Mrs. George M. Kaufman; On loan to the Metropoli-tan Museum of Art.*

123

124. Covered goblet, 1788, New Bremen Glassmanufactory, New Bremen, Maryland. *John Frederick Amelung (1741–98). Colorless glass; engraved on one side "New Bremen Glassmanufactory 1788/ North America State of Maryland" and on the other side above the arms of the city of Bremen, in a baroque shield, is "Old Bremen Success and the New Progress." H. 11¼ in., Dia. 5 in. The Metropolitan Museum of Art. Rogers Fund, 1928.*

125. Tumbler, 1789, New Bremen Glassmanufactory, New Bremen, Maryland. *John Frederick Amelung (1741–98). Colorless glass; engraved on one side "Made at the Glassmanufactory/ New Bremen in Maryland the 23 Jan. 1789/ by John Fr. Amelung & Comp" and on the other side "Our best wishes for every/ Glassmanufactory in the united States/ God bless the City of Boston." H. 5¾ in., Dia. at rim 4¾ in. Mabel Brady Garvan Collection. Yale University Art Gallery.*

125

Streets. From 1783 onward he had a pew in Christ Church, and in 1792 he became a Vestryman. It was in 1789, for his second wife, that he made the marvelous chest of drawers with accompanying dressing stand and glass[28] that closely relates to the design and workmanship of this font. By 1790 he moved his abode and shop to a house on High Street, and in 1793 he sold his city property and retired to a farm he owned on Ridge Road, where he died in 1795.

Specially commissioned furniture was occasionally made for official government or state use, as well as for use by various fraternal organizations such as masonic lodges and private societies. Today only a handful of pieces of furniture of this nature survive, and only recently have we begun to recognize them for their significance and what they can tell us about both the makers and the society. The oversized upholstered armchair in figure 121 was on display at the 1929 Girl Scouts Loan Exhibition (see fig. 4), yet it is still somewhat of a mystery as to how it got there and what it was doing there since it was not illustrated or even mentioned in the catalogue.[29] This grand chair is currently thought to have served as the governor's chair in the General Court in Williamsburg, and through recent research, it is thought to have been made in Williamsburg in the shop of the cabinetmaker Anthony Hay.[30] While the hairy paw feet, the asymmetrical leaf carving of the knees, and the carved lion's-head terminals of the arms are exceedingly English in inspiration, Wallace B. Gusler of Colonial Williamsburg feels "there is strong evidence to attribute the carving to a London-trained artisan, James Wilson, who worked for Hay in 1755."[31] Interesting also is the fact that this chair was pictured in *Frank Leslie's Illustrated Weekly Newspaper* on June 16, 1866, accompanied by the statement that it was "made in England, and sent over, with the stove, as a present to the House of Burgesses at Williamsburg." The illustration in *Leslie's* shows the chair with its arched back (recently restored) and crossed stretchers (these were not original and have since been removed). It should be noted that certain characteristics that are especially English also can be found on furniture made in Massachusetts, New York, and Philadelphia in the mid-eighteenth century, rococo style.

Masonic organizations in eighteenth-century America had among their members some of the finest minds and most successful men that our young nation had ever produced. They were serious, liberty-loving groups that held positions of great respect and dignity in their individual cities and towns. The two Masonic Master's chairs shown in figures 122 and 123 present the approaches of two cabinetmakers, one from Massachusetts and the other from Virginia, to this very special commission. The massiveness of the heavily ornamented Virginia chair (fig. 122) is in direct contrast to the thinness and refinement of the eastern Massachusetts example (fig. 123). The Virginia chair was originally made for the Falmouth Lodge, but when it dissolved in 1777, the chair was

126

127

129

130

126. Two-handled covered cup, 1749, Boston. *William Swan (1715[16]–74). Silver; marked twice "Swan" in rectangle at the side of each handle; engraved on one side with Pickman arms in cartouche, and on the other side inscribed in a foliate cartouche "THE/ Gift of the Province of the/ MASSACHUSETTS BAY/ TO/ Benjamin Pickman Esqʳ/ 1749." H. 12⅜ in., Dia. 11¼ in. Essex Institute, Salem, Massachusetts.*

127. George Washington at the Battle of Princeton, 1780–81, Philadelphia. *Charles Willson Peale (1741–1827). Oil on canvas. H. 95 in., W. 61 in. Yale University Art Gallery.*

128. Charles Cotesworth Pinckney (1746–1825), ca. 1773–74, Charleston, South Carolina. *Henry Benbridge (1743–1812). Oil on canvas. H. 30 in., W. 25 in. National Portrait Gallery, Smithsonian Institution.*

129. Richard Varick (1753–1831), 1787, New York. *Ralph Earl (1751–1801). Oil on canvas; signed and dated lower left "R. Earl pinxt 1787." H. 32¾ in., W. 28¼ in. Albany Institute of History and Art.*

130. Society of the Cincinnati Medal, ca. 1800, originally owned by Richard Varick. *Original design for medal by Pierre L'Enfant. Gold painted with enamels. Approx. 4 in. by 5 in. Albany Institute of History and Art.*

8

131

132

131. *Engagement Between the United States Constitution and the Macedonian, 1813, Philadelphia.* *Thomas Birch (1779-1815). Oil on canvas. H. 27¾ in., W. 35⅝ in. Museum of Fine Arts, Boston. Ernest W. Longfellow and Emily L. Ainsley Funds.*

132. *Centerpiece, ca. 1817, Baltimore.* *Andrew E. Warner (1786-1870). Silver, gilt on flag; inscribed on top surface of the base, "The Citizens of Baltimore to/Commodore Stephen Decatur/ Rebus gestis insigni Obvirtutes dilecto"; marked on base in rectangle "ANDREWWARNER BAL^T" with three pseudo-hallmarks. H. 20 in. Private collection.*

transferred to the Fredericksburg Lodge where it has remained ever since. While this chair creates an image of invincible strength, its elements are well integrated, the proportions are good, and the carving very well executed. The current question among southern furniture scholars is whether the chair was made in the Fredericksburg area by an as yet unidentified maker, or whether it was done in Williamsburg in the Anthony Hay shop where most certainly there were English pattern books that would have influenced its design and ornament. Some closely related carving on the overmantel of a house near Fredericksburg, "The Chimneys," helps support the former attribution, while close parallels in construction and ornament with other chairs from the Hay shop support the latter.[32]

The Massachusetts chair, which may have been made in Boston or north of Boston, has no specific provenance attached to it, but when it was sold at auction in 1928, the catalogue entry read, "Known to have been made to the order of a New Hampshire lodge of Free Masons."[33] A number of features of the lower portion of the chair suggest an eastern Massachusetts source, from the carefully and thinly carved talons with the side ones raked back and grasping a once-gilt ball, to the block and arrow-like stretchers and the hard-edged knees with precise, sinewy carving flowing downward over them. The serpentine-shaped arms are reminiscent of those found on earlier Massachusetts armchairs, and the integration of the various Masonic symbols in the splat, with part painted and gilt decoration, attests to workmanship of the highest order. While the upholstery of the seat is not the first, it appears to be perhaps the second, simply laid over the original haircloth and girt webbing. The year "1792," applied with white paint on the back of the splat, is possibly the date of the added decoration perhaps some ten or fifteen years after the fabrication of the chair itself.

Some aspects of eighteenth-century American glass manufacturing have already been dealt with in the first chapter. In a discussion of special commissions, the work of John Frederick Amelung of New Bremen, Maryland, has a primary place. Although not established until 1784, this glasshouse, with its corps of skilled German engravers, produced some of the most outstanding and superior pieces of presentation glass ever made in eighteenth-century America. Of course, considering Amelung's entrepreneurial sense, it is more than likely that most of these specially engraved objects were not commissioned but rather were ambitious gifts from Amelung to advantageous personalities who might have been in a position to muster political or economic support for his fledgling glassworks. A native of Germany, trained as a glassmaker and already experienced in administrative as well as manufacturing aspects of the business, Amelung carefully organized his move to America with the help of the Baltimore merchant Benjamin Crockett in 1783-84. With the financial support of several Bremen merchants, Amelung hired German workers, bought equipment and supplies, and settled his personal affairs before crossing the Atlantic. Finally, with letters of introduction from such notables as Franklin, Adams, and Thomas Barclay to important personalities like Thomas Mifflin, Charles Carroll, and William Paca, he left Germany by May or June of 1784. By the end of that year he had purchased a glasshouse in Frederick County, Maryland, from Conrad Foltz, one of six workers from the defunct Stiegel works (just forty miles north) who had been operating a glasshouse at New Bremen since 1775 when Stiegel went bankrupt. Amelung then had 82 German immigrants dependent on him, and by 1787 he had built not only houses for 135 Germans but also a German school and an English school. He had turned a small and struggling venture into an enterprising business, and by 1789 he advertised in the *Maryland Journal* and *Baltimore Advertiser* that:

> He makes Window-Glass transparent and substantial, equal to the London Crown, an inferior Quality equal to the Bristol Crown; all Kinds of Flint-Glass, such as Decanters, and Wine Glasses, Tumblers of all Sizes, and any Sort of Table Glass,—He also cuts Devices, Cyphers, Coats of Arms, or any other Fancy Figures on Glass, and in a short Time hopes to be able to furnish Looking-Glasses of all sizes.[34]

While this was certainly an encouraging and ambitious ad, by the early 1790s Amelung had suffered several disasters including a fire and subsequent financial difficulty. Finally he was forced to advertise his property and glassworks for sale, and he eventually deeded them to his son just before he died in 1798, thus ending the eighteenth-century's most sophisticated and enterprising glass manufactory.

It was not until 1928 that this magnificent covered goblet was discovered in Bremen,

Germany (figure 124), the first piece of signed Amelung glass to come to light. Because it is Germanic in both form and decoration, there was an initial suspicion that the piece was not American, but comparison with subsequently identified Amelung pieces (see also fig. 175) has led to the conclusion that this impressive goblet might have been sent to one of Amelung's wealthy merchant backers in Bremen as a tribute of thanks. One side of the bowl is engraved with the arms of the city of Bremen, which are flanked by whimsical lions, and the whole design is surmounted with the inscription "Old Bremen Success and the New Progress." The reverse side of the bowl bears the inscription "New Bremen Glassmanufactory 1788/ North America State of Maryland." The message of these lines is clearly one of celebration and thankfulness.

Amelung must have been a great promoter and a man who heartily believed in full encouragement and congratulation. Just one year after he made the extravagant "Bremen" covered goblet for his supporters on the other side of the Atlantic, he presented a simple tumbler (fig. 125) to, it is thought, Thomas Walley, a partner of the Boston Crown Glass Company, founded in 1787. This tumbler descended through the family of John Phillips, first mayor of Boston in 1822, who was the son-in-law of Walley. The inscriptions on both sides of this tumbler are quite competently engraved for the early date of this piece and read: "Made at the Glassmanufactory/ New Bremen in Maryland the 23 Jan.1789/ by John Fr. Amelung & Comp" and on the reverse: "Our best wishes for every/ Glassmanufactory in the united States/ God bless the City of Boston."

The striking covered sugar bowl in plate 18, blown in amethyst colored glass with a most whimsical bird finial, has to be one of Amelung's most enchanting commissions. Discovered in 1939 "in a farmhouse just a few miles over into Washington County,"[35] this was the first piece of colored Amelung to be identified. The sketchy provenance on the bowl states that it was owned by a Catherine Geeting, or Geeding, of Washington County. However, since she was not married until 1808, and the bowl was probably made between 1785 and 1795, it may have belonged to an older Catherine. One would guess that a piece of this quality and accomplishment must have been a special present upon a marriage or perhaps the birth of a child. While the form of this piece seems alien, it is related to Norwegian and German counterparts of similar date, and the engraved inscription "To Mis. C. G./ In Washington C=ty." is strongly related to the engraving on other documented Amelung examples.

Prior to the American Revolution, silver pieces and other special objects were commissioned in order to celebrate, commemorate, praise, and thank particularly laudatory acts or feats of accomplishment. For instance, a number of large, two-handled covered cups were presented to brave naval officers who had captured privateers, and before that, impressive silver oars, engraved with anchors and the arms of the Crown, were fashioned to be used in ceremonies just as a mace, or symbol of authority, was used when the Courts of Admiralty met. The massive silver covered cup (fig. 126) made by William Swan (1715/16–74) of Boston was presented to Benjamin Pickman by the Province of Massachusetts in 1749. Engraved on one side with a foliate cartouche surrounding an inscription and on the other with Pickman's arms, this cup is one of several closely related ones, four of which were made by Jacob Hurd.[36]

The American Revolution itself triggered a burst of military portraits, presentation swords, and decorative medals. Those who served in the army under Washington—and their male descendants—became members of the order of the Society of the Cincinnati (see fig. 130). In the years between the Revolution and the War of 1812, the emerging nation fostered other commissions, both for portraits and special awards. And in 1829 the final visit of General Lafayette to America caused the preparation of everything from commemorative ribbons and sashes to gold medals and miniatures.

Among the earliest commissions spawned by the Revolutionary War was that most familiar portrait of *General Washington at the Battle of Princeton* by Charles Willson Peale (fig. 127). Commissioned in January of 1779 by the Supreme Executive Council of Pennsylvania, it was begun at Valley Forge, continued at New Brunswick, and finished at Philadelphia. While it was not the first time that Washington had sat for Peale (the first had been in 1772 at Mount Vernon), this was the first official portrait. Thus it evoked the symbolic imagery of the American victory not only through the confident and serene countenance of the esteemed general but also through several painterly

133. *Thomas Macdonough (1783–1825),* 1815, New York. *Oil on canvas; signed "Jarvis." H. 96 in., W. 60 in. Art Commission of the City of New York.*

134. Presentation vase, one of a pair, 1824–25, Philadelphia. *Thomas Fletcher (1787–1866) and Sidney Gardiner (d. 1827). Silver; inscribed on front of base "TO THE HON. DEWITT CLINTON/ Who has developed the resources of the State of New York/ AND ENNOBLED HER CHARACTER/ The Merchants of Pearl Street offer the testimony of their/ GRATITUDE AND RESPECT/ Fletcher & Gardiner Makers . . . . Philadᵃ February 1825." H. 24 in., W. 21 in. New York Chamber of Commerce and Industry.*

133

134

devices like the American battle flag waving above crumpled Hessian standards and American soldiers marching off with British prisoners of war. This monumental and imposing portrait paved the way for numerous other paintings, engravings, and sculptures of Washington, including several dozen replicas of this same piece. Peale, who himself had served in the army until 1778, must have known the character of the general, since his contemporaries described him as "modest and gentle," and "even, quiet and composed in his occupations, sober in his speech." The image of this portrait, while perhaps a bit idealized, seems very true to the appearance and aspect of personality that Washington radiated. In 1779, the Marquis de Barbé-Marbois wrote of Washington: "His conversation is as simple as his manners and exterior; he does the honors of his house with dignity, but without haughtiness and without adulation . . . He sometimes plays ball for whole hours with his aides-de Camp."[37]

Until 1974 when the National Portrait Gallery staged a major exhibition and publication of the works of Henry Benbridge (1743–1812), this competent American painter was little known and less well understood. Born in Philadelphia, he apparently came under the influence of John Wollaston in 1758 when the English portrait artist painted in that city briefly (including a portrait of Henry's stepfather Thomas Gordon). By 1765 Benbridge came into his inheritance and was soon off to Italy, possibly stopping briefly in London. He remained in Rome and its environs for about four years. In 1769 he went to London for about a year where he studied with his fellow Pennsylvanian Benjamin West, whose wife was distantly related to Henry. Benbridge returned home in 1770, and little is known of his activities there except that early in 1772 he must have married Hetty Sage, an artist who specialized in miniatures, also of Philadelphia and by March 1772 he was in Charleston, South Carolina. The March trip south was exploratory, and by May he was back in Charleston to continue his commissions and find a home. Apparently Hetty Sage Benbridge did not come south until the following spring when she brought with her their infant son, Harry. She must have died not long after her arrival in Charleston, but the precise date of her death is unknown. Henry continued to make a respectable name and living for himself in Charleston until the city fell to the British and he, along with other patriots, was exiled to St. Augustine. Finally returning to Charleston in 1784, he remained there until at least 1790, for in 1788 he led the Limners in Charleston's Federal Procession. It was shortly after his arrival in Charleston that Benbridge painted the captivating and finely executed portrait of the handsome young Charles Cotesworth Pinckney (1746–1825) shown in figure 128. Benbridge's manner of painting his sitter from one side, with dramatic light on the side of the face and the other half of the face almost totally diminished and in shadow, succeeded with striking effect in this portrait. His articulation not only of the sitter's features but also of his body, his uniform, and the background demonstrates Benbridge approaching his finest. When Benbridge originally painted Pinckney, the subject was a lieutenant in the Charles Town Militia, and thus his uniform was red. However, in June 1775 South Carolina organized the First Regiment of the Continental Line, and Pinckney soon assumed the post of Captain of the Grenadier Company. It was at that time that he requested Benbridge to paint out the red of his old militia uniform with the blue of the new patriot force, an interesting instance of a "re-commission" that must have happened in more than one instance of American painting.[38]

In direct contrast to Benbridge's sophisticated presentation of a southern gentleman and officer is Ralph Earl's interpretation of the New York officer Richard Varick (1753–1831), painted in 1787 when Varick was attorney-general, just before he became mayor of New York in 1789 (fig. 129). Though Earl, like Benbridge, had studied with West in London and had been elected to the Royal Academy, there is a pointed stiffness and harsh linearity in his handling of Varick's features and anatomy. Looking at the backgrounds, one sees that while they are similar, there is a juxtaposition of softness and ease plus a rather amateur-like muddiness. While Earl represents the best of the New England provincial limners, Benbridge approaches a southern Copley. It is interesting that as late as 1787 Varick would have had himself painted in Revolutionary uniform wearing his coveted medal as a member of Washington's officers of the line organization, the Society of the Cincinnati (fig. 130). However, certain events explain Varick's possible insistence upon this specific posture and image. In 1780 Benedict Arnold appointed him as his aide, and when Arnold was convicted of treason, Varick petitioned

■ **Plate 18. Covered sugar bowl, 1785–95, New Bremen Glassmanufactory, New Bremen, Maryland.** *John Frederick Amelung (1741–98). Transparent, dark amethyst glass; engraved on bowl "To Mis. C. G./ In Washington C=ty." H. 8 in., Dia. 7⅛ in. The Henry Francis du Pont Winterthur Museum.*

Washington for a court of inquiry to clear his own name. Varick was eventually acquitted with honor. By the mid-1780s he was no longer an object of suspicion, and he became active and ultimately very successful in New York City politics. In the early nineteenth century he even served as president of the New York chapter of the Society of the Cincinnati, from 1806 until his death in 1831.[39]

While the patriotic spirit enveloped many Americans, and artists were busy recording images of our heroes and militiamen, the Indians, from whom we had usurped this land, were being sorely neglected. Images of American Indians had been drawn as early as the late sixteenth century, and during the eighteenth century several Indian portraits had been painted by artists like Smibert and Hesselius, but it was not until the 1820s and 1830s that the American government began to realize the importance of preserving and recording the images and culture of this important native group. As Charles Willson Peale amassed portraits of great and noteworthy Americans for the portrait gallery of his museum, he saw fit to include the image of at least one significant Indian, Chief Joseph Brant (1742–1807), a Mohawk chief called by his people Thayendanagea (pl. 19). As a bright young brave, Brant had accompanied Sir William Johnson on the Campaign of 1755 and then had attended Moor's Charity School in Lebanon, Connecticut, from 1761–63. A convert to the Anglican Church, and a competent translator, he was made secretary to the Superintendent of Indian Affairs in 1774. After the Revolution, Brant became an ambassador for the Indians and in 1792 journeyed to Philadelphia to speak for their land rights. It was at that time that his portrait was painted by Charles Willson Peale, eventually to be included in Peale's gallery of prominent Americans. Peale's strong and noble image of Brant, wearing a silver gorget and armband probably given him by the white men as a symbol of peace, was assuredly an important addition to this gallery of greats that Henry Wansey, an English traveler, described thus in 1794: "But what particularly struck me at this place was the portraits . . . of all the leading men in the late revolution . . . which, after a century hence, will be very valuable in the eyes of posterity."[40] And although Wansey did not have the advantage of seeing Chief Joseph Brant's image, which wasn't added until 1797, he could not have been more correct about the incomparable value of those images for posterity. In 1794 Peale's gallery, which was originally housed in a specially built structure with skylights, was moved to the hall of the American Philosophical Society, and in 1802 by act of the Pennsylvania Assembly, it was given free use of the State House, or Independence Hall. Today many of his original portraits, along with additional collections, occupy Latrobe's stately Second National Bank building on Chestnut Street under the administration of the National Park Service.

By the 1820s the United States government was beginning to negotiate treaties with the numerous Indian tribes throughout the country as the line of settlements pushed westward. Thus, it became a period of great "Indian activity" in Washington, and it seemed that every other week a new delegation would arrive in full regalia. The idea of the government preserving and collecting Indian artifacts and portraits for exhibition originated in about 1816 with Thomas McKenney, who was Superintendent of Indian Trade in Georgetown and eventual Chief of the Bureau of Indian Affairs in 1824. Calling upon the services of Rhode Island–born artist Charles Bird King, in 1821–22 the Department of War, via McKenney, commissioned its first group of Indian portraits that would eventually number over 135 by the time activity ceased in 1842. Over the next twenty years King created our most picturesque and romantic legacy of these native Americans and the first to be recorded in such a conscious and official way. The first delegation to come to Washington during the winter of 1821–22 was that of the Great Plains tribes from the Upper Missouri River, led by Benjamin O'Fallon, the Upper Missouri agent. As King painted the images of the various chiefs on wooden panels, he would also do a reduced-size painting for each Indian to take home with him. In a number of instances King painted replicas for himself and others, and it is because of this fortunate circumstance that we have the paintings that survive today. By 1858 the portrait gallery was moved to the new Smithsonian Institution building, but in 1865 fire destroyed that structure and almost all of King's paintings along with it. The handsome image of the virile young chief of the Pawnee Loups, Petalesharro, in plate 20, was one of five replicas originally owned by Patrick Macauley of Baltimore. In 1826 he sent them abroad to his friend Christopher Hughes, Chargé d'Affaires to the Netherlands, and it has only been in this century that they have returned to the United States. Petalesharro was one of the most popular figures among those of the first delegation, for he had demonstrated great bravery in rescuing a Comanche maiden from being burned at the stake by his own tribe. In a grand feminist gesture, the young ladies of Miss White's Seminary in Washington presented him with a silver medal engraved with depictions of the event and the words "To the Bravest of the Braves." In 1883 this medal was recovered in Nebraska and is now in the possession of the Nebraska Historical Society. The medal that appears around Petalesharro's neck in King's painting is a "peace" medal, which was given to all members of the delegation, with the image of President Monroe in profile relief on the front.

It seemed that no sooner had the War for Independence concluded with the Treaty of Paris in 1783 and the death of Washington occurred in 1799, than the War of 1812 with Great Britain erupted and again there was good occasion for artists, designers, goldsmiths, and numerous other craftsmen to seek patronage in the wake of disaster. Since this war revolved around dramatic naval encounters, the opportunity for further development of American marine painting had arrived. Not only were the faces of naval heroes like Decatur, Perry, and Macdonough being immortalized on canvas, but their vessels and the bloody battles they fought were also being captured in paint as well as being engraved later on paper.

Strategically this wholesale heroization of certain naval figures served to heighten the awareness of the American people and muster support for the efforts of various political figures. Thomas Birch (1779–1851), who had immigrated to the United States from England with his father in 1794, soon began to specialize in marine paintings and without any romantic embellishments was able to record with great accuracy numerous naval battles. His efforts to achieve true-to-nature accounts even took him so far as interviewing crew members shortly after encounters. One of the first scenes that he painted was the early defeat of the British frigate *Guerriere* by the *Constitution,* which was under the command at the time of Captain Isaac Hull of Boston. One of the next major victories at sea was the capturing of the *Macedonian* by the *United States* (fig. 131), which was under the command of Maryland-born Stephen Decatur (1779–1820). In 1804 Decatur had distinguished himself for his gallantry in the Mediterranean off Tripoli, action that had gained him great favor at home among his countrymen. After his capture of the *Macedonian,* which was repaired and equipped as an American frigate, he was praised throughout the country, and Congress, several state legislatures, and major cities showed their great respect by votes of thanks and costly presents. He was not the only naval hero to receive gifts and pieces of richly wrought silver, but Decatur was the fortunate recipient of the most extraordinary centerpiece with candelabra ever made by an American silversmith (fig. 132). Sometime after his triumphs of 1815 in the Mediterranean and his successful negotiation of a treaty in Algiers, the citizens of Baltimore presented him with a splendid six-light centerpiece made by Andrew Ellicott Warner. Inscribed on the top face of the pedestal, just in front of a freestanding figure of Neptune atop a dolphin and holding a gold flag, is the dedication: "The Citizens of Baltimore to/ Commodore Stephen Decatur/ *Rebus gestis insigni Obvirtutes dilecto.*" This centerpiece is remarkable in its design of three winged maidens springing from a tripod pedestal on hoofed supports, and joined by garland swags and a pierced ring, with removable two-part candle arms rising from the heads. Although there is no American precedent for this magnificent centerpiece, a strikingly similar one was made in 1806 in London by Digby Scott and Benjamin Smith and engraved with the Arms of Richard, 1st Earl of Howe.[41] It is not surprising to see silver designs so close to the furniture of French émigré cabinetmakers like Lannuier, as this piece is reminiscent of several of his card tables (see fig. 286) and the remarkable center table that is attributed to his shop (see pl. 48). Certainly for American silver of this date, the centerpiece exhibits a tremendous sense of the *avant garde* taste then in full favor in France and England, a fashion that had barely manifested itself in American cabinetshops.

Though the life of the portrait painter John Wesley Jarvis (1781–1840) ended sadly in dissolution, physical debility, and poverty, the earlier part of his career showed him to be a veritable Bohemian who delighted in cutting a picturesque figure, telling fabulous stories, and executing practical jokes. Likewise, during the better part of his career, he

Plate 19. *Chief Joseph Brant,* or *Thayendanegea,* (1742–1807), 1797, Philadelphia. *Charles Willson Peale (1741–1827). Oil on canvas. H. 25½ in., W. 21¼ in. Independence National Historical Park Collection, Philadelphia. Plate 19 is on page 108.*

Plate 20. *Petalesharro,* ca. 1821, Washington, D.C. *Charles Bird King (1785–1862). Oil on wood panel. H. 17½ in., W. 14 in. White House Collection. Plate 20 is on page 109.*

himself painted many picturesque national heroes, especially those from the War of 1812. He received a number of commissions from the city of New York, among which were the dramatic depiction of Stephen Decatur and the dashing and impressive full-length portrait of Thomas Macdonough (1783–1825) shown in figure 133. Jarvis received $400 on December 4, 1815 for doing this canvas, and judging from a watercolor by Charles Burton of the Governor's Room in City Hall in 1830,[42] this painting appears to have occupied a central position of honor in the room. Macdonough, almost as famous as Decatur, commanded the fleet on Lake Champlain during the War of 1812. By 1814 he had gained naval superiority of those waters, and with a fleet of 13 vessels and his 26-gun flagship *Saratoga*, he won one of the most sterling naval victories of all time in the Battle of Plattsburgh. This proved to be one of the most decisive engagements ever fought by the American navy, for it resulted in the Great Lakes remaining American territory. As a result of this victory he was not only made a captain, but also in 1815 he was made an honorary member of the Society of the Cincinnati, thus explaining the medal that he sports in the Jarvis portrait.

The prizes, gifts, and trophies that were presented to many heroes during and after the War of 1812 certainly gave many American silversmiths plenty of opportunity to sharpen their skills of design and execution. Thomas Fletcher and Sidney Gardiner were not only extremely successful in the market of domestic silver (see fig. 134) but also leaders in the field of presentation pieces.[43] One of their first major commissions after arriving in Philadelphia had been the large vase that was given to Isaac Hull for his valor in the defeat of the *Guerriere*. Though they were a Philadelphia-based firm, they were well-known up and down the Eastern seaboard as well as in New Orleans where they had family connections. Thus, when a group of merchants on Pearl Street in New York offered a $100 prize for the best design for a pair of vases to honor DeWitt Clinton for his role in the building of the Erie Canal, of course Fletcher and Gardiner entered the contest. In January of 1824 they won the competition and then began work on the vases. A contemporary broadside probably printed in New York in 1825, and perhaps even written by Thomas Fletcher, described in detail the intricate depictions on the vases, gave their source of design (the famous Warwick vase), and stated that they were designed by Thomas Fletcher. The completeness of the documentation on these objects is remarkable. But there is some room for questioning whether or not Fletcher really did design the vases, as there is a drawing of one in the collection of drawings in The Metropolitan Museum of Art that is signed by Hugh Bridgport. Bridgport apparently designed the Armistead presentation set in 1815, and he is also known to have illustrated *The Builder's Assistant,* published in three volumes in 1818, 1819, and 1821. Of course it is possible that Fletcher had him do the drawing for use as an advertisement after the vases were completed. Since Fletcher had journeyed to England in 1815, he was familiar not only with the Warwick vase but also with the work of goldsmiths like Paul Storr, who was then employed by Rundell, Bridge, and Rundell, the leading silver and jewelry firm in London. While elements of these vases are reminiscent of the coffee urn noted earlier in figure 106, the overall composition and successful integration of pictorial material makes these vases beyond comparison. As Philip Hone wrote in January 1838 when describing a piece that Fletcher had made to be given to Nicholas Biddle: "Fletcher & Co., are the artists who made the Clinton vases. Nobody in the "world" of ours hereabouts can compete with them in their kind of work."[44]

The immortalization of Washington as a classical folk hero after his death in 1799 and the public worship of naval and military heroes from the War of 1812 were mere preludes to the biggest drama on the early nineteenth-century stage of idolization and presentation of gifts and awards. Perhaps our country has never witnessed such a contagious national fever as that which swept the United States in 1824 and 1825 when General Lafayette traveled to America and made a grand triumphal tour along the eastern seaboard and into the interior. Reading Brandon's three-volume account of the entire tour and digesting the immense number of newspaper accounts about every waking moment of activity may overwhelm even the most capacious of minds. How Lafayette himself ever survived all the parades, reviews, galas, banquets, grand balls, and afternoon teas with the ladies is difficult to imagine. He should have been given the medal of honor for merely having survived that month-long round of both regimented and reckless chaos. His visit prompted the manufacture of everything from special gold

135. Medal, 1824, Baltimore. *Made by Charles Pryce. Engraved by J. Sands. Gold; engraved on face "OUR GRATITUDE / OCTOBER 19th 1781" and on the back with the names of the fourteen young men who presented it to Lafayette, and "C. Pryce Fecit" and "J. Sands Sc." H. 3 in., W. 2¼ in. Museum of Early Southern Decorative Arts.*

136. Lighthouse clock, ca. 1824–25, Boston. *Simon Willard (1753–1848). Mahogany and mahogany veneer, pine, brass, glass; signed on face, "SIMON WILLARD & SONS / PATENT." H. 29½ in., Dia. 9¼ in. White House Collection.*

135

136

medals to silk ribbons and sashes in commemoration of his trip. Throngs of people lined the roads along which his entourage passed, not to mention the enormous number of arches under which he must have passed as he moved from village to town to city. One of the many gold medals that were given to him was a gift "In behalf of the Young Men of Baltimore," and it was presented to him on October 11, 1824, during the five-day visit to that city (fig. 135). The medal is engraved on the face "OUR GRATITUDE/ OCTOBER 19th 1781," and the reverse side lists the fourteen names of the "Young Men of Baltimore" who subscribed to this gift; below those names are also inscribed the words "C. Pryce Fecit J. Sands Sc." Very little is known about either of these craftsmen, except that Sands is listed in the 1824 Baltimore directory as an "engraver and copperplate printer," and Pryce is also known to have been working in Washington, D.C., around 1834.[45] It was recorded that the medal was on exhibit on October 9, 1924 in the shop of Mr. Kirk, Silversmith (later Kirk and Son), and there has been some speculation Pryce was a journeyman in Kirk's shop, although this is undocumented as of this time.

While Lafayette must have been impressed with his reception in Baltimore, with the banquet, the ball, and the dinner given by the Society of the Cincinnati, not to mention his visit to Peale's museum and the fireworks that evening after all the events, he was probably more overwhelmed with his stay in that notably sophisticated and hospitable southern city of Charleston, South Carolina. On February 23, 1824, his party set out on their southern tour that was to cover fourteen states before it ended. Lafayette spent three days in Charleston, which in 1825 was the most socially and culturally aware city in the South. The high point of his visit there must certainly have been the splendid banquet at which magnificent dessert and confectionary by Madame Roumillat and Son was served. This extravaganza consisted of fifty pyramids and eight gilded fortresses, surmounted with laurel and myrtle and flags. On each pyramid were mottoes of sugar that said "Welcome! Lafayette!" and "To the Hero." At the conclusion of the dinner there were thirteen formal toasts and nineteen "volunteer" toasts after which there was a fireworks display. At the theater in Charleston on Lafayette's last night there, a "Grand Ball" held in his honor was accompanied by lavish decorations and elaborate arrangements. The guest of honor was announced with a trumpet flourish, and the evening that followed was affectionately described as "a splendid scene of confusion." While in Charleston, the governor gave Lafayette a miniature, set in a gold frame, of the Frenchman's good friend Francis Huger, a map of the state of South Carolina, and a handsome silver map case made by the Charleston silversmith Louis Boudo.[46] The city of Charleston also commissioned their best miniature artist, Charles Fraser (1782–1860), to paint a small image of Lafayette (pl. 21) that would remain in City Hall. Fraser, who ably carried out this commission, was born in Charleston and had had an early association with several noted artists like Sully, Edward Greene Malbone, and Washington Allston, all of whom worked or lived in Charleston. Though he studied to be a lawyer, was admitted to the bar, and practiced until 1818, he eventually abandoned law for his love of miniature and scene painting. Fraser has been described as "a man of exquisite taste and refinement, artist, scholar, and poet." With over three hundred works to his credit, he had his first exhibition of miniatures in 1857, just three years before his death.

The most sophisticated and elegant honor paid to Lafayette by an American craftsman of the early nineteenth century is the handsome lighthouse clock in figure 136. Inscribed on the face "Simon Willard & Sons/ Patent," this unique American creation appears to have been first patented in 1819 by Simon Willard of Roxbury, Massachusetts. The end of the patent has this description of the clock: "The whole of the clock work is inclosed with a handsome glass) (and it is wound up without taking the glass off, which prevents the dirt from) (getting into it. The whole plan of the clock I claim as my invention. The) (Pendulum is suspended upon and connected with the pivot."[47] Precisely when these handsome new clocks began to be known as "lighthouse" clocks is uncertain, but presumably that name derives from their likeness to the famous Eddystone light. With a veneered cylindrical case and an octagonal base resting on gilt brass balls, the clock has a front panel ornamented with a sulfide medallion displaying a portrait bust of Lafayette. While Lafayette sulfides were being produced in Pittsburgh by Bakewell, Page, and Bakewell, this one appears to be French in origin, probably made by Baccarat. Nevertheless, the Lafayette medallion of this distinctly American invention almost precisely dates the manufacture of this clock to about 1824 or 1825.

Chapter 4

Craftsmen and Ornament

Economics in Fashion and Workmanship

During the past hundred years myths have been both exploited and exploded in the ivory towers of American decorative arts scholarship. On the most superficial level, the popular image of Puritan plainness, in design, American simplicity, and lack of ornamentation has persisted. At best, if ornament was recognized, it was thought to be inferior to and more crudely handled than its English and continental counterparts. But there have always been three factors on this side of the Atlantic that have fostered a highly sophisticated repertoire of ornament: (1) knowledge of what was the current fashion or vogue abroad, (2) client demand and the attendant economic means, and (3) the presence of highly skilled craftsmen. Native craftsmen learned their skills through apprenticeship, by studying imported examples and design books, and on occasion from immigrant craftsmen arriving from abroad with knowledge of the latest foreign fashion. To compete with imported goods, American craftsmen (at least those in the major urban centers and port cities) strove to produce items as fine and as fashionable as, but cheaper than, imported goods. In many instances they were successful; they, not only survived but flourished, some amassing considerable wealth if blessed with an entrepreneurial sense. In other instances competition was too stiff, expenses of an infant industry too great, and losses too frequent, or else the craftsman was able to do well in some less risky occupation.

For centuries man has possessed the impulse to visually enhance everyday objects, to make them a little more appealing, a little richer, and a little more costly if he were the seller and more pretentious if he were the buyer. Numerous ways have evolved in which a craftsman can embellish or ornament an object, be it made of wood, metal, glass, clay, canvas, or ivory. He can apply ornament to the surface, or he can take something away from the surface, creating a texture or pattern. In certain instances the form and the ornament are one, as in the case of an object turned on a lathe, a completely carved piece of wood, or a blown or molded piece of glass.

During the first two hundred years of settlement in America, craftsmen employed a variety of ornamental techniques: carving, turning, painting, gilding, veneering, and engraving. Certain techniques were almost constantly in vogue, while others came and

■ Plate 22. Dressing table, 1710–30, Boston area. *White pine with gesso and japanned decoration. signed "Milton" three times on drawer backs. H. 30½ in., W. 34 in., D. 21½ in. Mr. and Mrs. George M. Kaufman.*

Plate 23. Dressing table, 1816, Bath, Maine. *Painted by Elizabeth Paine Lombard. Maple with painted decoration; inscribed on front of drawer "Elizabeth Paine Lombard Feb 1816," and written on the top is a poem entitled "Hope." H. 33 in., W. 31 in., D. 16 in. Shelburne Museum, Shelburne, Vermont.*

PL. 22

went depending on the fashion in London and on the Continent. At different times there were various regional preferences in ornament, and specific manners of painting, carving, or engraving became characteristic of regions, as will be discussed in chapter 5. The discussion here concerns objects selected because of their particularly superior or characteristic ornamental quality, or because of a specific craftsman or group of craftsmen whose work the objects illustrate. There are many objects cited elsewhere in this book that could have been included here, and there are many others not mentioned that could have been. The objects presented here are only a random selection, yet the concepts and principles of ornamentation discussed below can reasonably be applied to almost any American-made object with even the least amount of ornament. During the past two decades a renewed interest in objects with unusual or elaborate surface ornamentation and a reappraisal of individual craftsmen or groups of craftsmen have resulted in a number of important books, articles, theses, and exhibitions. Some of the subjects explored by students, scholars, and collectors have been: specific skills, early division of labor, craftsman specialization and versatility, shop practices, and both personal and professional interrelationships among craftsmen and their families. The following discussion will rely heavily on this new information while at the same time raising questions that scholars have not yet answered.

From at least the Centennial celebration onward, antiquarians have possessed an avid interest in Pilgrim furniture made and used during the first century of settlement in America. Due to this consuming interest, the three elaborately carved pieces in figures 137, 138, and 139 were known and illustrated at a very early date.[1] Today they still represent probably the earliest and definitely the finest high-style carved furniture produced in seventeenth-century America. Possessing a flawless provenance of direct descent in the family of Thomas Dennis (w. 1663–1706), joiner of Ipswich, Essex County, Massachusetts, these three along with two other related pieces (an almost identical chair and a chest) are the cornerstones of attribution for a regional school of joinery and carving. Irving P. Lyon, in a series of six articles in *Antiques* in 1937 and 1938,

PL. 23

137

■ **137. Wainscot chair, 1665–1700, Ipswich, Massachusetts.** *Attributed to William Searle (d. 1667) or Thomas Dennis (1638–1706). Oak. H. 48⅜ in., W. 24⅝ in., D. 17½ in. Bowdoin College Museum of Art, Brunswick, Maine*

■ **138. Tape loom, 1665–1700, Ipswich, Massachusetts.** *Attributed to William Searle (d. 1667) or Thomas Dennis (1638–1706). Oak. H. 38⅝ in., W. 9⅛ in., D. ⅝ in. H. Ray Dennis.*

138

got somewhat carried away with this cornerstone, however, and proceeded to attribute numerous other carved pieces not only to the same school but to Dennis himself. In 1938 Homer Eaton Keyes, then editor of *Antiques,* directly questioned Lyon's overambitious attributions, but it was not until the 1960s that scholars began to reassess the total picture of joiners working in Essex County and suggested the possibility of a number of craftsmen having produced this mass of "florid-style" carved furniture, as Lyon termed it. In 1960 Helen Park compounded the "Dennis Dilemma" by suggesting that perhaps some of the Dennis family furniture was made by the joiner William Searle of Ipswich, who had been the first husband of the wife of Thomas Dennis. More recent years have seen extensive and enlightening research by the scholar Benno M. Forman, which has further enlarged our knowledge of seventeenth-century craftsmen working in Essex County and neighboring communities in the Massachusetts Bay area.[2]

One of the most important insights provided by recent research is the varied nature of the work of the seventeenth-century joiner, who frequently functioned as a carpenter (or vice versa) and as a carver. The earliest reference to carved furniture thus far noted in Essex County records occurred in 1653 in the will of Thomas Emerson, baker of Ipswich. In that document he left his daughter, Elizabeth Fuller, "the great carued chest & the carued box . . . with all yt is in it and a small carued chest with what is in it."[3] Whether these carved articles were made in Essex County or had been brought from England when Emerson had come to America is unknown, but it is significant that there is no record of any craftsmen specifically called carvers in Essex County between 1638 and 1653. In fact, it was not until the 1660s that men were actually called carvers, indicating that carving had not been considered a primary occupation but rather something carried out as part of a joiner's regular work. Certainly, though, the earliest joiners must have possessed the ability to do a reasonably proficient job of scratch or sunken carving, if not the highly ornamental relief carving.

Judging from this well-documented survival of his/their workmanship, either Dennis or Searle (or both) was certainly a very capable carver. In her 1960 reexamination in *Antiques* magazine, Helen Park suggested the possibility that two craftsmen were at work in this group of five pieces and more specifically pointed out the difference in the carving of the two wainscot chairs, suggesting that one was by Searle and the other by Dennis, who might have been apprenticed to Searle. Benno Forman's research has not only broadened our knowledge of other Essex County joiners, but it has also added

140

139. Box, 1665–1700, Ipswich, Massa-chusetts. *Attributed to William Searle (d. 1667) or Thomas Dennis (1638–1706). Oak. H. 14⅜ in., W. 25¾ in., D. 17⅜ in. H. Ray Dennis.*

140. Armchair, 1660–90, Massachusetts. *Ash, pine replacement seat. H. 44½ in., W. 23½ in., D. 17 in. The Metropolitan Museum of Art. Gift of Mrs. J. Insley Blair.*

139

some important tidbits to the data about Searle and Dennis. Searle was born in Ottery St. Mary, Devonshire, England, and shortly after his marriage to Grace Cole of that same town, he must have immigrated to Boston. In May of 1663 he arrived in Ipswich, a "joiner from Boston," and not long after that Dennis, who was living in Portsmouth, bought land from Searle in Ipswich. Where Dennis had come from or when is still unknown. Perhaps both he and Searle had come from England together, gone to Boston, and then decided to go north, one to Portsmouth and the other to Ipswich. At any rate, they knew each other, and after Searle's death in 1667, Dennis moved to Ipswich and in 1668 married Searle's widow. Thomas Dennis died in 1706, and the earliest inventory in which these family heirlooms are mentioned is the 1757 inventory of Captain John Dennis, son of Thomas, where six pieces of carved furniture are mentioned, including "2 wooden carved chairs @ 2/" and "Carved box 2/8, carved salt box 8ᵈ." One final note of interest to further the intrigue of the "Dennis Dilemma" is the discovery in recent years of a carved chest in the town of Ottery St. Mary, Devonshire, that is strikingly similar, almost identical, to the one that has descended in the Dennis family.[4]

Clearly the carved ornament of the Searle/Dennis furniture was derived from English precedents and, in fact, probably executed by an English-trained craftsman who simply carved his ornament in the manner familiar to him and thus popular in his native region.[5] This craftsman joiner/carver was truly a highly skilled artisan who had ample ability not only to create great form but also to embellish it and to integrate ornament and form with a resounding degree of success. The two wainscot chairs are a rich and showy tribute to his artistry and the carved box a beautiful exercise of his carving vocabulary, but the true gem in this family group is the tape loom. The shaping and carving of something as simple and common as a tape loom into such a piece of sculpture is perhaps this craftsman's highest achievement.[6]

Another group of craftsmen whose work possessed innate ornamental qualities were those artisans who called themselves turners. Their principal piece of equipment was the lathe, in which the turner placed square lengths of wood that were then "turned" around as various chisels were held against them. In this way he would cut away extra wood and form variously shaped rounded parts that could be joined into chairs, stools, and tables or else split to make ornaments to be applied to case pieces of furniture. The turned armchair or "great chair" in figure 140 is one in a small group of closely related,

Plate 24. Lady's dressing table, 1800–1810, Baltimore. *Mahogany and mahogany veneer inlaid with satinwood, with painted and gilt decoration on wood and gesso, verre églomisé panels, baize cover on writing slide. H. 72 in., W. 54½ in., D. 25¼. Maryland Historical Society, Baltimore.*

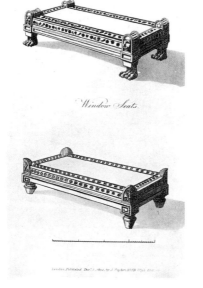

■ 141. *Kas, 1690–1730, New York.*
*Pine, maple, and probably gumwood; inde-cipherable signature inside right door; H.
67½ in., W. 61¼ in., D. 22½ in. The
National Society of the Colonial Dames in
the State of New York.*

142. Window seat, ca. 1823, New York.
*Duncan Phyfe (1768–1854). Rosewood ve-neer on pine with gilt decoration, original
silk damask upholstery. H. 19¼ in.,
W. 42½ in., D. 17 in. The Brooklyn Mu-seum. Gift of Mrs. J. Amory Haskell.*

143. *A Collection of Designs for Household
Furniture, plate 52, 1804, London.*
*George Smith (w. 1804–28). Joseph Downs
Manuscript Collection, The Henry Francis
du Pont Winterthur Museum.*

141

142

Plate 25. Girandole clock, 1816–20, Concord, Massachusetts. *Lemuel Curtis (1790–1857). Pine with gesso and gilt, brass, painted glass; inscribed on face "Warranted by L. Curtis" and on throat "PATENT"; "L. Curtis" also engraved on small brass crescent at base of lower glass. H. 43¼ in., Dia. 12¾ in., D. 4¼ in. Private collection.*

■ **Plate 26. Dressing stand with glass, 1790–1800, probably Boston.** *Mahogany with mahogany and satinwood veneers, white pine, gesso, and gilt, glass. H. 30¾ in., W. 20⅞ in., D. 13¾ in. Museum of Fine Arts, Boston. M. and M. Karolik Collection.*

PL. 25

mid-seventeenth-century turned chairs probably made in either Plymouth or Suffolk County, in the Massachusetts Bay Colony. Despite restorations on this chair, it embodies several distinguishing characteristics such as the tall, pyramidal finials, the repeated arrow-like spindles, and the flattened ball or vase turnings at intervals on the rear and front posts. Two chairs in Pilgrim Hall, Plymouth, as well as ones at the Museum of Fine Arts, Boston, and the Wadsworth Atheneum form the nucleus of this related group.

While studies of the four eastern Massachusetts coastal counties have revealed that between 1630 and 1730 in Charlestown alone there were "twenty-one turners and blockmakers"[7] and in Boston during the same period there were at least "sixteen turners, nine chairmakers," to date little extensive work has been done on identifying or grouping the work of these important craftsmen. Forman has enumerated several Essex County turners in his research, including Edward Browne of Ipswich who died in 1659 leaving in his shop ". . . work done toward chaires, 3 s.; 6 trayes, dishes, trenchers, & payles . . . ."[8] Patricia E. Kane, in her work on the New Haven Colony during the seventeenth century, has identified a number of craftsmen who owned turners' tools, including lathes, and noted that they were sometimes called "dishturners."[9] And in 1977 Robert F. Trent produced an illuminating study of a related group of Connecticut craftsmen/turners in his book *Hearts and Crowns.* Another study attempting to identify a specific maker with a related body of work is a recent article by Robert St. George entitled "A Plymouth Area Chairmaking Tradition of the Late Seventeenth-Century."[10] Not only has St. George found just one craftsman listed in the Plymouth records between 1633 and 1730 who possessed a lathe or turning tools (Ephraim Tinkham II, 1649–1713), but he has, in the course of attributing a group of chairs to Tinkham's hand, also recognized several important factors concerning the turner's craft and method of working. Perhaps central to understanding turned chairs of this period is recognizing that a craftsman probably produced preturned posts, or even a variety of parts, and thus was able to produce a variety of different chairs using preturned members interchangeably. Presumably future researchers will examine more turned pieces of furniture with this in mind and find records and inventories of other turners that illuminate production practices to a greater degree. The ability to produce a series of turned parts, fit them together using round mortise and tenon joints, and end up with a strong, well conceived, and integrated design was a skill that not all turners possessed. But certainly the craftsman who turned and joined the "great chair" in figure 140 was among those few who had the power to visualize and conceptualize a neatly proportioned and crisply executed product. Perhaps someday we will identify that craftsman.

In 1972 the publication of Dean Fales's *American Painted Furniture, 1660–1880* (New York: E.P. Dutton) called renewed attention to the use of paint as ornament throughout a period of changing styles and technology. This medium affords the widest variety of any type of ornament, and the European medieval tradition of painted furniture no doubt formed the basis for our seventeenth-century use of polychrome decoration as surface ornament. Presumably, just about the turn of the century or in the early 1700s, there was in New York City or its immediate environs a tradition of painting simple, tulipwood and pine *kasten* with elaborate *trompe l'oeil* grisaille decoration of festoons of fruit (fig. 141). While this group of related *kasten* have been recognized since the early part of this century, to date the identity of the painters of these large and lovely pieces has not been discovered. Definitely derived from a seventeenth-century Dutch tradition, related examples were made in Holland by *witwerkers* and decorated with scenes or similar festoons by a different craftsman, presumably a painter of some sort.[11] While at least a half-dozen of these great painted *kasten* with bold molded cornices are known, the decoration on four of them is so closely related as to suggest the work of the same hand.[12] Several of these *kasten* show evidence of small pin holes where compasses were used by the painter to lay out the festoon decoration. One cannot help but speculate on the identity of the New York craftsman responsible for decorating these masterpieces. Could the father and son Gerardus Duyckinck, Sr. and Jr., have been involved in this type of decorative work? In overall appearance these *kasten* closely parallel those being made on Long Island and in the Hudson Valley (see fig. 260),[13] but the board construction techniques of these are entirely different from the panel and joined construction of the others. While these painted *kasten* are definitely not unique American products, they must certainly be regarded as some of the most sophisticated early painted furniture produced in the colonies.[14]

When New Yorkers were ordering painted *kasten* in the first quarter of the eighteenth century, Bostonians were taken with the fashionable English practice of "japanning" furniture, that is, painting furniture with a black or tortoiseshell ground and then using gilt often underlaid with gesso to raise figures depicting Chinese scenes in an exotic mode. This manner of decoration had become popular in England during the last quarter of the seventeenth century and was widespread when Stalker and Parker's *A Treatise of Japanning and Varnishing* (Oxford) was published in 1688. Within the past five years extensive research in Boston's public records and the discovery of several signatures as well as several unknown pieces of furniture have spurred interest in and publications about this important group of early eighteenth-century decorators and their production in one of the most cosmopolitan colonial centers of the century.[15] The pioneering research on American japanned furniture dates from the 1930s and 1940s with the publications of Joseph Downs, Esther Stevens Brazier, and Mabel M. Swan. Within this decade Dean A. Fales, Jr., Richard H. Randall, Jr., Sinclair H. Hitchings, Brock W. Jobe, and Elizabeth A. Rhoades have made significant contributions to our existing body of knowledge. Before the Revolution at least a dozen japanners worked in Boston, and today scholars can identify signed examples from two of them; William Randle and Robert Davis. Unfortunately, the ravages of time and the fragile nature of the medium have left few pristine surviving examples, and conservators are currently using painstaking techniques to stabilize our surviving examples.[16] The earliest pieces of American japanned furniture are in the William and Mary style, and the dressing table in plate 22, a recent discovery, is to date the only one of its kind to survive. With fine decoration that remains almost untouched, this dressing table has extraordinarily well-turned legs with ball turnings complementing those of the feet and a handsome sweep rarely found on the trumpet portion of the turnings. Original decoration remains not only on the legs but also on the cyma-curved, crossed stretchers. Related to the high chest of drawers originally owned by the Quincy family and signed by Boston craftsman William Randle,[17] this piece might be from the same hand. The most florid and ambitious examples of American japanning are a group of high chests with broken scroll pediments, richly carved and gilt shells, and well-shaped cabriole legs. Winterthur Museum's example of this form is the well-known high chest signed by the cabinet-maker John Pimm.[18]

The early vogue for painted furniture ended by the 1750s, but by the 1790s and early 1800s painted decoration returned to fashion in both high-style and more simple furniture. The early nineteenth-century dressing table in plate 23 is an interesting contrast to the japanned one that is nearly a century older. Made in Maine of birch and maple, this simple piece of furniture with well-turned legs was then decorated much like a theorem painting, with birds, flowers, trailing vines, scenic views, shells, and a huge basket of fruit, and inscribed with a saccharine poem entitled "Hope" both on the top and around its edges. Probably completed as part of her training in a female seminary, this dressing table was signed across the front of the drawer "Elizabeth Paine Lombard Feb 1816." Presumably Miss Lombard was related to Rachel H. Lombard from Bath, Maine, who decorated an almost identical table that she signed similarly with the date January 1816. This second table and another related one signed "Executed by Wealthy P.S. Jones, Bath, Maine, March 6, 1815" are presently in the Winterthur Museum collection. While there were girls' schools in Portland, Wiscasset, and Brunswick, Maine, at this time, there is to date no knowledge of one in Bath or of anyone in that area teaching painting on furniture. These three outstanding painted objects represent an important aspect of schoolgirl art, an entirely different area of study from the subject of professional ornamental painters, and one that has yet to be fully explored and recognized.[19]

Although some fancy painted furniture was made in New York, the most important specialty of that city was the elaborate rosewood-veneered furniture with gilt stencil decoration. This type of furniture was often made in rather large shops where there was clearly some division of labor. The window seat in figure 142 is one of a pair (and possibly more) that was reputedly ordered in 1823 by Robert Donaldson of Fayetteville, North Carolina, along with a set of mahogany parlor furniture, known by a bill of sale

144. *View of Baltimore,* **1803, Baltimore.** *Francis Guy (1760–1820). Oil on canvas. H. 50⅞ in., W. 96 in. The Brooklyn Museum. Gift of George Dobbin Brown.*

dated 1823 by Duncan Phyfe. While the window seats are not recorded on that particular bill, one of them is inscribed in ink on the underside of the webbing "D. Phyfe." Two years after the furniture from Phyfe arrived in North Carolina, it was shipped back to New York where Donaldson established residence until 1836 when he moved to a country estate on the Hudson River near Tarrytown. With rosewood graining and gilt decoration similar to that on other attributed Phyfe pieces, the design of these window seats appears to have been drawn directly from George Smith's 1808 London publication of *A Collection of Designs for Household Furniture and Interior Decoration*, plate 52 (fig. 143). While Smith did not publish his collected plates until 1808, this particular plate was engraved and published in December 1804. Smith's description for "Plate 51. Tete-a-tete Seats" also applies to his "Plate 52. Window Seats: An article adapted to elegant apartments; the frames of rich wood or gold and bronze; the covering of fine cloth, velvet or calico; in dimension, it is calculated for two persons to sit on." According to Smith's dictates, Donaldson's window seats were upholstered in a "covering of fine cloth" and to this day retain their original upholstery of red damask with a loose cushion and original braid edging the lower portion of the seat. The gilt decoration on the seat rails and on the corner posts was meant to imitate more expensive ormulu mounts, and that on the feet and upper corners also imitates a richer treatment, as suggested by Smith's design, "the frames of rich wood or gold and bronze." In 1832 when George Cooke painted a portrait of Mrs. Robert Donaldson of New York, he put a corner of one of these seats in the lower right of the painting.[20] Also of interest is the fact that these window seats were acquired by the inveterate collector Mrs. J. Amory Haskell, who then gave them to the Brooklyn Museum in 1942.

By the end of the eighteenth century Baltimore had become the leading center for painted and highly ornamented furniture. The burgeoning economic success of this port, the boom in the building of new and elegantly stylish town houses, and the influx of skilled craftsmen all contributed to the development of a flourishing trade in painted furniture. Francis Guy's *View of Baltimore* (1803) is a striking visual image of this growing scene of new brick buildings (fig. 144). In 1972 a major examination of *Baltimore Painted Furniture 1800–1840* by William Voss Elder III resulted in not only a fine and beautiful exhibition but also a valuable and lasting publication.[21] Between 1800 and 1840 there were at least fifty-eight craftsmen listed in the Baltimore directories as "ornamental painters," "gilders," "Fancy painters," or "painter of decoration." The variety, volume, and quality of furniture that was produced in that center during a span of less than half a century was enormous. Of course, like many painted objects, few of these pieces have survived in good condition, but the ones that have present impressive testimony to the skill and competence of decorators working in Baltimore. Classical motifs were popular and were executed in both stencil and freehand gilt decoration.

Hugh and John Finlay were among the most competent craftsmen dealing in this type of ornamented furniture, though little is known about the size of their shop or the manner in which they employed their workmen. The Finlays were born and trained in Ireland and probably did not arrive in Baltimore until the 1790s. In 1805 they advertised in the *Federal Gazette and Baltimore Daily Advertiser*, describing at length that they painted furniture "... with real Views, Fancy Landscapes, Flowers, Trophies of Music, War, Husbandry, Love & c. & c . . . ." The card table in figure 145 might possibly have been produced in their shop or perhaps by decorators who were working for them, as it is similar to other firmly documented Finlay pieces of furniture and exemplifies what they professed in their advertisement. The delicate, linear quality of the early neoclassical form of this table relates it to others that were being made in New York and Boston using highly patterned veneers and elaborate inlaid medallions. An almost identical table, except with different decoration, incorporating a central painted scene is now in the collection of the Metropolitan Museum. The table illustrated originally belonged to the noted Baltimore collector Robert Gilmor II, whose wife, dressed in a strikingly fashionable dress and turban, was painted by Thomas Sully in 1823 (see pl. 47). The Gilmors must certainly have been people of great taste and fashion, no doubt with the means to outfit both themselves and their home in the most current styles.

In addition to handsome painted furniture, much richly veneered furniture was produced in Baltimore during the early Federal period. Baltimore cabinetmakers would frequently design a veneered piece of furniture to include églomisé panels, that is, glass

145. Card table, 1800–1810, Baltimore. *Possibly by Hugh and John Finlay (w. 1800–37). Wood painted black with gilt decoration, baize playing surface. H. 29⅝ in., W. 36⅛ in., D. 17⅝ in. Maryland Historical Society, Baltimore.*

146. Looking glass, 1800–1810, New York or Albany. *Pine with gesso and gilt, reverse painted glass. H. 86½ in. Albany Institute of History and Art. Gift of the Estate of Mrs. Abraham Lansing.*

■ **147. Card table (one of a pair), 1790–1800, Boston or Salem, Massachusetts.** *Mahogany and mahogany veneer with light wood inlay, pine, baize playing surface not original. H. 30 in., W. (closed) 49 in., D. 24¾ in. Museum of Fine Arts, Boston. M. and M. Karolik Collection.*

145

147

146

148

148. **Armchair, 1800–1810, Philadelphia.** *Ash, painted white with gilt. H. 36½ in., W. 20¼ in., D. 18¼ in. The Henry Francis du Pont Winterthur Museum.*

149. **Finial bust from a desk and bookcase, 1770–75, Philadelphia.** *Mahogany. H. 7⅞ in. Mr. and Mrs. George M. Kaufman.*

150. **Carved figure from desk and bookcase, 1780–90, Boston.** *Possibly by Simeon Skillin (1746–1800) or son John or Simeon, Jr. Mahogany; H. 12½ in. The Metropolitan Museum of Art. Gift of Mrs. Russell Sage, 1909.*

151. **Detail view of pediment of desk and bookcase, 1760–1800, Boston.** *Possibly by Simeon Skillin (1746–1800) or sons John or Simeon, Jr. Carved figures mahogany. Originally owned by Joseph Barrell. The Henry Francis du Pont Winterthur Museum. Figure 151 is on pages 132 and 133.*

152. **Bookplate of Joseph Barrell, 1780–1800, probably Boston.** *Joseph Downs Manuscript Collection. The Henry Francis du Pont Winterthur Museum.*

with painting on the reverse traditionally done in black and white and gilt. The lady's dressing table in plate 24 is one of a group of Baltimore Federal-style pieces of furniture of great accomplishment and exuberance[22] and is derived directly from plate 4 in Thomas Sheraton's 1802 edition of *The Cabinet-Maker and Upholsterer's Drawing-Book.* The base has the form of a sideboard, but its top drawer is fitted as a dressing table with small compartments, above which is a baize-covered writing slide, with the upper cabinets on each side also fitted with compartments for use in a lady's boudoir. The entire surface of this tour de force reverberates with the interplay of oval, circular, and diamond-shaped forms, articulated in veneers, églomisé, gilt, and polychrome. To date it is not known from which Baltimore cabinet shop this work might have come, but of interest is the label of the cabinetmaker William Camp (listed in directories from 1802 through 1809), which pictures a similar dressing table derived from the same plate in Sheraton.[23] Whatever shop completed this spectacular commission, a number of craftsmen must have been employed in its execution. Once the cabinetmaker finished the carcass, veneer cutters, inlay makers, ornamental painters, gilders, a carver, and a turner were all responsible for different parts. Did one shop have this total capability, or were elements bought from various craftsmen as piecework? Much remains to be learned about shop practices during this time of economic wealth and development.

The looking glass in figure 146 is another product of either a very large shop or a number of independent craftsmen. Since one of the oval views (upper left) in the vertical painted glass panels on each side is that of the Old Dutch Church (1715–1806) in Albany, the glass has always been considered the product of an Albany craftsman. However, the view was taken from a print engraved by Henry W. Snyder of Albany and published in New York in 1806 by the bookseller John Low, so it would have been available to any New York craftsman or could have been brought to him by an Albany client. The painted panels of this glass are very similar to those in an overmantel looking glass now in the Metropolitan Museum of Art, thought to have been made in New York. Regardless of the city of origin, it should be noted that the manufacture of this looking glass would have involved at least four different craftsmen: a cabinetmaker for the frame, a carver, a gilder and/or ornamental painter (possibly the same person), and a plate glass maker. In 1803 William Voight of New York City was importing from London and Hamburg "Elegant Gilt Frames, with pillars, balls, enamelled frieze and eagle of all sizes," while in 1804 John Dixey advertised his own "Newest Fashion. Chimney Glasses, a few very elegant ones ... As they are the first articles of this kind finished agreeably to the present prevailing fashion in Europe, it is hopeful they will merit the attention of persons of taste."[24] Though little is known of Dixey's establish-

149

150

152

ment, he was in business until at least the early 1820s, and he either employed a number of varied craftsmen or bought piecework from many. Possibly an immigrant craftsman like Dominica Clevenzana, who called himself a "varnisher and ornamental worker in glass" in the 1805–1806 New York City directory, might have been one of the men Dixey patronized.

While furniture painters flourished in Baltimore, and New York certainly had its quota of ornamental painters, Boston was the largest center for reverse painting on glass and other related arts. Names like John Ritto Penniman and John Doggett have been recognized for decades through the work of researchers like Mabel M. Swan, but only within the past few years has there been a more complete investigation of the group of interrelated craftsmen/painters/gilders in the Boston-Roxbury area.[25] During the first decades of the nineteenth century, versatility was the mark of these men, and several used their craft as a stepping stone to the higher accomplishments of portrait and landscape painting, like John Johnston, son of the Boston engraver and japanner Thomas Johnston. Some of these craftsmen established active trade along the Atlantic seaboard, like Samuel Curtis who exported his painted clock dials up and down the coast. Occasionally a researcher finds the signature of one of these men or evidence of a partnership. The painted glasses on the Willard banjo clock in plate 6 are fine examples of the work of Aaron Willard, Jr., and his partner Spencer Nolen. Their brief association ended after 1805, at which time Nolen became associated with Samuel Curtis, a partnership that lasted over a decade. Samuel Curtis was the brother of Lemuel, the noted clockmaker of Concord who presumably in 1816 patented what we today call the "girandole" clock (pl. 25), but what Curtis probably simply called his "Patent Time-piece." Though Lemuel Curtis moved to Burlington, Vermont, by 1821 and in June of that year announced his partnership with Joseph N. Dunning in an ad that pictured his famous girandole, he had probably been making these for several years before he left Concord. While Benjamin Curtis, another brother of Lemuel and also an ornamental painter, has always been thought to have painted the glasses for his brother's clocks, an advertisement in the December 1819 *Columbian Centinel* by Curtis and Nolen indicated they were shipping him painted tablets.[26] A box of goods had been shipped from Roxbury to Concord and left by the stage at a tavern but was not picked up immediately; someone else must have claimed it, and the shippers were begging the return of their merchandise. The Curtis girandole in plate 25 is among the most handsome and well preserved, with its original carved gilt eagle and complementing pendant leafage below. The painted, vertical "throat" glass is elaborately executed, and the popular scene on the round glass below depicting Aurora in her chariot is also exceptionally well done, though neither are signed. The sides of this particular clock are pine painted white, not the usual mahogany and gilt, and a narrow brass crescent below Aurora is engraved with the maker's name. This special embellishment is most unusual, and tradition has passed along the story that this clock was made as a present for a female of Curtis's family.[27]

John Doggett, perhaps best known as a looking glass maker from Roxbury, Massachusetts, was a pivotal figure in the group of Boston-Roxbury craftsmen. His account book, kept between 1803 and 1809, and a letter book from the 1820s present a fascinating record of the interrelationships, exchanges, and variety of work being done through his manufactory.[28] Doggett was buying painted tablets from Penniman and Curtis, selling gilt balls and books of gold leaf to Stephen Badlam, making dressing boxes, and silvering glass; he was also gilding clock cases for Simon Willard and selling supplies to the looking glass makers Cermenati and Monfrino. He was conducting business as both principal and middleman, with private persons as well as other craftsmen. Harrison Gray Otis and Mrs. Elizabeth Derby West were among his customers. Extant bills document Mrs. Derby's patronage of the Boston cabinet warehouse of Thomas Seymour. (After her divorce from Nathaniel West, she went by her maiden name.) In 1809, however, she also did a large amount of business with Doggett when she was redecorating Oak Hill, her country estate. While traditionally thought to be the product of a Salem cabinetshop with carving by Samuel McIntire, the dressing box with carved and gilt frame looking glass might well have been the joint effort of several Boston and Roxbury craftsmen (pl. 26). On March 2 Doggett charged Mrs. Derby $15.00 "To 1 round frame & eagle for Dressing glass," on March 18 he charged her another $4.00 "To regilding 1 Oval Dressing Glass frame," and on March 27 he billed her for $24.00 "To 1

151

Plate 27. Bust of Athena, 1760–1800, Providence or Boston. *Probably pine painted in polychrome. H. 11⅜ in. The Rhode Island Historical Society.*

Plate 28. Desk and bookcase, 1720–30, Boston. *Walnut, walnut veneer, white pine, maple, and light wood inlay; on insides of the upper case doors are pasted later specimens of penmanship: odes to "Liberty," to "Commerce," and "The Penman's Advice" signed by "Benjamin Gudworth and Thomas Blake, 1766." H. 88½ in., W. 29⅝ in., D. 20½ in. Museum of Fine Arts, Boston. M. and M. Karolik Collection.*

PL. 28

round Glass frame & Gilding the ornament for the top." In addition, Doggett made larger looking glasses for her as well as bed and window cornices. On March 11 he noted in his accounts "To Cash paid Whitman for Carving 4 Eagles @ 9/ . . . . $6.00." Whitman was also mentioned as a carver on the famous Seymour bill of 1809 to Madam Derby for her great commode and other items. He was clearly a free-lance craftsman doing piecework for a variety of shops, a situation demonstrating the pitfall of attributing an object to a certain cabinetshop on the basis of its carving. The oval, veneered and inlaid base of Mrs. Derby's dressing box is as rich and handsome as the carved and gilt frame above. All of Mrs. Derby's pieces of furniture were probably made in Boston rather than Salem, including the elaborate top of her commode from Thomas Seymour's cabinet manufactory and her pair of large, carved and veneered card tables (fig. 147). The carved cornucopia motifs on the tables (as well as on her sofa in pl. 9) could have come from the hands of a number of carvers doing piecework for entrepreneurs like Seymour and Badlam. In fact, there are noticeable differences in the carving on the pair of card tables, suggesting more than one carver at work. In many instances both Elias Hasket Derby and his daughter Elizabeth looked to Boston for their most fashionable goods, so there is ample reason to believe the products came from a thriving Boston warehouse that drew on the talents of a number of skilled artisans.

A small quantity of early nineteenth-century American furniture was made in the Louis XVI style with carved, gilt, and white painted ornament. French gilt furniture is known to have been imported into the major American style centers or brought back from abroad by ambassadors and diplomats, but little American production of this style and character seems to have occurred. However, a small group in this style has been attributed to Philadelphia, among which is the armchair in figure 148.[29] While at first glance it appears to be of French design, the translation is English, via Thomas Sheraton, who noted "These chairs are finished in white and gold or the ornaments may be japanned but the French finish them in mahogany with gilt moldings."[30] The carved ornament of this chair is closely related to designs published in English architectural books of the 1780s and 1790s, as well as to those being produced at Robert Wellford's American Manufactory of Composition Ornament in Philadelphia in the early 1800s.[31] Although the manufacture of a similar type of furniture in Boston has never been recognized, in March 1807 John Doggett billed Harrison Gray Otis $18.00 "To Gilding painting & composition of a Sopha," with a notation in the outside column, "Charged to Mr. Bass." On April 1, 1807, Doggett charged that sum against Benjamin Bass. Benjamin Bass, Jr., was a cabinetmaker who was working on Orange Street at least as early as 1798[32] and was listed in the Boston directories at least between 1806 and 1810. There was also a Moses B. Bass, perhaps a relation, listed as an upholsterer with a shop on Orange Street. To date Mr. Otis's "sopha" is not known to have survived, but perhaps it was like some of the French furniture that was sent to Boston and other East Coast ports by Major James Swan in the 1790s.[33] A final note of interest regarding Doggett's operation is that he appears to have hired and housed a man named James Evans, for whom he also purchased "sulpher-molds for composition"; this is another unknown and unexplored item in early nineteenth-century Boston furniture making.

Prior to the Revolution, and even before the nineteenth century, few pieces of sculpture were produced in America purely as artistic achievements. Most carving was an accompaniment to the cabinetmaking or building trades. The closest our craftsmen came to purely aesthetic, representational sculpture was the carving of busts or full length figures that ornamented the pediments of doorways, adorned the bows of ships, or graced the tops of elegant mahogany case pieces of furniture. Figural busts of this type were used as early as the first decades of the eighteenth century in England and France, and in Thomas Chippendale's 1754 edition of *The Director* he illustrated several instances of carved busts surmounting case pieces. In addition, many "builder's guides" of the eighteenth century, like William Pain's 1762 *The Builder's Companion and Workman's General Assistant*, suggested and illustrated "The manner of open Pediments with Busto's & shells for the open part of the PEDIMENT." The Philadelphia cabinetmaker Benjamin Randolph copied (but reversed) one of Chippendale's busts and incorporated it into his tradecard, which was engraved by James Smithers about 1770.[34] A variety of busts on Philadelphia case pieces presumably made before the Revolution have been

■ 153. Looking glass, ca. 1770, Philadelphia. *Attributed to James Reynolds (ca. 1736–1794). Yellow pine, painted white with partial gilt decoration. H. 60½ in., W. 30¼ in. Cliveden, Philadelphia, Pennsylvania; a property of the National Trust for Historic Preservation.*

154. *Josiah Quincy, Sr. (1709–84), ca. 1767, Boston. John Singleton Copley (1738–1815). Oil on canvas. H. 36 in., W. 28½ in. The Dietrich Fine Arts Collections, Philadelphia.*

154

studied, and they seem to exhibit a number of different hands at work (fig. 149). These pieces of sculpture seem quite English, which is consistent with the fact that many London-trained carvers were working in Philadelphia by that time.

Analogous sculptural figures from Boston area case pieces of furniture are of a quite different character, and all are post-Revolutionary (fig. 150). Frequently attributed to the shop of Simeon Skillin and his two sons, John and Simeon, Jr., many of these figures exhibit similar facial characteristics and drapery. Several case pieces of furniture with figures were owned by the Derby family, another by Joseph Barrell, and several bust figures for doorways were in the possession of wealthy Providence merchant John Brown. Conclusive evidence that any of these figures were made by the Skillins is lacking, although bills do document several garden figures made for Derby by that shop.[35] Exactly where the idea for these figures came from is speculative, but of interest is plate 52 in Chippendale's *Director* (1762). The composition of that illustration is similar to the top of Joseph Barrell's desk and bookcase (fig. 151), which was probably added several decades after the serpentine bombé base was made. However, even closer to the Barrell figures are those on his own engraved bookplate (fig. 152), yet it is impossible to know which came first as neither the bookplate nor the piece of furniture is dated.

The two carved and polychromed busts of Athena and Milton that John Brown owned and that were probably ordered during the construction of his Providence mansion in 1786–88 (pl. 27) have facial features rather different from other carved figures (fig. 150). They are similar to a face carved in relief on a wooden keystone that surmounts a great Palladian window in the back of Mr. Brown's house.[36] Perhaps future research and documentation will reveal the identity of other eastern New England carvers of comparable talent and ability and thus lighten the legendary production from the Skillins.

In the eighteenth century the art of carving was applied to a wide variety of objects from architectural elements and representational figures to looking glass frames. While the general belief is that all eighteenth-century looking glasses and most frames were imported into America, research over the years has revealed some important exceptions to this generalization. Since Philadelphia was the center par excellence of rococo carving in America, it is not surprising that the carvers of Philadelphia executed some ambitious looking glass frames. The papers of John Cadwalader reveal that in 1770 James Reynolds, a London-trained carver working in Philadelphia, billed him for "a Carved white frame," "Carv'd Burnish Gold frame," and "a Pier Glass 36:19 hd 13 partly Gold £18:10:0."[37] The "Pier Glass" by Reynolds is now in the collection of the Winterthur Museum, but the looking glass in figure 153 also descended through the same family, that of Joshua Francis Fisher, and was probably purchased from Reynolds by Cadwalader about the same time, though none of the measurements on the Cadwalader bills seem to match those of this glass. The two looking glasses are so nearly identical in composition, execution, materials, and surface treatment that there is little question that they came from the same hand. The design and ornamentation of these looking glasses is the work of a master artist and carver; here the light, flowing quality of the repeating C-scrolls with the clusters of flowers and leaves is truly exceptional. Reynolds clearly displays his debt to English design sources and most particularly to Thomas Johnson's *One Hundred and Fifty New Designs*, published in London between 1756 and 1758 in installments. While little is known of Reynolds's early training and apprenticeship, he was in Philadelphia by the end of 1766, and in September of 1767 he advertised in the *Pennsylvania Gazette* that he was "Just arrived" from London. Soon he had set up his own shop at the "Sign of the Golden Boy" where he did work not only for cabinetmakers like Thomas Affleck but also directly for private persons like John Penn, Joseph Pemberton, Samuel Powel, and George Washington.

Although Boston tastes and craftsmen never quite reached the florid heights of rococo accomplishment in Philadelphia, nevertheless some fine carving came out of that northernmost style center. Artists during the first half of the eighteenth century are

155

155. Dressing table, 1765–75, Philadelphia. *Mahogany and mahogany veneer, poplar, and pine. H. 31⅞ in., W. 36¼ in., D. 20⅜ in. Museum of Fine Arts, Boston. M. and M. Karolik Collection.*

156. Side chair, 1760–75, Philadelphia. *Mahogany, white cedar. H. 39¾ in., W. 25 in. Private collection.*

157. Side table, ca. 1770, Philadelphia. *Mahogany, pine, black walnut, and marble. H. 32¾ in., W. 48¼ in., D. 23⅛ in. The Metropolitan Museum of Art. John Stewart Kennedy Fund, 1918.*

known to have imported their frames from abroad, but a recent reevaluation of some Copley papers has led to the conclusion that Copley had at least some of his frames made in Boston by local carvers and gilders. In 1771 when Copley was in New York, he wrote to his brother Henry Pelham in Boston and added the following postscript: "I have parted with two small frames, but cannot yet give orders for more. because I would have none come but what are engaged. you must let me know the price of the small ones; I know that of the Large ones. let me know what you paid Welch for Carving and Whiting for Gilding and Give my compts. to Capt. Joy."[38] Copley was referring to John Welch (1711–89) and Stephen Whiting (1728–89), both of whom have long been recognized as Boston craftsmen.[39] In recent years Welch has been considered an important Boston carver and Whiting a varied craftsman who in 1771 advertised in the *Boston News-Letters*: "At (Whiting's Shop) Looking-Glasses are silvered, and Frames made for all sorts of Pictures, Looking-Glasses, Coats of Arms and Needle-Work, and gilt as best suits the Employer. New Frames made for old Glasses, or new Glasses put to old Frames. Also, Varnishing, Japanning and Gilding done to Frames of all Sorts, as well and reasonable as any are done in this Province."[40] While the handsomely carved and reticulated frame surrounding Copley's penetrating image of Josiah Quincy, Sr., painted around 1767 (fig. 154), is not the original frame from that portrait, it is nevertheless from a Copley painting and probably represents the work of a Boston carver, perhaps even the team of Welch and Whiting. Quite different in character from the elegant Reynolds looking glass with its abundance of C-scrolls, flowers, and foliage, this frame is visually more conservative but clearly a well executed piece of workmanship. There is so far no firm documentation for Copley's frames, but it is hoped that future research will delve deeper into the subject of carvers, gilders, and framemakers in colonial America.

The Philadelphia penchant for depicting Aesop's fables in architecture as well as on furniture will be discussed in detail in chapter 5, but the dressing table in figure 155 is an outstanding example of this practice and a very special example indeed considering the cabinetmaker's use of veneer on the drawer fronts and the carver's delicate handling of the ornament. The columns on both sides of the swan, the interlacing C-scrolls, and vines and flowers trailing down the quarter columns of the case echo the vocabulary and handling of the Reynolds looking glass frames. Despite the abundance of surface ornament, including carving on the rear cabriole legs, the ornament is neither heavy nor intrusive, but rather, it helps to lighten the dressing table and integrate the linear and curved components of the design.

The variety of design and ornament on Philadelphia chairs made in the rococo or Chippendale style is vast and the robust carving on the chair in figure 156 presents a dramatic contrast to the delicacy of that on the dressing table just cited. Copied directly

156

157

158. William Smith and his Grandson, 1788, Baltimore. *Charles Willson Peale (1741–1827). Oil on canvas. H. 51⅜ in., W. 40¼ in. Virginia Museum.*

159. Side table, 1760–90, Newport. *Mahogany, maple, pine, and marble. H. 28¾ in., W. 45 in., D. 21⅝ in. The Preservation Society of Newport County.*

159

from designs published in both the 1754 and 1762 editions of Thomas Chippendale's *Director*, this relatively simple chair has some of the most sculptural carving found on any piece of Philadelphia furniture. The cabriole legs of the chair, with their forward-sweeping leafy scroll feet and deeply carved, almost three-dimensional knees, appear to stand out as pieces of sculpture in their own right. The applied, carved gadrooning ornamenting the lower edge of the seat rails is unusual but not entirely unknown on Philadelphia chairs. Though minimal, the carving on the splat and crestrail is equally as sculptural as that on the legs.

Some even more monumental sculptural Philadelphia carving enhances the well-known marbletop side table originally owned by John Cadwalader and used in his elegantly appointed town house on Second Street in Philadelphia (fig. 157). Apparently, judging from information gleaned from the Cadwalader family papers, this table is one of two that were made for Cadwalader by Benjamin Randolph to whom Cadwalader supplied the marble slabs. The marble appears to have been purchased by Lambert Cadwalader, John's brother, at the household auction of Charles Coxe in May 1769. Whether or not Coxe sold the frames supporting these slabs is not specifically recorded, but in any case Cadwalader commissioned Randolph to make new ones. Whether or not this carving is the work of Hercules Courtenay is also undocumentable, but whoever of Randolph's employees carved this frame possessed an artful understanding of rococo design and its execution. Though missing some of the interlaced and reticulated scroll-work on the front of the skirt, the entire frame seems to be one continuous undulating wave of scrolls and leafage. While Chippendale included a number of elaborate "Frames for Marble Slabs," the "Slab Tables" shown in plates 73 and 74 of Ince and Mayhew's *Universal System of Household Furniture* are closer to this particular interpretation. This table remained in the Cadwalader family until the famous auction in 1904 when it was purchased by Charles Curran. It was later sold to George S. Palmer of Hartford and in 1918 purchased by the Metropolitan Museum of Art along with many other things from the Palmer Collection.

Marbletop "slab tables" survive today in limited numbers despite their frequent mention in eighteenth-century inventories and their appearance in some paintings. Perhaps Mr. Coxe's original frames were plain and unornamented, like the one that Charles Willson Peale depicted in this handsome and symbolic portrait *William Smith and his Grandson* painted in 1788 (fig. 158). With Smith's country seat "Eutaw" in the far background, and his orchard and an old mill facing the gentle slope, Smith reposes in a green rustic chair with his arm resting on the marble slab next to several scholarly books, including one on gardening. A grafting knife and peach branches lie on the table, emblematic of his experimentation with hybrid species. No doubt many marble slab tables like the one in this painting must have suffered from breakage, and afterwards, if the base was worthy, a mahogany top might have been fashioned; if not, perhaps the frame was simply discarded.

Fortunately the slab table in figure 159 has suffered only minor breakage; its marble has been successfully repaired, enabling it to remain with the original magnificent base. While this Newport table has no surface ornament save the carved claw-and-ball feet, it presents a fitting contrast to its Philadelphia contemporaries. The "ornament" of this table is found in its sweeping, undulating form and the beauty of the heavy, dense mahogany. Using a piece of wood at least four inches thick, the cabinetmaker, working possibly in the shop of John Goddard, skillfully shaped the front skirt of the table into a deep "cupid's bow." This table needs no further embellishment, for it repeats the same powerful, undecorated statement of the Newport corner chair once owned by John Brown (see fig. 182). The client's choice of simple pad feet in the rear could have been either aesthetic or economic. This table bears a close relationship to the documented one by John Goddard in chapter 1 (fig. 26), and it also incorporates elements as seen in the unusual Newport marbletop commode now owned by the Metropolitan Museum of Art.[41] The decidedly French influence that appears in the table, commode, and other Newport designs has yet to be fully understood and explained.

As is evident in the above table, ornament can be simple and subtle and still achieve its purpose. Two other eighteenth-century tables with comely, ornamental qualities yet simple, rather severe lines are the "China" tables in figures 160 and 161. The Newport example (fig. 160) is unique, although the pierced, crossed stretchers, stop-fluted legs, and lightly incised diaper work are characteristic of a group of Newport pembroke tables, one of which in the Winterthur Museum bears the label of John Townsend. Thomas Chippendale illustrated tables similar to these and called them "china tables," stating that they were "Tables for holding each a Set of China, and may be used as Tea-Tables." Though the pierced gallery, or fret, encircling the top of the Newport table does not correspond with any published designs, John Crunden did illustrate a wide variety of frets in his 1765 *The Joyner and Cabinet-Maker's Darling, or Pocket Director. . . . containing sixty different designs, . . . forty of which are gothic, Chinese . . . frets . . .* The term "china table" was used in colonial America, though probably interchangeably with tea table. The 1792 inventory of the Newport cabinetmaker Christopher Townsend lists "1 Old Blacknut China Table" and also an entry for "1 Fly tea table" and "1 Mahogany China Table 10/."[42] The table in figure 160 descended through the family of Jabez Bullock (1741–1808) and Mary Richmond Bullock (1740–1801), presumably of Newport, and tradition states the family was related to the Townsends. When John Townsend made his will in 1805, he left most of his elegant mahogany furniture to his eldest daughter, and judging from his listing he had some very fine things, among which might have been a table similar to this one:

I give unto my said Daughter the following Articles to Wit—One of my best Bedsteads with Clawfeet with the Bed thereon, ... Also my best Mahogany Bureau, which I made for her Mother, and one plain Mahogany Bureau, eight Mahogany Chairs with Claw feet, six Black walnut Chairs with hair bottom, my Easy Chair, two Mahogany Oval Pembroke Tables, One Square Mahogany four foot Table with fluted

160. China table, 1760–90, Newport. *Mahogany, chestnut, and pine. H. 27¼ in., W. 34¼ in., D. 21 in. The Henry Francis du Pont Winterthur Museum.*

161. China table, 1760–90, probably Portsmouth, New Hampshire. *Mahogany, mahogany veneer, maple, and pine. H. 28 in., W. 22 in., L. 32 in. Paper note pasted to the bottom reads: "Table belongs to Mary Anderson Poore of Greenwood, Maine" and was probably added in the late nineteenth or early twentieth century. Diplomatic Reception Rooms, Department of State, Washington, D.C.*

160

161

162. Card table, 1796–1800, New York. *Mahogany and mahogany veneer. H. 30 in., W. 38 in., D. 18 in. Private collection.*

162

legs, one Mahogany three feet square Table with fluted legs, one square Mahogany Pembroke Table with Stretchers, one Mahogany Tea Table with the set of China it Contains . . .[43]

Whether Townsend's tea table had stop-fluted legs and crossed stretchers will remain unknown, but certainly he was using it as Chippendale directed: to hold a set of china.

Although a few Philadelphia and New York cabinetmakers made similar gallery-top tea tables, a small but intriguing group (now totaling about six) seem to have been made in or around Portsmouth, New Hampshire. To date no particular cabinetmaker has been connected with these tables, which have in common a pierced gallery and brackets, veneered skirt, molded legs, and scrolled, arched stretchers with a reticulated finial at their crossing. They are most similar to Chippendale's designs in plate 51 of the 1762 edition of the *Director*. The 1929 Girl Scouts Loan Exhibition displayed the one that had been sold in the Reifsnyder sale in 1929 for $5,000.00, and was then owned by Matthew Sloan. Also of interest is the fact that Louis G. Myers owned two china tables, one of which is currently in the State Department Diplomatic Reception Rooms and thought to be of Virginia origin.[44] The history of the table in figure 161 is not specifically known, but an old piece of paper pasted to the underside of the top reads "Table belongs to Mary Anderson Poore of Greenwood, Maine." Several of these Portsmouth tables do have local histories, though only one specific eighteenth century reference is known. William Whipple, a merchant and general during the Revolution, died in 1788, and his inventory recorded a "raild Tea Table" valued at 48/ along with a "raild stand" worth 24/.[45] Currently on loan to the Warner House in Portsmouth is a table originally owned by Whipple and visually related to this group of china or tea tables; unfortunately its pierced gallery is missing and the matching stand apparently lost. Another "raild Tea Table," privately owned in Portsmouth, is still accompanied by its matching stand.[46]

Handsomely veneered pieces of furniture have been cited before in this book, but two more are worthy of mention at this point. One, a magnificent Boston desk and bookcase (pl. 28), was probably made before 1735, and the other, a seemingly simple yet exquisite New York card table, was made around 1800 (see fig. 162). The Boston example is one of the rarest gems in the M. and M. Karolik Collection at the Museum of Fine Arts, Boston. Belonging to a small group of early veneered furniture with stringing and star inlays, this piece is related to the blockfront dressing table in figure 232 and the early block-front bureau table in figure 233. Several pieces of similarly veneered and inlaid furniture have been associated with specific cabinetmakers because of their signatures. A high chest of drawers in the Museum of Fine Arts, Boston, was signed and dated 1739 by Charlestown cabinetmaker Ebenezer Hartshorne.[47] A solid walnut slantfront desk with stringing and star inlay was recorded a few years ago with the inscription: "Robt Burkes desk/draw'r October 19 1739/bot it of Wm Parkmn/at Clarks Wharf/Boston New England/price £ 14:10."[48]

While it is possible that one cabinetmaker alone may have made this desk and bookcase, it is more likely that several men worked on it, perhaps as many as four or five. Research into the Boston cabinetmaking trade in the early part of the eighteenth century has revealed that if a cabinetmaker was truly enterprising, as was Nathaniel Holmes, he might employ as many as ten joiners or cabinetmakers, three turners, two bed bottom makers, and one japanner.[49] All of these men might not be working under the same roof or even in the same town, but special skills were utilized and it was possible for a craftsman to make a living doing piecework. If a masterpiece like the veneered desk and bookcase is thought to be the work of a number of craftsmen, it is easier to understand it as the tremendous tour de force that it is. In the 1720s it was unlikely that one could buy premade inlay, such as the stars, so the task of cutting pieces out one by one and setting them in the veneered surface was far more time-consuming and demanding at that time than at the end of the century when a cabinetmaker could buy elaborate pieces of premade inlay and simply set them in a prepared surface.

The New York card table in figure 162 is an excellent example of early nineteenth-century inlay work on a form of superior design. While a cabinetmaker did not actually have to make the inlay himself, he or another in his shop was responsible for integrating it into the whole. While documentation exists for inlay or stringing makers working in Boston at this time, the little research done has not revealed any specific New York makers. The hazard of attributions to a specific cabinetmaker based on inlay alone is great for to our knowledge no one cabinetmaker had a copyright on any particular inlay. For instance, the eagle inlay in the central panel of this table is also found on a bureau labeled by Michael Allison in the Metropolitan Museum of Art, and though this table could have been made by Allison, it is likely that other cabinetmakers in New York at that time had access to the same inlay. The *New York Revised Book of Prices* for 1810 provides fascinating insight into how complicated the pricing was for pieces of furniture with any kind of veneer, banding, stringing, or other inlay work. Price depended not only on cost per foot but also on whether the work was done on a round surface, a hollow one, or an elliptical one. In the 1802 *Book of Prices* this table would have probably been called a "Veneer'd Ovalo Corner Card Table."[50] The base price for a table of this sort, being three feet long with straight middle and ends, was £2.10.0. However, if the client so desired, there were numerous extras that could be selected, including both slight variations in form as well as additional ornaments. The table in figure 162 has the additional feature of sweeping the front and sides oval or elliptic, which would have cost another ten shillings. All of the stringing on the legs and the inlaid panels and ovals would have also added greatly to the cost, especially the eagle inlay in the central panel, which must have been among the most extravagant.

In addition to furniture, many other kinds of articles were neatly ornamented and embellished, requiring either one craftsman with varied skills or the collaboration of several for the completion of a single work. The medium of silver, or "plate" as it was called in seventeenth- and eighteenth-century America, is as interesting as furniture because of the variety of ornament that was possible and the skills required. Although it is generally assumed that most goldsmiths or silversmiths executed every aspect of their production, there is evidence in a number of instances that they occasionally collaborated with engravers. While craftsmen like Nathaniel Hurd of Boston, William Rollinson of New York, and James Smithers of Philadelphia are known to have signed a few examples of their work on silver (figs. 107 and 277), they must have produced even more unsigned work. The possibility also exists that within a goldsmith's shop there were several apprentices or journeymen, each of whom was skilled in a specialty. It is hoped that future research and new documentation will enlighten our knowledge of the shop practices of more goldsmiths.[51]

An instance of Nathaniel Hurd engraving the work of another Boston goldsmith has been illustrated in the fine monteith fashioned by Daniel Henchman as a presentation to Dartmouth College in 1771 (fig. 107). In this past decade an exciting and unusual discovery has revealed two more pieces of Hurd engraving on silver, one of which is shown in figure 163. For several decades the daybooks of Paul Revere have been studied

163. Salver, one of a pair, 1762, Boston.
Paul Revere (1735–1818). Silver; marked "·REVERE" in rectangle on back at center point, and small "N·Hurd" in rectangle on face near rim; also engraved on face with Franklin arms in scroll cartouche. Dia. 8⅛ in., H. 1 in. Collection of The Paul Revere Life Insurance Company.

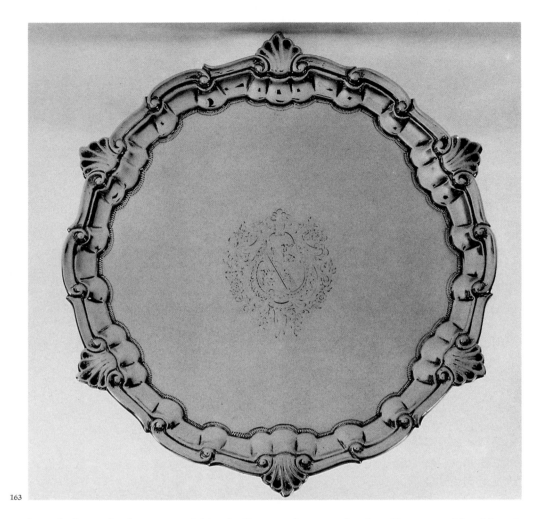

163

by scholars who have noted his dealings with several other Boston goldsmiths. A significant entry in the book is an item in April 1762 for charges against Nathaniel Hurd:

oz

To two Small Scolopd Salvers Silver Weight 23" 11—	8 – 5 – 2
To the Making of Salvers	4 – 4 – 0
	12 – 9 – 2

Several entries later Revere credited Hurd:

Mr. Nathaniel Hurd—Cr—oz	
—By Silver Received—24 - 0	8 - 8 - 0

Though this payment by Hurd did not cover the entire amount due to Revere, and in Hurd's next purchase of a chafing dish a full settlement was not recorded, scholars accept the fact that these daybooks have omissions and discrepancies. Revere marked each of the two salvers on the back at the center point with one of his pellet marks, and then Hurd, having engraved the face of each salver with the Franklin family arms, marked each one twice with his own small "N·Hurd" touch near the rim above and below the arms. The crest on the salvers is the same as one with a motto below that was cut as a bookplate for John Franklin, brother of Benjamin, by the eighteenth-century Boston engraver James Turner. Within this decade the salvers have returned from England, though their original owner is still unknown. Neither Benjamin Franklin nor his son William were the purchasers, as they were both in England at the time of the order. Possibly one Samuel Franklin, the son of Benjamin's cousin and a Boston cutler, might have ordered them. His inventory of 1775 included "132 ounces Plate £39 –12," though the only pieces specifically mentioned were "2 Silver Rattles 6/." Also of interest is Revere's entry in 1762 charging Samuel Minott six pounds for "two silver waiters chased"; their weight was similar to that of the Franklin salvers. The Minott "waiters"

are not known to survive today, and it is unclear what their form was; perhaps Revere was using the terms salver and waiter interchangeably, or salvers connoted a footed form while waiters were versions without feet.[52]

A tankard made by the Philadelphia goldsmith William Vilant around 1725 presents another fascinating puzzle. It was elaborately engraved in New York in 1750 by either Joseph Leddel or his son, Joseph Leddel, Jr., both of whom were pewterers (fig. 164). The tankard, typical of other Philadelphia-made ones of this period, has a low domed top, crenulated lip, broad sweeping handle with a segmented rib down the back, and a cast, applied thumbpiece. The body of the tankard is divided into three panels, each of which has engraved on it a highly detailed scene from Ovid. Figural portraits surmount each panel, and there is a mask at the bottom and a different Latin inscription below each scene. The caricature heads are said to represent Phillip, Earl of Hardwicke; Simon Fraser, Lord Lovat; and Philip, Earl of Chesterfield. In the 1930s the English author Edward Wenham suggested that these portraits derived from engravings (political prints) by Thomas Hudson, William Hogarth, and William Hoare, respectively. Their precise significance is still undefined, though in the Museum of the City of New York there is a French beaker also engraved by Leddel with a similar type of triptych motif.[53] Engraved on the handle of the tankard are the initials "I^LM," probably for Leddel and his wife, and the inscription "Joseph/Leddel./Sculp./1750." Though the inscription does not indicate whether the tankard was engraved by father or son, of interest is the 1752 advertisement of the son, stating that he "engraves on Steel, Iron, Gold, Silver, Copper, Brass, Pewter, Ivory or turtle-Shell . . . . . in a neat Manner." Clearly one of the Leddels was a very talented and competent engraver, but many unanswered questions remain. How did the Vilant piece come to New York, was it really owned by the Leddels, did father or son engrave it, and what is the significance of the engraving? In a larger vein, how much engraving was done on New York tankards by craftsmen like the Leddels, and how might we identify such pieces? Obviously free-lance engravers did not always sign their work, but how did goldsmiths and engravers interact in both their professional and personal lives? We have much to learn in this whole area of unknowns.

American-made candlesticks, and especially those dating from the seventeenth or early eighteenth centuries, are extremely rare. A pair fashioned by Jeremiah Dummer for the Lidgett family of Boston about 1680, and now in the Garvan Collection at Yale University, are the earliest known.[54] But the most ornate and sophisticated of the very early, seventeenth-century-style candlesticks are the exciting pair with accompanying snuffer stand that Cornelius Kierstede of New York made for Elizabeth and John Schuyler, probably between 1700 and 1715 (fig. 165).

Embellished around each base with exotic, whimsical Oriental figures and animals, these sticks and stand are among the earliest examples of chinoiserie taste in New York. Molded from wrought sheets of silver, the pieces are examples of such techniques as engraving or chasing, repoussé gadrooning, punching and stippling, drawn moldings, and applied meander wire and casting for the two-headed bird on the snuffer stand. Kierstede was an exceptionally competent craftsman (see also the Van Cortlandt tankard shown in figure 188), but whether he executed these pieces single-handedly is still a matter of conjecture, as is his possible ownership of any design books. The precise source of his figural engravings has not yet been discovered, but he was either working from a book of engravings or an imported piece of silver he might have been familiar with.

An equally elaborate but later set of four candlesticks were fashioned by the Boston goldsmith Thomas Dane (1726–95?), about whom little is known since few examples of his work survive (fig. 166). Probably made in the mid-1760s, these four ornate sticks were owned by Benjamin Hallowell and were mentioned in his will of 1773. The only other American candlesticks known of this style and elaborate fashion are a set of four made by the New York goldsmith Myer Myers.[55] The bases and shafts were cast in several sections, and the separate bobeches crowning the tops were raised by hand. Distinctly made in the manner that English goldsmiths often made their candlesticks, these candlesticks represent a superior achievement for an American maker.

John Coney was not only among Boston's earliest native-born goldsmiths (1655[6]–1722[3]), but he was also one of the most versatile, both in the variety of forms that he produced and in the different kinds of ornamentation he employed. Since Coney en-

148

165. Pair of candlesticks with snuffer stand, 1700–1715, New York. *Cornelius Kierstede (1675–1757). Silver; marked twice on top of base of each candlestick "CK" in rectangle, and engraved on underside of each "IᵉE"; stand marked twice "CK" on raised section of the base and engraved "IᵉE" on underside. Candlesticks, H. 11½ in., Dia. of base 6½ in.; Stand, H. 8 in., Dia. of base 5 in. The Metropolitan Museum of Art. Gift of Robert L. Cammann, 1957. Gift of Clermont L. Barnwell, 1964. Gift of William A. Moore, 1923.*

■ **166. Set of four candlesticks, 1760–70, Boston.** *Thomas Dane (1726–1795?). Silver; marked "T:Dane" in shaped rectangle, four times on bottom of each stick. H. 9 in. W. at base 4½ in. Historic Deerfield.*

165

166

167

168

170

167. **Plate, 1680–1700, Boston.**
John Coney (1655[6]–1722[3]). Silver; marked "JC" over fleur-de-lys in heart on rim. Dia. 11¼ in. Museum of Fine Arts, Boston. Pickman Collection.

■ 168. **Tankard, 1705–15, New York.**
Peter Van Dyck (1684–1751). Silver; marked "PᵛD" in trefoil at lip each side of handle; engraved on front with Wendell arms and crest in foliate cartouche. H. 7¼ in., Dia. of base 5½ in. Yale University Art Gallery. Mabel Brady Garvan Collection.

169. **Detail of Wendell arms on Van Dyck tankard in figure 168.**
Figure 169 is on page 150.

170. **Pair of salts, ca. 1737, New York.**
Charles LeRoux (1689–1745). Silver; marked twice on base "CLR" conjoined with bar, in oval; inscribed on base of each salt "IˢA" H. 2½ in., Dia. 3 in. The Metropolitan Museum of Art. Dodge Fund, 1935.

graved the first paper money for the Massachusetts colony and made a seal for Harvard College in 1693, it is reasonable to assume that he was an accomplished and competent engraver. The engraved motifs surrounding the rim of the large plate that he made probably for Caleb and Elizabeth Rawlins before 1691 bear witness to his extreme talent as an engraver (fig. 167). Though the source is not known, the flowers are similar to those found in sixteenth- and seventeenth-century emblem books from France and England. Since Coney may have been apprenticed to Boston's first goldsmiths, John Hull and Robert Sanderson, both from England, it is possible he learned some of these motifs in their tutelage. Coney's engraving on this plate is similar to that found on the top of Robert Sanderson's large, flat-topped tankard made about 1670–80 for Isaac and Mary Vergoose.[56] Timothy Dwight (1654–91/2), who is definitely known to have apprenticed with Hull and Sanderson, made a footed salver and engraved it with related trailing vines and flowers, among which were also an elephant, antelope, lion, and unicorn, somewhat exotic and Oriental in feeling.[57] Presumably Coney did not only the engraving on this plate, but also that on the salver Dwight wrought.

We have already noted the proficiency of New York goldsmiths in the early eighteenth century as exemplified by the work of Cornelius Kierstede, but the mastery of Peter Van Dyck must not be overlooked, for he produced some of the most sumptuous early tankards yet recorded. Among the greatest New York tankards is Van Dyck's masterpiece, probably made between 1705 and 1715 for Harmanus Wendell (1678–1731), Commissioner of Indian Affairs in Albany (1728–31), and bearing the Wendell family arms and crest along with the engraved intitials "H^Aw" on the handle (fig. 168 and 169). With the typical New York base molding of acanthus leaves and meander wire, engraved rim with crenulated lip, scroll thumbpiece, and cast cherub termination, this tankard also has less typical embellishments. The domed lid with repoussé decoration and gadrooned border, along with the handle's cast, applied ornament of mask, swags, and festoon, make this an exceptional piece of workmanship. Though little is known about Van Dyck except his abundant, superb production and his marriage to Rachel LeRoux, daughter of the goldsmith Bartholomew LeRoux (working 1689–1713), it has been suggested that perhaps he had been apprenticed to the elder LeRoux. As LeRoux was a French Huguenot émigré, this connection would account for the extremely French feeling and ornateness in some of Van Dyck's early production.

Closely related to Van Dyck's masterful tankard, but a little later in date and considerably smaller in size, are the delightful salts fashioned by Charles LeRoux (1689–1745) (fig. 170). As son of Bartholomew, the goldsmith, Charles may well have worked with Peter Van Dyck, and both could have been trained in the same French tradition as the elder LeRoux. Made for John and Ann Schuyler who married in 1737, each salt bears the initials "I^SA" on its bottom, and they may have been made as a wedding gift for the young couple. While circular salts of this same basic form were made in Boston and of course in England, the nature of this particular ornament, combined with its exceptional crispness and quality, make these a rare and desirable example of French influence as transmitted by émigré goldsmiths.

Only occasionally does American pewter occur with any significant amount of decorative engraving besides an inscription. This seems puzzling since pewter, more common and less expensive than silver, could have been embellished to imitate the rarer, more costly material. Among the small number of American pewter tankards surviving from about 1720 to 1750[58] is an exceptionally fine, elaborately engraved one with the "WB" touchmark, one of four attributed to William Bradford, Jr., of New York (fig. 171). Of early form, reminiscent of seventeenth-century styles, it has a flat top, crenulated lip, large strap-like handle, and lacks a mid-rib fillet. Engraved on the front of the tankard's body are the interlaced initials "C S," surrounded by an elaborate cartouche of C-scrolls, leafage, and flower garlands. While this tankard could have been made as late as the 1750s, its rococo ornament seems out of date with the earlier style of the tankard. Whether Bradford actually executed the ornament is uncertain, and there is no firm documentation indicating that he was even capable of it. However, possibly the original owner of the tankard took it to a separate engraver, like Joseph Leddel, Jr., sometime after his purchase of the item. Though Leddel, Sr., was Bradford's biggest competitor in New York pewtering circles, there were other engravers in New York who advertised. Henry Dawkins stated he "engraves in all sorts of mettals" in 1755, and Michael

DeBruls, in 1757, publicized that he did "Curious Chasing or other Raised Work, in general on Gold and Silver Watch-Cases, Snuff Boxes, & c. Engraving, Crests and Coats of Arms &c. on Gold, Silver and Copperplate, ..."[59] While many of these craftsmen seem like unknown entities to us today, their work may well be all around us, but because they never signed any pieces, their skills and art have gone unattributed for centuries. Perhaps someday an account book or additional signatures will enable more of these talented engravers to be recognized.

Calligraphy itself is an art, and a simple inscription on a piece of presentation silver or pewter can be quite artful, as in the case of Daniel Henchman's monteith, engraved by Nathaniel Hurd. Likewise, with a piece of pewter as monumental and important as this ecclesiastical flagon by William Will (1742–98) of Philadelphia (fig. 172), the inscription (fig. 173) had to be carefully planned and precisely executed. The bold, well-shaped form of the flagon demands a strong, robust handling of the engraving, and the German inscription with its swelling oval format aptly complements the overall form of this exemplary piece of American pewter.

Among the various metal objects that were well suited to and, in fact, actually demanded decoration were clock dials or faces. Therefore, it is not surprising that a number of talented, eighteenth-century clockmakers were also jewelers, silversmiths, engravers, and watchmakers. This seems to have been particularly true of a group of mid-eighteenth-century Connecticut clockmakers, including Enos Doolittle, Thomas Harland, and Daniel Burnap. On a clock face designed for his own personal use (fig. 174), Burnap completely filled the surface of the brass face with all manner of neatly executed scrolls, foliage, and flowers. With an unusual double chapter ring of both Roman and Arabic numerals, he has surrounded the minute hand and cleverly encircled his name and place of business, creating a four-part complement to the four quadrants of the face. The ultimate flourish that indicates his training in penmanship is the interlaced motif under the "E-Windsor" that is so gracefully and purposely done. Similar work by two of Burnap's apprentices, Thomas Lyman and Eli Terry, can be found on clocks by these makers in the Garvan Collection at Yale.[60] While it is possible that Burnap himself may have worked on their clock faces, their less skillful execution suggests the work of an apprentice instead.

The subject of American production of fine glass tableware before the end of the eighteenth century is now being adequately studied and ambitiously researched,· and the importance of skilled craftsmen who specifically advertised that they would engrave on glass is being formally recognized.[61] The earliest successful American glass manufactory, started by Caspar Wistar at Wistarburgh in Salem County, New Jersey, produced some sophisticated wares between 1739 and 1777 (see figs. 55, 56, 57 and pl. 7), yet it has not been firmly documented that engraving was done at that glasshouse. Though a letter from a friend congratulated Wistar on his successful "Glasschnitten" (literally glasscutting), examples of this have yet to appear.[62]

By 1773 a Jewish glass engraver, Lazarus Isaac, had arrived in Philadelphia from London. He advertised in the *Pennsylvania Packet* on May 17, 1773. That same day William Logan wrote a letter to Cornelius Fry saying: "As I Conclude thou may have heard of our new Glass houses erected here . . . . and We have some Glass Cutters lately Come over who cut Words—Grapes Coats of Arms or any Device that may be desired—"[63] Isaac announced to the public that he could be found at the house of Mary Wood, "nearly opposite to Mr. John Elliott's Looking Glass Store," and that "being just arrived . . . from London, . . . he undertakes to cut and engrave on glass of every kind, in any figure whatsoever, either coats of arms, flowers, names, or figures. to the particular fancy of those who may please to employ him: Patterns of his work may be seen at his dwelling. He cuts upon decanters a name of the wine, & c. for ls. tumblers for 6d. each, wine glasses for 2s. per dozen, and the stems cut in diamonds at 2/6 per dozen."[64]

Less than a month later Isaac contracted with Stiegel as a "cutter and flowerer," but by February of 1774 he left that failing venture and is believed to have returned eventually to England.

The Maryland glasshouse of John Frederick Amelung was the next successful venture to produce highly sophisticated wares. A large number of extant examples bear testimony to the fact that Amelung employed at least one or two highly talented, experi-

171. **Tankard, 1725–42, New York.**
William Bradford, Jr. (1688–1758). Pewter; marked with "WB" and fleur-de-lys touch; "CS" engraved on side. H. 7⅛ in., Dia. 7⅝ in. The Henry Francis du Pont Winterthur Museum.

172. **Flagon, ca. 1795, Philadelphia.**
William Will (1742–1798). Pewter; inscribed under spout as seen in figure 173. H. 13¾ in., W. 7½ in., Dia. of base 4⅝ in. square. Charles V. Swain.

173. **Detail of engraved inscription on flagon in figure 172.**

■ 174. **Clock face, 1790–95, East Windsor, Connecticut.** *Daniel Burnap (1759–1838). Brass. W. 12 in., H. 16¾ in. Wadsworth Atheneum. Gift of Efhine B. Hyde and Miss Mary E. Hyde. Figure 174 is on page 115.*

enced engravers during the years that his glasshouse flourished (see figs. 124, 125 and pl. 18). The handsome tumbler in figure 175 is one of the grandest and certainly most patriotic of all the Amelung products. With an impressive engraving of the Great Seal of the United States on one side and the inscription "New Bremen Glass-manufactory / 1792" on the other, this tumbler could have been a present to an important political figure. Unfortunately, any history of this piece before World War II has been lost, save for the report of a cover that was broken many years ago and discarded. While none of Amelung's engravers have been identified by name, the style of decoration on this tumbler resembles that of other engraved pieces from his manufactory. Since it is known that Amelung occasionally made promotional gifts for prominent and influential politicians, this tumbler might have been conceived as one of these.

In the 1790s patriotic feelings ran high, and it is probable that even imported glasswares arrived here with symbolic American motifs. There is an interesting advertise-

171

172

173

175

■ 175. Tumbler, 1792, New Bremen Glassmanufactory, New Bremen, Maryland. *John Frederick Amelung (1741–98). Colorless glass; engraved on front with the Great Seal of the United States, and on the reverse "New Bremen Glassmanufactory./ 1792." H. 8⅛ in., Dia. at rim 6⅛ in. Mr. and Mrs. George M. Kaufman.*

ment placed by John Moss, a London glass engraver who came to Philadelphia not long after Amelung's manufactory had closed, in the December 1796 *Pennsylvania Packet:*

> To the Merchants and Dealers in Glassware . . . he has lately arrived from London and commenced business at no. 67, Mulburry Street, where he carries on glass engraving in a superb elegant and masterly manner. The most fashionable borders, cyphers, coats of arms, crests, & c. engraved at the shortest notice and on the most reasonable terms. As elegance adds to the rapidity of the sale of goods, merchants will find it conducive to their interest, to have an engraving of something emblematical of their patriotic principles, which will be executed at a trifling expence. Patterns, to be seen at the shop of the subscriber, who trusts he will find succour in this city, where the arts and sciences are in a flourishing state.[65]

Philadelphia must have been a fertile employment area for free-lance engravers during this period, for there were several others who also advertised, including a "French glass engraver" named Mrs. Descamps. In a notice in the *Philadelphia Aurora* in April of 1800, she thanked her public "for the liberal support and encouragement . . . during more than six years, in the art of cutting and engraving on glass." She then indicated that she had others working with her whom she had apparently instructed "to be proficient in that art" and that "she will continue to engrave on glass of every kind, cyphers, devices, mottos, coats of arms." Apparently her work in Philadelphia continued for several more years, but by 1804 she had moved to Boston and was advertising in the *Columbian Centinel.*

Probably the most notable engraving and cutting on American glass during the first quarter of the nineteenth century occurred at the Pittsburgh manufactory of Bakewell, Page and Bakewell which was begun in 1808 by Benjamin Bakewell. Well aware of the public demand for imported glassware, these entrepreneurs figured that if they could offer their clients a comparable product at a lower price, they would corner the market. They took trips abroad to check out current trends and styles and were then able to closely imitate English and French imported wares. By 1820 the Bakewell manufactory was sizable, and many of the workmen, including cutters and engravers, must have been immigrants from England and France. The Pittsburgh directory for 1826 noted that the glass manufactory had sixty-one persons at work, of which twelve were constantly employed in engraving or cutting. While many of these workers are not yet known by name, at least one engraver did merit recognition because of his excellent work on a set of glassware made for President Monroe. The man's name was Alexander Jardelle, and in November 1818 the *Richmond Enquirer* reported:

> . . . During a visit a few evenings ago to the manufactory of Messrs. Bakewells & Page, we were much gratified by a sign of the splendid equipage of glass, intended for Mr. Monroe's sideboard. It consists of a full set of Decanters, Wine Glasses and Tumblers of various sizes and different models, exhibiting a brilliant specimen of double flint, engraved and cut by Jardelle . . . This able artist has displayed his best manner, and the arms of the United States on each piece are a fine effect. The glass itself must have been

■ **176. Tumbler, 1821, Pittsburgh, Pennsylvania.** *Bakewell, Page & Bakewell's Flint Glass Works. Colorless glass; engraved "VB" beneath swagged mantel on one side, with a greyhound chained to a pedestal with urn and doves above on the other. H. 3⅜ in., Dia. 3⅛ in. The Henry Francis du Pont Winterthur Museum.*

■ **177. Tumbler, ca. 1824, Pittsburgh, Pennsylvania.** *Bakewell, Page & Bakewell's Flint Glass Works. Colorless glass; engraved "MAS" on front with a sulfide bust of Benjamin Franklin in the base. H. 3⅜ in., Dia. 2⅞ in. The Henry Francis du Pont Winterthur Museum.*

selected with great care, or the spirited proprietors must have made considerable progress lately in their art, for we seldom have seen any samples so perfectly pellucid and free from tinct. Upon the whole, we think the present service equal, if not superior, to the elegant Decanters presented to the President when he passed through Pittsburgh last year.[66]

Though this Monroe service is documented by reports, orders, and bills, where that service is today is not known. Some elaborately cut glass pieces, including decanters, engraved with "the arms of the United States" and presently owned by the White House (and on loan to the Smithsonian Institution) seem too late in style to be the 1821 order, so the puzzle of the Monroe glass persists.

Although little Pittsburgh glass can be connected with the work of a specific engraver or cutter, recent research has definitely ascertained the exact date of manufacture of the diminutive little tumbler in figure 176. Engraved with the initials "VB" for Victorine Bauduy and with a common continental motif of a crouching greyhound chained to an urn with two doves, this tumbler was made in 1821 at Bakewell, Page and Bakewell's Flint Glass Works. The tumbler was a gift to Victorine Bauduy from her friend Antoinette du Pont, who in the spring of 1821 wrote to Victorine: "Mrs. Febigher is kind enough to take charge of a glass tumbler (which I hope you will use every day when you will be at home) of Mr. Bakewell's manufacture."

Apparently after Victorine received the gift, she wrote to thank Antoinette and probably to inquire about the design of the engraving, for Antoinette replied: "The engravings on your tumbler was not designed by me. . . . I saw a great many other ornamented [*sic*] glasses at Bakewells, most of which had like this one a place for a cypher. I found this very convenient and Mr. Bakewell's engraver is so expeditious that in the course of the same afternoon your cypher was put on."[67]

A second outstanding Pittsburgh tumbler is the one in figure 177, which has a sulfide portrait of Benjamin Franklin encased in its base. This sophisticated decorative use of "cameo encrustation" was adopted from European glassmakers and popularized by the Bakewell, Page, and Bakewell manufactory by the end of the first quarter of the nineteenth century. Images of other noted personalities such as Lafayette, DeWitt Clinton, George Washington, and Jenny Lind were also produced by Bakewell to compete with fancy imported French and English wares. The cut strawberry-diamond and fan motif was popular at Bakewell's manufactory, and this tumbler has the additional ornament of an engraved leafy border and interlaced cypher "MAS." A recent and illuminating article has presented valuable new information about Bakewell's use of this difficult decorative technique.[68] Studies which increase our knowledge of such decorative craftsmen as glass engravers, and their clients, must continue. Carvers, painters, turners, inlay-makers, engravers, etc., are still a great unknown quantity about whom much clearly remains to be discovered or reevaluated.

176

177

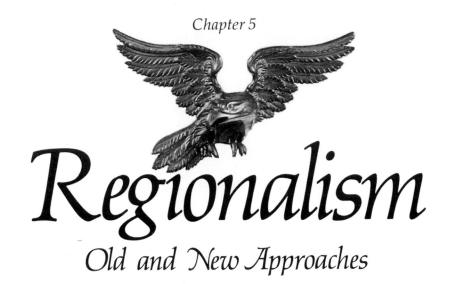

Chapter 5

Regionalism

Old and New Approaches

THE
UNITED STATES
of
AMERICA
laid down
From the best Authorities,
Agreeable to the Peace of
1783.
Published, April 3.d 1783.
by the Proprietor
JOHN WALLIS,
at his Map-Warehouse,
Ludgate Street
LONDON

The recognition of regional variations in different styles of furniture, silver, paintings, ceramics, and even some early American glass is not new. Even in the eighteenth century people were aware that distinctive interpretations of useful objects were being produced in various geographical regions. "New England" or "Boston" chairs were imitated in New York and Philadelphia and were also shipped along the coast and to the islands. Occasionally a merchant from one city would ask a friend in another to procure for him something more fashionable, if he felt that the latest styles could be obtained outside of his own region. While these regional differences have been acknowledged for centuries, what is new over the past fifteen to twenty years is the detailed study and attention that has been given to the reasons for and sources of these differences. Two important purposes of this section are: first, to present visual comparisons and contrasts that exemplify these often dramatic differences, and second, to cite and enumerate the recent and ongoing studies that are continually shedding new light on regionalism.

Regionalism is inherent and has existed for centuries, not only on this side of the Atlantic but also all over the world. Within different countries, the various interpretations of objects that are produced in separate geographical regions might be compared to the variety of dialects, or accents, that are also indicative of the regions.[1] The earliest collecting that occurred in America in the nineteenth century naturally had a distinct, regional focus. Those people who were antiquarian-collectors sought to preserve what was readily around them: things that had belonged to their immediate ancestors. In the early nineteenth-century antiquarians like William Bentley of Salem, Massachusetts, and John Fanning Watson of Philadelphia, were busily chronicling and collecting the cultural habits and possessions of their ancestors.[2] The later nineteenth-century New England collectors like Ben: Perley Poore, Henry Wood Erving, Cummings Davis, and George Sheldon all concentrated on preserving the artifacts from their own immediate culture. Sheldon was especially conscious of this, as noted in the Introduction to this book, for his establishment of the Pocumtuck Valley Memorial Association in 1870 was meant to record and preserve the heritage of those who had formerly inhabited the immediately surrounding area.[3]

In the early decades of the twentieth century the fullest manifestation of regional studies and groupings occurred with a series of "tercentenary" celebrations and exhibitions held in New England. In 1936 there was the Harvard Tercentenary, in 1935 the Connecticut Tercentenary, and in 1936 the Rhode Island anniversary. While the 1909 Hudson-Fulton Exhibition had not confined itself to New York products, a most important showing of New York furniture occurred a number of years later in 1934.[4] Also, by 1932 Louis Guerineau Myers was avidly studying the fine variations in Philadelphia chairs, including distinctive construction features.[5]

However, the greatest strides in studying and identifying regional schools of craftsmen have been made in the past fifteen or twenty years. The late 1940s and early 1950s witnessed several important regional furniture exhibitions, including the significant study of Baltimore furniture in 1947 and southern furniture in 1952. But not until the 1960s were comprehensive studies done using interior construction features as well as distinctive exterior design features as a basis of identification and comparison. Beginning in 1967 with an especially noteworthy exhibition of Connecticut furniture organized by John T. Kirk and held at the Wadsworth Atheneum, there have followed a series of valuable regional studies and exhibitions. These have covered the map from New Hampshire (1964, 1970, and 1978) to Boston (1973), Connecticut (the New Haven Colony in 1972 and New London County in 1974), Long Island (1976), Maryland (1968 and 1972), North Carolina (1976), Georgia (1976), and most recently eastern Virginia (1978). Scholars have also turned westward, away from the East Coast and the original thirteen colonies, and Kentucky, Tennessee, and Louisiana have received recent attention. Currently, the Museum of Early Southern Decorative Arts (established in 1960 in Winston-Salem, North Carolina) is systematically surveying various regions of the South in order to compile archival files of furniture and other decorative arts indigenous to the different geographic areas there. Finally, the Henry Francis du Pont Winterthur Museum, through its Decorative Arts Photographic Collection, is carrying out an extensive study of objects of interest from the Ohio and Delaware river valleys.

In addition to exhibitions and publications that have illuminated and defined new

178. Map of the United States of America, 1783, London. *Published by John Wallis. Paper and ink. H. 20½ in., W. 23¼ in. The Henry Francis du Pont Winterthur Museum. Figure 178 is on page 157.*

179. Chest of drawers, 1760–90, Boston.
Mahogany, with white pine and fire-gilt brasses; chalk inscription "Green" on inside of case. H. 31½ in., W. 35¾ in., D. 20¼ in. The Dietrich Fine Arts Collections, Philadelphia.

regional groups and distinctions, collectors and scholars must not overlook the many unpublished studies that have been completed over the years by students of American culture. These detailed studies of individual craftsmen, specific shops, and identifiable regional schools have added greatly to our knowledge, even though they have never been seen as published presentations. The only precaution that must be taken in identifying the work of an individual craftsman is that of interpreting the work of one man to be a regional style. While this may sometimes be the case, a survey of all known craftsmen who worked in the same area will more fully reveal the regional characteristics and practices.

Before turning to a discussion of regional contrasts and comparisons between objects, let us ask the basic questions of how regional differences manifest themselves and what the major factors are that determine these differences. Some of the most obvious differences occur in small details of form like turned pad feet or carved claw-and-ball feet, painted or inlaid decoration and carved ornamentation, as well as overall form and proportion. The specific methods of construction are another manner in which one can identify not only a geographical region but also sometimes even a distinctive maker. The way a craftsman makes his dovetails, the manner in which the drawers are joined, the style of corner blocks, and the manner in which moldings are applied can all be pertinent clues about both region and maker. Finally, the maker's choice of woods often indicates a broad geographical area of origin, depending on which woods are indigenous.

The factors that determine these differences can be almost as varied as the differences themselves, in addition to being occasionally inexplicable. Certainly the native origin and training of the craftsman is a prime factor, along with that of his client—as was especially true in the first century of our country's growth. The influences of both imported objects and design books (architectural and cabinetmaking), along with the raw materials available and the economic circumstances of the client, are other determining factors. Finally, the client's own personal preference had a great deal to do with an individual commission, but today that is the most difficult factor to document.

In addition to different regional interpretations of standard features, certain forms of furniture were either exclusively produced in one region, or the interpretation of a particular form in a region was unsurpassed by any other area. For example, Newport, Rhode Island, has at least in this century been acknowledged as the sole generator of the

179

so-called block and shell case furniture. The desk and bookcase in plate 29, originally owned by Joseph Brown of Providence (1733–85), is among the most notable of these pieces for its large number of carved shells—nine—and its richly figured imported mahogany.[6] This desk and bookcase is one of approximately a dozen known, though all the others have only six carved shells, lacking the three in the narrow top drawer. Supposedly each one of the four renowned Brown brothers of Providence owned a great Newport desk and bookcase. All of these are extant except the one owned by Moses Brown, which is believed to have burned in a fire at his homestead in the mid-nineteenth century. While all of these grandiose pieces appear similar, they do exhibit slight variations in carving, selection of mahogany, and construction techniques, suggesting that they either were produced in different shops or all came from a large shop with a number of journeymen or perhaps even craftsmen with specialized skills. Since none of the Newport block and shell desk and bookcases are signed or documented,[7] we have few clues as to who specifically was making them. However, in 1766 John Goddard corresponded with John Brown of Providence and queried in a postscript to his letter: "P.S. I should be glad if thou or some of thy Brothers & I could agree abought a desk & Bookcase which I have to dispose of."[8] This question suggests that perhaps one of the Browns had already purchased a handsome desk and bookcase from Goddard, as well as posing the possibility that these great creations were not necessarily special orders.

Not far from Newport, Rhode Island, in Boston, another quite distinctive form was being produced in the eighteenth century. Possibly derived from actual examples imported into Boston,[9] the bombé bureau in figure 179 is an important specimen of this "kettle-based" form found exclusively in Boston furniture (see also fig. 33). This form was used for a variety of case pieces including desks and bookcases, slant-top desks, chests of drawers, and chest-on-chests. To date few other Boston cabinetmakers except John Cogswell have been directly associated with the production of bombé pieces, though certainly other shops in Boston must have been making them.

In Philadelphia during the third quarter of the eighteenth century the finest expression in case furniture was the highboy or, in more correct eighteenth-century terminology, the high chest of drawers. By twentieth-century taste, one of the most celebrated Philadelphia high chests of drawers is the one in plate 30, which has been given the nickname the "Pompadour" because of its finely carved allegorical bust.[10] Alas, there is virtually no provenance for this piece except that it was purchased by the Hartford collector George S. Palmer shortly before 1918. Closely related to the noted dressing table with carved swan motif in its central drawer (see fig. 155), this high chest of drawers shows the Philadelphia cabinetmakers' knowledge of and reliance on English design books, especially Thomas Chippendale's *Director*.[11] The recent discovery of a less ornate Philadelphia high chest of drawers bearing not only the signature of a relatively unknown cabinetmaker, Henry Clifton, but also the date 1753 affirms the fact that this fully conceived rococo form was being produced in Philadelphia as early as the publication of Chippendale's first edition of *The Director*.[12] Another peculiarly Philadelphia feature is the adaptation of certain of Aesop's fables to carved decoration not only on pieces of case furniture but also in interior architectural woodwork.[13] In fact, La Fontaine's fable of the two pigeons appears in plate 179 of the 1762 *Director*, showing its use on a mantel block, in contrast to its use here on the lower drawer of the high chest of drawers.[14] In totality, the robust yet restrained decoration of this excellently proportioned piece, combined with its original fire-gilt brasses that so nicely carry out the feeling of the delicate rococo scroll carving, make this Philadelphia case piece a fine example of regional superlatives.

In contrast to the "Pompadour" high chest of drawers is a chest-on-chest made by a Charleston, South Carolina, cabinetmaker, perhaps Thomas Elfe, which reflects an even closer and stronger reliance on English prototypes (fig. 180). Whether by client demand, cabinetmakers' English training, or other unknown reasons, case furniture in that southern metropolis seems to have been directly derived from English examples, and it was also among the most widely produced forms. This impressive, mahogany chest-on-chest at first appears quite plain, but its maker has carefully used the most select, patterned mahogany to enhance the drawer fronts and cleverly draw the eye to the topmost part, which is then encircled with a fret and surmounted by a delicately pierced, broken scroll pediment. The graduation of the drawers in the upper case and the

180. Chest-on-chest, 1765–90, Charleston, South Carolina. *Possibly by Thomas Elfe, ca. 1719–1775. Mahogany, yellow poplar, cypress. H. 87 in., W. 44½ in., D. 24⅜ in. Colonial Williamsburg Foundation.*

181. Armchair, 1750–60, Philadelphia. *Walnut. H. 42 in., W. 31¾ in., D. at seat 19½ in. Private collection.*

182. Corner, or roundabout, chair, 1760–85, Newport. *Probably by John Goddard (1723–85). Mahogany, white pine, maple seat frame. H. 31¼ in., W. 29 in., D. 27 in. Peter W. Eliot.*

182

180

181

183. Chest of drawers with doors, 1670–80, Boston. *Oak, maple, walnut, chestnut, pine, cedar and an Asiatic tropical wood. H. 49 in., W. 45³⁄₁₆ in., D. 23³⁄₈ in. Yale University Art Gallery. Mabel Brady Garvan Collection.*

184. Court cupboard, 1680, northeastern Massachusetts. *Red oak, sycamore, maple. H. 57³⁄₄ in., W. 50 in., D. 21⅝ in. The Henry Francis du Pont Winterthur Museum.*

185. Court cupboard, 1640–60, Virginia. *Oak, yellow pine, walnut. H. 49⅞ in., W. 50 in., D. 18⅞ in. Museum of Early Southern Decorative Arts.*

184

185

186

186. Caudle cup, ca. 1690, Boston. *John Coney (1655[6]–1722[3]). Silver; marked on neck and bottom with "IC" with annulet between and fleur-de-lys below in heart-shaped stamp. H. 5⅝ in., Dia. 5¾ in. Museum of Fine Arts, Boston. Bequest of Mrs. Edward Jackson Holmes.*

187. Paneled bowl, 1700–1710, New York. *Cornelius Kierstede (1674[5]–1757). Silver; marked "CK" in rectangle, twice on outside of rim, and engraved near rim "ᵀQᵥ" for Theunis and Vroutje Quick. H. 5¾ in., Dia. 9¾ in. The Metropolitan Museum of Art. Samuel D. Lee Fund, 1938.*

188. Tankard, 1700–1710, New York. *Cornelius Kierstede (1674[5]–1757). Silver; marked "CK" in square on cover and engraved with the Van Cortlandt coat of arms and initialed "Iᶜᴇ" for Jacobus and Eve Van Cortlandt. H. 6½ in., Dia. 5 in. Museum of the City of New York.*

189. Tankard, 1700–1720, Boston. *John Coney (1655[6]–1722[3]). Silver; marked "I•C" over fleur-de-lys in heart and engraved with the Foster family arms. H. 6⅝ in., Dia. 4⅞ in. Museum of Fine Arts, Houston. Bayou Bend Collection.*

arrangement of three small drawers across the top help to control this visual climax. Clearly this southern urban center harbored capable and artistically gifted craftsmen, but since their clients' preference was for designs close to those produced in England, their distinctive regional production was limited.[15]

While both Philadelphia and New England produced armchairs and corner chairs in the mid-eighteenth century, figures 181 and plate 31 decisively demonstrate that Philadelphia surpassed all other areas in its capital production of a number of highly curvilinear and successful Queen Anne armchairs. However, Rhode Island probably produced the most beautifully and successfully designed corner, or roundabout (as they were called in eighteenth-century inventories), chairs (fig. 182). The integration and balance of cyma-curves as well as solids and voids in Philadelphia armchairs is thought by many to be the ultimate achievement in American design. Clearly Philadelphia chairmakers knew how to use the repeat of the volute to draw the eye from knee brackets, to arm terminals, to splat, and finally to the top of the crestrail in a masterful movement of graceful form. The stockinged trifid feet, the carved shells filling out the knees, and the central shell focusing attention on the crestrail all aid the movement of the eye upward. The famous Newport roundabout chairs achieve their design success in a similar way, using the technique of constant movement through reverse curves. They were sometimes ordered in pairs; this one and its mate were made for the Providence merchant John Brown. While the talented maker is not documented, Brown did do business with John Goddard and in 1766 ordered a close stool for a captain in Surinam. Brown wrote to Goddard:

> **Mr John Goddard—Sir—We have occasion for a handsome Mahogany Arm Chair as a Close Stool for Sick Persons with a Pewter pan please to make one & send it to us as soon as you Conveniently can & send a Bill with it as its for a Gentleman in the West Indies & you'l oblig [e].[16]**

Whether Goddard made these chairs or not, whoever was ordering the wood chose to use the densest and heaviest mahogany in order to enhance not only the visual but also the physical aspect of weight and density. Several other Newport roundabout chairs exhibit the same use of reverse curves, deeply shaped seats, beautifully scrolled arms, and strong, well-defined claw-and-ball feet.[17]

While the survival of seventeenth-century American objects is limited, and admittedly the majority of those objects known to date seem to have originated in the New England colonies, nevertheless scholars have still been able to identify distinct regional forms and preferences. Extensive work over the past ten years by several noted scholars

187

188

189

190. *David, Joanna and Abigail Mason*, 1670, probably Boston. *Oil on canvas; inscribed at the right of David's head: "Anno Dom. 1670," at the left "8," and "6" and "4" to the left of the girls' heads. H. 39½ in., W. 42⅝ in. The Fine Arts Museums of San Francisco. Gift Mr. and Mrs. John D. Rockefeller III.*

191. *Robert Gibbs*, 1670, probably Boston. *Oil on canvas; inscribed in upper right: "AE. 4½. A⁰ 1670." H. 40 in., W. 33 in. Museum of Fine Arts, Boston. M. and M. Karolik Fund.*

and students has focused attention on specific counties during the early years of settlement including Essex County, Middlesex County, Suffolk County, Plymouth County, and New Haven County. New York City and Long Island have also been given attention, as well as certain areas of the South. The chest of drawers with doors in figure 183 is probably the most sophisticated piece of furniture produced in seventeenth-century America. It was made in Boston, possibly even before 1650, and derives its design directly from London-made precedents. During the first one hundred years of settlement in Boston there were at least two hundred furniture craftsmen working, and this form represents the work of only one shop or group.[18] Presumably two craftsmen, a turner and a joiner, were responsible for this piece, and since the cabinet practices employed were those commonly used in London, these men must have been trained in London and then migrated to Boston. Though this form is believed to date from before 1650, it corresponds with a 1698 inventory description of "1 chist drawers with doors" valued at 20 shillings in the estate of Timothy Lindall of Salem.[19]

The seventeenth-century New England furniture form that is often thought to be the most expensive and extravagant is that of the so-called "court cupboard," though that phrase does not appear in Essex County inventories until after 1664. The massive, powerful cupboard in figure 184 is dated 1680 and bears the incised initials "PW" for Peter Woodbury, yeoman of Beverly, Massachusetts, in whose 1704 inventory this piece was listed as "one Winscut Cubard" valued at four pounds along with "one long Table one bench and two gines [?] [joined] stools." Until 1902 this cupboard had descended directly through the family of the original owner.[20] The sophistication of both design and construction in this important piece of furniture suggest that it was made in either Ipswich or Boston. Since little seventeenth-century furniture has been specifically identified with Beverly, the possibility of its having been made there is less likely. The popularity of Thomas Dennis, working in Ipswich from 1667–1706, was first fostered by Dr. Irving P. Lyon in a series of six articles in *Antiques* in 1937–38 on the oak furniture of Ipswich, but there is no plausible reason to arbitrarily attribute this piece to Dennis. It is hoped that the research of the next few years will yield further information about this cupboard and its possible makers and enrich our knowledge and understanding of seventeenth-century regionalism.

While less than a handful of pieces of southern furniture from the seventeenth century have survived, the cupboard in figure 185 presents a striking contrast to the Woodbury one from Massachusetts. Found in eastern Virginia, this cupboard is distinctly different in both overall form and ornamentation from its northern relatives. The totally open upper section is a feature not found in New England pieces, though it can be seen in English varieties. The massive turned upper supports, as well as the applied split spindles and the round turned bosses, also do not correspond with any northern counterparts. The use of yellow pine for the top, panels, and secondary wood, and walnut for the applied pieces, indicates a southern provenance. Perhaps the research currently being conducted by Colonial Williamsburg and the Museum of Early Southern Decorative Arts will yield related forms or corresponding turnings over the next few years. One might also wonder how many of the seventeenth-century joiners working from Virginia southward will come to light with the progress of research.

As with New England furniture, many examples of seventeenth-century New England silver still survive. Several forms were produced in this region that were not popular in areas to the south. Sugar boxes, spout cups, standing salts, caudle cups, and chocolate pots seem to have been favored more among the New Englanders. Yet there were correspondingly distinctive articles that were made in other areas and not in New England, such as New York paneled bowls, Dutch-inspired beakers, and octagonal teapots. The two-handled drinking vessels in figures 186 and 187 show an elaborate and possibly ceremonial New England drinking vessel and a corresponding New York alternative. John Coney's creation (fig. 186), made originally for John and Mary Mico (m. 1689), has a bulbous body with plain neck and lower portion embossed with flowers, trailing vines, and a demi-boy sprouting from a petal-like motif. The cast caryatid handles on Coney's cup are closely related to those on Cornelius Kierstede's bowl (fig. 187) that was originally owned by Theunis and Vroutje Quick (m. 1689), yet the New York goldsmith, with a clearly Dutch background, chose to execute a bowl of different form, in a style that he was more comfortable with. Divided into six lobes, or panels,

PL. 29   PL. 30

192

193

194

192. **Gateleg table, 1695–1720, probably Boston.** *Walnut and white pine. H. 28¾ in., Top 60¼ in. by 50⅜ in. Historic Deerfield.*

193. **Gateleg table, 1700–1725, New York State.** *Mahogany with tulip and red gum. H. 29½ in., Top 78½ in. by 71 in. Albany Institute of History and Art. Gift of Charles Hooper Nolt.*

194. **Gateleg table, 1710–40, Charleston, South Carolina.** *Cypress and yellow pine; oval brass plaque on one end reads "Gabriel Manigault/ 1739." H. 29½ in., Top 47¾ in. by 57¼ in. Charleston Museum.*

■ **Plate 31. Armchair, 1740–55, Philadelphia.** *Possibly by William Savery (1721[22]–87). Walnut. H. 41¾ in., W. 32¼ in., D. at seat 17½ in. Private collection.*
Plate 31 is on page 172.

Plate 32. *Mr. and Mrs. John Purvis (Anne Pritchard), 1775–77, Charleston, South Carolina.* Henry Benbridge (1744–1812). *Oil on canvas. H. 39½ in., W. 50 in. The Henry Francis du Pont Winterthur Museum.*
Plate 32 is on page 173.

each filled with a single embossed floral motif consistent with the distinct divisions of the bowl. Unlike the Boston vessel, Kierstede's bowl is mounted on a neat little stamped band of silver, giving extra lift and height to the predominantly horizontal body.

Presumably both Coney and Kierstede were totally versatile goldsmiths and therefore probably executed every step in the creation and completion of their masterpieces. Judging from the extensive variety of forms that Coney produced, he may well have been Boston's foremost goldsmith. When Coney died in 1722/3, Paul Rivoire, the father of the famous patriot, entrepreneur, and goldsmith, was serving an apprenticeship with Coney, so possibly Rivoire assisted in the completion or fabrication of some items. Little is known about the background or training of Kierstede, but apparently he worked in New York only until 1722 when he moved to New Haven to pursue copper mining, a venture that proved unsuccessful. However, during his New York period Kierstede produced some of the finest early New York tankards (fig. 188), with characteristics quite different from those made in Boston. Only six and a half inches in height, this diminutive tankard bears all the elaborate embellishments consistent with other New York tankards of this period by makers such as Boelen, Van Dyck (see fig. 168), Van der Spiegel, and Wynkoop. This tour de force of distinguished regional ornament includes an ample base molding with meander wire surmounted by a band of acanthus foliage, crenulated lip with lavishly engraved rim, scrolled thumbpiece, cast applied rampant lion on the handle, and cast cherub termination. The focus of ornament on the body is the engraved arms of the Van Cortlandt family, profusely encircled with a foliate cartouche, swagged garlands, and surmounted with an armor helmet and star. Curiously, the close similarity of this foliate engraving to that on a number of tankards by different makers suggests that perhaps there were one or two goldsmith-engravers who were doing specialized work for others. In a tankard almost as small (fig. 189), Coney produced a more simple Boston version in counterpoint to the Kierstede creation. A simple baseband, a lightly molded and less ambitious crenulated rim, a double-stepped top with ribbed banding and corresponding ribbed finial, a cast dolphin and mask thumbpiece, and applied cutcard work at the base of the handle make this a very different interpretation. The only obvious similarity is the cast cherub termination. Coney's fine engraving of the Henchman family arms seems somewhat restrained in comparison to New York engraving, even though a similar device of the armor helmet is employed. Obviously the ornamental devices used by Boston goldsmiths were derived from their English background, while those in New York were derived from Dutch ancestry and custom.

The number of surviving seventeenth-century American paintings is small and the majority of these were done in New England (Figs. 190 and 191). Though research has been ongoing in this area since the noteworthy work of Louisa Dresser in the 1935 exhibition and publication *17th Century Painting in New England* (Worcester Art Museum), we still do not know a great deal more about the artists who practiced in America during that early period. Although there were certainly far greater numbers of other craftsmen besides limners who migrated to the colonies, our present paucity of seventeenth-century canvases must have been caused by their inherent fragility and instability. Some of the most interesting and enlightening research that has been done in recent decades in the area of painting pertains to its English provincial roots.[21] Just as American furniture historians have turned to English precedents, so have art historians. Curiously though, what the American art historians found was that not even the English had done much work on their provincial, or what they called minor, portraiture. Now we can knowledgeably recognize a close relationship between English provincial painting, especially in East Anglia, and American. Both the ambitious and charming group portrait of the Mason children (fig. 190) and the single portrait of Robert Gibbs (fig. 191) derive from the same boldly linear and decorative tradition found in slightly earlier English bourgeois portraiture. The elaborate detailing and repetition of design elements in the clothing and accessories of these children, who are dressed as adults in miniature, create a charm and illusion that is almost akin to provincial limners' portraits of the 1830s and 1840s. Intricately embroidered ribbons, beads, bows, and laces all provide the artist with ample materials for the decorative counterplay of light and dark. While three of the Mason children were included in one portrait, the Gibbs children all received separate attention, and there still exist two other similar paintings depicting little Henry

PL. 31

and Margaret Gibbs. Another Mason child was also immortalized on canvas; the portrait of young Alice Mason is now owned by the Adams Memorial Society in Quincy, Massachusetts. The artists of these portraits are still unknown. It is interesting to note that in 1935 when the exhibition was held at Worcester, the publication included an extensive technical section by Alan Burroughs, then director of X-ray research at the Fogg Art Museum, and it even included X-ray shadowgraphs, an early technological aid to determining authenticity and condition. There is a project currently in progress at the Museum of Fine Arts, Boston, with the assistance of the Polaroid Corporation, to form a complete archive in full-size color Polaroid prints of every known seventeenth-century American painting.

The art of the turner is an ancient craft and was practiced in this country from the first years of settlement. Craftsmen in both urban and rural areas used lathes for a variety of purposes, sometimes creating entire pieces of furniture from turned parts, and other times making special parts and ornaments to be applied to different objects. While studies have been done on a wide variety of craftsmen and on regional variations, only a select few have ever focused on specific turners or on regional schools of turning.

Variations in the turnings of gateleg tables, both large and small, are fascinating. Both geographical origin and date had a great deal to do with determining form and configuration. However, perhaps more so than with any other feature of American furniture, turning styles can span vast ranges of time up to almost a century. The three gateleg dining tables in figures 192, 193, and 194 are monumental examples produced by some ambitious turners for three distinguished families—Bowdoin, Johnson, and Manigault—from the North, the Middle Colonies, and the South. Probably all of them were made before 1750; in fact, the robust quality of the turnings on the Boston and New York examples suggests an even earlier date, but that is difficult to document. With a history of having descended through the family of James Bowdoin III (1752–1811), founder of Bowdoin College, the unusually large walnut table in figure 192 was almost certainly made in Boston. Bearing a close resemblance to another walnut gateleg table owned by Governor Josiah Winslow and now at Pilgrim Hall in Plymouth, the bulbous vase and ring turnings of this table suggest that it was probably made for Bowdoin's father or perhaps even grandfather. Equally as robust, the New York State table in figure 193 has quite different vertical turned members, in addition to the unusual feature of double swinging gates. The massive cup turning below the vase is reminiscent of turnings in the

PL. 32

195

William and Mary style, and is a feature that appears later in New York on pedestal tea tables. Owned originally by Sir William Johnson (1715–74), Superintendent of Indian Affairs, this table may have been made just prior to 1749, the date when Johnson built his first log house, Fort Johnson, near Amsterdam. The table in figure 194 was presumably made in the urban center of Charleston, South Carolina, as it was owned by Charlestonian Gabriel Manigault (1704–81) and bears an oval brass plaque that reads "Gabriel Manigault/1739." Made of yellow pine and cypress, the vertical members of this table are sparsely turned with only one long vase turning between an unturned square shaft. On the other hand, the stretchers are fully turned with symmetrical vase and ring turnings.

At the same time that commodious tables were being produced by talented turners for well-to-do merchants and entrepreneurs, immigrant artists were obtaining commissions from that same flourishing class of the populace. Mann Page II (1718–78), the affluent Virginia planter (fig. 195), was painted around 1744 or 1745 by the English immigrant artist Charles Bridges (1670–1747), who came to Virginia at the age of sixty-three with the specific intention of seeking portrait commissions. Working there for a little more than ten years and producing a substantial body of paintings, he then returned to England shortly before his death at the age of seventy-seven. The nature and source of Bridges's artistic training in England remain a mystery, and to date only one English portrait has been firmly attributed to his hand. However, Graham Hood's

195. *Mann Page II (1718–78), ca. 1744–45, Virginia. Charles Bridges (1670–1747). Oil on canvas. H. 46½ in., W. 36½ in. The College of William and Mary in Virginia.*

recently published study has examined and assembled a large number of Virginia portraits that, on the basis of a small group of documentable Bridges paintings, must have been executed by the artist during his Virginia sojourn.[22] This study convincingly ascertains the presence of a competent artist working in Virginia at the same time that the Scottish-born and London-trained John Smibert was painting in Boston. Though frequently uncertain of anatomy and faltering in his articulation of volume and space, Bridges had an appealing style of intensity and directness when it came to recording the facial characteristics of his sitters. Certainly the image of Mann Page II is one of the strongest of these statements, and as Graham Hood has concluded, "the best of these portraits—in the context of provincial painting—convey an unmistakable sense of individual presence and identity, of a distinct posture and preference."[23]

Arriving in Newport, Rhode Island, only a few years before the London-trained Bridges came to Virginia, artist John Smibert (1688–1751) rendered a strikingly similar image of the notable Francis Brinley (1690–1765) of Boston (fig. 196). Although the poses and backgrounds are different in these two paintings, the rendering of the heads warrants comparison. Little specific documentation concerning the career of this Scottish-born artist was available before 1966 when the existence of his notebook in the London Public Records Office was brought to the attention of Stephen T. Riley, then director of the Massachusetts Historical Society. The notebook clearly indicates that Smibert left England in September 1728 and in May of 1729 began painting portraits in Boston. "Francis Brinly Esqr." and "Mrs. Brinly and son Fras" appear in this diary as the third and fifth pictures that were painted by Smibert, and they cost £40 and £50 respectively. The close similarity between the works of Bridges and Smibert is a clear indication that the same English painting tradition fostered the talents of both men. When Francis Brinley died in 1765, he left a fairly extensive estate, the total value being £572.11.0½ exclusive of property.[24] Among Brinley's household goods were a number of handsome objects, including several large looking glasses, a pair of sconce glasses, two marbletop tables, and over one hundred ounces of silver, including a pair of candlesticks and a pair of "Chaffin" dishes. The pair of paintings by Smibert are not specifically mentioned in the inventory, but near the end there is an entry that records "a Number of Prints £13:0:8 _____ 5 p^ies. of Paint £6_____." Since this is the only mention of any wall hangings owned by Brinley (with the exception of "7 Prints 4/"), it is possible that the portraits were among those five "pieces of painting."

Smibert's portrait of Mrs. Brinley and her infant son Francis (fig. 197), painted in 1729 and recorded by the artist in his notebook in May of that year, is similar to his later portrait of Mrs. Oliver and her young son Andrew done in 1732. Smibert appears to have had a difficult time adequately capturing the image of a wriggling infant in a less than natural position. The artist sought to unite his composition with the device of an orange blossom held by Mrs. Brinley and gestured at by the babe, thus completing a strong diagonal across the canvas almost in a gesture of honor toward the pendant portrait of the father Francis.

Before Smibert even set foot on American soil in Newport, Rhode Island, a woman artist had arrived in Charleston, South Carolina, from England and was drawing pastel portraits of children from wealthy Carolinian families. Henrietta Johnston (d. 1728/29), a presumably unschooled artist, came to Charleston in 1708 with her husband, Gideon Johnston, who was a representative of the Bishop of London and commissary for the Society for the Propagation of the Gospel in Foreign Parts. The young couple had been married just three years before in Dublin, and certainly their early years in Charleston must have been a physically trying experience. Nevertheless, working in the delicate art of crayon, or pastels, Henrietta recorded the images of numerous prominent Charlestonians. Today at least three dozen signed or attributed pastels by her survive, including several that were executed on a trip that she made to New York around 1725. While many of her images bear a resemblance to each other, they all have a simple delicate charm that is tremendously winsome, like the small portrait of Henriette Chastaigner, done about 1711 (fig. 198). Of Huguenot extraction and the daughter of a man prominent in affairs of the province, Henriette later married Nathaniel Broughton.

As has already been illustrated, from the seventeenth century on, artists on American soil were commissioned to record images of the young. Almost a century after an anonymous artist in or near Boston painted little Robert Gibbs, the native-born

Plate 33. *Mrs. Thomas Lynch (Elizabeth Allston),* **ca. 1755, Charleston, South Carolina.** *Jeremiah Theus (1719–94). Oil on canvas. H. 29⅞ in., W. 24⅞ in. Reynolda House Museum of American Art, Winston-Salem, North Carolina.*

Plate 34. Bureau table, 1760–85, Newport. *Mahogany, poplar, and white pine. H. 34¾ in., W. 38¼ in., D. 21 in. Museum of Fine Arts, Houston. Bayou Bend Collection.*

196. *Francis Brinley,* **1729, Boston.** *John Smibert (1688–1751). Oil on canvas. H. 50 in., W. 39¼ in. The Metropolitan Museum of Art. Purchase, Rogers Fund, 1962.*

197. *Mrs. Brinley and her infant son Francis,* **1729, Boston.** *John Smibert (1688–1751). Oil on canvas. H. 50 in., W. 39¼ in. The Metropolitan Museum of Art. Purchase Rogers Fund, 1962. Figures 196 and 197 are on pages 178 and 179.*

Plate 35. *James Boutineau (1711–78),* **ca. 1748, Boston.** *Robert Feke (w. 1741–50). Oil on canvas. H. 50 in., W. 40 in. Nova Scotia Museum.*

Plate 36. *Mrs. James Boutineau (1712–99[?]),* **1748, Boston.** *Robert Feke (w. 1741–50). Oil on canvas. H. 50 in., W. 40 in. Nova Scotia Museum. Plates 35 and 36 are on pages 180 and 181.*

36

198

198. *Henriette Chastaigner*, **ca. 1711, Charleston, South Carolina.** *Henrietta Johnston (d. 1728[9]). Pastel on paper. H. 11¼ in., W. 9 in. Carolina Art Association. Gibbes Art Gallery.*

199. *James Badger* **(1757–1817), 1760, Boston area.** *Joseph Badger (1708–65). Oil on canvas; inscribed on back of canvas, "July 8, 1760." H. 42½ in., W. 33⅛ in. The Metropolitan Museum of Art. Purchase, Rogers Fund, 1929.*

Charlestown, Massachusetts, artist Joseph Badger painted a likeness (fig. 199) of his own grandson James Badger (1757–1817), seemingly in the same tradition of linear and decorative painting as the Gibbs portraits. Apparently untrained and working mainly as a house and sign painter, Badger may have seen the work of earlier artists including that of Smibert, Feke, Copley, and Blackburn. Using a pose similar to that of Robert Gibbs, again the artist chose to play on the decorative aspects of the costume, in lieu of his skill as an anatomical draftsman or proficient face painter. In keeping with eighteenth-century practice, Badger has placed his subject before a landscape background instead of using a patterned floor like the anonymous limner of the Gibbs boy.

During the early centuries of settlement in America, children not only received attention in the rendering of their images on canvas and paper, but occasionally some were also fortunate enough to have specialized pieces of silver or furniture fashioned for their use. Windsor chair-makers produced a wide variety of seating furniture, and not only did each geographical region exhibit specialized features and turnings, but different areas also sometimes preferred different forms. The sack-back chair was a form favored more in Philadelphia, as already noted in chapter 1 (see fig. 37) with the example marked by Francis Trumble. While the child's sack-back armchair in figure 200 is not marked, it definitely came out of a Philadelphia shop, for its overall form as well as the distinctive turnings of the legs identify it as a product of that city. Although this was made as a low armchair for a child, the same arm supports would have been used for a child's high chair in which case the cylindrical turning at the top would have been drilled for a rod to fit across to keep the child from falling out.

Somewhere in New England, probably about the same time, another windsor chair-maker fashioned a child's armchair but came up with a very different interpretation (fig. 201). With a high comb-back having nicely defined scrolled ears, decoratively shaped armrests, arrow turned arm supports, and short stubby legs, the stance and proportions of this chair demand a disciplined and upright position from its occupant. Though this chair may have lost an inch or so from its legs, it nevertheless affirms the ability of windsor makers to yield distinctive forms as well as repetitive ones.

Research has firmly ascertained that the earliest windsor chairs made in America were produced in Philadelphia.[25] The comb-back chair in figure 202 represents what is felt to be the earliest form made in that city, and its robust turnings put the date of manufacture at around 1750. Though the legs are somewhat related to the child's sack-back in figure 200, notice that the stretchers on this full-sized chair are very different, and the

spindles suggest almost a seventeenth-century form. The stiff and almost linear quality of the crest is repeated in the forward scrolled arm terminals and the hard, squared-off corners of the seat. As windsor chair-making developed in Philadelphia, crestings and arm supports took on a more pleasing, curvilinear quality.

Precisely when windsors were first made in Rhode Island is not yet known, but certainly by the end of the Revolution a distinctive style had emerged among that specialized group of craftsmen. Continuous bowback armchairs, similar to those of New York makers like Walter MacBride (see figs. 38 and 39), were perhaps their most successful and commanding form. The armchair in figure 203 was recognized in the 1929 Girl Scouts Loan Exhibition as a superlative windsor, and even today that distinction holds true. The thirteen precisely turned spindles and the bulbous vase-shaped arm supports whose turnings are duplicated in large proportion on legs that sharply taper as they terminate are now recognized as characteristics of Rhode Island manufacture, though few examples are identified as to maker. While Rhode Island and New York makers favored similar forms, it is evident when comparing figures 203 and 38, that even in a form as simple as a continuous arm windsor, regional distinctions prevailed.

Not only do windsor chairs provide a good barometer of regional differences, but also almost any period of side chair can be used to demonstrate this same variation. Each region produced at least several different variations of rococo or Chippendale-style side chairs, and almost any one selected will exhibit characteristic regional differences. The chairs that have been specifically identified as Charleston products prior to and just after

■ **Plate 37. Tea service, 1792, Boston.**
*Paul Revere (1735–1818). Silver with
wooden handle on teapot; marked "RE-
VERE" in rectangle on bottom of pot,
caddy, each stand, inside sugar tongs, on
side of plinth of sugar urn and creampot;
and each piece (except tongs) engraved
"JMT" for John and Mehitable Templeman. Teapot, H. 6⅛ in., L. 11¼ in.; tea
caddy, H. 5¾ in., L. 5½ in.; covered
sugar urn, H. 9⅝ in., Dia. 3⅛ in.;
creampot, H. 7½ in., Dia. 2⅝ in.; sugar
tongs, L. 5½ in.; tea shell, L. 2½ in., W.
1¾ in.; strainer (not shown), L. 11⅛ in.
The Minneapolis Institute of Arts.*

the Revolution seem to be relatively simple in form and detailing but still exhibit some reliance on English prototypes (fig. 204). While this example has a well-designed and articulated splat, with crisp yet simple leaf carving, the crestrail and other vertical and horizontal members of the chair are quite plain and devoid of any distinguishing ornament. Though no direct English design source can be cited, there are ornate English side chairs that utilize a similar figure eight and diamond motif set in a broadly spreading splat.[26] In New York, an area that is not necessarily noted for its proficiency in rococo furniture design, a different diamond motif was employed in an interlaced scrolled splat with vertical piercings below (figure 205). This chair, still retaining a compass-shaped seat and a cyma-curved front rail that is usually used in the Queen Anne style, has shaped rear feet, solidly square, claw-and-ball front feet, and trailing leaf carving on the knees bisected by a V-shaped section of crosshatching.

In Philadelphia, where the rococo style thrived and excelled, chairs like the one in figure 206 were not out of the ordinary and exhibited a high degree of ornamentation of the finest and most sophisticated order. The rear stiles rounded below the seat rail and fluted above were characteristic. The cyma-curved crestrail with fine central carved shell, delicately carved trailing foliage, and large shell-shaped ears was a consistent part of Philadelphia chairmakers' and carvers' vocabulary. The carving on the scrolled splat repeats a similar theme, and the shell in the front seat rail and those pushing upward from the carved cabriole knees continue the rococo image. Finally, the double-voluted knee brackets with ruffle and leafage and the asymmetrical scroll and leaf carving with trailing vine on the legs make this one of the more fully ornamented high-style Philadelphia chairs.

In contrast to Philadelphia preferences, Boston chairs were frequently devoid of lavish rococo ornament and did not follow English design sources as closely. However, Bostonians were just as much Englishmen as Philadelphians, and frequently there are some strong English characteristics that appear in Boston chairs. In addition to the fact that the splat on the chair in figure 207 is directly derived from plate 13 of Chippendale's 1762 edition of the *Director* (fig. 208), the seat of the chair also exhibits the broad proportions and open corner braces characteristic of English specimens. The precise, striated carving of the characteristic hard-edged knees and the high, ball feet with thin elongated talons, slightly raked back, are additional eastern Massachusetts features. Several years ago a chair of this sort, even with a firm Massachusetts history, would have been suspect as an English immigrant. However, the recognition of these features on other confirmed Massachusetts chairs and the presence of maple and birch in the overupholstered seat frame and cross braces reaffirm its American origin.

At about the same time that Boston chair-makers were attempting to produce the most high-style, English-influenced pieces, Boston's own native portrait artist, John Singleton Copley, was turning out some of his most expressive creations in crayon, or pastel. Since the splendidly serene image of Mrs. Joseph Henshaw (née Sarah Henshaw) in figure 209 has a hint of the neoclassical in it, there is the possibility that Copley derived his composition and pose from a current English print that introduced the latest "Roman" attire and motifs.[27] But the rococo still persisted, with delicate lace encircling Mrs. Henshaw's bosom and her triple string of pearls around her neck. This was one of Copley's latest American pastels, and it is clear he had mastered the technique and attained maximum expression through a delicate and difficult medium.

Henry Benbridge (1744–1812) produced some of his finest portraits while working in Charleston, South Carolina (see fig. 128). While he did not have the talent that Copley possessed, some of his accomplishments came close to Copley's intense reality and inner perception of his sitters' personalities. Benbridge's ambitious double portrait of Captain and Mrs. John Purvis (pl. 32), executed around 1775, must be considered one of his most mature and accomplished paintings. While the artist clearly had some difficulty with anatomy and tried to cloak his shortcomings in drapery, he was successful in capturing pensive facial expressions. With the light source coming from the left of the painting, the captain's face is seen almost half in shadow, while Mrs. Purvis's face receives almost full light. Here the similarity to Copley's *Mrs. Henshaw* is remarkable and leads one to question whether perhaps they were working from similar print sources. Or could Benbridge have seen Copley's work if he visited Boston soon after his return from England? In his typical manner, Benbridge almost totally diminished the right side of his lady's face, where Copley reached a more pleasing solution showing a fuller view of the face. With Benbridge and Bridges as examples, it must be recognized that the South attracted some artists with considerable competence who have left us with rich and strong images of the cultured society that dominated centers such as Charleston, South Carolina.

Eighteenth-century society and attendant fashionable customs no doubt placed many demands on the craftsmen of the day. A number of polite social pastimes necessitated the manufacture of specific pieces of furniture and accessories. Card playing, tea drinking, music making, needlework, and general polite entertaining were enjoyed throughout the colonies in both urban and rural areas. Certain types of amusement seemed to be favored over others in specific regions, judging from the number of surviving forms necessary for the various entertainments. Card tables seem to have been made in America from about the 1730s on, but Philadelphia turned out the greatest number around the time of the Revolution, while production of Massachusetts ones appears to have decreased at that period. Massachusetts produced its most successful and beautiful card tables in the Queen Anne style with well-turned pad feet, somewhat straight cabriole legs, and commodious turret corners with shaped blocks connecting the corners with the straight sides. The table in figure 210 is one of a small number of closely related eastern Massachusetts turret-cornered card tables. While these diminutive tables are most charming, the same form was made in a larger version, several of which survive with their original needlework tops.[28]

Though knowledge of pre-Revolutionary manufactures in the South is just beginning to emerge fully, the card table in figure 211 is now thought to be the product of a Norfolk, Virginia, cabinetmaker. With oak and poplar as its secondary woods, this table has a long history of ownership in that southeastern coastal Virginia city. Slightly more English in form with its C-scrolls on the inside of the knees and differently shaped pad feet, this table does have certain features in common with the Massachusetts example. Is

200

201

200. Child's sack-back windsor armchair, 1760–80, Philadelphia. *Maple and hickory with 19th-century black paint over original green. H. 27¾ in., W. 15½ in., D. 11 in. Olenka and Charles Santore.*

201. Child's comb-back windsor armchair, 1750–1800, New England. *Maple and ash, painted black. H. 27¼ in., W. 14¾ in., D. 11 in. Museum of Art, Rhode Island School of Design.*

202. Comb-back windsor armchair, 1735–50, Philadelphia. *Poplar, hickory and maple with red paint, over yellow, over original green. H. 42½ in., W. 24 in., D. 16 in. Olenka and Charles Santore.*

203. Windsor armchair, 1770–1800, Rhode Island. *Hickory, white pine, and maple, with blue-green paint and traces of original red paint underneath. H. 37 in., W. 16½ in., D. 17⅛ in. Colonial Williamsburg Foundation.*

this table characteristic of those produced in the Norfolk region? This question remains to be answered through future research.

In the full-blown rococo style, New York and Philadelphia vie for first place in the creation of card tables. However, if a choice is to be made, New York might win in the name of robustness and movement, while Philadelphia would take first place for overall integration of design and ornament, and especially for profuseness and quality of the execution of the ornament. Like most New York furniture from the middle half of the eighteenth century, the card tables manifest a power and forcefulness all their own. Undoubtedly the most successful form produced in New York during this period (see fig. 212), these bold, compact tables are characterized by deeply serpentine-shaped sides, gadrooned skirts, carved knees, and a fifth leg to support the open top. This particular example also retains its original baize playing surface. A detailed study of this form in the early 1970s[29] recognized two basic types and then defined several groups under each type. Though we are always seeking truly American creations, and at first one might think these card tables to be without English or other precedents, alas, the Heckscher study concludes with the disappointing news that an English precedent exists for this form at Temple Newsam in Leeds, England!

Aside from the magnificent and unique Cadwalader family card tables,[30] the epitome of the Philadelphia card table is seen in the pair of tables that originally were owned in the Vaux family, one of which has recently been acquired by the Colonial Williamsburg Foundation from the Reginald Lewis collection (fig. 213). With a gracefully shaped and expertly carved skirt on three sides, the ornament of the skirt becomes one with that of the knees and also with that which rises up almost totally covering the turreted corners. The secret to the success and beauty of this piece assuredly lies in the total unity of form and ornament, a masterpiece of harmony between cabinetmaker and carver.

The polite social custom of tea drinking seems to have been more popular in the New England colonies than was card playing, though there are several superlative tea tables from regions south of New York. The Philadelphia specimen in figure 214 is a special example, and like the card table in figure 213 from the same city, the success of this tea

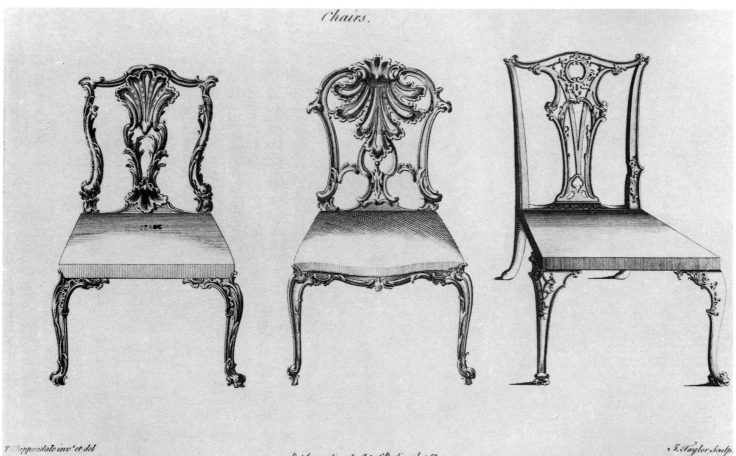

Chairs.

T. Chippendale inv.t et del

Pub.d according to Act of Parliam.t 1753.

J. Taylor Sculp.

208

204. Side chair, 1760–90, Charleston, South Carolina. *Mahogany. H. 38½ in., W. 21⅞ in., D. 22 in. Charleston Museum.*

205. Side chair, 1765–85, New York. *Mahogany, white pine, seat frame red oak. H. 39⅜ in., W. 29⅝ in., D. 18⅝ in. Mabel Brady Garvan Collection. Yale University Art Gallery.*

206. Side chair, 1755–85, Philadelphia. *Mahogany. H. 40⅜ in., W. 22½ in., D. 17½ in. Museum of Art, Rhode Island School of Design.*

207. Side chair, 1760–85, Boston. *Mahogany, maple, and birch. H. 38 in., W. 23¾ in., W. 20 in. Private collection.*

208. The Gentleman and Cabinetmaker's Director, plate 13, 1762, London. *Thomas Chippendale (1718[?]–79). Joseph Downs Manuscript Collection. The Henry Francis du Pont Winterthur Museum.*

table lies in the understated yet complete integration of form and ornament. Delicate C-scrolls and cyma-curved scrolls lightly trail across the skirt and inconspicuously unite with the leaf carving flowing down the legs and the inside curve of the cabriole leg as it flows upward into the skirt. The simplicity of the sides and molded tray top is broken only by the gentle overlapping of a carved flower easing up from the top of each leg. The design quality and crisp control of this carving suggests that it may have come from the hand of Hercules Courtenay, who was working in the shop of Benjamin Randolph in 1774 when Vincent Loockerman, the original owner of this table, purchased over £38 worth of merchandise. When Loockerman, whose home was in Dover, Delaware, died in 1785, his household inventory indicated an elegant parlor in which this tea table stood along with "1 mahogany china table."

In Newport, Rhode Island, the most handsome and probably the most expensive tea tables that a wealthy patron could acquire were of a distinctly different form (fig. 215). Essentially rectangular in shape, the tables had sides that were shaped with reverse curves all cut from a solid piece of rich mahogany and topped with a single piece of mahogany with molded edge following the configuration of the sides. The characteristic Rhode Island cabriole legs, square in section with well-defined edges, were ornamented with stylized, incised carving with only a hint of relief and were symmetrical on each side. To date only a half dozen of these tea tables are known to have survived, and the inspiration for their form is unknown.

In Boston, where tea was favored over cards, there were some extraordinary turret-top tea tables made that might compare with the expensive Newport ones;[31] however, the most characteristically American form produced in Boston was like the table in figure 216. Not always possessing the extra feature of slides that pulled out from either side to hold extra tea equipage or possibly candles, these unornamented rectangular tables usually had slender cabriole legs, simple pad feet, plain or lightly shaped skirts, and

209. *Sarah Henshaw* (Mrs. Joseph, 1732–
1822), ca. 1770, Boston. *John Singleton
Copley (1738–1815). Pastel on paper. H.
24 in., W. 17¾ in. Museum of Fine Arts,
Houston. Bayou Bend Collection.*

molded tray tops. In this form the emphasis was on austerity and definitely not ornament. Most tables of this type retained the use of pad feet, possibly right up to the
time of the Revolution. However, this is as yet undocumented since no examples exist
with labels, dates, or signatures on them.

The equipage that graced the tops of these tables during the eighteenth century was a
varied array of silver, possibly pewter, imported English ceramics, and Chinese porcelain. Sometimes mahogany or japanned waiters covered the tops of these tables for
protection and for the servant's ease in carrying the service in and out of the room.[32] The
earliest known silver teapot made in this country is a small pear-shaped one by John
Coney for the Mascarene family of Boston and now in the Metropolitan Museum of Art.
Early New York teapots also followed a similar pearform style, yet the most common
early form was the small globular pot with a curved spout usually found in New
England, and in several New York examples with a straight spout. The simplicity and
balance of this form is seen in the example (fig. 217) made by Bartholomew Schaats
(1670–1758) of New York about 1728, presumably as a birth present for Sarah Bogert,
the original owner. While this pot appears essentially as a horizontal form with its
generous curving wooden handle and its forward-reaching tapered spout, Schaats balanced that dimension with a neatly stepped lid of two graduated flattened rings surmounted by a cast finial. The only hint of embellishment found on the pot is a narrow
ring of engraving on the body encircling and framing the lid.

The typical New England globular pot is seen in two examples by Joseph Clark, a little-
known maker thought to have been working in Boston as early as 1737 (fig. 218).
According to their history, both pots were made for Nicholas Easton, a Newport cabinetmaker and merchant who may have been working in partnership with Thomas
Townsend.[33] Totally globular in form and raised on a molded foot, these pots suggest a
date in the late 1730s or 1740s. Though close in form, the pots show variations in the
treatment of spouts, finials, handle sockets, and engraving. The small circular lids are
flush with the body, and delicate engravings of leafage, strapwork, masks, and bell-
flowers encircle the shoulder of each pot. One side of the larger pot bears an asymmetrical rococo cartouche with the initials "N*E" for Nicholas Easton, and the smaller pot
has a nineteenth-century inscription "1841/Mary Hazard/ to/ Dr. Enoch Hazard."
Before the end of the eighteenth century, silver for tea service was not usually made in
matching sets, but occasionally a sugar and a creamer would be made at the same time.[34]
The occasion for these very similar pots by Clark is still unknown, though clearly they
must have been made within a year or so of each other. By the 1770s the form and
ornamentation of teapots and other equipage had changed; pots were larger in size, and
instead of being globular they had evolved into an inverted pearform shape. Boston
goldsmiths like Benjamin Burt, Samuel Minott, and Paul Revere must have filled a large
number of orders for these commodious pots with their higher, more generous stance.
The one that Revere made for the Reverend Jonathan Parsons (fig. 219) typifies a
number of similar pots, yet its exceptionally well articulated engraved cartouche surrounding the Parsons coat of arms and the scroll and foliate engraving around the
slightly domed lid make it a superior example. In Philadelphia, perhaps a little earlier, a
similar inverted pearform teapot was being made (figure 220), quite like those from
Boston. The most significant visual difference between these two geographical regions is
seen in the distinctive manner of engraving frequently ornamenting the pourer's side of
the vessel. While the engraved interlocking reverse cipher on this example was presumably executed at a date later than the pot's manufacture, the style of the cipher is
wholly compatible with the rococo form of the pot.

A very special example of this form produced in New York is seen in the teapot with
embossed decoration made by Peter deRiemer for Philip Schuyler (fig. 221). Also shown
are a covered sugar bowl and a footed creampot by deRiemer for the same family.
However, if one examines all three pieces closely it is apparent that there are differences,
and quite possibly all three were not made at the same time *as a set.* While the robust and
powerful nature of this embossed decoration also complements the massive quality of
much New York furniture in the rococo style, it should be noted that this form of
ornament was not peculiar to New York goldsmiths. Paul Revere made a matching sugar
bowl and creampot as a wedding gift for Lucretia Chandler and also a similarly embossed teapot later engraved with the Ross family crest.[35]

210

211

212

213

214

215

210. Card table, 1740–60, Boston area.
Mahogany with white pine. H. 27¼ in.,
W. 25¾ in., D. 13¼ in. Private collection.

211. Card table, ca. 1750, possibly
Norfolk, Virginia. *Mahogany with oak*
and poplar. H. 27¼ in., W. 32⅞ in., D.
21⅞ in. Colonial Williamsburg
Foundation.

212. Card table, 1760–80, New York.
Mahogany with oak and poplar. H. 26½
in., Top open, 34 in. by 33¼ in. Museum
of Fine Arts, Boston. Gift of Mr. and
Mrs. H. H. Edes, Catherine W. Faucon
and Dudley L. Pickman by exchange of
Charles H. Tyler Residuary Fund.

213. Card table, 1760–80, Philadelphia.
Mahogany, with white cedar, poplar and
oak. H. 29½ in., W. 35½ in., D. 33⅛ in.
(open). Colonial Williamsburg Foundation.

214. Tea table, 1774, Philadelphia.
Attributed to Benjamin Randolph (1721–
91) and Hercules Courtenay (1744[?]–84).
Mahogany with cherry and pine. H. 29½
in., W. 25¾ in., D. 17½ in. Philadelphia
Museum of Art. Given by Mr. H. Rich-
ard Dietrich, Jr.

215. Tea table, 1760–80, Newport.
Mahogany, pine. H. 27 in., L. 33¼ in.,
D. 19½ in. Eric M. Wunsch.

216. Tea table, 1750–75, Boston area.
Mahogany. H. 27½ in., W. 19 in., D.
30¼ in. Private collection.

216

219   220

Compared to the large amounts of surviving silver made in the North before the Revolution, southern production was sparse. Yet the fact that quite proficient goldsmiths were working in Charleston, South Carolina, is attested to by pieces known to be from the hands of men like Daniel You, his son Thomas, and Alexander Petrie. The covered sugar bowl in figure 222 was originally fashioned for Daniel and Mary Cannon by Thomas You, probably about 1760. Similar in form to those made in Boston, New York, and Philadelphia, the relatively simple floral and vine incised motif is distinctive and is either an expression of the client's plain taste or the craftsman's limited decorative abilities. The impressive coffee pot (figure 223) bearing an unidentified coat of arms is part of an ever-growing body of work by perhaps Charleston's finest goldsmith, Alexander Petrie. Modeled directly on English coffee pots from the 1740s and 1750s, this is one of several similar pots known to bear the mark "AP," struck two times on the base. Probably made in the late 1750s or early 1760s, this pot is as English in its derivation as the Jeremiah Theus painting of Mrs. Thomas Lynch, which was directly copied after a mezzotint of the Duchess of Hamilton by Richard Houston (pl. 33). While Mrs. Lynch is exceptionally pretty (unlike many of Theus's sitters), she is representative of the mid-eighteenth-century society in Charleston that was so closely emulating, consciously or unconsciously, their English and French Huguenot counterparts. If Mrs. Lynch had not died in 1755, she might well have owned silver by Petrie or You, for she was an Allston by birth and a member of the rapidly growing group of wealthy rice plantation owners around Charleston. Theus, who arrived in Charleston from Switzerland in 1735, began painting portraits and all manner of other objects including coaches with coats of arms in 1740. During his career as the leading portrait artist in the South, he recorded the images of many of that society's most prominent and wealthy inhabitants.

While Alexander Petrie was turning out austere, unembellished coffee pots in Charleston, Philip Syng (1703–89) of Philadelphia must have been faced with a different demand from some of his clients. In about 1753 he produced perhaps his greatest tour de force in the rococo style (fig. 224). A large pot standing almost a foot high, this masterful creation is skillfully embellished with floral, scroll, and foliate chased and repoussé decoration that unites with the overall form of the vessel in much the same manner as the carving on a great piece of Philadelphia rococo furniture. Originally owned by Joseph Galloway of Philadelphia, this pot is testimony to the direct derivation from high-style London forms and ornamentation that was occurring in America. Though such an elaborately decorated pot was unusual for Syng, in 1748 Laurence Hubert, an engraver from London, joined his shop. Did Hubert bring designs or actual examples with him that may have inspired this piece? Certainly high-style English rococo silver was owned in Philadelphia at that time.[36]

With the same demand for exuberance and overall florid ornamentation, the Philadelphia goldsmith Philip Hulbeart (d. 1763), a Swiss immigrant, created this vigorous and whimsical footed creampot (fig. 225). Typical in overall form, it has feet, embossed decoration, and an ornate cast handle that make it unique among Philadelphia cream-

221

222

223

224

225

226

221. Tea set, 1760–80, New York. *Peter deRiemer (w. 1763–96). Silver with wooden handle on pot; marked "PDR" in rounded rectangle on base of each piece. Teapot, H. 6¾ in., Dia. 9 in.; Creampot, H. 5½ in., Dia. 3⅞ in.; Sugar bowl, H. 4⅝ in., Dia. 4½ in. Museum of the City of New York.*

222. Covered sugar bowl, ca. 1760, Charleston, South Carolina. *Thomas You (w. 1735–86). Silver; marked "TY" three times on center of bottom and engraved near rim of bowl "D^CM" for Daniel and Mary Cannon. H. 6⅛ in., Dia. at rim, 4½ in. Museum of Early Southern Decorative Arts.*

223. Coffee pot, 1750–60, Charleston, South Carolina. *Alexander Petrie (d. 1768). Silver with wooden handle; marked "AP" twice on base; unidentified arms on side of pot. H. 10¼ in., Dia. of base, 4¼ in. The Minneapolis Institute of Arts.*

224. Coffee pot, 1760–70, Philadelphia. *Philip Syng, Jr. (1703–89). Silver with wooden handle; marked "PS" in rectangle on base three times, separated by two leaf motifs. H. 11⅞ in., Dia. of base 5¼ in., Dia. 8¾ in. Philadelphia Museum of Art. Purchased: John D. McIlhenny Fund.*

225. Creampot, ca. 1760, Philadelphia. *Philip Hulbeart (d. 1763). Silver; marked "PH" in rectangle on bottom. H. 4¾ in., Dia. 4¼ in. Philadelphia Museum of Art. Given by Walter M. Jeffords.*

226. Creampot, 1740–55, Boston. *Jacob Hurd (1702[3]–58). Silver; marked "HURD" on bottom with Vassall arms and initials "ECP" on bottom. H. 3¾ in., L. 3½ in. Cleveland Museum of Art. Gift of Hollis French.*

227. Caster, 1710–20, Boston. *John Coney (1655[6]–1722[3]). Silver; marked on bottom "IC" crowned, over a coney in a shield; engraved on body with Charnock arms in cartouche. H. 6¼ in., W. of base, approx. 2 in. Museum of Fine Arts, Boston. Marion E. Davis Fund.*

228. Caster, 1700–1710, New York. *Bartholomew LeRoux (ca. 1663–1713). Silver; marked twice on bottom "BR" in oval. H. 8 in., Dia. of base, 3¾ in. Yale University Art Gallery. Mabel Brady Garvan Collection.*

pots. Most enchanting are the cast feet that appear to resemble Indian women with huge feather headdresses and the top of the handle in the form of a caryatid figure, much like the handles on the Coney cup and Kierstede bowl. New England goldsmiths produced some equally powerful and charming counterparts to the Hulbeart creation, like Samuel Casey's stout-bodied pot with cast claw-and-ball feet and unusual monogram derived from Samuel Sympson's 1726 *Book of Cyphers* (see figs. 257 & 258). In Boston, Jacob Hurd (1702/3–58) fashioned at least four[37] standard bulbous footed creampots, which he then carefully and minutely engraved and embossed with a trilogy of scenes (fig. 226). While these Hurd pots are unique in American silver, there is precedent for them among English and Irish silver of the mid-eighteenth century. This particular example bears the arms of the Vassall family and the engraved initials "ECP" on the bottom.[38]

Another form of silver hollowware that might have graced tea tables of the eighteenth century, and most certainly would have been seen on dining tables, was the caster. This vessel, with pierced, removable top, might have held spices, pepper, or perhaps even sugar that had been cut from a cone and crushed. John Coney's hexagonal, baluster-shaped example (fig. 227) is perhaps the grandest New England rendition of this form, which usually appeared as a straight-sided cylindrical shape with domed or stepped top. Combining both linear and curved forms, the proportion and ornament, both engraved and pierced, demonstrate yet another aspect of the skill and expertise of Boston's most versatile goldsmith. Distinctly representative of New York casters of about the same time is the one in figure 228 by Bartholomew LeRoux. Though not as luscious or vibrant as Yale's caster by Peter Van Dyck, this example has the traditional, broad gadrooned foot, applied mid-molding, ribbing around the base of the upper portion, and chased as well as pierced ornament on the top. A number of New York goldsmiths fashioned similar casters, and some even utilized stamped bands of acanthus applied around the base in the same manner as on the great early New York tankards and beakers.[39]

Turning away from tea table's, let us focus on another popular form of American furniture that was produced in quantity from 1725 to 1775: the lowboy, or dressing table, as it was called in contemporary terms. Of the New England dressing tables, perhaps the most sprightly and well balanced is the one shown in figure 229 and made north of Boston, possibly in the Salem area. This piece of furniture is a powerful example of understatement in design. Hogarth would have praised it for the craftsman's masterful handling and the varied use of his proverbial "line of Beauty." The outermost curve of the cabriole leg, combined with the repeated cyma-curves of the skirt and the undulating lobes of the central shell make this an exciting piece of furniture. Typical of numerous other pieces of Salem area furniture are the disc-like pad feet, the hard-edged, square in section legs (much like Newport), almost spur-like scrolled knee brackets, diamond cutout in the center front and center of each side, and the carved

227

228

shell, also similar to Newport workmanship. The generous overhang of the thin, molded-edge top neatly balances the spread and weight of the cabriole legs.

Like the unexplored similarities between eighteenth-century Salem and Newport furniture that were pointed out above, there are certain correspondences between New England furniture and specific examples of furniture made from Virginia southward. The large number of coastwise shipments of furniture from Massachusetts and Rhode Island[40] clearly had some influence on production in the South, but sources of this influence have yet to be specifically pinpointed. The dressing table in figure 230 was discovered in the last few years in northeast North Carolina, where it was originally made for Martha Anne Blount Skinner of Mulberry Hill, Chowan County, North Carolina. Martha Blount married Joshua Skinner in 1780, and although this style might seem *retarditaire* for that date, possibly the dressing table was part of their wedding furniture. Made of American walnut with red cedar, yellow pine, poplar, and cypress as the secondary woods, the dressing table is reminiscent of New England examples with its central shell, cyma-curve skirt, scrolled knee brackets, and plain pad feet raised on a disc. Until further research has been completed on the immigration of northern cabinetmakers into the South, and specific objects of New England manufacture owned in the South have been identified, the inspiration for furniture like this dressing table will continue to remain a puzzle.

The interpretation of a mid-eighteenth-century Philadelphia area-dressing table was very different from those made in the North or South. One high-style version was shown in figure 155, and figure 231 shows yet another, one that is more closely parallel to the same form interpreted north of Boston. With perfect proportion, a subtle interplay of mass and voids, and fine craftsmanship in every detail, this dressing table is indisputably of superior quality. The entire composition is a symphony of repeating rhythms that complement and coordinate, from the unusual trifid feet, through the convex shells on the front knees, to the notched corners of the molded edge top, and finally back to the concave shell in the central drawer (the inner scrolls of which are echoed by the double pendent drop). The canted corners of the case section not only lighten the mass but also draw the eye upward from the shells to the generous overhanging top. As was evident in the Philadelphia armchairs in figure 181 and plate 31, the artistry and achievement of the Philadelphia eighteenth-century style was in its constant movement and total integration of form and ornament.

While figure 229 illustrates a north-of-Boston dressing table of about 1750–60, in figure 232 is an equally exciting and recently discovered dressing table probably made in Boston as early as 1730 or 1735. With its blockfront style and concave center section, this piece is related to a small group of other similar blockfront Boston-area dressing tables, as well as to the notable Boston desk and bookcase signed by Job Coit and reputed to be one of the earliest pieces of American blockfront furniture.[41] Exceptional because of its vibrant crotch veneers and checkered string inlay,[42] plain original brasses, and surviving original pendent drops, this dressing table is a close relation to the diminutive desk and bookcase (see pl. 28) with similar veneer and inlay now in the M. and M. Karolik Collection at the Museum of Fine Arts, Boston.

Scholars now believe that blockfront American furniture was first made in Boston, not in Newport, Rhode Island, the cabinetmaking center that achieved the fullest manifestation of this special form. By the 1760s and 1770s bureau tables were a popular form in Boston, and they usually had blocked fronts and straight bracket feet. The survival of several earlier Boston blockfront bureau tables reinforces the conclusion that blocking originated in America in Boston.[43] The earliest documented reference to a bureau table was in 1737 when Richard Woodward, a craftsman working for Nathaniel Holmes, cabinetmaker of Boston, noted making one for Holmes.[44] While the history of this particular bureau table is not known (fig. 233), it is possible that it has always resided in Boston since it was previously owned by the noted Boston collector Susan Higginson Nash.

Though none of the Newport block and shell bureau tables are dated, judging from the dates on several labeled chests and desks, this form was probably being made in Newport in 1760 or shortly thereafter. There are less than a dozen extant, and the only one with a maker's label is the bureau table in the M. and M. Karolik Collection made by Edmund Townsend (1736–1811). Since all of these bureau tables exhibit variations in

229. Dressing table, 1740–60, Salem, Massachusetts, area. *Mahogany and white pine. H. 30¾ in., W. 35 in., D. 22½ in. The Art Institute of Chicago.*

230. Dressing table, 1750–80, Albemarle area, northeast North Carolina. *Walnut, red cedar, yellow pine, poplar, and cypress. H. 28⅜ in., W. 34 in., D. 21⅝ in. Private collection.*

231. Dressing table, 1740–60, Philadelphia. *Mahogany, tulip poplar, white cedar and yellow pine. H. 29¾ in., W. 33¾ in., D. 21¼ in. Private collection.*

■ 232. Dressing table, 1730–35, Boston. *Walnut and walnut veneer with light wood inlay and white pine. H. 30 in., W. 34 in., D. 22 in. Mr. and Mrs. George M. Kaufman.*

visible details as well as in construction, they were obviously not the single product of one craftsman, but were either from a variety of shops or a very large shop where a great deal of division of labor resulted in several journeymen producing just one or two specific parts. The bureau table shown in plate 34, originally believed to have been owned by William Vernon (1719–1806), son of the goldsmith Samuel Vernon, features a vibrant, figured mahogany that has aged to a deep mellow tone.

While furniture craftsmen like Richard Woodward and Nathaniel Holmes were busy in and around Boston making a wide range of furniture and other objects, limners like John Greenwood and Robert Feke were seeking portrait commissions from the same circle of patrons and clients. Mr. and Mrs. James Boutineau (pls. 35 and 36) presumably were among Robert Feke's Boston sitters in 1748 when he was working in that city. Though neither of these paintings is signed, the strong similarity to other works by Feke, the quality of workmanship, and Boutineau family history leave little doubt that they are from the hand of America's first native-born artist. It is believed that since the Revolution these paintings, presumably in original frames, have resided, unrecognized, in Uniacke House (or Mount Uniacke), until a year or so ago when a program of recataloguing by the Nova Scotia Museum led to their rediscovery.[45] James Boutineau, a Boston lawyer, married Susannah Faneuil, sister of Peter, in 1738. Being devoted Loyalists, the Boutineaus fled to England in 1775, where they lived the remainder of their lives. However, their daughter married a Francklin from Halifax in 1762, and several other relatives had fled to Nova Scotia by 1776. By the early nineteenth century the paintings were owned by James Boutineau Francklin, who left them to his only daughter who married the Reverend Robert F. Uniacke in 1830. Typical of other of Feke's portraits, especially *Isaac Winslow* and *James Bowdoin II*, these works exhibit not only the artist's shortcomings with anatomy, but also the richness with which he rendered both fabrics and flesh. The rediscovery of these Loyalist portraits gives curators and collectors cause to ask how many more ancestors now reside in silent seclusion in Nova Scotia.

Though portrait artists of the eighteenth century customarily placed minor landscape views in the backgrounds of their portraits, until the end of the century there was no established tradition of landscape painting in America. Occasionally a landscape overmantel might have ornamented a chimney breast, or an English-inspired conversation piece might rely heavily on landscape backgrounds and details, but that was the extent of artists coping with the wonders of nature on large-scale canvases until about the 1790s. Figures 234 and 235, while dramatically different in representation and technique, show two of the earliest attempts at landscape painting by American artists. As with furniture, the fact that John Trumbull (1756–1843) was from Connecticut and James Peale (1749–1831) from Philadelphia, and the fact that each had different backgrounds and training, resulted in their work being quite divergent. The sources of their training and the inspirations for their particular styles were largely responsible for the differences in their work.

Both the Connecticut-born Trumbull and the Maryland-born Peale were destined to become artists, the former in spite of his father's wishes, and the latter because of his elder brother's (Charles Willson Peale) influence and tutelage. The major difference between the careers of these two contemporaries, in addition to their inherent talents, was the fact that in the 1760s Trumbull traveled to England where he worked in the studio of Benjamin West and then traveled and painted on the Continent, whereas Peale never left the Middle Atlantic colonies of America. From the beginnings of their interest in art, though, both men seem to have had an interest in landscape as well as in historical painting. Trumbull's interest dates from 1770 when he began to copy engraved English landscapes, and then in the 1780s both here and abroad he sketched and painted the terrain as he traveled about. In a detailed notebook that he kept prior to 1789, he wrote, "in America, in 1783 / 72. a Small Landscape with one figure." One cannot help but wonder if that small canvas at all resembled the one that is ascribed to the year 1791 (fig. 234), probably done after his return from England and when he visited with his family in Connecticut for a short time. Reminiscent of a rocky Italian landscape, the scene is purported to be *Monte Video*, the Connecticut country seat of Daniel Wadsworth. This early landscape evokes a tremendously romantic feeling, with the impending storm on the right, the central focus of the dead tree overshadowing the young sapling, and the

234

233. Bureau table, 1730–50, Boston.
Walnut and white pine with light wood stringing. H. 31¼ in., W. 33¾ in., D. 19⅜ in. Gore Place Society, Waltham, Massachusetts.

234. *Monte Video*, ca. 1791, near Hartford, Connecticut. *John Trumbull (1756–1843). Oil on canvas mounted on wood. H. 19 in., W. 24⅞ in. Yale University Art Gallery.*

235. *Pleasure Party by the Mill*, ca. 1790, Philadelphia. *James Peale (1749–1831). Oil on canvas. H. 26 in., W. 40 in. Museum of Fine Arts Houston. Bayou Bend Collection.*
Figure 235 is on pages 202 to 203.

233

236

lone inhabitant gazing off toward the flowing river on the left. Totally unlike any of Trumbull's tumultuous Revolutionary battle scenes, this painting secretly heralds the advent of romantic neoclassicism and foreshadows works to follow by the first great romantic landscape artist, Washington Allston.

James Peale's large and detailed *Pleasure Party by the Mill*, ca. 1790 (fig. 235) evokes a dramatically different feeling from that created by the Trumbull landscape. This painting has an almost separate conversation piece in the lower right-hand corner, and the foreground shows tremendous attention to naturalistic detail of the surrounding flora. While Peale is known to have painted still lifes and landscapes later in his career, the discovery of this early view only a few short years ago has added a new dimension to the repertoire of James Peale. While he executed a number of historical paintings in the 1780s, including the important view of *The Generals at Yorktown* (ca. 1781), the only other semi-landscape of his 1790s period is his group portrait of himself with his family painted in 1795. *Pleasure Party* was originally thought to have been painted by Charles Willson Peale; the suggestion that this might be the work of his younger brother James led to the examination of the latter's sketchbooks in the American Philosophical Society Library in Philadelphia. The discovery of sketches identical to portions of this landscape, including details of plants and flowers, confirmed the James Peale attribution.[46] Furthermore, the younger Peale noted several visits to a site along the Delaware River near Easton, Pennsylvania, where he often visited relatives and where descendants of the Peales still reside today.

While it took a decade or so for American painters to embrace fully the neoclassical style, craftsmen working with three-dimensional objects were quicker to shift their methods, for by the 1770s and 1780s English and continental objects were coming into America heralding the newest fashion. Although Philadelphians were perhaps the first to adopt the new forms and shapes (see fig. 277), Bostonians were not far behind. By 1782 the goldsmith Paul Revere was making round, drumform teapots with straight spouts, and a year later he was using rows of small neoclassical beaded ornament to enhance their bases and upper portions. By 1785 he made elliptical teapots and shortly thereafter began turning out ones with fluted sides and engraved swag and tassel motifs. The 1790s brought many important commissions to this accomplished goldsmith and respected entrepreneur, and fortunately the largest and most complete one that he

237

executed during those years still survives in its entirety (pl. 37). Made in 1792 for John Templeman, the complete order is fully recorded in Revere's daybook.[47] As noted earlier, in the rococo period only rarely was more than one piece of silver for tea service ordered at a time, so consequently whole sets or complete services rarely exist in that style. However, the advent of the neoclassical style also brought with it new and quicker methods of manufacture using rolled sheets of silver so that each piece did not have to be raised by hand. Thus a whole service could be produced more expediently and the expense reduced. In the Templeman service Revere included his usual covered sugar urn and urn-shaped creampot and added some unusual items: a locked tea caddy raised on a separate tray similar to the teapot's, a shell-shaped tea scoop to accompany the caddy, and a pierced strainer that could be used for either tea or punch.

Philadelphia and New York goldsmiths and their clients chose rather different interpretations for the form and ornament of their neoclassical tea services. Christian Wiltberger (1766–1851) of Philadelphia executed an impressive five-piece tea and coffee service for Captain Bernard and Mary Raser (fig. 236), and though the urn-shaped covered sugar and the creampot were essentially like those that Revere fashioned, the coffee pot and teapot were unlike any Revere ever produced. Raised on fluted bases, both pots have urn-shaped fluted bodies, long, gracefully curved spouts, and great sweeping wooden handles. Each covered piece in the service is crowned with a cast urn finial and ornamented with a liberal amount of beaded decoration. The engraving encircling the top of the fluting on each piece consists of a circular medallion surrounding a sunburst motif. The "BMR" monogram on each piece is encircled with a wreath of crossed, tapering branches. The inclusion of a low, footed slop bowl in this service was also more common in Philadelphia than elsewhere.

The New York neoclassical style as interpreted by the goldsmith William G. Forbes (1751–1840) exhibits a sugar urn and creampot not unlike those made in Boston (fig. 237). However, the oval teapot is distinctively New York with its characteristically dished or concave shoulder and raised lid surmounted with cast finial. Also, the engraved decoration on all three pieces in the set differs from Boston and New York bright-cut engraving in this neoclassical style. The engraved lunette banding, shield surrounded with swagged drapery, and flowing floral garlands encircling the body of each piece can be found not only on other objects by Forbes but also on those by other New York makers.

In furniture making, New York was soon to take the country by storm with classical furniture by Phyfe, Lannuier, and others becoming the rage by the early nineteenth century. Before the full-blown advent of neoclassicism in New York, styles were more restrained, and as in New England, great attention was paid to veneered and inlaid surfaces that exhibited a balanced play of light and dark because of the different figured woods. Among the more indigenous and distinctive forms made by New York craftsmen in this brief, early neoclassical period was the clothes press, or wardrobe, as it was termed in the American price books (fig. 238). Though this form was large and cumbersome, with the risk of being massive and boring, some craftsmen were perceptive enough to realize this danger and aptly compensated by breaking the monotony of the vast surface. Sensuous, figured mahogany, almost resembling woven silk moiré, combined with bands and ovals of crotch mahogany and enlivened with diamond and oval inlays of urns and eagles were techniques skillfully employed by men like Michael Allison, who may have been the creator of this magnificent wardrobe. While any New York cabinetmaker could buy stock inlays, either imported or made locally, the true genius came in successfully integrating them into surfaces and creating a unified and interesting facade.

In 1793 the Scottish-trained cabinetmaker Robert Walker (1772–1833) arrived in New

■ **Plate 38. Armoire, 1815, Louisiana.** *Cherry and cypress with light wood inlays; chalk inscription on inside reads "October 1815." H. 85 in., W. 56 in., D. 21½ in. Mrs. Chester A. Mehurin.*

Plate 39. Tall clock, 1790–1810, Charlestown, Massachusetts. *Works by James Doull (w. 1790–1820). Mahogany and mahogany veneer, curly maple, satinwood inlay, white pine; face inscribed: "James Doull/CHARLESTOWN." H. 111¾ in., W. 37¼ in., D. 14½ in. Mrs. Jeannette Jones Balling.*

PL. 38

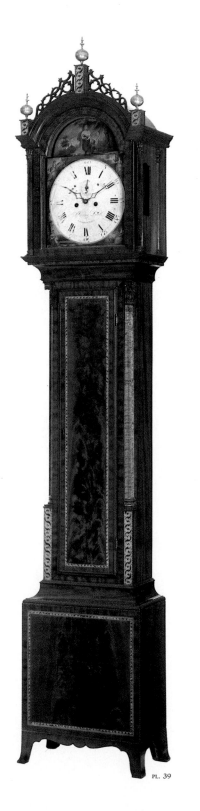

PL. 39

York. Among the possessions that he brought with him was his *London Book of Prices* for 1793, which he proceeded to use as a guide to pricing, noting what New York cabinetmakers were then charging. By 1795 when Walker decided to continue his work as a cabinetmaker in Charleston, South Carolina, he again took his price book with him.[48] In Charleston he worked in partnership at least during 1802 with Charles Watts, but shortly thereafter he had his own "Cabinet ware-room workshop" on Church Street. Prior to 1810 he advertised:

ROBERT WALKER
LATE WATTS AND WALKER
CABINET-MAKER
No. 39, Church-Street, Charleston

has, at all times, on hand, a large and handsome Assortment of every Article in his Line, Orders from the Country speedily and carefully executed in the neatest manner.[49]

Walker used this advertisement apparently also as a label, for a card bearing this information was found attached to the wardrobe in figure 239. Whether it was in New York or through his previous training on the other side of the Atlantic, Walker undoubtedly learned the value of selecting and using highly figured veneers in careful juxtaposition to enliven broad, massive surfaces. Judging from the current search for and study of Charleston-made furniture, this form of large wardrobe with sliding shelves inside was most popular in the Charleston area, and its popularity lingered on into the nineteenth century.

Another area of the South that has recently received study and attention is Louisiana and the lower Mississippi River Valley.[50] The French influence was understandably stronger in this region than in any other part of America, and it is not surprising that this influence marked the forms of furniture made there. Tall, large-scale armoires, closely akin to the wardrobes of New York and Charleston, were extremely fashionable and practical in the late eighteenth century and first quarter of the nineteenth. Like the one in plate 38, their facades were frequently ornamented with lavish arrays of string inlay, oval paterae, trailing vines, and light and dark banding. As expected, native woods were used, such as cherry, cypress, Spanish cedar, and walnut. One group of armoires that are even more directly related to French style are devoid of inlay and have handsomely shaped panels in the manner of Louis XV furniture. The interior of the armoire in plate 38, like many others, is fitted with shelves and a mid-level belt of drawers, thoughtfully outlined in corresponding light and dark inlay.

Neoclassicism brought the introduction of some new, more specialized forms of furniture, and naturally along with them came the opportunity for different regional interpretations. Rooms especially for dining were now more popular than ever, and furniture to serve specific purposes in that ritual began to appear. A sideboard or a smaller hunt board became the most important focus in the room, and these forms were conceived in a myriad of styles. To compare just two interpretations, let us look at the form in Baltimore and again in Boston. Baltimore was a burgeoning federal center of industry and trade by 1795 (fig. 144). As early as November 26, 1782, John Brown, a merchant of Providence, observed: ". . . that most Flourishing Markantile Town [,] I mean Baltimore, it will soon be the Graitest Trading Town in America."[51] To suit the needs of well-to-do new house owners, Baltimore cabinetmakers offered a handsome assortment of furniture in the newest fashion. One peculiar feature of the architecture of Baltimore houses of this period was the introduction of small alcoves and niches, and in an effort to meet clients' special requests, cabinetmakers occasionally fashioned furniture to fill particular spaces. The diminutive demi-lune sideboard in figure 240 probably fit comfortably into just such a niche. To complement the deep sweep of the back and the light serpentine of the front, the cabinetmaker has treated the facade with a masterful interplay of ovals and has integrated trailing vine and rich bellflower inlays on the square tapered legs. Notice that instead of the awkward and less functional construction of drawers on the sides, the cabinetmaker has simply made a pretense of drawers to control the facade and has hinged the side panels to open into a large cupboard space.

In Boston-area homes of the same period and slightly later, sideboards were more varied, frequently following the styles defined by Thomas Sheraton rather than the more linear, Hepplewhite-inspired ones preferred in Baltimore, Philadelphia, and New

238. Wardrobe, 1790–1800, New York. *Mahogany and mahogany veneer with satinwood inlay; H. 100 in., W. 45 in., D. 21 in. Mrs. Northam Warren.*

239. Wardrobe, 1800–1810, Charleston, South Carolina. *Robert Walker (1772–1833). Mahogany and mahogany veneer; advertisement/label inside drawer reads: "ROBERT WALKER/ LATE WATTS AND WALKER/ CABINET-MAKER/ No. 39 Church Street, Charleston/ .... H. 82½ in., W. 54½ in., D. 23⅝ in. Charleston Museum.*

240. Sideboard, 1790–1800, Baltimore or Annapolis. *Mahogany and mahogany veneer with satinwood inlays. H. 39 in., W. 59 in., D. 25¼ in. The Baltimore Museum of Art. Gift of Mr. and Mrs. Kenneth S. Battye.*

241. Sideboard, 1795–1810, Boston area. *Mahogany, mahogany and bird's-eye maple veneers, ebonized banding, white pine, and cherry. H. 45 in., L. 73¾ in., D. 27½ in. Fenton L. B. Brown.*

242. Tall clock, 1795–1805, Baltimore. *Works by William Elvins (w. 1796–1808). Mahogany and mahogany veneers with light wood inlay; face inscribed: "WILLIAM ELVINS/FELLS POINT/ BALTIMORE." H. 98¼ in., W. 20¾ in., D. 10¾ in. Museum of Early Southern Decorative Arts.*

241

242

York. The sideboard in figure 241, while differing from the more popular boxlike, tambour sideboards, is representative of a small related group of highly sophisticated dining room pieces. Having a gracefully undulating facade and neatly stepped-back top surface, the whole is lightly perched on six finely turned and reeded legs. The central section is lightened with an arch, suggesting that perhaps a cellarette or wine cooler was originally intended to slip back into that space. Instead of using intricate inlays and planned patterns, the craftsman has simply relied on the basic formula of contrasting lights and darks and has selected a handsome, rippling bird's-eye veneer as the light element. Framing the light-flickering panels with slightly striped, darker bands, he has created the effect of overall movement and brilliance.

To conclude this survey with two timely examples of regional distinction, let us have a look at how Baltimore and Boston fashioned tall clocks and their cases at the end of the eighteenth century. William Elvins, of Fells Point, Baltimore, used his fine sense of balance and proportion when he gave instructions to his cabinetmaker for the case for the massive clock in figure 242. Basically understating the base and trunk of the case, the craftsman used carefully selected crotch-grained mahogany to draw the eye upward to the real focus of purpose and ornament, the bonnet and face. With great delicacy and simplicity he topped the hood with a pierced, broken-scroll pediment and refined inlaid urn resting on a plinth with, again, urn inlay. But the most regionally distinctive and enchanting element is the skillfully placed grapevine inlay held in the center with a small bowknot. Just below the bonnet, balancing the mass of ornament above, is a row of simple interlocking lunette stringing, which lightly complements that of the upper portion in an understated manner.

Finally, the grandest (and possibly tallest) timepiece of all is the monumental clock and case in plate 39, with its dial proudly signed "James Doull/Charlestown." Although Doull was working in Charlestown, Massachusetts, it is possible that the painted face and superior case came out of shops in Boston, just across the Charles River. However, to date there is no documentation concerning the sources of Doull's cases or whom he might have been working with—whether in semipartnership, or for trading services or necessities. The painted face suggests the hand of John Ritto Penniman and is assuredly one of the most ambitious and artistic clock faces known, with classical figures in each spandrel representing the four seasons, and in the crescent above, a charming romantic landscape view also with a classical maiden in the foreground. The superlative case bears every mark of the finest Boston cabinetmaking tradition, and the integrated use of crotch mahogany veneers, lunette inlay, and light and dark stringing is a remarkable feat to sustain on a piece of case furniture so tall and narrow. One of the most remarkable and understated details is the use of tiger maple for the fluted quarter columns topped with carved Corinthian capitals. Not only in size but also in richness of ornament and power of statement, this timepiece is a rare and wonderful tribute to the artistic daring of American craftsmen in an era of tremendous national exuberance and economic growth.

Chapter 6

Design with a Difference

Production Outside of Major Style Centers

The majority of objects discussed in this book were made in the major East Coast urban style centers. Port cities like Boston, Newport, New York, Philadelphia, and Charleston, where access to imported objects and design sources was the greatest, were natural leaders in the production of sophisticated and tasteful objects. However, many aesthetically pleasing and useful objects were made in smaller urban areas, as well as in rural towns and villages. These objects were not necessarily derived from elite art forms but were often creations influenced and fostered by other forces. Ethnic backgrounds, economics, craft techniques, available materials, patronage, and inherent skills of the craftsman were all major factors in the conception and execution of these objects. Although most of the lenders to the 1929 exhibition appeared to favor "masterpieces" of high-style objects—and thus they set the "taste" of many collectors during the decades that followed—nevertheless during this century there has been a growing interest in and appreciation for less highly styled creations.

In the last half-century scholars and connoisseurs have applied a wide variety of terms to those arts and objects made outside of major urban style centers. Terms such as country, folk, provincial, rural, and even primitive have been used time and again with and without appropriate definition. Our purpose is not to compound this problem of definition and terminology but simply to present a group of objects, view them on their own terms, and not try to pigeonhole them into derivative patterns or seek high-flown sources. The study of the sources of inspiration for these objects will be left to future scholars; here we shall deal only with immediate facts surrounding their places of origin and, in some cases, the school or specific craftsmen who produced them.

Of primary interest for each object considered here will be the geographical area from which it has come. To a lesser degree there is also the consideration of the population of the area, though frequently that is unknown; eighteenth-century surveys and censuses were infrequent and to an extent unreliable. Any area with a population of at least three thousand was considered urban, even if the inhabitants were spread over a sizable region. But certain towns that were large and densely settled in the eighteenth century might be considered provincial backwaters today if they ceased to grow in population since the mid-nineteenth century.

Thus this section becomes an extension of the chapter on regionalism, for distinctive geographical areas are again being examined. The purpose of this look at more "provincial" areas will ultimately be to show that quite sophisticated and superior objects could be produced outside of major style centers. In fact, in many instances some of the most singularly "American" expressions and creations came from the hands of craftsmen not living in the traditional, Anglo-oriented, high-style centers. While many forms were derivative, not everything flowed outward in a rainbow of influence from the major port cities and style centers. Some of the freshest and most visually delightful objects were products of nonurban societies.

New Hampshire was never a style-setter in fashions or even a leader in quality of craftsmanship and design, yet today there survives a body of objects with amazing boldness and sophistication that were produced in both Portsmouth and inland areas. Robust and gutsy are words that appropriately describe the large, Spanish-foot armchair (fig. 243) that has been attributed to the shop of John Gaines III who worked in Portsmouth from 1724 to his death in 1743. John was the son of John II and the brother of Thomas, both of whom worked in Ipswich, Massachusetts. Although he was born and trained in Ipswich, at the age of twenty he decided to move to Portsmouth and work on his own. The discovery, in 1953, of an account book for John II and Thomas of Ipswich has provided a vast amount of data about the type of work these craftsmen did from 1710 until 1762.[1] Basically turners by trade, they seem to have been jacks-of-all-trades, and Thomas in particular seems to have been a carver of sorts, for among other accounts in 1739 he charged Nathaniel Dutch "to carving a top to May^r Apleton's couch." Unfortunately, no signed or labeled pieces by the Gaines family exist, and the cornerstones for most attributions have been a set of four Spanish-foot side chairs.[2] Closely related to the "grait" chair in figure 243, the side chairs descended in the Brewster family of Portsmouth (Mary, daughter of John III, married David Brewster [1739–1818], a joiner of Portsmouth), and tradition states that they were made by John III about 1728

243. Armchair, 1725–45, Portsmouth, New Hampshire. *Attributed to John Gaines III (1704–43). Maple. H. 42 in., W. 24 in., D. 17 in. Peter W. Eliot.*

244. Dressing table, 1725–50, possibly Portsmouth, New Hampshire. *Walnut with white pine. H. 30⅜ in., W. 37⅝ in., D. 22¾ in. Private collection.*

245. Chest-on-chest, 1790–95, New Hampshire. *School of Major John (1746–1792) and Lieutenant Samuel Dunlap (1752–1830). Curly maple, white pine. H. 82⅝ in., W. 36 in., D. 16⅞ in. The Currier Gallery of Art.*

246. Chest of drawers, ca. 1786, Deerfield area. *Cherry with white pine. H. 35½ in., W. 36 in., D. 24 in. Historic Deerfield.*

243

244

245

246

for a new house that he had built.[3] It is ironic that history has left us so much written documentation yet so little physical evidence, but this is often the situation. Perhaps at a future date some signed or stamped Gaines products will be discovered. No matter who made this strongly conceived armchair and where it was made, it represents a truly masterful integration of ornament and good design. The sculptural, carved front feet, the bulbous, turned front stretcher, the turned baluster arm supports, and the lightly carved and pierced crest are all strong and distinguished features. Yet the most outstanding feature is the marvelous curved and scrolled arms with their bulbous "ram's horn" terminations.[4] If John Gaines III did in fact make this fine armchair, he was both a skilled turner and a competent carver.

Except for the supposed work of John Gaines III, little is known of furniture produced in the Portsmouth area prior to 1750. However, a delightfully interesting group of blockfront dressing tables may possibly have been made in that small northern center. The dressing table in figure 244, though unconventional, is an intriguing and lively interpretation of a popular eighteenth-century form. This piece, which has a history of ownership in a Portsmouth family, exhibits a number of unusual yet successfully integrated features. The square, toed feet, slender cabriole legs with high relief carving, fluted corner columns, deeply blocked drawers, and unusually carved central shell and leafage are all rare features. In the 1900–1901 publication *The Furniture of Our Forefathers* Esther Singleton published a sketch of a similar dressing table "Owned by Miss Sherburne, Warner House, Portsmouth, N.H."[5] Precisely where Miss Sherburne's dressing table is now is unknown, but a third one of somewhat more conventional design and bearing the signature of one Joseph Davis on a drawer bottom is privately owned.[6] The

- Plate 40. **Chest-over-drawers, 1695–1720, area of Hadley, Massachusetts.** *Oak with white pine and hard pine, painted. H. 47 in., W. 45 in., D. 19½ in. Pocumtuck Valley Memorial Association, Memorial Hall Museum, Deerfield, Massachusetts.*
- Plate 41. **Tall clock, 1775–88, Norwich, Connecticut.** *Works by Thomas Harland (1735–1807). Case by Abishai Woodward (1752–1809). Cherry, pine, brass, and ivory; dial inscribed "Abishai Woodward/ Harland/ Norwich"; handwritten note on inside of door reads: "This clock was made by Thomas Harland of Norwich, Connecticut, sometime between 1775 and 1795, was bought by my grandfather Elias Brown, of Preston, Ct., and was left to his youngest son, Billings Brown, of Preston, who gave it to me in 1865. Washington 1898. H. B. Brown." H. 87½ in. The Detroit Institute of Arts.*

Plate 42. *Catherine Ogden (1709–97), ca.* **1730, Newark, New Jersey.** *Attributed to Pieter Vanderlyn (1687–1778). Oil on canvas. H. 57 in., W. 37¼ in. The Newark Museum.*
Plate 42 is on page 211.

PL. 40

247

248

only information about Davis is on a receipt dated 1725[6] indicating he was serving an apprenticeship under Job Coit, Jr., of Boston. Since no other mention of him is found in Boston records, it is possible that after he had served his time in Boston, he moved to Portsmouth, taking with him the concept of blockfront furniture. Although the carving, the side pilasters, and the unusual feet on these pieces are not typical, they do relate to elements found on other forms of New Hampshire furniture and thus add strength to the hypothesis that these dressing tables might be among some of the most sophisticated early Portsmouth productions.

As imaginative and distinctive as any piece of American furniture, the delightful chest-on-chest in figure 245 is another New Hampshire triumph, this time from the school of Major John and Lieutenant Samuel Dunlap. Actually a chest-on-chest on frame, this piece has squared pad feet similar in form to those on the preceding dressing table. Owing little to the direct inspiration of high-style urban furniture, the craftsman who created this grand tour de force clearly knew how to combine the decorative elements he used: not only is there a perfect balance and proportion from top to bottom, but also the eye is cleverly drawn upward across the facade to the bold, stepped-out molding and whimsical cornice. The shaping and movement of the base is strong, and it is complemented by the unusual cornice that echoes some of the same forms of the base, including the shells and also the scrolls, which are much like the knee brackets. The case section of this chest-on-chest could have been a problem, but the maker cleverly relieved the facade by creating an immediate upward thrust with the shell in the center of the bottom drawer (note that although visually subdivided, it is all one drawer), and then he used distinctly striped maple drawer fronts to pull the eye upward with a series of graduated drawers. The work of the Dunlaps has been known and published since 1922, and over the past fifty years many articles and other publications have illuminated the numerous objects attributed to them. But ironically, only a handful of firmly documented Dunlap pieces exist, so we are probably dealing with a whole school of craftsmen and not just the work of one or two shops. Nevertheless, found in Weare and possibly made in Henniker or Salisbury, New Hampshire, this chest-on-chest remains the finest example from this innovative school.

The Connecticut River Valley, like any major avenue of transport, was influenced by the styles of other regions, but it also spawned some exceptionally diverse styles of its

247. *Cephas Smith, Jr.*, ca. 1806, Rutland, Vermont. *William Jennys (w. 1795–1806). Oil on canvas. H. 41½ in., W. 31½ in. Museum of Fine Arts, Boston. Ainsley, Hopkins, Shuman, and Luard Funds.*

248. *Mrs. Cephas Smith and daughter Mary*, ca. 1806, Rutland, Vermont. *William Jennys (w. 1795–1806). Oil on canvas. H. 41¼ in., W. 31½ in. Museum of Fine Arts, Boston. Ainsley, Hopkins, Shuman, and Luard Funds.*

own. The popular carved chests from Wethersfield, also called "Sunflower" chests, and the Hadley-type carved chests have been studied and well published over the past half-century. Surviving in fewer numbers (probably because many were stripped and cleaned) are the polychrome painted chests with geometric motifs. As early as 1870, George Sheldon, founder of Deerfield's Pocumtuck Valley Memorial Association, recognized the quality and regional significance of the uniquely decorated pieces like the chest-over-drawers in plate 40. In that year he purchased it and added it to the association's collections. It is surprising that although a handful of similarly decorated forms has been identified,[7] little information has been gleaned regarding the craftsman who might have been decorating these pieces. Clearly the chests were made by a joiner and then decorated by another craftsman. What his precise occupation was is speculative, but he owned a compass and had a supply of paint. Though geometric and not floral, these painted motifs took the place of carving and may well have been produced simultaneously with the carved chests, which also often had several colors of paint highlighting the carving. Though the "S.W." who owned this chest-over-drawers is not known, Hannah Barnard, who died in 1717, had an elaborately painted press cupboard, probably from the same hand. Thus, there is one extant piece providing us with a date span. Perhaps a future study will focus on the craftsmen in the upper valley or Deerfield area who might have been painters and who recorded in their inventories a compass and a variety of colors. What has heretofore been interpreted as a regional school might simply be the production of one man working in the Hadley-Hatfield area.

Another lively expression indigenous to the upper Connecticut River Valley is the "scallop-top" style of furniture. The most commonly found form is the scallop-top chest of drawers on frame (fig. 246). The sharply pointed pad feet with pronounced mid-rib are also found on some Connecticut desks-on-frames. The scallop-top of this particular chest is exceptionally well cut, and the overall patina of the cherry has mellowed to a rich color, even though many years ago the chest was cleaned. As in the case of the New Hampshire chest-on-chest, the craftsman has carefully balanced the mass and ornament of the base with the overhang and shaping of the top. The graduation of the drawers helps draw the eye upward to the top. While scallop-top pieces were probably made by a number of cabinetmakers in the upper valley during the last three decades of the eighteenth century, the chest in figure 246 was presumably made in 1786 upon the marriage of Mary Hoyt to Dr. William Stoddard Williams.[8]

Just as little is known about many of the "provincial" cabinetmakers who produced some of our most American pieces of furniture, similarly we have little evidence and documentation for the numerous itinerant painters. Yet, for the most part, these self-taught craftsmen have given us the most expressive, two-dimensional images of our American culture. William Jennys was working in Connecticut and northern New England from about 1795 to at least 1807. He must have traveled up through the Connecticut River Valley, for he is known to have worked in the Deerfield area before going to Rutland, Vermont, where probably around 1806 he painted his ambitious, highly descriptive portraits *Cephas Smith, Jr.* and *Mrs. Cephas Smith and daughter Mary* (fig. 247 & fig. 248). These two images are so realistic and piercing that they appear almost sculptural or photographic. Though Jennys's style was harshly linear, he knew how to model the face with light and dark, which suggests he may have had some formal training. Precisely where he came from is still unknown, but he was probably related to Richard Jennys and they might have emigrated from England together. Both Jennys's competence with the brush and his tremendously sophisticated manner of presentation enable him to be considered among the more interesting nonacademic artists. Although he was probably not native-born, he was rendering images of native Americans in a wholly individual manner, so his production cannot be cast aside as "un-American." Jennys's portrayal of Mr. Smith embodies all the signs of the prosperity and success that this young lawyer had achieved, and the face also expresses strength and determination. Richer and more extravagant are the images of Mrs. Smith and her infant daughter Mary, decked out in yards of fabric and lace ruffles. Though the child is stiffly and awkwardly posed on the mother's lap, with a similar stern stare on her face, she nevertheless clutches a gold whistle and coral with bells in her hand (note it is also tied to the child with a ribbon), symbols of affluence no doubt. Assuredly William Jennys left a distinctive mark on American provincial portraiture, whatever his background and training. Perhaps future research and new discoveries will further document his career.

The highboy, or more properly the high chest of drawers, was a form that enjoyed great popularity in America throughout the eighteenth century, though it had not been as favored in England. While each region exhibited stylistic differences and variations, on the whole the form evolved as an American superlative. The high chest of drawers in figure 249 is among the simplest yet most outstanding examples of this form ever produced in America. Probably not the product of a major urban center, this high chest was made in Connecticut and possesses lines and proportions that flow together into a harmony achieved only by gifted and sensitive craftsmen. Unlike many Connecticut examples that exhibit exaggerated proportions or features, this high chest embodies a compatibility of parts that are delicately and finely conceived and integrated. The diminishing repetition of fans from the bottom to the pinwheel in the center of the broken pediment and the curves of the bonnet echoing those of the legs and the shaped skirt are elements of refinement and great design. Here is a piece of American furniture that owes nothing to English sources and represents the quintessence of fine American design.[9]

A sophisticated Connecticut companion to the New Hampshire chest-on-chest (fig. 245) is this imposing chest-on-chest made by Samuel Loomis of Colchester, Connecticut, before 1785 (fig. 250). One of two almost identical chest-on-chests, it would appear that Loomis derived his concept of the block and shell form directly from that popularized by Newport cabinetmakers. Yet he added elements of his own choosing and invention such as the pendent shell in the center of the base, the engaged, twisted columns, more incising above the carved shells, the double-dentil pediment molding, the central pendant shell, and the spiral, cone-like finials. This creation is truly a tour de force, embellished with almost every decorative element Loomis had in his vocabulary, yet it is amazingly well integrated and handsomely proportioned. Although today we think of the Norwich/Colchester area as being rural and not a style center, it must be remembered that by 1775 Norwich did have a population of around three thousand and was therefore considered a city.[10] Its proximity to New London gave it a direct link with other East Coast seaports and thus probably influenced craftsmen's production as well as clients' demands. The 1974 study and exhibition of *New London County Furniture* provided valuable insight into the specific nature of furniture and craftsmen in that area, especially in the discussion of construction techniques and unusual design features.

The tall case clock in plate 41, with works and engraved dial by Thomas Harland, and mahogany block and shell case probably by Abishai Woodward, is another example of superior design and craftsmanship from this Connecticut center. The most elaborate and outstanding Connecticut clock case of the eighteenth century, this piece exhibits blocking and engaged twisted columns similar to the Loomis chest-on-chest. The shells of the base and blockfront door are finely executed, in imitation of Newport craftsmanship. A most unusual element is the use of ivory to stop the flutes in both the engaged quarter columns and the colonnettes of the bonnet. The ogee bracket feet and pendent scroll and shell skirt surmounted with elaborate moldings provide a delicate balance to the mass of the bonnet. While Thomas Harland is well-known both as a clockmaker and as an engraver of clock faces, it is most unusual to find the names of two craftsmen on the face of a clock. However, conclusive evidence has been put forward supporting the fact that Abishai Woodward was a skilled craftsman and probably made the case. Upon his death in 1809 his inventory revealed an extensive number of joiner's tools and three architectural books.[11] Originally from Preston, in 1788 Woodward moved to New London where he was involved in the building trade and is known to have made picture frames and exterior ornamental urns and pillars for the Shaw family. The clock has an unquestionable provenance of original ownership by Elias Brown of Preston. Of especial interest is the entry in Brown's 1806 inventory for "Mahogany Case and Clock $70," an extraordinary sum for a clock. Curiously though, whoever made the inventory was more taken with the elaborate case than with the clock, since he noted the case first, not the usual practice in making an inventory.

While today New Haven is a sizable urban area and certainly a center for the study of American arts, in the early years of settlement the situation was different. However, by the 1640s New Haven's jurisdiction had expanded to include Guilford, Milford, Stamford, and Southold, Long Island. It was the hope of the London merchants who had settled the colony that New Haven would become a large port and center for transat-

■ **249. High chest of drawers, 1750–90, Connecticut.** *Cherry with pine. H. 86 in., W. 40 in., D. 18 in. Mr. and Mrs. Joseph H. Hennage.*

250. Chest-on-chest, 1769–88, Colchester, Connecticut. *Samuel Loomis (1748–1814). Mahogany with tulip poplar and pine. H. 88 in., W. 45 in., D. 26 in. Wadsworth Atheneum. Gift of Mr. and Mrs. Arthur L. Shipman, Jr.*

lantic trade. But a terrible tragedy occurred in 1646 when the "Great Ship," carrying many of the colony's leading citizens back to London, was lost at sea. The colony never really recovered from this, and by the 1660s it was absorbed into the Connecticut Colony. Even though the earliest settlement existed as a small rural society, with a limited demand for labor as well as for woodworking craftsmen, nevertheless some extraordinary objects were produced. Two important factors made this possible: (1) there existed a craftsman with excellent training, and (2) there was a client with the money and/or the taste to demand a sophisticated product. It is believed that sometime between 1640 and 1650 the joiner Thomas Mulliner of Branford made the chest in figure 251 for Thomas Osborne, a tanner of New Haven, before he left to settle in Easthampton, Long Island, in 1650. Mulliner was not only a joiner (probably trained by his father, a joiner from Ipswich, England) but also a competent and recognized carver.[12] This three-panel chest-over-drawers is one of the earliest documented pieces of American furniture known. The three panels with architectural arches are typically English in derivation, and much of the carving is representative of the kind of work done in Ipswich, England. Yet among American seventeenth-century chests it is one of the finest examples of early carving with a precise and interesting provenance.

The cherry Connecticut armchair in figure 252 is among the strongest and most handsome New England armchairs in the rococo style. Tradition relates that it was part of the wedding furniture of Anna Barnard of Northampton, Massachusetts, in 1772 when she married Joseph Hawley Clarke. This armchair, two others closely related to it,[13] and a large group of side chairs have all been attributed to the shop of Eliphalet Chapin, a cabinetmaker in East Windsor, Connecticut. The attribution to Chapin dates back to a statement made in 1891 by Irving Lyon about a set of side chairs he had seen with an accompanying bill from Chapin dated 1781.[14] Although Lyon's chairs had an entirely different splat, on the basis of the shape of the legs and feet on the chairs he noted, many other chairs have been attributed to Chapin, perhaps with a little too much zeal. Whether or not we know who created this armchair, its distinctive curvilinear splat with diamond and cross motif, great scrolled ears of the crest and central shell, and wonderfully curved and scrolled arms all make it an exceptionally sophisticated chair. However, although East Windsor and Northampton might today seem like "provincial" areas, in the eighteenth century when the Connecticut River was an active avenue of transport, the river towns were more *avant garde* than one might suspect.

Windsor furniture was made in both urban and rural areas, but the precise geographical locations for many of the pieces are difficult to establish. Windsor chairmakers were at work throughout New England, and it was probably some ingenious Connecticut craftsman who made the strong and delicately balanced writing armchair in figure 253. In addition to a nicely shaped and deeply curved comb-back crest, the chair has a thick plank seat that balances the gracefully cantilevered, ample writing arm. The well-shaped turnings of the arm supports and the more robust shaping of the legs and stretchers add a dimension of quality to this armchair. Writing arms are often difficult to integrate into a well-composed chair, but the turner-chairmaker who conceived this one had no trouble whatsoever.

The Connecticut windsor side chair with braced fanback in figure 254 is quite different from the writing armchair, but like the armchair, it has good proportions and a sprightly design. The seat is small but vigorously shaped, and the upper and lower turned elements splay outward with a dramatic thrust. Notice that the rake of the legs complements the angle of the braces supporting the back. The broad sweep of the crest with well-defined ears at each end of the easy cyma-curve adds a strong horizontal element to a composition that is largely vertical. This side chair and its mate were part of the small but select group of windsor seating furniture in the 1929 exhibition.

Another exciting example of windsor furniture that may or may not have been made in a nonurban area is the typical Rhode Island, yet very rare, child's high chair with turned arm supports and solid mahogany arms (fig. 255). Quite similar to the full-sized armchair (fig. 203) that was in the original 1929 exhibition, this chair is simply a smaller version with longer legs, elongated vase-shaped turnings, and separate mahogany arms instead of a continuous arm. The turned arm supports, instead of being lengthened, have been compressed and have thus become somewhat squatter and plumper. Though

250

very few Providence or Rhode Island–made windsor chairs are specifically documented, this rare child's chair is related to a set of six side chairs and two windsor armchairs, all of which descended in the Corey family of East Providence and are now in the collection of the Museum of Fine Arts, Boston.

Though not a windsor chair, the child's high chair in figure 256 was the product of a clever and imaginative turner. The lively pattern created by the rear stiles, banisters, and double-arched crest is the focal point of the chair; all four stiles cant inward and upward leading to the marvelously vigorous banisters and fine finials. The forward scroll arms of the chair are simple, and the turned arm supports echo shapes seen in silhouette on the banisters. The lower portion of the chair is relatively simple with just ball turnings on the front stiles and baluster and ball turnings on the two front stretchers, which were clearly used by many tired feet. Regardless of the provenance and geographical area from which this chair has come, it ranks as one of the most sophisticated chairs ever "turned" out for a child.

Although South Kingston, Rhode Island, is just across the Narragansett Bay, not far from Newport, it is surprising that a goldsmith working there around the middle of the eighteenth century created such a splendid and delightful creampot (fig. 257). The "personality" of this pot is immediately evident, with its three cast and applied claw-and-ball feet, its stout bulbous body, and its delicately curved and scrolled handle. But the most refined aspect of Samuel Casey's (c. 1724–80) wondrous creation is the extraordinary embossed and chased decoration of a cipher monogram "IC" and foliate scroll motifs. He was probably apprenticed to the Boston goldsmith Jacob Hurd,[15] so he may have been familiar with some of the embossed scenic creampots that Hurd made, like the one in figure 226. Casey's monogrammed "IC" (fig. 258) is identical to that illustrated in a 1726 London book entitled *A New Book of Cyphers More Compleat and Regular than any yet extant . . . Compos'd and Engrav'd by Samuel Sympson.* Possibly he was familiar with this publication from his apprenticeship in Boston, or maybe he even purchased a copy for himself. By the 1760s Casey must have been a goldsmith of some repute and fortune, for in 1764 when his home was destroyed by fire, notices appeared in papers in Providence, Newport, and Boston. The *Providence Gazette* printed the following report on September 29, 1764: " . . . the very valuable Dwelling-House of Mr. Samuel Casey . . . unhappily took fire, and was entirely consumed with a great Quantity of rich Furniture. The whole Loss, 't is said, amounts to near Five Thousand Pounds, Lawful Money."[16] Clearly Casey was making a handsome living goldsmithing, which makes it even more difficult to understand why he had become involved with the counterfeiting business in 1770. Though he was arrested and sentenced to hang, he was pardoned and released by 1779, though supposedly he died shortly thereafter.

251. Chest, 1640–50, Branford, Connecticut. *Attributed to Thomas Mulliner (w. 1639–58). White oak (with restorations to feet, drawers, and top). H. 33 in., W. 51 in., D. 23 in. Home Sweet Home Museum, East Hampton Village.*

252. Armchair, 1770–1800, Connecticut. *Possibly by Eliphalet Chapin (1741–1807). Cherry with white pine. H. 40 in., W. 37 in. Mr. and Mrs. Christopher Granger.*

251

252

Albany, New York, lies about 150 miles up the Hudson River from New York City, and although during the eighteenth century it was readily accessible by water, it never developed into a major urban style center because it was always overshadowed by Manhattan. Albany however enjoyed a certain degree of economic wealth, and the city supported a number of craftsmen capable of fairly sophisticated production. The silver tankard in figure 259 was made probably between 1720–50. Jan Cluett, the goldsmith who presumably made this piece, is a relatively unknown craftsman, although he must have been as accomplished as any goldsmith working in New York. Although there are references during the second half of the eighteenth century to a Jan Cluett, Jr., working as a goldsmith, he must have been the son of the maker of this tankard. With many characteristics of a typical New York tankard, this piece lacks the elaborate base molding and applied acanthus leafage that adorns many New York pieces. Whoever engraved the body of the tankard must have had some good design sources, for the foliate cartouche is quite close to those found on New York City pieces, and the pendant· pomegranates resemble those on the New York *trompe l'oeil kas* in figure 141. Though the engraved arms on this tankard has not yet been identified, it has descended through a New York family related to the Van Cortlandts and the Van Rensselaers.

Throughout New York large pieces of storage furniture known as *kasten* were produced, similar to the painted *kas* in figure 141. Made for the Isaac Perry house in Orangetown, New York (now part of Pearl River), probably between 1740–60, the *kas* in figure 260 is one of two that were originally in the house.[17] A chalk inscription on the underside of the top reads "Made by Roeloef Demarest / March 17," identifying the maker but unfortunately omitting the year of fabrication. The remarkably elaborate applied moldings and the great, stepped-out cornice are the distinguishing features of this large piece. Using bilsted (sweet gum) and poplar, woods frequently found in New York furniture, Demarest, probably at his client's request, chose to cover up the bilsted with simulated graining, thus imitating several richer woods. As a result, what could have been a massive and boring piece of furniture became a triumphant geometric interplay of varying surface textures. In addition to graining the wood, Demarest broke the mass of the great cornice by gilding and ebonizing sections of the bold, stepped-out molding. He also ebonized and gilded the moldings which frame the great doors and the base. Perhaps the original owner wished to imitate some grand Dutch *kas* he had seen abroad or in a neighbor's house.

At about the same time that Dutch-inspired *kasten* were being produced on Long Island, in the New York City area, and up along the Hudson, wealthy patroon families were having their portraits painted for display in their grand homes. Research over the past fifty years has led to the grouping of many of these paintings by artist, but still little is known regarding the actual limners who were active in the Hudson River Valley

253

254

255

256

253. Windsor writing armchair, 1770–90, probably Lyme, Connecticut. *Pine, maple and birch with original green paint. H. 40 in., W. 21 in., D. 16½ in. Olenka and Charles Santore.*

254. Windsor brace-back side chair, one of a pair, 1795–1810, Connecticut. *Soft maple painted black with traces of red, white and green paint underneath. H. 34 in., W. 15⅛ in., D. 18½ in. Yale University Art Gallery. Mabel Brady Garvan Collection.*

255. Child's windsor high chair, 1775–1810, probably Rhode Island. *Ash, maple, white pine, hickory and mahogany. H. 35⅜ in., W. 15⅛ in., D. 16¼ in. The Henry Francis du Pont Winterthur Museum.*

256. Child's high chair, 1725–50, New England. *Maple and ash. H. 35⅛ in., W. 13 in., D. 10½ in. Yale University Art Gallery. Mabel Brady Garvan Collection.*

during the first half of the eighteenth century. Because very few of these stern and linear images are signed, specific names of the artists are usually not known, although the name of Pieter Vanderlyn has been associated with a certain group of paintings. The well-known portrait *Pau de Wandelaer* (fig. 261) is one work that might be from the hand of Vanderlyn,[18] who came from Holland to New York in 1718 and worked in the Kingston-Albany area. It has been estimated that there were at least eighteen artists working in the Albany area between about 1713 and 1744. The clients they catered to were merchants and landowners who had made their fortunes in furs, lumbering, and milling. The distinctive images that survive of this singular regional class are simple, linear expressions with a directness found in many American paintings. While these artists lacked formal training and perhaps even innate skill, their angular, hard-edged expressions have a pleasing and delightful aspect. Frequently the compositions demonstrate a good sense of proportion and balance, along with a play of light and dark and also mass and void. *Pau de Wandelaer* has a fascinating central triangle formed by the opening of the coat, which both reveals the vest and draws the focus of the eye up to the sitter's face. Attention is also drawn to the nautical background landscape, because both arms of the sitter move your eyes to the left where they focus on the bird and boat.

A similar interplay of mass and void and also form and pattern is achieved in the captivating painting of Catherine Ogden (1709–97), daughter of Colonel Josiah Ogden and Catherine Hardenbrueck of Newark, New Jersey (pl. 42). As with the preceding likeness, this one has also been attributed to "the Gansevoort limner," who may have been Pieter Vanderlyn. The focus of this painting is Catherine's vast and boldly patterned red dress, with its rich and scrolling foliate pattern. The boldness of the skirt filling the lower half of the painting is balanced by the refinement and delicacy of the sitter's upper torso, hands, and face. The detailed lace surrounding her neck, her necklace with its ornate clasp, and the small spray of flowers in her hair are all foils to the brilliant red gown. Her features are finely drawn with the faintest hint of shadow to give dimension and roundness to her face. The light, semi-landscape background on the left is balanced on the right with darkness. While rather simple and devoid of tremendous painterly acumen, the limner who captured Catherine's image had a sophisticated sense of design and a lively enjoyment of his subject matter.

The geographical area of Long Island provides another fascinating study of rural craftsmen working in relatively close proximity to a major urban area, with some being profoundly affected and others not at all.[19] On the island there were basically two areas of influence: the Dutch on the western half, and the English on the eastern end. In addition, craftsmen fell into two categories: those who had been trained in urban areas outside of Long Island, and those who had never left the island but rather acquired their skills from a fellow islander. The Southampton goldsmith Elias Pelletreau (1726–1810) received his training in Manhattan, under the highly skilled direction of the master goldsmith Simeon Soumaine (1685–1750). Hence, Pelletreau was not only well trained, but he was also familiar with the sophisticated production of urban craftsmen and was fully able to satisfy the demands of the wealthy clients in his area who wanted the finest and most fashionable wares that money could buy. Pelletreau's inverted pearform teapot in figure 262 illustrates his skill in handling hollowware forms. Pelletreau's account books document the fashioning of seventeen teapots, sixteen of which were made before the Revolution. The initials "ɟMP" on the bottom of this pot may possibly stand for John Mitchell, who is recorded in the accounts as having purchased teapots in 1763 and 1769 at a cost of £9.11s for the silver and £5.4s for the fashioning. Many of Pelletreau's teapots and other pieces of hollowware are reminiscent of New England styles, much like furniture made on the eastern end of Long Island.[20]

Unlike Pelletreau, the Dominy family of Easthampton, Long Island, were trained on the island and passed their traditions of craftsmanship through four generations of the family. Working as turners, chairmakers, cabinetmakers, and clockmakers, this family of craftsmen was typical of many rural makers in both their methods of production and their output. The rare survival of family accounts and a workshop complete with tools, templates, and a few unfinished pieces, along with a good-sized body of extant objects attributable to the Dominys, has provided the basis for an enlightening study of rural craftsmen.[21] Unlike such towns as Lancaster, Pennsylvania, and Norwich, Connecticut,

257

258

Easthampton had no major economic or cultural link with any of its closest urban neighbors—Newport, New Haven, or New York. Since it was over 150 miles by land from Manhattan, communication with the rest of the world was essentially via waterways. Consequently, Easthampton became a town that time passed by, where tradition persisted because there were no economic or cultural forces to impose change and where a "sense of stillness and sequestration from the world" lingered on.[22] The armchair in Figure 263 was probably made by Nathaniel Dominy V (1770–1852), who would have called it a "fiddle-back" armchair. Stylistically this armchair would seem to have been made earlier in the century, with its eared crestrail, solid splat, and pad feet. However, this is a classic example of traditional skills, tools, and designs or patterns being passed on through a family of craftsmen with little regard for fashionable styles. While this phenomenon was not true of all rural craftsmen, it did occur at the same time that other rural craftsmen were keeping abreast of new styles. The singular quality of this armchair expresses the entire character of the Dominys' work, as well as the milieu of Easthampton itself. In 1811 when Timothy Dwight, the president of Yale College, visited Easthampton, he observed: "A general air of equality, simplicity, and quiet, is visible here in a degree perhaps singular."[23]

Because few examples of the work of eighteenth-century New Jersey cabinetmakers survive today, a specific regional style has not yet been clearly identified. The high chest of drawers in figure 264 was originally made for Joshua Smith as a gift for his daughter, Catherine Smith Stephens of Maidenhead, New Jersey. Since today Maidenhead is called Lawrenceville, which lies northeast of Trenton, halfway to Princeton, it is possible that this highly sophisticated, flat-top high chest of drawers may have been made in Trenton. While a significant list with the names of over one thousand New Jersey craftsmen was compiled in 1958,[24] a signed or documented piece is rarely noted. However, the current concern of scholars for regionalism and documentation should help in this study and search. Meanwhile, the best that one can do is to note the distinguishing characteristics of this fine walnut high chest. First, the proportions are excellent, and there is an interesting balance across the facade with the use of the small original engraved brasses to break up the surface. The deep, coved cornice with corners broken out to surmount the fluted corner columns is a handsome and unusual detail. Also, the paneled and molded ends of the upper case are quite rare, although they are reminiscent of certain workmanship found on Long Island pieces of furniture. Finally, the treatment of the cabriole legs and pad feet is most distinctive and is not found on any other known New Jersey work. It is hoped that, on the basis of pieces like this high chest of drawers, the work of other New Jersey craftsmen will eventually be identified.

259

The work of competent and skillful Pennsylvania craftsmen in the counties west of Philadelphia, especially Chester and Lancaster, illustrates the incorporation of some distinct native traditions brought over from Germany. The Pennsylvania Germans favored a form of storage furniture called a *shrank*, similar to the Dutch-inspired *kasten* in New York. Because of an instinctive desire to ornament plain surfaces, these craftsmen frequently decorated the impressive and monumental *shranks* with elaborate painting or inlay. Among the most highly developed and intricately decorated pieces in this group is one that was made for "GEORG HUBER" and is conveniently dated "ANNO 1779" (pl. 43). The elaborate inlay of flowers, urns, trailing vines, stars, and pinwheels is actually a mixture of powdered white lead, sulphur, and beeswax set into the wood after the desired pattern has been cut into the surface. Perhaps the inlaid motifs of the upper panels of the doors have a special significance, as the paired birds and the large crowns suggest possible religious or marital symbolism. There is no precise provenance for this *shrank*, but it is thought to have been made in Lancaster County. The large number of Hubers in that area makes it almost impossible to trace back to the original owner, and the maker has left no clues. The mystery behind this magnificent object remains for some future scholar to research and interpret.

A more formal and definitely English-inspired rococo piece of Lancaster County furniture is the clock illustrated in figure 265. While the works are signed on the face "Christian Forrer/Lampeter," the name of the craftsman who fashioned the case is unknown. Christian Forrer, along with his brother Daniel (also a clockmaker), emigrated from Switzerland about 1754, and by 1756 had settled in Lampeter, Pennsylvania, just about five miles southeast of Lancaster. By 1774 Christian had moved to Newberry Township, still in Lancaster County, where he ran a ferry on the Susquehanna and

257. Creampot, 1750–60, South Kingston, Rhode Island. *Samuel Casey (ca. 1724–80[?]). Silver; marked "S:CASEY" in rectangle on bottom. H. 4 in. Museum of Fine Arts, Boston. Gift of Mrs. Charles Gaston Smith's Group.*

258. Detail of cipher monogram "IC" on Casey creampot.

259. Tankard, 1720–50, Albany, New York. *Probably by Jan Cluett, n.d. Silver; marked "I-C" once on each side of the handle; unidentified arms engraved on front of body, and "E*V*R" engraved on butt of handle. H. 7¾ in., Dia. 6¼ in. Philadelphia Museum of Art. Gift of Mrs. Courtlandt S. Gross and Mr. Antelo Devereux in memory of Alexander van Rensselaer.*

260. Kas, 1740–60, probably New York or Hudson River Valley. *Roeloef Demarest n.d. Bilsted or sweet gum and poplar, with paint and gilding; signed in chalk on underside of top "Made by Roeloef Demarest/March 17." H. 78 in., W. 73 in., D. 25 in. Private collection.*

260

261

262

261. Pau de Wandelaer (1713-?), 1725-30, Albany County, New York. *Attributed to the Gansevoort limner, possibly Pieter Vanderlyn (1687-1778). Oil on canvas. H. 44⅞ in., W. 35¾ in. Albany Institute of History and Art.*

262. Teapot, 1760-75, Southampton, New York. *Elias Pelletreau (1726-1810). Silver, with wooden handle; marked "EP" over centerpoint on base; initials "ⅰMⅰ" engraved on bottom. H. 6 in., Dia. of base 3 in. The Minneapolis Institute of Arts.*

possibly operated a tavern. Either he had decided to retire, or his clockmaking no longer provided an adequate income. The mahogany case that houses Forrer's clock shows some of the finest Lancaster cabinetwork. Not an exceptionally tall clock, it is well proportioned, and its overall demeanor is hardy and robust. The heavy cornice, broken scroll pediment, carved rosettes, and applied leafage are reminiscent of Philadelphia styles but evoke a very different feeling. Carved flame finials were used in other Lancaster-area pieces with ornamental carving. The additional refinements of the carved tops and bases of the colonnettes and quarter columns, along with the vigorously shaped panel on the base and the small doors that cover the side light windows on the bonnet, are all sophisticated embellishments executed by a highly skilled craftsman. While many case pieces of this type have been attributed to the Bachman family of cabinetmakers, there were certainly many other competent craftsmen in the Lancaster area who were capable of this type of production.[25]

Although to date few Lancaster County windsor chairmakers have been identified, specific characteristics of their work can be noted and certain chairs definitely attributed to that region. The comb-back armchair in figure 266 is a well-turned and nicely proportioned representative of this group, being essentially a sack-back armchair with five back spindles raised higher to receive the undulating comb. The comb has nicely scrolled ears and the distinct type of incising found only in this area. The forward scrolled, knuckle arms are an added refinement, and the shallow, slightly oval-shaped seat is found on other windsors from Lancaster. The most unusual characteristic of this chair can be seen when comparing the front legs with the rear legs. Notice that the front ones terminate in almost egglike bulbs below a straight cylinder, while the rear ones end in a long, slender, turned taper. No other windsor chairmakers appear to have exercised this incongruity, so perhaps these Lancaster County craftsmen used this difference almost as a trademark.

Another Lancaster-made article that exhibits a robust rococo feeling similar to that of the tall case clock in figure 265 is the handsome silver coffee pot made by Charles Hall (1742-83), goldsmith of Lancaster (fig. 267). The wonderfully florid, repoussé decorations of flowers and foliage are reminiscent of some Philadelphia workmanship and definitely related to the coffee pot by Philip Syng (fig. 224). However, this baluster-shaped pot is rather stout and does not have the refined, slender height that can be seen in examples from the major style centers. Furthermore, the ornament appears to be thicker and more coarsely executed. Since Hall was born in Philadelphia and probably apprenticed there, it is likely that he was familiar with the talents and work of Philadelphia's finest goldsmiths. Presumably he was associated in the goldsmithing business with his older brother David for several years in Philadelphia, before he settled in Lancaster by 1763. As with many goldsmiths, Hall became both an active citizen and a respected leader in his community. During the Revolution he participated in several committees and aided in many causes. He was even called upon by the burgesses of the town in 1774 to make "a silver Tea Sett as a present to Mr. Atlee for his trouble relative to the Borough Law."[26] By the second half of the eighteenth century Lancaster grew to be the largest inland community in the colonies. The economic wealth that was generated—and the accompanying social prestige—was able to support numerous skilled craftsmen. In 1764 Jasper Yeates went to Lancaster to work in the office of Edward Shippen, and he wrote back to his father about his new area of residence: "As far as I can discover this country will be very opulent. It is already rich, and from the protection afforded it by our great Men and the Borough's Convenience for Inland Trade, bids fair to be a Place of great Consequence."[27]

While the counties west of Philadelphia seem rural today, two hundred years ago they were the center of skillful and sophisticated production. The slantfront desk in figure 268 may have been made in either Chester County or Lancaster County, and it is hoped that through future research its origin will eventually be known. Under the inlaid date "1771" on the lid the name "REESE" is branded twice. This clue, along with another undeciphered signature inside, may ultimately lead scholars to greater insight.[28] More research is needed regarding the meaning or symbolism of the inlaid decoration both on the lid and on the interior door. Is the date 1771 significant? Does it mark a marriage or a birth date? Do the birds and the crown on this piece have the same significance as the ones that appear on the Huber *shrank*, which is dated only eight years later? The

263

264

265

266

263. Armchair, 1790–1820, Easthampton, New York. *Nathaniel Dominy V (1770–1852). Maple with rush seat. H. 44 in., W. 26 in., D. 20. Mr. and Mrs. Morgan MacWhinnie.*

264. High chest of drawers, 1740–60, Maidenhead, New Jersey. *Walnut, secondary woods unexamined. H. 71 in., W. 21⅜ in., D. 42½ in. The Newark Museum.*

265. Tall clock, 1760–74, Lampeter, Pennsylvania. *Works by Christian Forrer (ca. 1737–83). Mahogany, with tulip poplar, brass face; inscribed on face, "Christian Forrer/ Lampeter." H. 99 in., W. 23⅝ in., D. 13¾ in. Virginia Museum.*

266. Comb-back windsor armchair, 1780–1800, Lancaster, Pennsylvania. *Maple, tulip and hickory. H. 44⅝ in., W. 25½ in., D. 23⅛ in. The Henry Francis du Pont Winterthur Museum.*

267. Coffee pot, 1765–80, Lancaster, Pennsylvania. *Charles Hall (1742–83). Silver, with wooden handle; marked "C•Hall" in rectangle twice on bottom. H. 10¾ in. Greenfield Village and Henry Ford Museum.*

267

meanings of the star inlay and the crescent may also be of significance and will certainly someday be tackled by an enterprising scholar. Meanwhile, this desk can be appreciated and understood on its known merits: the strong, well-shaped feet, the delightful division of the surface with fine, inlaid decoration, and the finely designed and executed interior. The interior is worth a closer look (fig. 269), for it is here in the small, thoughtful details that the greatest refinements are found: the cyma-curve molding below the drawers, the shaped, concave drawer fronts, the tripart string inlay on each drawer front, the use of tiger maple for the fronts of the narrow document drawers, and the intricate inlay on the central drawer. The craftsman who created this desk was being paid well for his work, and he was eminently capable of extremely high-quality craftsmanship.

A charming, diminutive form that was peculiar to the Chester County area was the spice box or spice chest (fig. 270). Usually small and square or rectangular in shape, it was designed to sit atop another piece of furniture, and it might have held everything from spices to silver spoons. The 1750 inventory of Jacob Hibberd, yeoman from Darby Township, contained a spice box that held gold sleeve buttons, silver shoe clasps, a pin cushion with silver belt and chain, a thimble, and some silver spoons.[29] The spice box seen here is typical of a number found in the Chester County area, with door and side panels that are embellished with the distinguishing "string and berry" inlay of the region. In this example there are also modified tulips and light and dark herringbone banding. The nicely molded top cornice and the central arched portion of the door are simple design elements that enhance the quality of this delicate, specialized box.

The slip- and sgraffito-decorated red earthenware that was produced in the counties west of Philadelphia by German immigrant potters has always been considered "folk art," and it can be counted among some of the most beautiful, imaginative, and sophisticated ceramic production in America. The early American ceramic scholar Edwin Atlee Barber was the first to truly appreciate and write about this area of craft production as early as 1903 when he wrote *Tulip Ware of the Pennsylvania-German Potters.* Even today this publication remains the most informative and complete book on the subject. On the basis of a signed and dated plate published by Barber, this dated 1787 plate (pl. 44) has been attributed to George Hübener (d. 1846) of Montgomery County. With an ambitious and tightly conceived decorative motif of tulips, vines, and a peacock decorating the center, the plate is incised on the outer circumference with a German inscription that when translated reads: "When there are no men or roosters left, cradles and chicken pens will stand empty; September 14th 1787." The overall surface is washed with white slip, with scratched in (incised) decoration and some lead glaze applied. A very differently decorated plate is seen in figure 271; it is attributed to David Spinner (d. 1811), a potter

268

■ **268. Slantfront desk, 1771, Chester or Lancaster county, Pennsylvania.** *Walnut, light wood inlay, original brasses; inlaid date "1771" on slant front, and "REESE" branded under inlaid date. H. 44 in., W. 38½ in., D. 20 in. Private collection.*

269. Detail of interior of slantfront desk in figure 268.

270. Spice box, 1740–75, Chester County, Pennsylvania. *Walnut, with light wood inlay. H. 23½ in., W. 16½ in., D. 10¾ in. Chester County Historical Society.*

271. Plate, 1800–1810, Milford Township, Bucks County, Pennsylvania. *Attributed to David Spinner (d. 1811). Red earthenware with white slip, sgraffito decoration, lead glaze; "Hansel und/ Gretel" incised above figures on plate. Dia. 12 in., H. 1⅜ in. The Henry Francis du Pont Winterthur Museum.*

269

270

271

from Milford Township, Bucks County. Above the charmingly incised pair of figures that adorn this plate is the inscription "Hansel and Gretel." Flanking the figures are a pair of birds atop what appear to be fuchsias, flowers that symbolize spring. The implication is that this may have been a marriage present, but since there is no provenance on the plate we will never know. Spinner was one of the few potters to draw human figures on his plates, though they were not uncommon on Swiss and German pottery. The attribution of this plate is based on its close resemblance to two signed examples in the Brooklyn Museum and several in the Philadelphia Museum of Art. As can be seen in this instance, the effect of these whimsically decorated plates is one almost of fantasy and delight.

The German Moravians who immigrated to Pennsylvania soon moved south from Bethlehem to the area that is known today as Winston-Salem, North Carolina. Like the German potters in Pennsylvania, the North Carolina group also produced highly ornamented slip-decorated earthenwares. The main difference in the work of these southern potters, however, is that their work was not incised with the sgraffito decoration characteristic of the Pennsylvania pottery. The Moravian potters in Salem merely painted motifs on their plates with slip and various glazes. A large plate made by Gottfried Aust and dated 1773 is the most impressive piece of this redware known, and it was probably used as the shop sign for this noted Salem potter.[30] The large redware plate shown in plate 45 is probably also the work of Aust, and it is related to a group of similarly decorated plates with wavy borders and central motifs of flowers and foliage. Completely different in feeling from the Pennsylvania redware, each one has an individual charm and beauty all its own. Well balanced and neatly drawn, each plate is a variation on a continuing theme.

At the same time the Moravians were making slip-decorated earthenware, they were also trying to produce molded tableware to compete with the English creamware that

272

273

272. Group of shards (1773–88) exca-vated at Bethabara and Salem, Moravian settlements near Winston-Salem, North Carolina. *Attributed to two potters, Rudolf Christ (1750–1833) and William Ellis (w. 1773–74); show reliance on English prototypes as well as desire to create sophisticated local wares. Old Salem.*

273. Fish bottle, 1800–1819, Salem, North Carolina. *Attributed to Rudolf Christ (1750–1833). Earthenware with green glaze. L. 6½ in., W. 3⅝ in., D. 1½ in.* **Heart-shaped inkwell, 1810–20, Salem, North Carolina.** *John Holland (1781–1843). Earthenware with lead glaze; signed inside right cavity, "IH." Dia. 5 in., H. approx. 2 in. Old Salem.*

Plate 43. Shrank, 1779, probably Lancaster County, Pennsylvania. *Black walnut with pine, oak, poplar, sulphur and white lead inlay, and brasses; inlaid inscription on front doors," GEORG HUBER/ANNO 1779." H. 83 in., W. 78 in., D. 27½ in. Philadelphia Museum of Art. Purchased.*

PL. 43

274. Tea table, ca. 1710, possibly Williamsburg, Virginia. *Walnut. H. 27½ in., W. 26½ in., D. 21½ in. Colonial Williamsburg Foundation.*

275. *Frances Peyton (1753–1828), 1770–75, Virginia. John Durand (w. 1766–82[?]). Oil on canvas. H. 35 in., W. 28 in. Private collection.*

■ **276.** Sideboard, 1790–1810, Georgia, possibly Athens. *Mahogany and mahogany veneer, with southern yellow pine. H. 37¾ in., L. 64 in., D. 23⅜ in. Mr. and Mrs. Henry D. Green.*

had become so popular in the colonies. Precisely how successful this production was is uncertain, for few examples survive, and they are seen mostly in the shards and pieces of molds discovered during recent archaeological excavations.[31] The most remarkable observation concerning many of these surviving examples is how similar they are to their English antecedents. However, this is not too difficult to understand when it is noted that in 1773 a man named William Ellis, from Hanley, England, arrived in Salem, having first stopped near Charleston, South Carolina.

Among the surviving fragments of objects that were being produced in Salem by Gottfried Aust, William Ellis, and one Rudolf Christ are pieces of Whieldon-type Queensware plates, globular teapots with crossed-strap handles and applied sprigs, bulbous-bodied canns (again with crossed handles and sprigs), and delicately molded sauceboats with embossed floral decoration (fig. 272). Whether large amounts of these highly sophisticated tablewares ever graced many tables in Salem must be left to conjecture, but the venture must have been moderately successful or we might not have even these few remaining examples. In addition to these refined products, it is only fair to note two other unusual examples from Salem potters. The marvelous little green-glazed fish bottle and the heart-shaped inkstand (fig. 273), by potters Rudolf Christ and John Holland respectively, are distinctive forms not encountered elsewhere. Their delicacy and whimsey are two characteristics of this genre of American production.

Although much of the South was rural and agrarian, ties with both England and closer centers of culture were strong. The aesthetic taste of the South does not appear to have suffered because of its geographical and topographical nature. Only a limited number of southern-made objects have been specifically identified, but many of those that are known do exhibit a simple sense of good design and proportion. The visually enchanting, stretcher-based tea table in figure 274 is presumed to be of Virginia origin and has cautiously been attributed to Williamsburg.[32] The rarity of any early southern furniture makes this table's existence extremely important, yet the object clearly stands on its own merit. The lively, shaped skirt is the first aspect to catch one's eye, and the finely turned legs and stretchers seem to temper the exuberance of the skirt. One cannot help wonder how many similar tables may still exist in houses in Virginia.

The painters, or limners, working in the South from the seventeenth century until the early nineteenth have never been fully studied or documented. Currently a number of scholars are working in different geographical areas, concentrating on a variety of artists,

276

PL. 45

■ **Plate 44. Plate, 1787, Montgomery County, Pennsylvania.** *Attributed to George Hübener (d. 1846[?]). Red earthenware with white slip, sgraffito decoration and inscription, and lead glaze; incised around outer edge of rim, "Wann das manngen, und das hengen nicht wehr, so standen die wiegen und hickel heusser Lehr; September, de ? 14.ͭᵐ 1787," which when translated reads: "When there are no men or roosters left, cradles and chicken pens will stand empty." Dia. 13¾ in., H. 2 in. The Henry Francis du Pont Winterthur Museum.*

■ **Plate 45. Plate, 1770–1820, Wachovia, North Carolina.** *Attributed to Gottfried Aust (1722–88). Earthenware with slip decoration and lead glaze. Dia. 14 in., H. 2¾ in. Old Salem.*

in the hope that during the next few years there will be a major colloquium on painting in the South, with significant research presented.[33] Several English-trained artists working in the South, such as Charles Bridges and Henrietta Johnston, have already been discussed in this book. John Durand, an artist of possible French ancestry, was first noted in 1766 as "Monsieur Duran" in the account book of James Beekman of New York. Essentially itinerant, Durand worked in New York and Connecticut before going south. He seems to have been in Virginia as late as 1782 but after that disappears from all records.[34] Presumably about 1775 Durand was working in Virginia where he painted the fascinating yet simple likeness of Frances Peyton, later Mrs. John Tabb (1753–1828) (fig. 275). As early as 1917 this painting was exhibited at the Brooklyn Museum when it was owned by John Hill Morgan and again in 1929 both in Richmond and in New York at the Girl Scouts Loan Exhibition. Like other untrained, nonacademic painters, Durand worked in a very hard-edged, linear style. Lacking an understanding of anatomy, he painted portraits with a curious stiffness and an awkward handling of limbs and extremities. Yet like Jennys, Durand's directness and attention to dress and detail always resulted in an engaging likeness. Forthcoming studies of southern artists and newly discovered works by Durand should supply us with more information.

In 1976 the High Museum of Art in Atlanta presented a pioneering exhibition of furniture made in the Georgia Piedmont before 1830. The sideboard in figure 276 was one of the finest pieces of furniture shown, and in some respects it is difficult to imagine this gracious piece, with its deeply serpentined front, coming out of the hinterlands. However, a great deal of high-style furniture was imported through the port of Savannah, and thus there were opportunities for some of it to have migrated inland and influenced craftsmen working there. Much furniture was imported from New York City sources,[35] and there were even some cabinetmakers trained in New York who went south to Savannah. It is interesting to note that the 1793 *London Book of Prices* was not only known but also owned in New York and that plate 4 in that publication seems to be a direct source for the Georgia sideboard. Is it possible that somewhere in Georgia there existed a *London Book of Prices*? What about the copy that Robert Walker brought with him from Scotland to New York and then to Charleston?[36] Or perhaps an English-made sideboard was owned in Georgia, admired, and thus copied? Whatever the circumstance may have been, there is no denying the facts that skilled craftsmen existed in Georgia (as well as in other provincial regions) who could successfully copy a design, whether from a drawing or a full-sized example, and there were clients with the economic resources to order or purchase such sophisticated pieces.

Chapter 7

The Classical Impulse
Early Nineteenth-Century Style in America

Although the preceding chapters have been organized thematically and have crossed barriers of time, geography, and media, this final chapter will return to the format of the 1929 Loan Exhibition and explore a specific period of time in which a precise style was adopted throughout America. However, unlike the first exhibition's section that dealt with the Phyfe style, this chapter will attempt to deal with the classical taste in a broader manner and illustrate the many areas that scholars have explored over the past fifty years.

By 1929 Duncan Phyfe and his prolific fellow cabinetmakers in New York were all the rage among collectors, and thus the first Girl Scouts Loan Exhibition had not only a section entitled "Sheraton and Hepplewhite" but also a separate one for "Duncan Phyfe" (see fig. 10 in the introduction). Of course, Phyfe's popularity had been heightened by the Metropolitan Museum's 1922 exhibition and the subsequent publication by Charles Over Cornelius of *Furniture Masterpieces of Duncan Phyfe.* The 1934 exhibition of New York furniture at the Metropolitan also had a large complement of furniture in that distinctive manner, and by 1939 Nancy McClelland had written for the collectors and scholars of this famous immigrant Scotsman a book called *Duncan Phyfe and the English Regency.*

However, just in the past twenty years, scholars have taken a more broadly cultural look at this post-Revolutionary classical period and have tried to understand the direct sources of inspiration as well as the numerous aspects of life and art on this side of the Atlantic. The Newark Museum's 1963 exhibition entitled *Classical America* heralded this exciting rediscovery and exploration, and it brought numerous objects to the attention of scholars and collectors that had lain dormant for many years. By 1970 the popular groundwork had been laid for the Metropolitan Museum's spectacular presentation of *Nineteenth Century America,* and as a result of the exhibit the decade of the seventies has witnessed a phenomenal growth in the scholarship and collecting of American objects made between about 1780 and 1840.

The introduction of the "classical taste" into France and England can be easily documented through the travels and publications of many artists and archaeologists, but its parallel appearance in America is still a matter of scholarly exploration. The earliest expression of the classical impulse abroad seemed to manifest itself in the adoption of primarily decorative motifs and light, almost watered-down translations of Greek and Roman forms, but the second phase embraced a more archaeological and robust copying of forms and motifs. The urn form seems to have been one of the first and most popular adoptions both for importation and domestic manufacture. Traditionally it has been recognized that only after the American Revolution did our artists and craftsmen begin to adopt the new-style classical motifs and forms. This seems to hold true in style centers such as Boston and New York, but contradictory evidence in other sophisticated urban areas suggests an earlier, pre-Revolutionary introduction of classical influence into American art. Recent research into the life and possessions of certain citizens of Williamsburg, Virginia, has indicated that objects incorporating classical motifs were imported into Williamsburg as early as 1771.[1] However, the earliest known and most outstanding extant specimen of an American-made object fully embracing classical form and ornament is the monumental silver urn made in Philadelphia by Richard Humphreys (fig. 277). Presented in 1774 to Charles Thomson, Secretary of the Continental Congress, "in Testimony/ of their Esteem and/ Approbation/1774," this piece possibly copied an English piece of silver that had already been imported into Philadelphia or was perhaps derived from sketches from someone's travels abroad. To date the presence of any English silver of similar form in Philadelphia is not known, but the possibility does exist.[2] According to the records of the Continental Congress, on October 25, 1774, the Committee on Rights, "made some resolves, ordered a piece of plate for the Secretary, 50 sterling." Unfortunately these records don't provide any other clues regarding the specifics of this illustrious order; nevertheless, it is fascinating that one of the most avant garde and stylish objects of its day emanated from a political body as a commission to recognize personal commitment and achievement.

After Richard Humphreys completed the urn for Thomson, almost a quarter of a century passed before Americans fully embraced the classical taste in almost every aspect of life and art. Henry Sargent's well-known, often exhibited, large paintings of

277. Presentation Urn, 1774, Philadelphia. *Richard Humphreys (1750–1832). Silver; marked "R.HUMPHREYS" in script in conforming rectangle on lid and base, twice on bezel; inscribed in foliate cartouche on body, "the conti*[l] *Congress/TO/ Cha*[s] *Thomson/ Secr*[y] *in Testimony/ of their Esteem and Approbation/ 1774/ Smither Sculp; NIL DESPERANDUM" (on scroll below). H. 21½ in. Philadelphia Museum of Art. Gift of the Dietrich Brothers Americana Corporation (funds contributed).*
Figure 277 is on page 239.

Plate 46. *The Tea Party,* ca. 1823, Boston. *Henry Sargent (1770–1845). Oil on canvas. H. 64¼ in., W. 52¼ in. Museum of Fine Arts, Boston. Gift of Mrs. Horatio A. Lamb, in memory of Mr. and Mrs. Winthrop Sargent.*
Plate 46 is on page 240.

Plate 47. *Mrs. Robert Gilmor, Jr. (nee Sarah Reeve Ladson, c. 1790–1866), 1823, Baltimore. Thomas Sully (1783–1872). Oil on canvas; signed, lower left, "TS 1823." H. 36⅛ in., W. 28⅛ in. Carolina Art Association. Gibbes Art Gallery.*
Plate 47 is on page 241.

278. *On the Beach,* 1827–28. *Thomas Doughty (1793–1856). Oil on canvas; signed and dated lower left, "T. Doughty/ 1827–8." H. 35 in., W. 51⅘ in. Albany Institute of History and Art.*

279. *On the Delaware,* ca. 1830, Philadelphia. *Thomas Birch (1779–1851). Oil on canvas. H. 20 in., W. 30⅛ in. Historical Society of Pennsylvania.*

278

279

The Dinner Party and *The Tea Party* (ca. 1823) provide some of the most important visual documents from which scholars may reconstruct the manners, possessions, and lifestyle of early nineteenth-century Americans. That these paintings were popularly known in the artist's own day (*The Tea Party* was exhibited as early as 1828 at the Boston Athenaeum) reveals society's conscious image of itself in a period of growing social pretension and awareness. The paintings, aesthetic triumphs in their own right, serve as rare gems for both the decorative arts historian and the art historian. The attentive detail that Sargent has given to the overall interior decoration including floors, walls, textiles, furniture, and furnishings—in addition to the placement of not only objects but also persons—is socially introspective. Consequently, it will be most illuminating if we take a close, detailed look at *The Tea Party* (pl. 46) and use it as an illustrative frontispiece and point of direct reference as we proceed with the manifestation of neoclassicism in America.

Tradition has related that *The Tea Party* was painted to commemorate an event that took place at the artist's own home around 1798. However, both the nature of the furniture and perhaps even the style of the costumes suggest that the artist was depicting (or at least remembering) visual images of a slightly later date in Boston's sophisticated era of Bulfinch-inspired architecture. Whenever and whatever the occasion was, the dress of both gentlemen and ladies was elegant and fashionable. Empire dresses, colorful shawls, and chic turbans characterized the ladies' costumes, while the men cut handsome figures in their slim, form-fitting pantaloons and neatly trimmed waistcoats with tails. This stylish manner of dress was popular throughout the new Federal republic, having been adopted directly from the latest French and, perhaps more specifically, English fashions. In Philadelphia and Baltimore, fashions were much the same, even in 1823 when Thomas Sully (1783–1872), then working mostly in Philadelphia, painted this captivating likeness of Mrs. Robert Gilmor, Jr., Charleston-born wife of the well-established Baltimore art collector and merchant (pl. 47). Sully's exquisite portrayal of Mrs. Gilmor's face is heightened by the exotic richness of her ermine-lined cloak and her colorful turban with cascading fringe. One is made to think that Mrs. Gilmor, Jr., has such assured poise that she would surely flourish in any demanding social situation in Charleston, Baltimore, New York, or Boston. Her lifestyle was a cultured and sophisticated one, as Philip Hone, New York's celebrated diarist and onetime mayor (see fig. 287), indicated during his 1830 visit to Baltimore:

> I then walked out to pay a few visits, and dined with a very agreeable party at Mr. Robert Gilmor's. This gentleman lives in handsome style; nobody in America gives better dinners or more exquisite wines. His collection of pictures is very fine, and his house is filled with specimens of the fine arts and objects of taste and *virtu*.[3]

PL. 48

PL. 49

PL. 50

280

280. *View of Mount Pleasant, ca. 1830, Philadelphia.* *Attributed to Thomas Birch (1779–1851). Oil on canvas. H. 25¾ in., W. 35½ in. The Dietrich Fine Arts Collections, Philadelphia.*

281. *A Quilting Frolic,* **1813, Philadelphia.** *John Lewis Krimmel (1789–1821). Oil on canvas. H. 16⅞ in., W. 22⅜ in. The Henry Francis du Pont Winterthur Museum.*

Hone's brief comments about Gilmor are especially significant when considered in combination with several other factors. First of all, look closely at the pictures that Sargent so clearly delineated on the walls in *The Tea Party.* They seem to be romantic, sensitively illuminated landscapes and seascapes, perhaps something like the 1790s landscapes by Trumbull and James Peale that have already been discussed (figs. 234 and 235). If we can speculate about the type of paintings Hone might have seen at the Gilmors', some works by Thomas Doughty (1793–1856) such as *On the Beach* (fig. 278) were probably included in his fine "collection of pictures." The early decades of the nineteenth century had witnessed the budding careers of a number of talented young artists; and patrons like Robert Gilmor, Jr., had further encouraged specific individuals including Thomas Doughty with commissions and financial support. With virtually no formal training, Doughty had taught himself, frequently copying old master paintings, a number of which were in Gilmor's collection. By 1824 Doughty had been elected a "Pennsylvania Academician" by the Pennsylvania Academy of Fine Arts. In addition, he frequently went on sketching trips with his friend and fellow artist Alvan Fisher (1792–1863). As an important pioneer in American landscape painting, Doughty shows a broad range of moods and talents in his work. Some art historians believe that his best work was done between 1822 and 1830,[4] and certainly his scene *On the Beach,* painted in the Adirondacks, combines the best of his most positive and innovative qualities. With a most romantic and sublime background, the canvas contains a genre scene in the central portion, while the foreground frames the whole with a detailed and highly naturalistic bower. Dated in the lower left "1827-8," this canvas might be the one (or be derived from it) that he exhibited in 1827 at the Pennsylvania Academy of Fine Arts entitled *Landscape, Fishermen drawing their Nets & a composition.*

Another Philadelphia-based artist who contributed much to the body of landscape and seascape paintings (figs. 279 and 280) was the English-born Thomas Birch (1779–1851). Trained by his father, William, in the 1790s, he had a variety of skills and talents. The War of 1812 brought naval commissions and popularity to competent painters like Birch (see fig. 131), and after the war a number of these artists settled down to painting harbor scenes and pleasant, bucolic landscapes. Birch's marine landscapes of the post war years clearly demonstrate that he was following the seventeenth-century Dutch marine painting tradition of the Ruisdaels and Van de Veldes. Of course, it is not surprising that Birch followed this established tradition, for his father (and teacher) had an impressive collection of Dutch art including copies that he had made himself. Significant is the fact that Birch was the first marine painter to achieve widespread popular favor. His view *On the Delaware* (fig. 279) is typical of his "mature style" in harbor scenes, being very fine in its composition and detailed delineation of the wharves, ships, and small craft in the foreground. Unlike the work of Doughty and other early landscape artists like Washington Allston (1779–1843), Birch rarely verges on the romantic or

281

sublime in his marine scenes or landscapes, as is clearly evident in figure 280. Supposedly a view of Mt. Pleasant along the Schuylkill River in Philadelphia, this pastoral scene is one of precise detail showing a broad panorama of landscape but nevertheless remaining distinctly topical in orientation. Reminiscent of his 1821 *Fairmount Water-Works,* this work exhibits a similarly rendered "bright luminous sky."[5]

Nineteenth-century American art saw the fascinating development of a lively strain of genre painting. In 1935 the Whitney Museum of American Art held an exhibition entitled *American Genre: The Social Scene in Paintings and Prints, 1800–1935.* Included in that exhibition were three scenes by the German-born artist John Lewis Krimmel (1789–1821), who settled in Philadelphia in 1810. His small but extraordinarily detailed interior scene of *A Quilting Frolic* (fig. 281) presents an interesting contrast to Sargent's *The Tea Party.* Clearly concerned with the presentation of a totally different economic level of society, Krimmel's decorative detail is always most illuminating. The intricacies of his compositions, plus his social commentary, are unequaled by any other genre artists at this early date. Possibly influenced by the engravings of William Birch, Krimmel probably also knew the work of William's son Thomas, and it is interesting that he has included in his painting a pair of naval engagement scenes, similar to Birch's work, over the mantel.

At approximately the same time that Birch and Krimmel were diligently at work on popular and topical scenes, artists like James Peale and other Peale family members were working on the creation of an American still-life tradition. Restrained and classical in its pristine and realistic quality, *Still Life No. 2* (fig. 282) illustrates the style that James Peale developed in the early decades of the nineteenth century. Still-life painting continued to grow in popularity, and it went through an evolution of styles throughout the rest of the century, but never was it as controlled and serenely ideal as with James Peale.

The most demonstrative American expression of classicism on canvas produced during the first two decades of the nineteenth century came from the brush of John Vanderlyn (1775–1852) in his *Ariadne Asleep on the Island of Naxos* (fig. 283). Vanderlyn's talent was initially fostered under the patronage of New York's Aaron Burr, who financed Vanderlyn's early studies in Paris and elsewhere abroad from 1796 to about 1800. Vanderlyn came back to the United States at intervals (when he worked on his Niagara series), but essentially he lived abroad until about 1815. He studied in Rome between 1805 and 1807, where he copied some of the masters like Titian and Correggio. Before he began to paint *Ariadne* in 1809, he copied Correggio's *Antiope* for the New York lithographer John Murry. It is a strikingly sensuous depiction of Jupiter mas-

■ **Plate 51. Pole screen, 1810–15, New York.** *Mahogany with silk embroidery. H. 53⅛ in., W. 17¾ in. White House Collection.*

■ **Plate 52.** *Secrétairé à abattant,* **1815–25, Philadelphia.** *Rosewood veneer, with ebonized sides, gilt feet, cut-brass inlay, marble top, ormolu mounts, pine and tulip poplar secondary woods. H. 60 in., W. 40 in., D. 19 in. Decatur House, Washington, D.C.; a property of the National Trust for Historic Preservation.*

querading as a satyr and unveiling the naked Antiope as she reposes under a bower. When Murry saw it he is supposed to have exclaimed: "What am I to do with it? It is altogether indecent. I cannot hang it up in my house, and my family reprobates it."[6] Vanderlyn's *Ariadne*, no doubt inspired by the works of the old masters, was the artist's own composition, painted between 1809 and 1812, though dated 1814. As the first classical likeness of a nude by an American artist depicting "female beauty," it was exhibited by Vanderlyn at the Paris Salon in 1810 and 1812. After he returned to America in 1815, it was shown in New York in 1819, New Orleans in 1821, and Charleston in 1822. In September 1822 the *Charleston Courier* approvingly reported that "no man of taste and sensibility, no student of love and beauty, no connoisseur of graceful form should fail to gladden his eyes, to charm his fancy and refresh his imagination with the exquisite performance of Mr. VanDerlyn where the sleeping and unconscious Ariadne is sweetly reclining."[7] In 1831 the artist sold it for $600.00 to Asher B. Durand, who eventually engraved it and later sold it for $6,000.00 to a Philadelphia widow, who ultimately gave it to the Pennsylvania Academy of Fine Arts. Thus another blow for sublime, sensuous, and romantic painting in nineteenth-century America was struck, a trend that was to grow and mature throughout the century.

In addition to the costumes and paintings that are clearly drawn in *The Tea Party*, elaborate pieces of furniture are depicted. Even with a close look it is difficult to determine whether individual pieces of furniture were made in Boston or New York. Assuming that Sargent painted what he actually saw or knew in some way to exist in Boston, one might speculate that the furniture could be French in origin. Perhaps it was some of the furniture that Major James Swan sent over from France during the 1790s, property from estates that were confiscated during the Revolution.[8] The center table in the middle foreground is very much like one that was purchased by President James Monroe in France in 1817 for the Washington White House.[9] That table, which is still in the White House, was described on the 1817 bill as "une table ronde en bois d'acajou." While Sargent's center table looks French, it is also reminiscent of a specific group of early nineteenth-century Boston pieces characterized by sleek veneered columns with ormolu capitals and bases, sweeping veneered surfaces with rich mounts, and flattened ball feet with mid-bands of ormolu beading. The diminutive, marbletop pier table in figure 284 is a representative example of this style of Boston furniture, though unusual in its small size. Bearing the stenciled mark of "EMMONS & ARCHBALD/No. 39 Orange Street/(BOSTON)/Cabinet, Chair & Upholstery/Manufactory" on the top side of the bottom board, the table was made between 1813 and 1825 when Thomas Emmons and George Archibald were partners at that address.[10] It is quite possible that imported French furniture did influence the production of craftsmen in the Boston area during the first decades of the nineteenth century.

Although President Monroe had a French center table, the form was also made in this country, perhaps most successfully in New York. The extraordinary table in plate 48 was either inspired by an imported piece or possibly by some of the designs published by Pierre La Mésangère in Paris between 1796 and 1830 (fig. 285). The four carved and gilt, winged figural supports of this New York center table are almost identical to those found on similar labeled and attributed card tables by Charles-Honoré Lannuier (see fig. 286). In combination the decorative embellishments of this grandiose creation, including mahogany veneer, ormolu mounts, cut brass inlay, and ebony, make it an outstanding triumph. The enormous white marble top unites the elements and balances the design and masses below.

The New York card table in figure 286 is directly related to the center table, and though it does not bear Lannuier's label, it is so much like several other labeled ones that it must be from his shop. In addition, this table was owned by Philip Hone, entrepreneur and onetime mayor of New York, who seems to have been a man of impeccable taste and notable aesthetic perception (fig. 287). Closely related to three other pairs of Lannuier card tables that are documented, this table is perhaps the richest and most elaborate. The varied use of popular French design motifs plus the vibrant and striking variety of surface treatments, including cut brass inlay, bird's-eye maple veneer, rosewood, and satinwood, contribute to the lush ostentation of this superb card table. The winged caryatid and hocked animal leg are found in plates 19 and 20 published in 1802 in La Mésangère's *Collection des Meubles et Objets de Goût*. The cut brass ornaments inlaid around the top edge are a special element found in other work by Lannuier, including the very different card table illustrated in figure 302.

While the armchairs, or *fauteuils,* that Sargent illustrated are truly unlike any known American upholstered chairs of that period, both New York and Philadelphia makers are known to have produced some handsome armchairs. A pair of them owned by the Baltimore merchant James Bosley were part of a large suite of furniture he ordered from New York, possibly from Lannuier (fig. 288). Unusual chairs with straight arms supported by winged caryatids, these may have been inspired by imported ones like Sargent's, or perhaps by designs published in 1805 and 1807 by George Smith of London in *A Collection of Designs for Household Furniture and Interior Decoration.* Plate 55 from Smith's publication (fig. 289) offers a choice of four "Drawing Room Chairs in Profile." The first one in the upper left corner seems closest to the armchairs attributed to the shop of Charles-Honoré Lannuier. The curve of the front legs, the tablet back cresting and reverse curve of the rear legs, and the arrow-straight arms with winged female figures supporting them all suggest a strong direct source from George Smith. While the inspiration for the New York armchairs is essentially French, the immediate source seems to be an English translation. This is true in other instances also, for while La Mésangère or even Percier and Fontaine designs can be cited, frequently there will be a more immediate English version, derived from the French.

The Philadelphia-made armchair in figure 290 is one of an unusual pair and might be considered the direct counterpart to the New York version just cited. The use of the dolphin motif is seen in both New-York and Philadelphia furniture, and earlier design sources for the use of dolphins as arm supports are found in La Mésangère's plates 443 (fig. 291) and 483 published in 1817 and 1819 respectively. While the armchair on the left in plate 443 has dolphins with curled tails and open mouths related to the Philadelphia chair, it is actually George Smith's plate 55 (fig. 289) that exhibits the closest parallels. A combination of the two topmost armchairs, but integrating the La Mésangère dolphins, is most like the Philadelphia examples. These chairs seem stout and massive in appearance; their proportions are strong but the decorative carving is delicate and highly articulate. Of extremely dense, heavy mahogany, they were originally made for George Harrison of Philadelphia who lived on Locust Street. The chairs were inherited by his adopted son Joshua Francis Fisher and can be seen *in situ* in an 1892 photograph in a house built by Brinton Coxe on Spruce Street.

Other examples of Philadelphia furniture sport dolphins as supports on pier tables,[11] and in one grand instance they are supports for a center table. On the other hand, a small group of New York sofas have dolphins as feet, with their tails gracefully curving up and tapering outward to form languid, rolling arms.[12] The superior example shown in plate 49 has the additional feature of twin eagles with wings outspread and necks curved inward, rising up from either side of the sofa back. The expressively articulated dolphins are *verd-antique* with gilt heads and foliate fins. The straight, horizontal crestrail is skillfully carved with a trailing vine and leaf motif bound in the middle with a bowknot. The broad, veneered, front seat rail provides a necessary balance to the robustness of the other framing elements of this extraordinary sofa.

While New England furniture does not often boast of dolphins and eagles, an interesting Boston counterpart to the New York sofa is the elegantly refined and understated "Grecian" couch in plate 50. One of a pair, and of a distinctly diminutive size, this same couch was also made in a larger version.[13] Of particular interest is the ornament, with fine strings of ormolu beading and cut brass inlay in the central and end panels. Although a number of Boston cabinetmakers advertised "Grecian couches,"[14] George Smith called a similar design, without a back, a "Chaise Longue." Smith's design does vary in several details but is close enough to this Boston version to suggest an English source or interpretation of an originally French form. Of the "Chaise Longue" Smith made the following comments:

> . . . . an article admissible into almost every room. The present Designs are intended for Drawing Rooms, or Boudoirs, in which case the Frames may be of satin-wood, inlaid with other woods, and the ornaments of bronze, as Plates A and B; or in gold, with bronzed ornaments, as Plates 63 and 64. For covering, silks or cloth may be used; and in more moderately furnished apartments calico may suffice, provided the pattern be small and of the chintz kind. The same Designs will answer extremely well for Libraries, Parlors, or Dressing Rooms, executed in mahogany, and divested of the ornaments.[15]

282. *Still Life No. 2,* **1821, Philadelphia.** *James Peale (1749–1831). Oil on canvas. H. 18 in., W. 26½ in. Pennsylvania Academy of the Fine Arts.*

283. *Ariadne Asleep on the Island of Naxos,* **1809–12, Paris.** *John Vanderlyn (1775–1852). Oil on canvas; signed lower left, "J.Vanderlyn fact/Parisiis 1814." H. 68 in., W. 87 in. Pennsylvania Academy of the Fine Arts.*

Another form of seating furniture that became popular in the early nineteenth century and derived its inspiration from Greek and Roman sources was the settee, or window seat. These could be used in a variety of ways as illustrated in *The Tea Party*. The primary place where one would be used was, of course, in a window niche or alcove. However, they could also be used on either side of an arched entry, or placed out in full view in a room, as Sargent has shown us. The New York "curule"-form window seat in figure 292 has a crossed or X-shaped base derived from ancient Greek stools. This form was also used on New York chairs, and in Sargent's painting there is a similar stool to the right of the center table. In 1800 Pierre La Mésangère illustrated a related Grecian crossed stool, and by 1807 the English designers Thomas Hope and George Smith published similar designs. This particular New York window seat is one variation on a theme that was applied to side chairs, armchairs, window seats, settees, and sofas. Many examples of this form are attributed to the workshop of the famed cabinetmaker Duncan Phyfe, based on several documented suites of furniture. Indeed the quality of this window seat is so exquisite as to suggest the hand of this master. The finely tapered reeding, the concave curve of the back, the delicate, trailing laurel carving of the crest, and the gilt lion's mask and applied ormolu paw feet all add to the refinement of this superb little seat—and, no doubt, increased the original price!

The generously curvilinear armchair in figure 293 is another variation of this popular New York style. With a back almost identical to that of the window seat, this chair has different carving, instead employing thunderbolts tied in the center with a bowknot. In the 1810 *New-York Revised Prices for Manufacturing Cabinet and Chair Work*,[16] this form was called "A Scroll Back Chair." Judging from the base prices listed and all the extras that embellished a chair and thus added to its overall cost, this armchair was among the most expensive that a client could order. The base price for a scroll-back chair "with straight rails for stuffing over, one cross bannister in the back" was £1.2.8 However, it appears that this chair had the following extras:

Bell seat, extra from sweep rails	0	4	3
Ditto when mahogany rails, extra	0	0	9
Rabetting ditto for stuffing	0	0	9
Each rose in the centre of the cross	0	0	9
Scroll sweep elbows arms	0	11	0
An ogee splat instead of a straight one	0	2	9
Springing the front legs one way, each leg	0	0	6
Preparing the front legs for lion's paws, each	0	1	0

In addition to these standard choices, various price tables at the back of the price book included "Price of Putting on BrassWork." In the case of this armchair, the most expensive type of termination was used.

Ditto lion's paw ditto	0	0	7

Another price table calculated the "Price of Claws, Therming Legs, Reeding ditto and Claws," and the charge for "Reeding chair legs, each" was £0.1.6. Thus, when all the additional costs are tallied, an armchair like that in figure 293 could cost as much as £2.10.1 A client had a wide range of choices, and depending on his taste and his pocketbook, he could order any variety of combinations he desired, all of which had predetermined, fixed costs. Consequently, an understanding of these important price guides provides an explanation for the numerous variations that are found in New York chairs of this type.

Two other variations on New York "scroll back" chairs are illustrated in figures 294 and 295. The chair with a lyre-back splat has the exceptional features of not only carved leafage on the legs but also carved and gilt paw feet. The leaf and rosette carving on the lyre-backs is also a fine feature that no doubt added a few more shillings to the base price. The provenance of this chair (one of a set of at least six side chairs) is particularly interesting as they have descended in the Middleton family of South Carolina. By the early nineteenth century a great deal of furniture was being shipped from New York to southern ports such as Norfolk, Charleston, and Savannah.[17] These chairs were probably shipped back north to Rhode Island, where many South Carolinians spent the summer, once they were out of fashion and the Middletons decided to use them in the

285

1, Table à Manger 2, Table de Nuit. 3, Table de Jeu.

284. Pier table, ca. 1813–20, Boston.
Thomas Emmons and George Archibald (w. 1813–25). Mahogany veneer on chestnut and pine, marble top, ormolu mounts; stenciled label on top of bottom board under marble, ''EMMONS & ARCHBALD/ No. 39 Orange Street/ (BOSTON)/ Cabinet, Chair & Upholstery/Manufactory.'' H. 31½ in., W. 32¼ in., D. 16¾ in. Museum of Fine Arts, Boston. Gift of Mr. and Mrs George C. Seybolt.

285. Collection des Meubles et Objets de Goût, plate 19, published 1802, Paris. *Pierre La Mésangère (1761–1831). Joseph Downs Manuscript Collection. The Henry Francis du Pont Winterthur Museum.*

284

287

288

286

286. Card table, ca. 1815, New York. *Charles-Honoré Lannuier (1779–1819). Veneers of bird's-eye maple, rosewood, and satinwood, carved and gilt pine, cut-brass inlay, and ormolu mounts. H. 31 in., W. 35 in., D. 18 in. The Metropolitan Museum of Art. Purchase, Funds from Various Donors, 1966.*

287. Philip Hone (1780–1851), 1826, New York. *John Vanderlyn (1775–1852). Oil on canvas. H. 36 in., W. 30 in. Art Commission of the City of New York.*

■ **288. Armchair (one of a pair), ca. 1815, New York.** *Attributed to Charles-Honoré Lannuier (1779–1819). Mahogany and mahogany veneer with carved and gilt pine, brass inlay, and ormolu mounts. H. 35½ in., W. 22 in., D. 20½ in. Maryland Historical Society, Baltimore.*

289. A Collection of Designs for Household Furniture, plate 55, published 1805, London. *George Smith (w. 1804–28). Joseph Downs Manuscript Collection. The Henry Francis du Pont Winterthur Museum.*

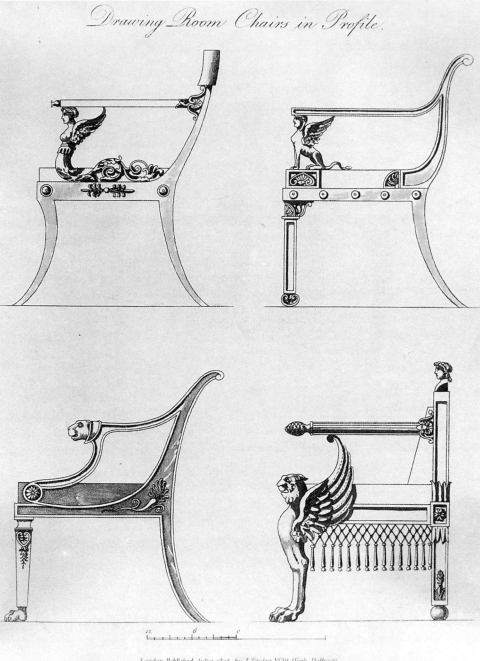

289

summer home they had purchased in Bristol, "Hey Bonnie Hall," originally built by William DeWolfe.

As we have seen, the use of carved eagle motifs on various forms of furniture was most popular during the closing years of the eighteenth century and the first decades of the nineteenth. The dolphin sofa (pl. 49) illustrates one very unusual use of this motif, and the scroll-back side chair in figure 295 shows us a different use. Governor DeWitt Clinton has traditionally been cited as the original owner of this large set of at least twelve side chairs, which may have come from the workshop of Duncan Phyfe. The overall simplicity of this classic form heightens the striking focus of the carved eagle backs. One must assume that these chairs were probably a special order from Clinton since this particular form of eagle splat is neither listed in New York price books nor found on any other chairs. Although carved eagles are traditionally associated with patriotism and thought to be symbolic of our early Federal republic, it must be remembered that great winged creatures are often found in the popular French and English design sources.[18]

In the early decades of the twentieth century when New York furniture in the style made by Duncan Phyfe was being studied and collected, the work of contemporaneous

290

292

Fauteuils Garnis.

291

■ **290. Armchair (one of a pair), 1815–25, Philadelphia.** *Mahogany and oak. H. 33 in., W. 21⅞ in., D. (at seat) 26 in. Mr. and Mrs. Charles H. Carpenter, Jr.*

291. *Collection des Meubles et Objets de Goût*, plate 443, published in 1817, Paris. *Pierre La Mésangère (1761–1831). Joseph Downs Manuscript Collection. The Henry Francis du Pont Winterthur Museum.*

292. Window seat (one of a pair), 1810–15, New York. *Mahogany and maple. H. 30¼ in., W. 37¼ in., D. 14½ in. Edward V. Jones.*

293. Armchair, 1805–15, New York. *Mahogany and ash. H. 32 in., W. 20½ in., D. 20 in. Fenton L. B. Brown.*

294. Side chair, 1810–15, New York. *Mahogany with ash seat rails and seat frame. H. 32½ in., W. 19½ in., D. 17¼ in. William Nathaniel Banks.*

295. Side chair (one of a set of twelve), 1810–15, New York. *Mahogany with ash. H. 31¼ in., W. 18 in., D. 17 in. Mr. and Mrs. George M. Kaufman.*

296. Side chair, 1810–15, Boston. *Mahogany and mahogany veneer. H. 32⅝ in., W. 18¼ in., D. 21¼ in. Private collection.*

Boston cabinetmakers went virtually unrecognized. However, over the past decade collectors and scholars have begun to study and recognize the distinctive products made in Boston in the first quarter of the nineteenth century. Unfortunately, Henry Sargent has not shown us any identifiable examples in *The Tea Party*, though his companion painting *The Dinner Party* illustrates recognizable Boston furniture. The side chair in figure 296 is the Boston tablet-back version of the New York scroll-back chair. A serenely handsome example of the Grecian klismos form, this chair has a draped and swagged splat found on other Boston chairs, as well as a handsomely veneered panel in the tablet that has scrolled acanthus carved ends.[19] Although none of these presumably Boston-made chairs are labeled, several large sets have histories of ownership in Boston and thus can be firmly identified as the work of Boston craftsmen.

The compositional framework and diminishing perspective in Sargent's painting is fascinating, and it is especially significant that the focal point to which one's eye is drawn is the grand pier glass between the windows in the front parlor. This expensive and elegant piece is positioned almost in the center of the canvas, though Sargent has been careful to balance his composition without making it wholly symmetrical. Looking glasses, pier glasses, mirrors, and girandoles, all similarly expensive items, were practically essential, for they served a number of functions in addition to being ornamental. When candles or lamps were placed in front of them, they reflected the light and increased the room's illumination. By the end of the eighteenth century well-to-do citizens were using grand glasses placed between the windows, or "piers" as John Brown did in the new mansion he was just completing in Providence in 1788:

> . . . . On Friday, Mr. Brown gave a smart ball at his home on the hill. Indeed, it will be a most elegant place. We had four rooms lighted up on the second story—one for supper, another for cards, and two for dancing. . . . the rooms are already genteel but will be elegant when finished and furnished. Two of the largest and most elegant mirrors I ever saw ornamented the rooms. Standing in the door which is in the middle of the partition you are just in line with them, so that at the head of the dance you can look down through a variegated crowd of sprightly dancers, . . .[20]

Brown probably obtained some of his pier glasses from abroad, yet magnificent examples of American manufacture were also available. Harrison Gray Otis of Boston and Mrs. Elizabeth Derby of Salem both purchased huge, elegant glasses from John Doggett of Roxbury in the first decade of the nineteenth century, and several of these are known to exist today. As has already been noted, New York manufacturers were copying the most current London fashions, and the pier glass in figure 297 is an excellent example of the finest type made in New York. Of special quality are the reverse painted tablet across the top and the trapezoidal glass surmounted by the carved and gilt eagle at the top. The composition urns on both upper corners and the swagged wire with composition flowers are also characteristic embellishments of New York pier glasses.

A popular alternative to the rectangular pier glass was the circular, convex girandole mirror, which was frequently surrounded with elaborate composition ornaments, flanked with candleholders, and surmounted with an appropriate cresting like the example in figure 298. Although this particular example seems to have been made in New York, it is interesting to note that the label of John Doggett, the Roxbury, Massachusetts, looking-glass manufacturer, illustrated a girandole mirror with intertwined dolphins below, an eagle above, and cascading leafage flowing from the top. A number of New York makers advertised girandoles in the first decade of the nineteenth century, including John Dixey and John Sandford, who called himself a carver and gilder. On the other hand, in 1803 and 1804, William Voight of No. 92 Maiden-lane boasted that he had received "by the latest importations from London and Hamburg, a superb assortment of Looking Glasses, made after the newest London fashion."[21] In 1807 George Smith illustrated several of these grand round "Mirrors" in plates 135A and 136B and noted:

> In apartments where an extensive view offers itself, these Glasses become an elegant and useful ornament, reflecting objects in beautiful perspective on their convex surfaces; the frames, at the same time they form an elegant decoration on the walls, are calculated to support lights . . . . in general, they will admit of being executed in bronze and gold, but will be far more elegant if executed wholly in gold.[22]

Although there is no girandole with sconces for candles depicted in *The Tea Party*, there are several classical candelabra placed about the room to provide illumination. Appropriately, one is positioned on the mantel over the fireplace, in front of a long horizontal chimney glass. While it is difficult to distinguish the specific form of these candelabra, they do seem to be figural with a central, tapering support. Perhaps French or English in origin, they were probably similar to the restrained yet elegant pair of silver candlesticks made in Philadelphia between 1809 and 1812 by the partnership of Simon Chaudron (1758–1846) and Anthony Rasch (1778–1857) (fig. 299). Neoclassic in both the chaste simplicity and the refined classical ornament, these candlesticks are outstanding examples of the finest American silversmithing of the early nineteenth century. Neither Chaudron nor Rasch was a native American, the former having emigrated from Santo Domingo after uprisings there, and the latter having arrived in Philadelphia in 1809 from Hamburg, Germany. Both men must have been familiar with European styles; soon after he began his business in Philadelphia in 1796, Chaudron advertised that he imported French silver. Curiously, while both men continued to work in Philadelphia until 1820, at that time each of them departed to points south, Chaudron to Demopolis, Alabama, and Rasch to New Orleans, Louisiana.

During the three years that Chaudron and Rasch were in partnership, they appear to have produced a limited quantity of extraordinarily high-style neoclassical silver.

297

297. Looking glass, 1790–1810, New York City or possibly Albany, New York. *Pine, gesso, gilt, painted glass. H. 76½ in., W. 33½ in., D. 4½ in. The Henry Francis du Pont Winterthur Museum.*

■ 298. Girandole mirror, 1805–15, probably New York. *Carved pine with gesso and gilt. H. 55 in., W. 33 in. Mr. Edward V. Jones.*

Though Sargent did not illustrate a silver tea service in *The Tea Party,* it would have been appropriate to put in a service like the one in figure 300. Probably the most sophisticated American service of the second decade of the nineteenth century, the service consists of five bulbous-bodied pieces of silver that were made for George Mifflin Dallas (1792–1864) presumably upon his marriage to Sophia Nicklin in 1813 in Philadelphia. Since the Chaudron and Rasch partnership had been terminated by the end of 1812, Dallas probably ordered the service several months prior to his marriage the following year. The body of each piece bears the crest and motto of the Dallas family: a crescent above a heraldic wreath, below and flanking which is a wavy banner with the motto "LUX VENIT AB ALTO" (translated "Light cometh from on high"). The form and decoration of this service are chaste and delicately handled, just like the candlesticks by the same makers. While the whole service is rather unusual for American silver of the period, the most strikingly different form is that of the covered sugar bowl. Raised high above its tripod base, supported on three slender, curved legs terminated by cloven hoofs, and surmounted at the top by ram's heads, this piece seems to have been derived from the late eighteenth-century English "pastille burner" or "cassolette," in which perfume or "sweet gale" (bog myrtle) was burned to produce a fragrant odor.[23] Traditionally these burners were about ten to twelve inches in height, with a small, circular burner fitted into the triangular platform at the base. The source for this form can be seen in Robert Adam's designs and drawings, especially in his work at Osterley Park. A particularly handsome cassolette by Boulton and Fothergill, dated 1779, is in the collection of Temple Newsam, Leeds, England.[24]

Whether or not there would have been any card playing at a formal tea party is difficult to ascertain, but the multitude of tables made specifically for that purpose in the early nineteenth century suggests that it was a popular pastime. We have already seen one of the grandest forms of New York card tables (fig. 286), but figure 301 presents an almost equally grand example. This one is a Philadelphia, lyre-based card table made about 1815. From the striped satinwood banding around the top edge all the way down to the cast brass paw casters, this table provides a panoply of surface textures utilizing brilliant veneers as well as ornate ormolu mounts. The ever-popular lyre motif was also used in Boston for the bases of card tables, but the Philadelphia examples had a very special quality. The fact that this form of card table was not mentioned in the 1811 *Philadelphia Cabinet and Chairmakers Book of Prices* suggests that it did not become popular until later in that decade.

One of the most sophisticated and expensive forms of New York card tables seems to have been what was referred to as "A Veneered Eliptic Pillar and Claw Card Table" in the 1810 edition of *The New-York Revised Prices For Manufacturing Cabinet and Chair Work*

299

301

299. Pair of candlesticks, 1809–12, Philadelphia. *Simon Chaudron (1758–1846) and Anthony Rasch (1778–1857). Silver; marked "CHAUDRON'S & RASCH" on outer edge of each base. H. 12 in., Dia. 5⅝ in. The Henry Francis du Pont Winterthur Museum.*

■ **300. Tea service, 1809–12, Philadelphia.** *Simon Chaudron (1758–1846) and Anthony Rasch (1778–1857). Silver, with wooden handles on teapot and coffee pot; each piece marked on base in banners, "CHAUDRON's & RASCH" and "STER·AMER·MAN"; each piece also engraved with the crest and motto (LUX VENIT AB ALTO) of the Dallas family of Philadelphia. Coffee pot, H. 13 in., W. 12⅝ in.; teapot, H. 10 in., W. 10¾ in.; covered sugar bowl, H. 10⅝ in., Dia. 6 in.; creampot, H. 6⅞ in., W. 5½ in.; waste bowl, H. 6¼ in., Dia. 7¼ in. The Henry Francis du Pont Winterthur Museum.*

301. Card table, ca. 1815, Philadelphia. *Mahogany, with veneers of mahogany, rosewood, satinwood, or birds'-eye maple, brass, ivory, and ormolu mounts. H. 29¼ in., W. 35¾ in., D. 18⅛ in. Private collection.*

302. Card table, ca. 1815, New York. *Attributed to Charles-Honoré Lannuier (1779–1819). Mahogany and mahogany veneer on pine and tulip poplar with brass inlay. H. 29¾ in., W. 36 in., D. 17½ in. Ronald Kane.*

302

(fig. 302). As has already been demonstrated in the case of the New York scroll-back chair, there were variations that could be chosen depending upon how much money the client was willing to spend. This table, which is one of a pair, seems to have almost every feature and embellishment possible. The essential description given for this table in the price book is "Three feet long, the top jointed, clamp'd and slip'd; both sides of each top veneered, or inside lip'd for cloth; the edges banded, 5.8.0." However, if you wanted a "Treble eliptic ditto" as seen on this table, it cost six shillings more. Furthermore, "An eliptic rail veneered, with four flush stumps, a bead or band on lower edge" was an additional fourteen shillings, and to have all that done "treble eliptic" added one pound four shillings to the price. Then, of course, the carving, the brass inlay, and the paw feet and casters would have also cost extra. The quality of workmanship on this table appears to be of the highest order, including the superior carving and the delicate brass inlays, which are also occasionally found on furniture by Charles-Honoré Lannuier.

Another form used for card tables and other types of small tables had a central cluster of four turned and carved columns. The work table in figure 303 is a dazzling example of this form and was constructed entirely of rich satinwood. In 1810 *The New-York Revised Prices for Manufacturing Cabinet and Chair Work* noted the following: "All work made of solid satin, or similar hard/wood, (or that part of any work which is) to be three shillings in the pound extra from mahogany; and all plain veneering with ditto to be one-third extra from the price in the table of veneering; and when panelled with band, or strings one-half extra, for veneering only."[25] Clearly this work table was one of the most expensive versions, and in the 1817 New York price book it would have been called a "Canted Corner Work Table." In this particular instance, instead of having a silk bag below, the enclosed bottom section has what today are called tambour doors and what the early nineteenth-century price books referred to as "enclosing with reeds." This special feature would have cost extra, just as the satinwood, casters, carved legs and columns, and fluted base did. The designation "work table" implied that this form was not only suitable for sewing activities, but when fitted with a writing slide and various compartments, it could also be used for more intellectual pursuits.

While the small marbletop table in figure 304 is related in basic form to the satinwood work table, the overall effect is entirely different, and quite probably they are the work of two distinctly different shops or schools. The slender, elongated vase forms of the columns on the marbletop table are a direct contrast to the short, robust ones of the work table. The carving of the leafage is singularly distinct and does not overlap as on the work table. The mass and weight of the former table make it appear quite different from the springy, delicate quality of the marbletop one. Even the use of carved paw feet instead of brass paw feet affects the overall aesthetic, as well as the cost. Finished on all four sides, this sprightly table might have been used out in a room for mixing or serving drinks, or simply as an occasional table to be pulled up to a chair or sofa when neces-

303   304

303. Work table, 1810–15, New York. *Satinwood and satinwood veneers. H. 31 in., W. 22¾ in., D. 14½ in. Mrs. Jeannette Jones Balling.*

304. Marbletop table, 1810–15, New York. *Charles-Honoré Lannuier (1779–1819). Mahogany and green marble; engraved paper label under top reads: "Honore Lannuier/ Cabinet Maker,/ (From Paris)/ Keeps his Warehouse and Manufactory/ And Cabinet Ware of the Newest Fashion,/ At No. 60 Broad Street./ Honore Lannuier/ Ebeniste/ (De Paris)/ Lient Son Magasin/ De Meubles, Les Plus/ A La Mode,/ Broad Street No. 60/ New York." H. 28¼ in., W. 23¾ in., D. 16¼ in. White House Collection.*

305. Encoignure, or corner table (one of a pair), ca. 1817, New York. *Charles-Honoré Lannuier (1779–1819). Mahogany and mahogany veneers with gilt, paint, and ormolu mounts; one of the pair bears the label of Lannuier. H. 35⅝ in., D. 19⅞ in. Albany Institute of History and Art. Gift of Mrs. Roger E. Hooper.*

306. *Collection des Meubles et Objets de Goût,* **plate 143, published 1804, Paris.** *Pierre La Mésangère (1761–1831). Joseph Downs Manuscript and Microfilm Collection, The Henry Francis du Pont Winterthur Museum.*

305

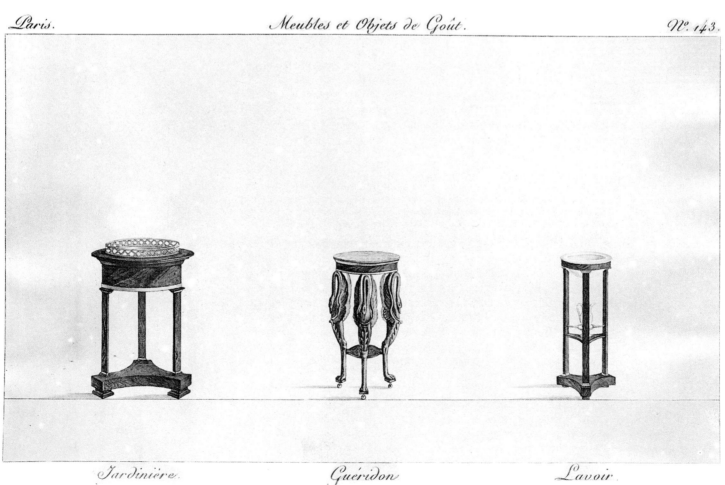

Paris.   *Meubles et Objets de Goût.*   *Nº. 143.*

Jardinière.   *Guéridon.*   *Lavoir.*

306

Secrétaire.   *Secrétaire.*

308

sary. The label "Honore Lannuier/Cabinet Maker,/ (From Paris)," on the underside of the top support of this table may be a clue to distinguishing between the work of Duncan Phyfe and Lannuier. However, the same carvers and other specialized journeymen may have been doing piecework for a number of New York shops.

   Possibly one of the most unusual forms of New York neoclassical furniture is the elegant pole screen in plate 51. Occasionally the English designers used the terms "fire screens" and "pole screens" interchangeably, but customarily fire screens were double-based, rectangular forms. In 1792 Thomas Sheraton illustrated three ornate "Tripod Fire-Screens" in plate 38 of his book and stated that:

> The rods of these screens are all supposed to have a hole through them, and a pulley let in near the top on which the line passes, and a weight being enclosed in the tassel, the screen is balanced to any height. . . . Such screens as have very fine prints, or worked satin, commonly have a glass before them. In which case a frame is made, with a rabbet to receive a glass, and another to receive the straining frame, to prevent it from breaking the glass; and to enclose the straining frame a bead is mitered round.[26]

This particular screen is fitted with a charming piece of worked satin enclosed in an oval, but it moves up and down the pole by means of a metal clamp and not an intricate pulley system. The base of the tripod stand is composed of a platform with a carved pineapple—as is sometimes found on cluster-column card tables—and three reeded, tapered scrolls, similar to elements of scroll-back chairs. The turned and carved base of the pole, which is supported by the three scrolls, is reminiscent of sections of the columns of the preceding marbletop table. The fluting around the base of the pole is another common characteristic found around the bases of numerous tables in this style. Curiously, this pole screen embodies many of the characteristic elements of other objects combined together to result in a successful and interesting composition.

307

   The introduction and persistence of the neoclassical style in America witnessed the creation of many new and unusual forms in the country's useful arts. While these objects at first seem unprecedented in many instances, upon close examination an English or continental source for almost everything can be found. The idea of a suite of three tables, a central pier table and two flanking corner tables, was not common in America, but in the early nineteenth century several of these suites were made in

307. Corner table (one of a pair), 1790–1810, Baltimore. *Possibly by Hugh and John Finlay (w. 1800–1837). Mahogany with satinwood inlay, painted gilt decoration, églomisé glass panel, marble top. H. 37 in., W. 21½ in., D. 21½ in. The Maryland Historical Society, Baltimore.*

308. Collections des Meubles et Objects de Goût, plate 563, published 1823, Paris. *Pierre La Mésangère (1761–1831). Joseph Downs Manuscript Collection. The Henry Francis du Pont Winterthur Museum.*

different geographical regions. One of the most ambitious examples of this form (fig. 305) was ordered by Stephen Van Rensselaer IV, who in 1817 built a house in Albany for his new bride Harriet Elizabeth Bayard. The most unusual features of this suite of three tables are the very dramatic supports, which are swans deeply arched necks. While the English designer George Smith used some swan motifs for things like armchair supports, the most direct source for the swan supports chosen by Charles-Honoré Lannuier for the Van Rensselaer suite is found in La Mésangère's plate 143, published in 1804 (fig. 306). The central piece in this plate is a "Gueridon" with three grand swan supports, the bases of which terminate in paw feet. The similarity to Lannuier's swans is remarkable; again he must have been familiar with the plates in *Collection des Meubles et Objets de Goût*. The corner tables in this suite seem angular except when viewed from a side perspective; seen from the side, the deep curves of the swan's neck and the paw foot are captured and echoed in the mirrors set at right angles and facing in, under the top section. Exquisitely carved, and with gilt and painted decoration, these swans are closely related to the winged female supports of other labeled Lannuier card tables.

Pairs of corner tables with matching pier tables were also produced in the Baltimore area, though probably in quite limited numbers, as was also true in New York. However, the Baltimore ones, while slightly earlier in date, are very different from the New York examples in overall form and aesthetic character. The corner table in figure 307 is very light and delicate in all of its elements, with the only real mass or weight coming from the marble top. With turned legs and sprightly arched stretchers, this table has a combined ornament of inlay, veneer, gilt decoration, and a finely painted glass panel set in the central portion of the skirt. This style of decoration was definitely part of the repertoire of the famed school of Baltimore ornamental painters, and this table and its mate might even have come from the shop of John and Hugh Finlay of Baltimore. While there is no surviving pier table with these corner tables, similar tables do exist, and in fact one of those tables was exhibited in the 1929 exhibition. Though Baltimore could very well have been the source of these tables, recent scholarship has built an equally strong case for tables of this type coming from the Philadelphia shop of Joseph B. Barry.[27] In 1803 Barry published an advertisement in Baltimore that remains the only known American reference to matching pier and corner tables. With shops in both Philadelphia and Baltimore, Barry might have been making things in Philadelphia and taking, or importing, them to Baltimore.

Finally, among the new and totally foreign forms that were adopted on this side of the Atlantic was the *secrétaire*, popularized through La Mésangère's designs. Presumably produced in most of the major style centers, the *secrétaire* in its American interpretation is just now being discovered and fully recognized. In the nineteenth century the cabinetmakers and patrons of Philadelphia seem to have embraced this form wholly in the French manner. Plate 563 (fig. 308) shows two of La Mésangère's 1823 designs, which appear to be very massive and almost architectural. Although the form of this desk is exceedingly bold and essentially a large rectangular box, the ingenious cabinetmaker, using a judicious selection of veneers, bandings, and ormolu mounts, can redefine and ornament the facade so as to create an exciting and sophisticated object, as demonstrated in plate 52. Probably made in Philadelphia, this American *secrétaire*, with its rosewood veneers, ebonized sides, cut brass inlay, a white marble top, and ormolu mounts, is a rival to any French production.

Although great advances have been made over the past few decades in what we know about the early nineteenth century, there still remains much to be explored and discovered. We have gone beyond the Phyfe myth, and we have recognized numerous valuable design sources, but more work has yet to be accomplished in the subject of regional distinctions and more must be learned about the various makers and specialized craftsmen. The southern and the western reaches of our country were realizing tremendous growth at that time, and both exportation of goods and movement of craftsmen out of the northeast must have had a great effect on production in newly settled areas. The kind of insights gleaned from Sargent's *The Tea Party* must now be sought out in the smaller works of lesser artists, in less sophisticated geographical areas. Sargent's and Krimmel's paintings are rare documents, but as pieces to the puzzle of our history keep being discovered, our knowledge will increase, and the endless search for a total pictorial understanding of the culture of our past will go on.

Introduction

1. Transcript of verbatim minutes, Board of Directors Meeting, April 17, 1929, Library and Archives, Girl Scouts of the United States of America, p. 281.
2. Ibid.
3. Charles F. Montgomery, "Classics and Collectibles: American Antiques as History and Art," *Art News* 76, no. 9 (1977): 129.
4. Unpublished letter to the author from Mrs. Edmund B. Ross, grand-daughter of Mrs. J. Amory Haskell.
5. Dianne H. Pilgrim, "Inherited from the Past: The American Period Room," *The American Art Journal* 10, no. 1 (May 1978): 14–15.
6. The Collection of Luke Burnell Lockwood (son of Luke V. Lockwood), New Leaf Associates, Greenwich, Conn., Sept. 29 and 30 and Oct. 1, 1978.
7. Marshall B. Davidson, "Those American Things," *Metropolitan Museum Journal* 3 (1970): 228.
8. Richard H. Saunders III, "American Decorative Arts Collecting in New England, 1840–1920" (M.A. thesis, The Winterthur Program, University of Delaware, 1973).
9. George Sheldon, "Note to Visitors," *Catalogue of the Collection of Relics in Memorial Hall*, 3rd ed. (Deerfield, Mass.: Pocumtuck Valley Memorial Association, 1920), n.p.
10. Charles F. Montgomery, "Some Remarks on the Science and Principles of Connoisseurship," *Walpole Society Notebook*, 1961, pp. 7–20.
11. The culmination of this research (funded by the National Endowment for the Humanities) will be a major travelling exhibition, "New England Begins, 1630–1720," opening in 1982 at the Museum of Fine Arts, Boston, accompanied by an important two-volume catalogue.

Chapter One

1. Houghton Bulkeley, *Contributions to Connecticut Cabinetmaking* (Bloomfield, Conn.: Connecticut Historical Society, 1967), pp. 12–13.
2. Irving Whitall Lyon, M.D., *The Colonial Furniture of New England* (Boston and New York: Houghton Mifflin, 1924), p. 121, fig. 50.
3. Bulkeley, pp. 28–33.
4. This sideboard is now owned by the Wadsworth Atheneum, Hartford, Conn. See Phillip Johnston, "Eighteenth- and Nineteenth-Century American Furniture in the Wadsworth Atheneum," *Antiques* 115, no. 5 (1979): pl. 9.
5. Patricia E. Kane, "The Seventeenth-Century Furniture of the Connecticut Valley: The Hadley Chest Reappraised," in *Arts of the Anglo-American Community in the Seventeenth Century*, ed. Ian M. G. Quimby, Winterthur Conference Report 1974 (Charlottesville: University Press of Virginia, 1974), pp. 79–122.
6. Homer Eaton Keyes, "Cobwebs & Dust," *Antiques* 2, no. 5 (November 1922): 201.
7. Walter A. Dyer, "John Goddard and His Block-Fronts," *Antiques* 1, no. 5 (1922): 203–8.
8. Transcript of verbatim minutes, Board of Directors Meeting, April 17, 1929, Library and Archives, Girl Scouts of the United States of America, p. 286.
9. It is believed that this is one of Lannuier's earliest engraved labels—further evidence for the table's having been made shortly after his arrival in this country.
10. La Mésangère's plate 348, published in 1811, has a related swan mount on a "Vide Poche," and plate 360, published in 1812, shows a bed with the sunburst medallion mount.
11. The 1964 Winterthur M.A. thesis *New York Cabinetmaking Prior to the Revolution* by J. Stewart Johnson explored the Delaplane family in particular; a 1977 Winterthur M.A. thesis (incomplete) by Neil D. Kamil is exploring New York William and Mary furniture.
12. Katharine G. Farnham, "The John Fulton Sideboard and Knifeboxes," *Bulletin of the Friends of the Decorative Arts*, The High Museum of Art, Atlanta, Fall 1977, pp. 20–24.
13. In the 1805-6 New York directory there is a listing for a William Whitehead, shipmaster, 445 Pearl Street. Could this be the same man? Also of interest is an inventory in the Downs Manuscript Collection (Winterthur Museum) dated August 9, 1806, of one Rubin Paddack, taken and signed in the presence of "Mical" Allison (presumably the cabinetmaker) and others. Appended to this inventory, dated January 19, 1807, is a notation that "There is an unsettled Acct. between this Estate and Capt. William Whitehead who was in Partnership with Rubin Paddack in several voyages to the West Indies—Whitehead says that Paddack's Estate will have nothing coming from this Partnership and that it is largely indebted to him." If this is the same Whitehead as our cabinetmaker, or a son or relative, was there a coastwise furniture trade going here, and how was "Mical" Allison involved in the whole thing?
14. Mr. du Pont did not purchase this desk directly at the Philip Flayderman Sale (American Art Association–Anderson Gallery, January 2–4, 1930, Lot 451) but rather several months later from a noted dealer, Collings and Collings.
15. One of the most notable Seymour bills is the one that documents the grand half-round commode ordered by Mrs. Derby in 1809 and now in the M. and M. Karolik Collection, Museum of Fine Arts, Boston. See Edwin J. Hipkiss, "A Cabinetmaker's Bill," *Museum of Fine Arts, Boston, Bulletin* 45, no. 259 (Feb. 1947), pp. 12–14.
16. *Paul Revere's Boston: 1735–1818* (Boston: Museum of Fine Arts, 1975), p. 180, fig. 271.
17. Page Talbott, "Boston Empire Furniture, Part I," *Antiques* 107, no. 5 (1975): 881. For further discussions of Boston Empire cabinetmakers see also Page Talbott, "Boston Empire Furniture, Part II," *Antiques* 109, no. 5 (1976): 1004–13.
18. Dyer, p. 207.
19. Joseph K. Ott, *The John Brown House Loan Exhibition of Rhode Island Furniture* (Providence: Rhode Island Historical Society, 1965), p. 40, fig. 34.
20. Sotheby Parke Bernet, Inc., New York, Sale 3215, May 22, 1971, Lot 199.
21. Ralph E. Carpenter, Jr., *The Arts and Crafts of Newport, Rhode Island* (Newport: The Preservation of Newport County, 1954), p. 9.
22. Ott, fig. 40.
23. Stanley Stone, "Documented Newport Furniture: A John Goddard Desk and John Townsend Document Cabinet in the Collection of Mr. and Mrs. Stanley Stone," *Antiques* 103, no. 2 (1973): 319–21.
24. Israel Sack, Inc., *American Antiques from Israel Sack Collection*, vol. 3, (Washington, D.C.: Highland House, 1972), pp. 732–33.
25. R. Peter Mooz, "The Origins of Newport Block-front Furniture Design," *Antiques* 99, no. 6 (1971): 882–86.
26. Two more chairs from this group are in the Bayou Bend Collection, Museum of Fine Arts, Houston, Texas; one is also in the collection of the Henry Francis du Pont Winterthur Museum.
27. Charles F. Montgomery, *American Furniture: The Federal Period* (New York: Viking, 1966), p. 107, fig. 53.
28. *Paul Revere's Boston*, p. 229, fig. 267.
29. Montgomery, p. 96.
30. For a discussion of an eighteenth-century Philadelphia price book see Martin Eli Weil, "A Cabinetmaker's Price Book," *Winterthur Portfolio 13* (Chicago and London: University of Chicago Press, 1979), pp. 175–92.
31. For an extensive discussion of the labeled Randolph side chairs see John T. Kirk, *American Chairs, Queen Anne and Chippendale* (New York: Alfred A. Knopf, 1972), pp. 172–74.
32. From March 14–April 30, 1978, the Virginia Museum of Fine Arts and the Colonial Williamsburg Foundation co-sponsored an exhibition in Richmond entitled "Furniture of Eastern Virginia: The Product of Mind and Hand." As a result of that research and project, Wallace B. Gusler published the book *Furniture of Williamsburg and Eastern Virginia 1710–1790* (Richmond: Virginia Museum, 1979). See pp. 75–79.
33. Bradford L. Rauschenberg, "Two Outstanding Virginia Chairs," *Journal of Early Southern Decorative Arts* 2, no. 2 (November 1976): 1–23.
34. Gilbert T. Vincent, "The Bombé Furniture of Boston," in *Boston Furniture of the Eighteenth Century*, ed. Walter Muir Whitehill (Boston: Colonial Society of Massachusetts, 1974), pp. 176–79.
35. Edwin J. Hipkiss, *Eighteenth-Century Arts, The M. and M. Karolik Collection* (Boston: Harvard University Press, 1950), pp. 60–61.
36. I would like to thank Robert Sack for sharing his research in the Essex Institute manuscript collections with me.
37. Nancy A. Goyne, "Francis Trumble of Philadelphia: Windsor Chair and Cabinetmaker," *Winterthur Portfolio 1* (Winterthur, Del.: Henry Francis du Pont Winterthur Museum, 1964), pp. 221–42.
38. Rita Susswein Gottesman, *The Arts and Crafts in New York 1777–1799* (New York: New-York Historical Society, 1954), p. 123, no. 386.
39. This is the case with the tall clock whose dial is inscribed "Warranted for Mr. Joshua Seaver/ 1806/ Aaron Willard/ Boston" and cited in *Paul Revere's Boston: 1735–1818*, p. 183, fig. 277.
40. For further information about the Willards' fellow craftsmen see Alice Knotts Bossert Cooney, "Ornamental Painting in Boston, 1790–1830" (M.A. thesis, The Winterthur Program, University of Delaware, 1978).

41. Mantle Fielding, *Catalogue of Exhibition of Portraits by John Neagle* (Philadelphia: Pennsylvania Academy of the Fine Arts, 1925), p. 10.

42. Henry J. Kauffman, "Pennsylvania Locks Made by the Rohrer Family," *Spinning Wheel Magazine*, 21, nos. 7–8 (July–August 1965): 11–12. This article begins to pinpoint makers and opens the way for future research.

43. For an illustration of this pair of pipe tongs see the *Bulletin for the Society of the Preservation of New England Antiquities* 59, no. 1 (Summer 1968): 25.

44. Richard H. Randall, Jr., "Benjamin Gerrish, Brazier," *Antiques* 85, no. 3 (1964): 320–21.

45. Charles F. Montgomery and Gerald W. R. Ward, "Iron Candlestands: Made Where, When and by Whom?" *Antiques* 112, no. 2 (1977): 282–84, fig. 2.

46. John Bivins, Jr., "Decorative Cast Iron on the Virginia Frontier," *Antiques* 101, no. 3 (1972): 535–39, fig. 9.

47. Robert Greenhalgh Albion and Leonidas Dodson, eds., *Philip Vickers Fithian: Journal, 1775–76* (Princeton: Princeton University Press, 1934), pp. 14–15.

48. George Francis Dow, *The Arts and Crafts in New England 1704–1775* (1927; reprint ed., New York: Da Capo, 1967), p. 226.

49. Ibid., p. 228.

50. I would like to thank Dean F. Failey for calling my attention to the inventory of William Taylor and for sharing it with me. This inventory is located in the Queens College Historic Documents Collection, Queens College, Flushing, New York.

51. Nicholas B. Wainwright, *Colonial Grandeur in Philadelphia: The House and Furniture of General John Cadwalader* (Philadelphia: Historical Society of Pennsylvania, 1964), p. 37.

52. James R. Mitchell, "Marked American Andirons Made Before 1840" (M.A. thesis, The Winterthur Program, University of Delaware, 1965).

53. An important and interesting documented example of Rollinson's work is on a large presentation punch bowl by Hugh Wishart, ca. 1799, which recently sold at auction. See Sotheby Parke Bernet, New York, Sale 4268, June 20–23, 1979, Lot 102.

54. Wainwright, p. 38. It is interesting to note that Cadwalader paid King just four shillings less than he paid Peale for painting the marvelous 1771 portrait of himself with his wife and infant daughter.

55. The Hendricks papers are in the manuscript collections of the New-York Historical Society. I wish to thank Charles F. Hummel, Winterthur Museum, for calling my attention to this information.

56. *Philadelphia, Three Centuries of American Art* (Philadelphia: Philadelphia Museum of Art, 1976), p. 79.

57. Rupert Gentle and Rachael Feild, *English Domestic Brass, 1680–1810* (New York: E. P. Dutton, 1975), p. 163, fig. 212.

58. Arlene M. Palmer, "Glass Production in Eighteenth-Century America: The Wistarburgh Enterprises," *Winterthur Portfolio 11* (Charlottesville: University Press of Virginia, 1976), pp. 75–101.

59. Ibid., p. 86.

60. Ibid., p. 92.

61. *Journal of Glass Studies*, Corning Museum of Glass, vol. 18 (1976). This entire special bicentennial issue is devoted to the discussion of Amelung and his work, and it is a major contribution to twentieth-century glass scholarship.

62. Kenneth Wilson, *New England Glass and Glassmaking* (Sturbridge, Mass.: Old Sturbridge Village, 1972), p. 198.

63. *Journal of Glass Studies*, vol. 18, p. 17.

64. Graham S. Hood, "Career of Andrew Duché," *Art Quarterly* 31, no. 2 (Summer 1968): 168–84.

65. Ibid., p. 170.

66. *South Carolina Gazette* (Charleston), October 11, 1770.

67. Ibid., April 11, 1774.

68. Graham Hood, *Bonnin and Morris of Philadelphia; The First American Porcelain Manufactory, 1770–1772* (Chapel Hill, N.C.: University of North Carolina Press, 1972), p. 11.

69. Ibid., p. 13.

70. Sotheby Parke Bernet, Sale 4103, April 1, 1978, Lot 28.

71. I am indebted to Gary and Diana Stradling for their thoughts on this piece of stoneware.

72. Susan H. Myers, "Handcraft to Industry: Philadelphia Ceramics in the First Half of the Nineteenth Century" (M.A. thesis, George Washington University, 1977).

73. Phillip H. Curtis, "Tucker Porcelain, 1826–1838: A Reappraisal" (M.A. thesis, The Winterthur Program, University of Delaware, 1972), pp. 4–5.

74. Ibid., p. 10.

75. Curtis, "Tucker Porcelain."

76. Lowell Innes, *Pittsburgh Glass, 1797–1891* (Boston: Houghton Mifflin, 1976), pp. 17–19.

77. Again I am indebted to the Stradlings for this information and insight into Vowdrey since they are currently involved with the transcription of his diary and are doing further research on him.

78. Laura Woodside Watkins, "Henderson of Jersey City and His Pitchers," *Antiques* 50, no. 12 (1946): 388–92.

79. I would like to thank Ms. Arlene Palmer for sharing her research on early lustrewares and for pointing out this newspaper reference.

80. *Philadelphia: Three Centuries of American Art*, pp. 247–48.

81. Newark Museum, *The Pottery and Porcelain of New Jersey, 1688–1900* (Newark, N.J.: Newark Museum, 1947), p. 15.

Chapter Two

1. Brock W. Jobe, "The Boston Furniture Industry, 1720–1740," in *Boston Furniture of the Eighteenth Century*, ed. Walter Muir Whitehill (Boston: Colonial Society of Massachusetts, 1974), p. 24.

2. John Ash, *The New and Complete Dictionary of the English Language*, vol. 2 (London: Printed for Edward and Charles Dilly in the Poultry; and R. Baldwin in Pater-Noster Row, 1775), s.v. "upholsterer."

3. Robert Campbell, *The London Tradesman* (1747: reprint ed., London: David & Charles, 1967), pp. 169–70.

4. *Colonial Furniture: The Reifsnyder Collection*, American Art Association, April 24–27, 1929, Lot 674.

5. Wendy Ann Cooper, "American Chippendale Double-Chairback Settees," *American Art Journal* 9, no. 2 (November 1977): 34–35.

6. *Important Early American Cabinetwork from the Estate of the Late Mrs. Charles Hallam Keep*, Parke Bernet Galleries, October 19, 1963, Lot 183.

7. Louis Guerineau Myers, ed., *Girl Scouts Loan Exhibition* (New York: American Art Galleries, 1929), no. 617.

8. Homer Eaton Keyes, "The Editor's Attic," *Antiques* 16, no. 5 (November 1929): 363.

9. Raymond V. Shepherd, Jr., "Cliveden and Its Philadelphia Chippendale Furniture: A Documented History," *American Art Journal* 8, no. 2 (November 1976): 6–7.

10. Thomas Sheraton, *The Cabinet-Maker and Upholsterer's Drawing-Book* (1794; reprint ed., New York: Praeger, 1970), pl. 35 and p. 388.

11. Joseph Downs, *American Furniture: Queen Anne and Chippendale Periods* (New York: Viking, 1952), figs. 16 and 18.

12. Edwin S. Hipkiss, *Eighteenth-Century American Arts: The M. and M. Karolik Collection, Museum of Fine Arts, Boston* (Cambridge: Harvard University Press, 1950), fig. 14.

13. Thomas Sheraton, *The Cabinet Dictionary* (1803; reprint ed., New York: Praeger, 1970), pl. 8 and p. 19.

14. In the fall of 1977 the Furniture History Society of England held a one-day symposium in London on eighteenth-century upholstery practices, and in March 1979, the Decorative Arts Society of the Society of Architectural Historians co-sponsored a similar four-day meeting with the Museum of Fine Arts, Boston and Old Sturbridge Village. The proceedings from that symposium are scheduled for publication in the near future. See also Peter Thornton, "Upholstered Evidence," *Furniture History* 10 (1974): 17–19; and Peter Thornton, "Fringe Benefits," *Connoisseur* 196, no. 787 (September 1977): 2.

15. Nicholas B. Wainwright, *Colonial Grandeur in Philadelphia: The House and Furniture of General John Cadwalader* (Philadelphia: Historical Society of Pennsylvania, 1964), pp. 40–43.

16. Percy MacQuoid and Ralph Edwards, *The Dictionary of English Furniture*, vol. 2 (London: Charles Scribner & Sons, 1924), p. 160 and pl. 7.

17. Ibid., p. 159, fig. 3.

18. Robert F. Trent, "The Endicott Chairs," *Essex Institute Historical Collections* 114, no. 2 (April 1978): 115. See also Richard H. Saunders III, "Collecting American Decorative Arts in New England, Part I, 1793–1876," *Antiques* 109, no. 5 (May 1976): 1000, pl. 2.

19. William Bentley, *The Diary of William Bentley, D.D., Pastor of the East Church, Salem, Massachusetts* (Salem, Mass.: Essex Institute, 1905–1914), 4 (1914): 594–95.

20. Robert F. Trent, "A History of the Essex Institute Turkey Work Couch," *Essex Institute Historical Collections* 113, no. 1 (January 1977): 29–37.

21. A major documentary study of seventeenth-century New England is now being compiled by Boston University and the Museum of Fine Arts, Boston. The study, which is funded by a grant from the National

Endowment for the Humanities, will culminate in a major exhibition in Boston in 1982.

22. Trent, "Endicott Chairs," p. 104.

23. Ibid., p. 105.

24. Ibid., pp. 105–6.

25. Two other closely related chairs are located in the collections of the Smithtown Historical Society, Smithtown, New York, and the Munson-Williams-Proctor Institute, Utica, New York.

26. Thomas Fitch letter book, New England Historic Genealogical Society, February 8, 1714/1715, Thomas Fitch to Madam Hooglant, n.p. I wish to thank Benno M. Forman, Winterthur Museum, for sharing with me his research notes on the Thomas Fitch and Samuel Grant accounts.

27. Thomas Fitch account book, 1719–1732, Massachusetts Historical Society, p. 84.

28. Brock W. Jobe, "The Boston Furniture Industry, 1725–1760" (M.A. thesis, The Winterthur Program, University of Delaware, 1976), p. 42.

29. Ibid.

30. Again, I would like to thank Benno M. Forman for sharing with me his recent research and observations on the subject of New York chairs.

31. Richard Randall, "Boston Chairs," Old Time New England 54, no. 1 (July 1963): 12–20, fig. 4.

32. An M.A. thesis on New York seventeenth-century and William and Mary styles by Neil D. Kamil is currently in preparation for the Winterthur Program, University of Delaware.

33. Fitch account book, p. 217.

34. Randall, pp. 12–14.

35. Jobe, "Boston Furniture Industry," p. 39.

36. Fitch account book, p. 80.

37. William MacPherson Hornor, Blue Book of Philadelphia Furniture (1935; reprint ed., Washington, D.C.: Highland House, 1977), p. 191.

38. Inventory of Thomas Nevett, 1749, Dorchester County Probate Records, Liber 40, pp. 350–92, Hall of Records, Annapolis, Maryland.

39. Inventory of John Scott, 1750, Dorchester County Probate Records, Liber 44, p. 304, Hall of Records, Annapolis, Maryland.

40. Wendy Kaplan, "Catalogue Entry for the Williams Room Easy Chair (58.1504)," (research paper, The Winterthur Program, University of Delaware, May 1978).

41. For a list of repositories where Fitch and Grant materials may be located, see Jobe, "Boston Furniture Industry, 1720–1740," in Boston Furniture of the Eighteenth Century, p. 27, n. 45.

42. Samuel Grant account book, July 10, 1731, Massachusetts Historical Society, p. 106.

43. I am indebted to Donald L. Peirce of the Brooklyn Museum for calling my attention to this letter in the museum files.

44. David B. Warren, Bayou Bend: American Furniture, Paintings and Silver from the Bayou Bend Collection (Houston: Museum of Fine Arts, 1975), pp. 50–51, pl. 90.

45. Wendell D. Garrett, "Providence Cabinetmakers, Chairmakers, Upholsterers, and Allied Craftsmen, 1756–1838: A Checklist," Antiques 90, no. 4 (October 1966): 516.

46. The Cabinet-makers' Philadelphia and London Book of Prices (Philadelphia: Snowden and M'Corkle, 1796), p. 133.

47. Account of John Relfe with Plunket Fleeson, April 13, 1764, John Carter Brown Library, Brown University, Providence, quoted in Wendy A. Cooper, "The Purchase of Furniture and Furnishings by John Brown, Providence Merchant: Part I, 1760–1788," Antiques 103, no. 2 (February 1973): 329, fig. 4.

48. Wendy A. Cooper, "The Furniture and Furnishings of John Brown, Merchant of Providence, 1736–1803" (M.A. thesis, The Winterthur Program, University of Delaware, 1971), p. 24.

49. Wainwright, pp. 40–43.

50. Six chairs from this set are known to exist today: Two are at the Brooklyn Museum, two at the Museum of Fine Arts, Boston, and two at the Historic Deerfield Foundation.

51. Though not mentioned in this comparison, there are numerous similarities between Newport and New York chairs of this style. Clearly what is needed is a thorough study of the interrelationships between these two busy commercial centers, especially with respect to trade and social relationships, in the mid-eighteenth century.

52. Ralph E. Carpenter, Jr., The Arts and Crafts of Newport, Rhode Island 1640–1820 (Newport, R.I.: Preservation Society of Newport County, 1954), p. 37, fig. 11.

53. George G. Channing, Early Recollections of Newport, Rhode Island (Newport: A. J. Ward; Charles E. Hammett, Jr., 1868), pp. 251–52.

54. Wallace B. Gusler, Furniture of Williamsburg and Eastern Virginia 1710–1790 (Richmond: Virginia Museum, 1979), p. 143, fig. 98.

55. Note that an eighteenth-century reference to "canvas" as a chair covering most probably meant linen, as canvas was first of all defined as "a coarse unbleached cloth made of hemp or flax."

56. Wainwright, p. 41.

57. Florence M. Montgomery, Printed Textiles, English and American Cottons and Linens 1700–1850 (New York: Viking, 1970), fig. 214.

58. Ibid., p. 78.

59. Conover Hunt-Jones, Dolley and the "Great Little Madison," (Washington, D.C.: American Institute of Architects Foundation, 1977), pp. 90–95. See also H. M. Fede, Washington Furniture at Mount Vernon (Mount Vernon: Mount Vernon Ladies' Association of the Union, 1966), pp. 34–35.

60. The original bill for the account of Andrew Craigie, Esqr., with Nalbro and Frazier of Philadelphia, dated July 9, 1793, is in the American Antiquarian Society, Worcester, Massachusetts.

Chapter Three

1. John Hill Morgan, "Address on Copley to Walpole Society," in Walpole Society Notebook, 1939, p. 1.

2. Copley-Pelham Letters, Massachusetts Historical Society Collections, 71 (1914): 97.

3. Ibid., p. 35.

4. Ibid., p. 41.

5. This painting was shown in a 1975–76 exhibition at Hirschl and Adler Galleries, New York, and published in the catalogue for the show entitled American Portraits by John Singleton Copley.

6. Copley, Stuart and West in America (Boston: Museum of Fine Arts, 1976), p. 21.

7. In 1761 Revere made a similar salver for Sarah Tyng, now in the Fogg Art Museum, Harvard University, Cambridge, Mass., and another one for Lucretia Chandler, which is now in the Museum of Fine Arts, Boston. See Kathryn C. Buhler, American Silver in the Museum of Fine Arts, Boston, 1655–1825, vol. 2 (Boston: Museum of Fine Arts, 1973), pp. 394–95, figs. 344 and 345.

8. I am indebted to Kathryn C. Buhler for this information and for sharing with me the unpublished manuscript of her catalogue of the silver collection of the Paul Revere Insurance Company.

9. This teapot is also in the collection of the Museum of Fine Arts, Boston. See Buhler, American Silver, vol. 1, pp. 377–78.

10. Philadelphia, Three Centuries of American Art (Philadelphia: Philadelphia Museum of Art, 1976), pp. 151–52, fig. 120.

11. I am indebted to Deborah Dependahl Waters, Winterthur Museum, for this information. See also Deborah D. Waters, "A Closer Look—Elegance in the Dining Room," Winterthur Newsletter 24, no. 6 (November 1978): 5–6.

12. Katharine Morrison McClinton, "Fletcher and Gardiner, Silversmiths of the American Empire," Connoisseur 173, no. 697 (March 1970), p. 221, fig. 15.

13. The Oxford English Dictionary (Oxford: Oxford University Press, 1970), 6: 633, cites the following derivation for the term "monteith": "1683 Wood Life Dec. (O.H.S.) III. 84 This year . . . came up a vessel or bason notched at the brim to let drinking glasses hang there by the foot so that the body or drinking place might hang in the water to cool them . . . Such a bason was called a 'Monteigh,' from a fantastical Scot called 'Monsieur Monteigh,' who at that time or a little before wore the bottome of his cloake or coate so notched. . . ."

14. I would like to thank Mrs. Margaret Hubbard of the Franklin Delano Roosevelt Library at Hyde Park for bringing to my attention an unpublished letter containing this information, sent to George Roach from Bruce T. McCully, Department of History, College of William and Mary, June 29, 1951. Photostats of the Samuel Vetch manuscripts are now in the collection of the New-York Historical Society.

15. Nina Fletcher Little, Paintings by New England Provincial Artists: 1775–1800 (Boston: Museum of Fine Arts, 1976), p. 162.

16. George Francis Dow, ed., The Holyoke Diaries 1709–1856 (Salem, Mass.: Essex Institute, 1911).

17. Ibid., p. ix.

18. There exists a small group of similarly related objects in the William and Mary style having side flanking pilasters and presumably made in northeastern Massachusetts, see figure 244.

19. W. Nicholas Dudley, "Nicholas Sever's Plate Returns to Harvard," *The American Collector* 2, no. 1 (June 1934): 3, 8.

20. Phillip H. Hammerslough, *American Silver Collected by Phillip H. Hammerslough*, vol. 2 (Hartford, Conn.: privately printed, 1960), p. 86a.

21. Diary of Samuel Sewall, July 1701, quoted in *American Art at Harvard* (Cambridge, Mass.: Fogg Art Museum, Harvard University, 1972), fig. 173.

22. Clifford K. Shipton, ed., *Sibley's Harvard Graduates*, vol. 6 (Boston: Massachusetts Historical Society, 1942), p. 581.

23. E. Alfred Jones, *The Old Silver of American Churches* (Letchworth, England: The Arden Press, 1913), p. 146, pl. 53.

24. These remarkable candlesticks were discovered after the publication in 1940 of Ledlie Irwin Laughlin's *Pewter in America: Its Makers and Their Marks* (Boston: Houghton Mifflin). They are included, however, in the volume 3, published in 1971 by Barre Publishers, Barre, Massachusetts.

25. This significant account book, kept by Henry Will between 1763 and 1793, was owned in recent years in Charleston, South Carolina, and is now in the collection of the Museum of Early Southern Decorative Arts, Winston-Salem, North Carolina. A microfiche copy is in the Joseph Downs Manuscript Collection, Winterthur Museum.

26. Thomas Hamilton Ormsbee, "Three Pieces Show Gostelowe's Individuality," *The American Collector* 1, no. 13 (June 14, 1934): 3, 5.

27. Stephen P. Dorsey, *Early Churches in America 1607-1807* (New York: Oxford University Press, 1952), p. 135.

28. *Philadelphia: Three Centuries of American Art*, pp. 152-153, fig. 121.

29. One possible answer to this mystery is provided by Colonial Williamsburg's records, which show that in 1928 the chair was sent to New York for restoration, probably under the care of Louis G. Myers. Perhaps he decided to use it in the exhibition simply to fill a vacant spot in the corridor before returning it to Williamsburg.

30. Wallace B. Gusler, *Furniture of Williamsburg and Eastern Virginia 1710-1790* (Richmond: Virginia Museum, 1979), pp. 70-71.

31. Ibid., p. 61.

32. Ibid., pp. 92-95 and p. 56, n. 21. See also Bradford L. Rauschenberg, "Two Outstanding Virginia Chairs," *Journal of Early Southern Decorative Arts* 2, no. 2 (November 1976): 1-23.

33. Anderson Galleries, *George S. Palmer Collection Removed from Westomere, New London with Additions from the Collection of I. Sack*, Sale 2280, October 18-20, 1928, Lot 209.

34. Dwight P. Lanmon and Arlene M. Palmer, "John Frederick Amelung and The New Bremen Glassmanufactory," *Journal of Glass Studies* 18 (1976): 32.

35. Ibid., pp. 104-5.

36. "The Pickman Silver, Deposited with the Essex Institute December, 1902," *Essex Institute Historical Collections* 39, no. 2 (April 1903): 97-120.

37. Mantle Fielding and John Hill Morgan, *The Life Portraits of Washington and their Replicas* (Philadelphia: privately printed, 1931), p. xix.

38. A similar situation is evident in Copley's portrait of Mr. and Mrs. Isaac Winslow, now at the Museum of Fine Arts, Boston. A recent cleaning and restoration has revealed an earlier and original costume on Mrs. Winslow. The later style dress, long thought to be original, was probably added in England after the painting was taken there sometime before 1800. Copley himself may have made the change.

39. William S. Thomas, M.D., *The Society of the Cincinnati 1783-1935* (New York: G. P. Putnam's Sons, 1935). See this source for additional information on the Order of the Cincinnati.

40. John C. Milley, *Faces of Independence: Portrait Gallery Guidebook* (Phila.: Eastern National Park and Monument Association, 1974), pp. 2-3.

41. Michael Clayton, *The Collector's Dictionary of the Silver and Gold of Great Britain and North America* (Middlesex, England: Hamlyn Publishing Group, 1971), p. 129.

42. Harold E. Dickson, *John Wesley Jarvis 1780-1840, American Painter* (New York: New-York Historical Society, 1949),fig. 22.

43. Donald L. Fennimore, "Elegant Patterns of Uncommon Good Taste: Domestic Silver by Thomas Fletcher and Sidney Gardiner" (M.A. thesis, The Winterthur Program, University of Delaware, 1972).

44. Elizabeth Ingerman Wood, "Thomas Fletcher, A Philadelphia Entrepreneur of Presentation Silver," *Winterthur Portfolio 3* (Charlottesville: The University Press of Virginia, 1967), pp. 136-71.

45. Jennifer Faulds Goldsborough, *18th and 19th Century Maryland Silver in the Collection of the Baltimore Museum of Art* (Baltimore: Baltimore Museum of Art, 1975), p. 193.

46. This map case is now in the Clearwater Collection of American silver at the Metropolitan Museum of Art.

47. John Ware Willard, *Simon Willard and His Clocks*, new and rev. ed. (Mamaroneck, N.Y.: Paul P. Appel, 1962), pp. 16-17.

Chapter Four

1. A similar chair, owned by the Essex Institute and closely related to the one in figure 137, was illustrated in Clarence Cook's *The House Beautiful* (Scribner's, 1877), although the text did not mention it at all.

2. Benno M. Forman, "The Seventeenth Century Case Furniture of Essex County, Massachusetts, and its Makers" (M.A. thesis, The Winterthur Program, University of Delaware, 1968). The same author is presently completing for publication a catalogue of Winterthur Museum's seventeenth-century and William and Mary style furniture.

3. Ibid., p. 86.

4. This chest was brought to the attention of Abbott Lowell Cummings, of the Society for the Preservation of New England Antiquities, who subsequently shared its discovery with other American furniture scholars.

5. Anthony Wells-Cole, of Temple Newsam, Leeds, England, who is currently doing research on carvers working in the area of Exeter, England, has found that their work is strikingly similar to that of the Searle/Dennis school. The most important mason/carver Mr. Wells-Cole has identified to date is John Deymond, who worked in Exeter and died in the 1620s. Since Ottery St. Mary is not far from Exeter, the craftsman who did the chest might have been part of or have been influenced by the Exeter school of mason/carvers.

6. See Nina Fletcher Little, *Country Arts in Early American Homes* (New York: E. P. Dutton, 1975), p. 52, for an almost identical tape loom.

7. Robert F. Trent, "The Joiners and Joinery of Middlesex County, Massachusetts, 1630-1730," in *Arts of the Anglo-American Community in the Seventeenth Century*, Ian M. G. Quimby, 1974 Winterthur Conference Report (Charlottesville: The University Press of Virginia, 1974), p. 125.

8. Forman, p. 34.

9. Patricia E. Kane, *Furniture of the New Haven Colony, The Seventeenth Century Style* (New Haven: New Haven Colony Historical Society, 1973), p. 6.

10. Robert St. George, "A Plymouth Area Chairmaking Tradition of the Late Seventeenth Century," *The Middleborough Antiquarian* 19, no. 2 (December 1978): 3-12.

11. For a discussion of Dutch precedents see T. H. Lunsingh Sheurleer, "The Dutch and Their Homes in the Seventeenth Century," in *Arts of the Anglo-American Community in the Seventeenth Century*, ed. Ian M. G. Quimby, Winterthur Conference Report 1974 (Charlottesville: University Press of Virginia, 1975).

12. Examples of painted *kasten* can be found at Winterthur Museum, Monmouth County Historical Association, the Metropolitan Museum of Art, the Van Cortlandt Mansion, and in the Taradash Collection. The *kasten* at the first four institutions mentioned are closely related.

13. Dean F. Failey, *Long Island Is My Nation: The Decorative Arts and Craftsmen 1640-1830* (Setauket, N.Y.: Society for the Preservation of Long Island Antiquities, 1976), pp. 109-15.

14. In the near future an article by Patricia O'Donnell that discusses these painted *kasten* will be published in *Antiques* magazine. I am greatly indebted to Mrs. O'Donnell for sharing her research and observations with me and for calling my attention to the Van Cortlandt Mansion *kas*.

15. Boston is regarded as a center for American japanning, but a limited production of japanned work is known also from New York during the first quarter of the eighteenth century. Clock cases with japanning on oak seem to be the predominant New York survivors. Unquestionably this topic needs the kind of attention recently given Boston japanners.

16. John H. Hill, "The History and Technique of Japanning and the Restoration of the Pimm Highboy," *American Art Journal* 8, no. 2 (November 1976): 59-84.

17. Richard H. Randall, Jr., "William Randle, Boston Japanner," *Antiques* 105, no. 5 (May 1974): 1127-31.

18. Other examples of this form are in the collections of Colonial Williamsburg, Bayou Bend, and the Metropolitan Museum of Art.

19. I would like to thank Jane Nylander of Old Sturbridge Village for sharing with me her knowledge of female seminaries in Maine.

20. William Nathaniel Banks, "George Cooke, Painter of the American Scene," *Antiques* 102, no. 3 (September 1972): 448.

21. William Voss Elder III, *Baltimore Painted Furniture 1800-1840* (Baltimore: Baltimore Museum of Art, 1972).

22. Other notable examples of this elaborate Baltimore furniture include

two pieces at the Metropolitan Museum, a sister's cylinder secretary desk and a sideboard with knifeboxes; a lady's cabinet and writing table at Winterthur Museum; and a desk and bookcase at Gore Place, Waltham, Mass.

23. While Joseph Barry of Philadelphia used the same illustration of a dressing table on his label, his overall label was not exactly like that used by William Camp.

24. Rita Susswein Gottesman, *The Arts and Crafts in New York 1777–1799* (New York: New-York Historical Society, 1954), p. 164, no. 409.

25. Alice Knotts Bossert Cooney, "Ornamental Painting in Boston, 1790–1830" (M.A. thesis, The Winterthur Program, University of Delaware, 1978).

26. Ibid., p. 72.

27. In May 1948 this clock was sold as part of *The George M. Curtis Collection of Early American Furniture and Silver*, Parke Bernet Galleries, Catalogue 971, Lot 255. It was also illustrated in Luke V. Lockwood, *Colonial Furniture in America*, vol. 2 (1931), fig. 859.

28. John Doggett Daybook, Roxbury, Mass., 1802–9. Joseph Downs Manuscript Collection, Winterthur Museum.

29. Other related examples include a carved and gilt armchair in a private collection and a set of carved and gilt furniture in the Philadelphia Museum of Art.

30. Thomas Sheraton, *The Cabinet-Maker and Upholsterer's Drawing-Book* (1794; reprint ed., New York: Praeger, 1970), pl. 6, p. 387.

31. I am indebted to Donald L. Fennimore for this information, which is contained in an unpublished research paper in the files of Winterthur Museum.

32. Walter Muir Whitehill, ed., *Boston Furniture of the Eighteenth Century* (Boston: Colonial Society of Massachusetts, 1974), Appendix A, "Eighteenth Century Boston Furniture Craftsmen," p. 271.

33. Eleanor P. DeLorme, "James Swan's French Furniture," *Antiques* 107, no. 3 (March 1975): 452–61.

34. Robert C. Smith, "A Philadelphia Desk and Bookcase from Chippendale's *Director*," *Antiques* 103, no. 1 (January 1973): 131.

35. One of these Skillin figures is now in the Peabody Museum, Salem, Mass. See Mabel M. Swan, "A Revised Estimate of McIntire," *Antiques* 20, no. 6 (December 1931): 342–43.

36. Tom Armstrong et al., *200 Years of American Sculpture* (New York: David Godine in association with the Whitney Museum of American Art, 1976), p. 28, fig. 25.

37. Nicholas B. Wainwright, *Colonial Grandeur in Philadelphia: The House and Furniture of General John Cadwalader* (Philadelphia: Historical Society of Pennsylvania, 1964), p. 46.

38. Barbara M. Ward and Gerald W. R. Ward, "The Makers of Copley's Picture Frames: A Clue," *Old Time New England* 67, nos. 1–2 (Summer-Fall 1976): 18.

39. Mary Louise Brown, "John Welch, Carver," *Antiques* 9, no. 1 (January 1926): 28–30.

40. Ward and Ward, p. 19.

41. Israel Sack, *American Antiques from Israel Sack Collection*, vol. 3 (Washington, D.C.: Highland House, 1972), pp. 732–33.

42. Wendell D. Garrett, "The Newport Rhode Island Interior, 1780–1800" (M.A. thesis, The Winterthur Program, University of Delaware, 1957), p. 163.

43. Will of John Townsend, 1805, Wills and Inventories, Newport, R.I., March 17, 1803 to November 1, 1819, p. 600. On microfilm, Joseph Downs Manuscript Collection, Winterthur Museum.

44. Wallace B. Gusler, *Furniture of Williamsburg and Eastern Virginia 1710–1790* (Richmond: Virginia Museum, 1979), pp. 82–84, fig. 52.

45. Elizabeth Adams Rhoades, "Household Furnishings in Portsmouth, New Hampshire" (M.A. thesis, The Winterthur Program, University of Delaware, 1972), p. 41.

46. James Biddle, *American Art from American Collections* (New York: Metropolitan Museum of Art, 1963), p. 46, fig. 84.

47. Richard H. Randall, Jr., *American Furniture in the Museum of Fine Arts, Boston* (Boston: Museum of Fine Arts, 1965), frontispiece, pp. 68–70. Several years ago John T. Kirk and Albert Sack decided that they thought the legs on the Hartshorne high chest were replacements. In 1978 an X-ray examination of the piece proved that the legs had been replaced and new ones secured with dowels.

48. Dorothy E. Ellesin, "Collector's Notes," *Antiques* 107, no. 5 (May 1975): 952–53.

49. Brock W. Jobe, "The Boston Furniture Industry 1720–1740," in *Boston Furniture of the Eighteenth Century*, ed. Walter Muir Whitehill (Boston: The Colonial Society of Massachusetts, 1974), pp. 14–15.

50. *The New-York Book of Prices for Cabinet & Chair Work* (New York: Southwick & Crooker, September 1802), p. 22.

51. Martha Gandy Fales, "Heraldic and Emblematic Engravers," in *Boston Prints and Printmakers, 1670–1775* (Boston: Colonial Society of Massachusetts, 1973), pp. 185–220. This excellent article discusses engravers who were working on silver as well as other metals and begins to shed new light on the probable relationships between goldsmiths and engravers. Another fine recent study by the same author focuses on a single family of goldsmiths; see Fales, *Joseph Richardson and Family: Philadelphia Silversmiths* (Middletown, Conn.: Wesleyan University Press, 1974).

52. I would like to thank Kathryn C. Buhler for calling my attention to these salvers and for sharing with me her unpublished research on them.

53. Edward Wenham, "American XVIIIth Century Silver in England," *Connoisseur* 94 (July 1934): 16–22. Also, a beaker by Fueter, made after 1754 and not signed by the engraver, is now in the Winterthur Museum.

54. Kathryn C. Buhler and Graham Hood, *American Silver: Garvan and Other Collections in the Yale University Art Gallery*, vol. 1 (New Haven: Yale University Press, 1970), pp. 14–17, no. 9.

55. The Metropolitan Museum of Art owns one pair of Myers sticks, and their mates are in the collection of Yale University.

56. Buhler and Hood, pp. 2–3, no. 1.

57. Ibid., pp. 31–32, no. 26.

58. Donald L. Fennimore, "A True American Stuart Tankard—Maybe," *Bulletin of Pewter Collector's Club of America*, no. 74, vol. 7, no. 5 (April 1977), pp. 168–74.

59. Rita Susswein Gottesman, *The Arts and Crafts of New York 1726–76* (New York: New-York Historical Society, 1938), pp. 8–12.

60. Patricia E. Kane and Edwin A. Battison, *The American Clock 1725–1865* (Greenwich, Conn.: New York Graphic Society, 1973), pp. 34–41.

61. I would like to thank Ms. Arlene Palmer, Winterthur Museum, for sharing with me her research on glass engravers in America.

62. One tumbler, privately owned, may be an example; it is engraved "Margareta / Wistar in / 1751." For an illustration see Arlene M. Palmer, "Glass Production in Eighteenth-Century America: The Wistarburgh Enterprise," in *Winterthur Portfolio 11*, ed. Ian M. G. Quimby (Charlottesville: The University Press of Virginia, 1976), figs. 25 and 27, p. 97.

63. *Journal of Glass Studies* 18: 18.

64. I wish to thank Arlene Palmer for sharing with me this unpublished research on Lazarus Isaac.

65. *The Pennsylvania Packet*, December 1, 1796, advertisement of John Moss. I am indebted to Arlene M. Palmer for this information.

66. *Richmond Enquirer*, November 10, 1818. Again, I thank Ms. Palmer for this information.

67. Karol A. Schmiegel, "Tokens of Friendship," *Antiques* 115, no. 2 (February 1979): 367–69.

68. Arlene M. Palmer, "American Heroes in Glass: The Bakewell Sulfide Portraits," *American Art Journal* 11, no. 1 (January 1979): 4–26.

Chapter Five

1. John T. Kirk, *American Chairs: Queen Anne and Chippendale* (New York: Alfred A. Knopf, 1972), Appendix.

2. For a closer study of John Fanning Watson see Deborah L. Dependahl, "John Fanning Watson, Historian 1779–1860" (M.A. thesis, The Winterthur Program, University of Delaware, 1971).

3. See n. 9, Introduction.

4. Joseph Downs and Ruth Ralston, *A Loan Exhibition of New York State Furniture with Contemporary Accessories* (New York: Metropolitan Museum of Art, 1934).

5. Louis G. Myers, "Queen Anne Chairs of Colonial Days," *Antiques* 22, no. 6 (December 1932): 213–17.

6. Currently in preparation by Joseph K. Ott is an article on the importation of mahogany with emphasis on Rhode Island trade.

7. The only exception known to the author is the desk and bookcase formerly owned by the Lyle family and now in the collections of The Rhode Island School of Design Museum. While it was not labeled or signed contemporaneously with its making, in 1813 it was repaired by Thomas Goddard and presumably at that time signed "Made by John Goddard/ 1761 and Reapered by/ Thomas Goddard 1813/ . . ." See Hedy B. Landman, "The Pendleton House at the Museum of Art, Rhode Island School of Design," *Antiques* 107, no. 5 (May 1975): 934.

8. Wendy A. Cooper, "The Furniture and Furnishings of John Brown, Merchant of Providence, 1736–1803" (M.A. thesis, The Winterthur Program, University of Delaware, 1971), p. 26.

9. *Paul Revere's Boston: 1735–1818* (Boston: Museum of Fine Arts, 1975), p. 44, fig. 49.

10. Robert C. Smith, "Final Busts on Eighteenth-Century Philadelphia Furniture," *Antiques* 100, no. 12 (December 1971): 900–905.

11. Charles F. Hummel, "The Influence of English Design Books Upon the Philadelphia Cabinetmaker" (M.A. thesis, The Winterthur Program, University of Delaware, 1955).

12. This high chest of drawers is now in the collection of Colonial Williamsburg.

13. David Stockwell, "Aesop's Fables on Philadelphia Furniture," *Antiques* 60, no. 6 (December 1951): 522–25.

14. Hummel, p. 74.

15. This seems to be a general rule, although an exception to it can be found in the two known great bookcases from Charleston. While the one presently owned by MESDA in Winston-Salem, N.C., was inspired by a plate in Chippendale's *Director*, the other, owned by the Charleston Museum and in the Heyward-Washington House, seems unlike any produced in either England or America. For an illustration see E. Milby Burton, *Charleston Furniture 1700–1825* (Columbia, S.C.: University of South Carolina Press, 1955), frontispiece.

16. Cooper, p. 26.

17. Another Newport corner chair of equal eminence is illustrated in Ralph E. Carpenter, Jr., *The Arts and Crafts of Newport, Rhode Island 1640–1820* (Newport, R.I.: Preservation Society of Newport County, 1954), p. 46, fig. 20, and is now privately owned.

18. I am indebted to Benno M. Forman for sharing his insights with me regarding not only this piece of furniture but also furniture craftsmen in Boston during the seventeenth century.

19. Benno M. Forman, "Urban Aspects of Massachusetts Furniture in the Late Seventeenth Century," in *Country Cabinetwork and Simple City Furniture*, ed. John D. Morse, Winterthur Conference Report 1969 (Charlottesville: University Press of Virginia, 1970), p. 8.

20. Benno M. Forman, "The Seventeenth Century Case Furniture of Essex County, Massachusetts, and its Makers" (M.A. thesis, The Winterthur Program, University of Delaware, 1968), pp. 118–19.

21. Louisa Dresser, "The Background of Colonial American Portraiture," in *Proceedings of the American Antiquarian Society* 76, pt. 1: 28 (Worcester, Mass., 1966); Samuel M. Green, "English Origins of 17th Century Painting in New England," in *American Painting to 1776—A Reappraisal*, ed. Ian M. G. Quimby, 1971, Winterthur Conference Report (Charlottesville: University Press of Virginia), pp. 15–70.

22. Graham S. Hood, *Charles Bridges and William Dering* (Williamsburg: Colonial Williamsburg Foundation, 1978).

23. Ibid., p. 97.

24. Francis Brinley Probate Inventory, Suffolk County Probate Records, vol. 65, docket 13839, pp. 269–73.

25. I wish to thank Nancy Goyne Evans for sharing her ideas and unpublished research on windsor furniture. See also Nancy Goyne Evans, "A History and Background of English Windsor Furniture," *Furniture History: The Journal of The Furniture History Society* 14, 1979.

26. Ralph Edwards, *English Chairs* (London: Her Majesty's Stationery Office, 1970), intro., fig. 67.

27. David B. Warren, *Bayou Bend: American Furniture, Paintings and Silver from the Bayou Bend Collection* (Houston: Museum of Fine Arts, 1973), p. 134, fig. 251.

28. One superb example of this larger form with original needlework top was originally owned by Mercy Otis Warren and is now in the collection of the Pilgrim Society, Plymouth, Massachusetts. (See *Paul Revere's Boston*, p. 82, fig. 95.) Another was originally in the Faneuil family of Boston and is now in the Bayou Bend Collection, see Warren, pp. 30–31, fig. 57.

29. Morrison H. Heckscher, "The New York Serpentine Card Table," *Antiques* 103, no. 3 (May 1973): 974–83.

30. *Philadelphia, Three Centuries of American Art* (Philadelphia: Philadelphia Museum of Art, 1976), pp. 115–16, figs. 91a and 91b.

31. Five of these so-called turret-top (not a contemporary term in the eighteenth century) tea tables are known to the author today—two at the Museum of Fine Arts, Boston, one at Historic Deerfield, one at the Winterthur Museum, and one in the Bayou Bend Collection.

32. Israel Sack, *American Antiques from Israel Sack Collection*, vol. 3, brochure 19, November 1970 (Washington, D.C.: Highland House, 1972), P3225, p. 710.

33. The only known, labeled piece of Thomas Townsend furniture is a chest-on-chest that bears the name "Nicholas Easton" inscribed on the top board of the lower case. See Dean F. Failey, *Long Island Is My Nation: The Decorative Arts and Craftsmen 1640–1830* (Setauket, N.Y.: Society for the Preservation of Long Island Antiquities, 1976), p. 162, fig. 188.

34. Kathryn C. Buhler and Graham S. Hood, *American Silver: Garvan and Other Collections in the Yale University Art Gallery*, vol. 2 (New Haven: Yale University Press, 1970), pp. 394–95, nos. 344 and 345.

35. Ibid., pp. 395–96, no. 346.

36. The Frank family of Philadelphia owned some superb English rococo silver in the eighteenth century. One grand piece, a bowl by the London goldsmith Paul de Lamerie, is now in the collection of the Metropolitan Museum of Art.

37. Of these four unusual teapots by Jacob Hurd, two are at Yale, one at Bayou Bend, and one at the Cleveland Museum, as illustrated.

38. Hollis French, *Jacob Hurd and His Sons, Nathaniel and Benjamin, Silversmiths, 1702–1781* (Cambridge, Mass.: Riverside Press, 1939), pp. 37–38.

39. For example, a marvelous caster by Gerrit Onckelbag, which is now in the collection of Mrs. Edsel Ford of Detroit, has a gadrooned foot and acanthus leaf banding. See Graham S. Hood, *American Silver: A History of Style, 1650–1900* (New York: Praeger, 1971), p. 87, fig. 79.

40. Joseph K. Ott, "Rhode Island Furniture Exports 1783–1800, Including Information on Chaises, Buildings, Other Woodenware and Trade Practices," *Rhode Island History* 36, no. 1 (February 1977): 3–13.

41. Nancy Goyne Evans, "The Genealogy of a Bookcase Desk," *Winterthur Portfolio 9* (Charlottesville: University Press of Virginia, 1974), pp. 213–22.

42. The survival of original veneer on the top of this early dressing table is most remarkable, though there is some minor restoration in the central portion.

43. Nancy Goyne, "The Bureau Table in America," *Winterthur Portfolio 3* (Charlottesville: University Press of Virginia, 1967), pp. 24–36.

44. Brock W. Jobe, "The Boston Furniture Industry, 1720–1740," in *Boston Furniture of the Eighteenth Century*, ed. Walter Muir Whitehill (Boston: The Colonial Society of Massachusetts, 1974), p. 20.

45. I would like to thank Stuart Feld for calling my attention to these paintings and Marie Elwood of the Nova Scotia Museum for sharing her research with me, and also for her cooperation and helpfulness.

46. I wish to thank Dean F. Failey for sharing with me his research on this painting.

47. The daybooks of Paul Revere kept between 1761 and 1797, along with other Revere family papers, are in the Massachusetts Historical Society. John Templeman's order was recorded on April 17, 1792, p. 119.

48. This price book is now in the collections of the Greenville County Library, Greenville, South Carolina. I wish to thank Bradford Rauschenberg for sharing with me his information about Walker and this extraordinary survival of a cabinetmaker's price book.

49. Burton, p. 125.

50. Jessie J. Poesch, "Early Louisiana *Armoires*," *Antiques* 94, no. 2 (August 1968): 196–205. And Jessie J. Poesch, *Early Furniture of Louisiana* (New Orleans: Louisiana State Museum, 1972).

51. Cooper, p. 125.

Chapter Six

1. Robert E. P. Hendricks, "John Gaines II and Thomas Gaines I, 'Turners' of Ipswich, Massachusetts" (M.A. thesis, The Winterthur Program, University of Delaware, 1960). Using the Gaines account book as a basis, this thesis presents a detailed analysis of the variety of work being carried on by these craftsmen.

2. Stephen Decatur, "John and George Gaines of Portsmouth," *American Collector* 7, no. 10 (November 1938): 6–7.

3. Ibid. As early as 1858 Charles Warren Brewster wrote about these chairs in his *Rambles about Portsmouth*.

4. Two other closely related armchairs can be found in the collections of the Metropolitan Museum of Art and Winterthur Museum.

5. Esther Singleton, *The Furniture of Our Forefathers* (1900–1901; reprint ed., New York: Benjamin Blow, 1970), p. 331.

6. Walter Muir Whitehill, ed., *Boston Furniture of the Eighteenth Century* (Boston: Colonial Society of Massachusetts, 1974), pp. 98–100, fig. 68.

7. Two other similarly decorated and well-known pieces of furniture are

Hannah Barnard's press cupboard at the Henry Ford Museum, Dearborn, Michigan, and a four-drawer chest of drawers at Winterthur Museum.

8. Michael K. Brown, "A Study of Scallop-Top Furniture from the Connecticut River Valley" (research paper, Historic Deerfield Summer Fellowship Program, 1974).

9. Another closely related high chest of drawers is in the collection of the Henry Ford Museum and was exhibited in 1976 at Yale University and the Victoria and Albert Museum, London. See Charles F. Montgomery and Patricia E. Kane, eds., *American Art: 1750–1800 Towards Independence* (Boston: New York Graphic Society, 1976), pp. 160–61, fig. 112.

10. Lester J. Cappon, *The Atlas of Early American History, The Revolutionary Era, 1760–1790* (Princeton: Princeton University Press, 1976), p. 97.

11. Minor Myers supports the conclusion that Abishai Woodward (1752–1809) of Preston and New London actually did make the case. See Minor Myers, Jr., *New London County Furniture 1640–1840* (New London: Lyman Allyn Museum, 1974), no. 46, pp. 57 and 130.

12. Patricia E. Kane, *Furniture of the New Haven Colony, The Seventeenth Century Style* (New Haven: New Haven Colony Historical Society, 1973), pp. 6–11.

13. The Wadsworth Atheneum, Hartford, Connecticut, and the Connecticut Historical Society both have closely related armchairs in their collections. However, the one at the Atheneum is made of mahogany, and the other two are of cherry.

14. Patricia E. Kane, *300 Years of American Seating Furniture* (Boston: New York Graphic Society, 1976), nos. 117–19, pp. 138–42.

15. Kathryn C. Buhler, "Samuel Casey's Apprenticeship," *Museum of Fine Arts, Boston, Bulletin* 37, no. 226 (1940): 33–35.

16. William Davis Miller, *The Silversmiths of Little Rest* (Boston: Merrymount Press, 1928), p. 4.

17. For an illustration of the house from which this *kas* came see Rosalie Fellows Bailey, *Pre-Revolutionary Dutch Houses* (1936; reprint ed., New York: Dover, 1968), pp. 203–4, pl. 56.

18. Mary C. Black, "Pieter Vanderlyn and Other Limners of the Upper Hudson," in *American Painting to 1776: A Reappraisal*, ed. Ian M. G. Quimby, Winterthur Conference Report 1971 (Charlottesville: University Press of Virginia, 1971), pp. 217–50.

19. Dean F. Failey, *Long Island Is My Nation: The Decorative Arts and Craftsmen 1640–1830* (Setauket, N.Y.: Society for the Preservation of Long Island Antiquities, 1976).

20. For a more detailed account of the work of Elias Pelletreau see Dean F. Failey, "Elias Pelletreau, Long Island Silversmith" (M.A. thesis, The Winterthur Program, University of Delaware, 1971).

21. Charles F. Hummel, *With Hammer in Hand: The Dominy Craftsmen of East Hampton, New York* (Charlottesville: University Press of Virginia, 1968).

22. Ibid., p. 5.

23. Ibid.

24. *Early Furniture Made in New Jersey* (Newark, N.J.: Newark Museum, 1958), pp. 40–89.

25. John T. Snyder, Jr., "A Study of Lancaster County Clock Cases," in *Clockmakers of Lancaster County and Their Clocks 1750–1850*, ed. Stacy B. C. Wood, Jr., and Stephen B. Kramer III (New York: Van Nostrand Reinhold, 1977), pp. 31–67.

26. Vivian S. Gerstell, *Silversmiths of Lancaster, Pennsylvania 1730–1850* (Lancaster: Lancaster County Historical society, 1972), p. 44.

27. Ibid., p. 1.

28. It should also be noted that Reese is a Welsh name; Benno M. Forman has recently theorized that some Chester County furniture may be derived from Welsh or West England precedents.

29. Margaret Berwind Schiffer, *Furniture and Its Makers of Chester County Pennsylvania* (Philadelphia: University of Pennsylvania Press, 1966), pp. 265–66.

30. John Bivins, Jr., *The Moravian Potters in North Carolina* (Chapel Hill: University of North Carolina Press, 1972), p. 224, fig. 233 and pl. opposite p. 242.

31. Ibid., pp. 7–14.

32. Wallace B. Gusler, *Furniture of Williamsburg and Eastern Virginia 1710–1790* (Richmond: Virginia Museum, 1979), p. 22–23, fig. 15.

33. In 1978 the Virginia Museum of Fine Arts, Richmond, received National Endowment for the Humanities Planning Grant to hold two conferences to explore organizing a major research project on Southern painting from the seventeenth century to the present. Pending future finding, the museum proposes a project which would result in a comprehensive catalogue and exhibition in 1983–84.

34. Wayne Craven, "Painting in New York City," in *American Painting to 1776: A Reappraisal*, ed. Ian M. G. Quimby, Winterthur Conference Report 1971 (Charlottesville: University of Virginia Press, 1971), pp. 281–87.

35. Marilyn A. Johnson, "John Hewitt," in *Winterthur Portfolio 4* (Charlottesville: University Press of Virginia, 1968), p. 186.

36. See n. 48, chap. 5.

Chapter Seven

1. Graham Hood of Colonial Williamsburg has recently been researching the papers and inventory of Lord Botetourt, the last royal governor of Virginia. One significant discovery of his has been the importation of an iron plate stove with Adamesque motifs to Williamsburg from England in 1771.

2. In Boston, by the 1780s, the Whipple family owned an English silver urn made in London by John Schofield in 1786, and it is possible that this piece of imported silver served as a model for presentation urns made by Paul Revere and other Boston goldsmiths.

3. Bayard Tuckerman, ed., *The Diary of Philip Hone, 1828–1851*, vol. 1 (New York: Dodd, Mead, 1889), pp. 13–14.

4. Frank H. Goodyear, Jr., *Thomas Doughty 1793–1856: An American Pioneer in Landscape Painting* (Philadelphia: Pennsylvania Academy of the Fine Arts, 1973), p. 15.

5. John Wilmerding, *A History of American Marine Painting* (Boston: Little, Brown, 1968), p. 106.

6. A. Hyatt Mayor and Mark Davis, *American Art at the Century Club* (New York: Century Association, 1977), p. 2.

7. Marius Schoonmaker, *John Vanderlyn Artist, 1775–1852: Biography* (Kingston, New York: Senate House Association, 1950), p. 26.

8. Eleanor P. Delorme, "James Swan's French Furniture," *Antiques* 107, no. 3 (March 1975): 452–61.

9. *The White House: An Historic Guide* (Washington, D.C.: 1963), p. 76.

10. Page E. Talbott, "Boston Empire Furniture, Part I," *Antiques* 107, no. 5 (May 1975): 879, fig. 3.

11. Robert C. Smith, "The Furniture of Anthony G. Quervelle, Part I: The Pier Tables," *Antiques* 103, no. 5 (May 1973): 992, pl. 3.

12. Two other examples of this form are in the collections of the White House and the Metropolitan Museum.

13. Talbott, p. 881 and pl. 3, fig. 10.

14. A billhead of the Boston cabinetmaker and upholsterer William Hancock, now in the collections of the American Antiquarian Society, Worcester, Massachusetts, illustrates a "Grecian couch" and notes one on the bill.

15. George Smith, *A Collection of Designs for Household Furniture* (1808; reprint ed., New York: Praeger, 1970), pl. 64.

16. Duncan Phyfe's own copy of the *1810 New-York Revised Prices for Manufacturing Cabinet and Chair Work* is in the Joseph Downs Manuscript Collection of the Winterthur Museum Libraries.

17. Marilynn A. Johnson, "John Hewitt," in *Winterthur Portfolio 4* (Charlottesville: University Press of Virginia, 1968), p. 187.

18. George Smith, pl. 46, 55, 91, & 115.

19. Page E. Talbott, "Boston Empire Furniture, Part II," *Antiques* 109, no. 5 (May 1976): 1004–13, figs. 16, 16a, and 17.

20. Wendy A. Cooper, "The Furniture and Furnishings of John Brown, Merchant of Providence, 1736–1803" (M.A. thesis, The Winterthur Program, University of Delaware, 1971), p. 131.

21. Rita Susswein Gottesman, *The Arts and Crafts in New York 1800–1804* (New York: New-York Historical Society, 1965), pp. 165–66.

22. Smith, p. 25.

23. Michael Clayton, *The Collector's Dictionary of Silver and Gold* (New York: World, 1971), pp. 192 and 197.

24. Eric Delieb, *Mathew Boulton: Master Silversmith, 1760–1790* (New York: Clarkson N. Potter, 1971), pp. 71–72.

25. *The New-York Revised Prices For Manufacturing Cabinet and Chair Work* (New York: Southwick and Pelsue, 1810), p. 7.

26. Thomas Sheraton, *The Cabinet-Maker and Upholsterer's Drawing-Book* (1791–94; reprint ed., New York: Praeger, 1970), pl. 38, pp. 390–91.

27. Charles F. Montgomery, *American Furniture: The Federal Period* (New York: Viking, 1966), pp. 369–70.

Acknowledgments

The generous and unselfish devotion of numerous collectors, dealers, and professional colleagues has made the publication of this book possible. From the initial concept, through the development of overall theme and final selection processes, the constant support and assistance of many outstanding individuals have made this volume a reality. In 1974, the original idea of an exhibition and publication to celebrate the 1929 Girl Scouts Loan Exhibition was proposed by Mrs. Harold L. Frank, a member of the National Board of Girl Scouts of the United States of America. With the assistance of Harold Sack, Mrs. Frank assembled a distinguished committee which guided the project and resulting publication. For her relentless faith and perseverance, I extend immeasurable thanks to Mrs. Frank; her co-chairmen, Mrs. Robert L. McNeil, Jr., and Eric M. Wunsch; and the committee, Clement E. Conger, Lawrence Fleischman, Wendell D. Garrett, Joseph H. Hennage, Graham S. Hood, Charles F. Hummel, Julie Kammerer, the late Charles F. Montgomery, Jules D. Prown, Harold Sack, and Berry Tracy. I would like to add an extra note of thanks to Messrs. Hummel, Hood, Tracy, and Sack who in addition to committee participation served as close advisors and critics in the selection of objects as well as on matters of scholarship. I extend special thanks to Dori Parker and Helen Lee from Girl Scouts of the United States of America, for all their hard work. And special recognition must go to the generosity of Jonathan L. Fairbanks, Curator of American Decorative Arts and Sculpture, Museum of Fine Arts, Boston, who not only supported the project, but also allowed me to take a two-year leave of absence from the museum to prepare the exhibition and this publication.

A major contribution from the Ford Motor Company Fund has helped to finance the research and writing of this book, and for that generosity I wish to sincerely thank both Mr. Ray C. Kooi, Director of the Ford Motor Company Fund, and Mr. Philip Caldwell, President of the Ford Motor Company. In addition to this grant, the kind contributions of Dick Button, Lawrence Fleischman, Mr. and Mrs. Harold L. Frank, Joseph H. Hennage, Mrs. Robert L. McNeil, Jr., Harold Sack, and Eric M. Wunsch have also added enormously to this undertaking from beginning to end.

For assistance in locating objects, sharing and suggesting research resources, and supplying various and sundry bits of data, I sincerely thank and recognize the following colleagues: The Reverend James Kenneth Allen, First Parish Church of Dorchester; Louise Ambler, Fogg Art Museum; Mrs. Jeannette Jones Balling; William Nathaniel Banks; Michael Birdsall, Minneapolis Institute of Art; Roderic Blackburn, Albany Institute of History and Art; Russell Blanchard, Paul Revere Insurance Company; Nicholas Bragg, Reynolda House; Fenton L. B. Brown; Michael K. Brown, Museum of Fine Arts, Boston; Mrs. Yves Henry Buhler, Museum of Fine Arts, Boston; Arthur W. Campbell, Fredericksburg Lodge No. 4, A.F. & A.M.; Mr. and Mrs. Charles H. Carpenter, Jr.; Ralph E. Carpenter, Christie, Manson and Woods, Inc.; Mary Jane Clark, Dartmouth College Museum; John Cherol, Preservation Society of Newport County; Margaret B. Clunie, Bowdoin College Museum of Art; The Reverend Edwin Coleman, St. Michael's Church, Charleston; Carl L. Crossman, Childs Gallery, Boston; David Curry, Yale University; Phillip H. Curtis, Newark Museum; H. Ray Dennis; Richard Dietrich; Charles Dorman, Independence National Historic Site; Allison Eckhardt, *Antiques* magazine; William Voss Elder, III, Baltimore Museum of Art; Marie Elwood, Nova Scotia Museum; Nancy Goyne Evans, Winterthur Museum; Dean F. Failey, Christie, Manson and Woods, Inc.; Dean and Martha Fales; Ann Farnam, Essex Institute; Katharine Gross Farnham, The High Museum; Stuart P. Feld, Hirschl and Adler; Donald L. Fennimore, Winterthur Museum; Benno M. Forman, Winterthur Museum; Donald R. Friary, Historic Deerfield; Alexandra Rollins Garfield; Beatrice Garvan, Philadelphia Museum of Art; James L. Garvin, New Hampshire Historical Society; Averill D. Geus, Home Sweet Home, Easthampton, New York; Anne Golovin, Smithsonian Institution; Frank H. Goodyear, Jr., Pennsylvania Academy of the Fine Arts; Donald Gormley, New York City Hall; Mr. and Mrs. Christopher L. Granger; Henry D. Green; Barry A. Greenlaw, Bayou Bend Collection, Houston; Frances Gruber Safford, Metropolitan Museum; Wallace B. Gusler, Colonial Williamsburg; Philip Hamerslough, Jr.; Charles A. Hammond, Gore Place Society; Kathy Headberg, Minneapolis Institute of Art; Morrison H. Heckscher, Metropolitan Museum; Donald G. Herold, Charleston Museum; Dale Herman; Mrs. Eleanor Hunnewell, Gore Place Society; Louise Hale, College of William and Mary; Pamela T. Hodgkins, Historic Deerfield; Mark Hollander; Frank L. Horton, Museum of Early Southern Decorative Arts; D. Roger Howlett, Childs Gallery, Boston; Mrs. Margaret Hubbard, Franklin D. Roosevelt Museum and Library; Brock W. Jobe, Society for the Preservation of New England Antiquities; Mr. and Mrs. Edward C. Johnson, III; William L. Johnson; Philip M. Johnston, Wadsworth Atheneum; Edward V. Jones; J. Kenneth Jones, Charleston Museum; Karen Jones, *Antiques* magazine; Mr. and Mrs. J. Howard Joynt; Ronald Kane; Patricia E. Kane, Yale University Art Gallery; Mr. and Mrs. George Kaufmann; Dorothy Kemper, de Young Museum; Peter Kent, Newport Restoration Foundation; Mr. and Mrs. Edward A. Kilroy; Mr. William Kilroy; Joe Kindig III; John T. Kirk, Boston University; Albert T. Klyberg, Rhode Island Historical Society; Dwight Lanmon, Corning Museum; Ann LeVeque, Rhode Island Historical Society; Mrs. Everell M. Le Baron; Bernard and S. Dean Levy; Dr. Jane Lockwood; Laura Luckey, Museum of Fine Arts, Boston; Mr. and Mrs. Morgan MacWhinnie; David Revere McFadden, Cooper-Hewitt Museum; Robert L. McNeil, Jr.; Peter Manigault; Mr. and Mrs. Chester Mehurin; Susan Meyers, Smithsonian Institution; John C. Milley, Independence National Historic Site; Christopher Monkhouse, Rhode·Island School of Design Museum; Florence Montgomery; Margaret Moody, Dartmouth College Museum; Dr. R. Peter Mooz, Virginia Museum of Fine Arts; Mrs. Donald Mullins; Milo M. Naeve, Chicago Art Institute; Christina H. Nelson, Henry Ford Museum; Timothy C. Neumann, Pocumtuck Valley Memorial Association; Jane Nylander, Sturbridge Village; Richard Nylander, Society for the Preservation of New England Antiquities; Patricia O'Donnell, Philadelphia College of Textiles and Sciences Museum; Mr. and Mrs Joseph K. Ott; Arlene Palmer, Winterthur Museum; Donald C. Peirce, Brooklyn Museum; Dianne Pilgrim, Brooklyn Museum; Jessie J. Poesch, Sophie Newcomb College; Robert Porter, Van Cortlandt Mansion; Sumpter T. Priddy III, Colonial Williamsburg; Bradford Rauschenberg, Museum of Early Southern Decorative Arts; Dagmar Reutlinger, Worcester Art Museum; Nancy Richards, National Trust for Historic Preservation; Norman S. Rice, Albany Institute of History and Art; Nancy Rivard, Detroit Institute of Arts; Rodris Roth, Smithsonian Institution; Edward B. Russell, U.S. Army Engineer Museum, Fort Belvoir; Albert Sack, Donald Sack and Robert Sack; Charles and Olenka Santore; Stanley Sax; Karol A. Schmiegel, Winterthur Museum; Mr. and Mrs. Irvin Schorsch; Marvin Schwartz, Metropolitan Museum; Jan Seidler, Museum of Fine Arts, Boston; Martha Severens, Gibbes Art Gallery, Charleston; Raymond V. Shepherd, Jr., Cliveden, Philadelphia, Pa.; Deborah Shinn; Romaine Somerville, Maryland Historical Society; J. Peter Spang, III, Historic Deerfield; Lynn Springer, St. Louis Art Museum; Margaret Stearns, Museum of the City of New York: Theodore E. Stebbins, Jr., Museum of Fine Arts, Boston; William W. Stahl, Sotheby Parke Bernet, Inc.; Kevin Stanton, Yale University; Robert St. George, University of Pennsylvania; Garrison and Diana Stradling; Mrs. P. Gordon Stillman, National Society of Colonial Dames in the State of New York; Mr. and Mrs. Edward L. Stone; Charles V. Swain; Joseph Tarica, Congregation Shearith Israel, New York; Neville Thompson and the staff of the Winterthur Libraries; Robert F. Trent, Museum of Fine Arts, Boston; Jane Van Nostrand Turano, American Art Journal; The Reverend James A. Trimble, Christ Church, Philadelphia; Mr. and Mrs. Frederick Vogel III; John and Mary Walton; Barbara and Gerald Ward, Yale University Art Gallery; Mrs. Edward R. Wardwell; David B. Warren, Houston Museum of Fine Arts; Mrs. Northam Warren; Rebecca D. Warren; Deborah D. Waters, Winterthur Museum; Dr. Katharine Watson, Bowdoin College Museum of Art; Melvin Watts, Currier Gallery; Carolyn J. Weekley, Abby Aldrich Rockefeller Folk Art Collection; Gregory Weideman, Maryland Historical Society; Paula Welshimer, Old Salem; Alice Winchester; Miss Elizabeth Morris Wistar.

The organization and research of a manuscript requires a team of devoted specialists, and for their ceaseless efforts I thank my research and manuscript assistants Elisabeth Kaplan Boas, Jane Desmond Crawford, and Wendy Kaplan. For new and outstanding photographs, Richard Cheek must be thanked. And for enduring the task of typing and proofreading the manuscript I thank Freida Place, Walter Spencer, Norman Herreshoff, and especially Kathryn Buhler. But above all my utmost gratitude goes to Anthony Schulte and Jane Garrett at Alfred A. Knopf; Jane has stalwartly shepherded this publication through its various stages, along with her colleagues, Katherine Hourigan, Ellen McNeilly, Carole Frankel, John Woodside, and Janet Odgis, who have worked with enthusiasm and determination.

Finally, the generous support of J. Carter Brown, Director of the National Gallery of Art, has provided an appropriate and splendid opportunity for the presentation of this volume—the first exhibition of American decorative arts ever to occur at the National Gallery. Like the 1929 Exhibition in New York, this show in Washington is also a landmark in several respects. Not only is it a first, but it is also a summation of the major developments in the growth of knowledge in this field over the past fifty years. To Mr. Brown and his staff I owe special gratitude, and thank John Wilmerding, Senior Curator of the National Gallery for

his guidance and support, and Linda Ayres, Assistant Curator of American Art, for her infinite organization and assistance. Gil Ravenel and his design staff must be commended for their excellent installation, and Frances Smyth for her support of the Gallery Guide.

In concluding, my very personal thanks go to my parents who have sincerely supported me in this venture, and to Bill who encouraged me always with tremendous understanding and objectivity.

Wendy A. Cooper

Photo Credits

Joe Adams: 263
Allentown Art Museum Collection: Plate 1
Arden Photographers and the Newark Museum: 112, 264
E. Irving Blomstrann: 168, 169
Edward A. Bourden: 217
Courtesy of The Brooklyn Museum: 62, 67, 114, 142, 144
George Henderson Brown Photo Lab: 28, 30
Will Brown: 259; Plates 13, 31
Will Brown, courtesy of The Dietrich Fine Arts Collections: 52, 179, 280
Carolina Art Association, Gibbes Art Gallery: Plate 47
City Hall, Charleston, S.C.: Plate 21
Richard Cheek: 6, 12, 14, 15, 21, 24, 25, 29, 44, 48, 59, 68, 75, 76, 84, 85, 89, 94, 95, 96, 97, 99, 100, 102, 109, 113, 116, 120, 123, 126, 129, 130, 132, 133, 136, 137, 138, 139, 140, 146, 147, 149, 150, 153, 155, 156, 159, 161, 163, 164, 166, 174, 182, 192, 193, 194, 204, 206, 212, 215, 216, 219, 233, 236, 239, 240, 243, 244, 246, 250, 261, 275, 276, 278, 287, 295, 296, 298, 301, 304, 305; Plates 5, 6, 8, 11, 12, 22, 25, 26, 27, 28, 29, 39, 40, 47, 48, 49, 52
Richard Cheek for The Metropolitan Museum of Art: 83, 86, 157; Plates 3, 30
Chester County Historical Society: 270
Cleveland Museum of Art: 226
College of William and Mary: 195
Colonial Williamsburg: 32, 60, 72, 91, 121, 122, 180, 203, 213
Colonial Williamsburg / Delmore A. Wenzel: 63, 88, 211, 274
Colonial Williamsburg / Hans E. Lorenz: 92
The Corning Museum of Glass: 58
Joseph Crilley, courtesy of New Jersey State Museum: 65
George M. Cushing Photography: 34
Dartmouth College Museum and Galleries: 107; Plate 17
Detroit Institute of Arts: Plate 41
Barry Donahue: 198
Richard P. Eells: 80, 207
Bill Finney: 81, 245
George Fistrovich: 37, 125, 200, 202, 253
Courtesy of the Henry Ford Museum: 267
Girl Scouts of the U.S.A. (Lawrence X. Champeau): 1, 2, 3, 4, 5, 7, 8, 9, 10
Harvard University Portrait Collection: 108, 110, 111
Helga Photo Studio, Inc.: 26, 27, 77, 104, 106, 141, 188, 241, 284, 292, 293, 302; Plates 19, 24, 51
Helga Photo Studio, Inc., courtesy of Bernard and S. Dean Levy: 260
Helga Photo Studio, Inc., courtesy of Ginsburg and Levy, Inc.: 290
Historical Society of Pennsylvania: 53, 279
Historical Society of Western Pennsylvania: 66
Home Sweet Home Museum: 251

Maddox Studio: 172, 173
Maryland Historical Society, Baltimore: 74, 145, 288, 307
R. E. Merrick Media Sources: Plates 35, 36
The Metropolitan Museum of Art: 105, 124, 134, 165, 170, 187, 196, 197, 199, 286; Plate 4
Allen Mewbourn: 209
Meyers Studio, Inc.: 103, 237
The Minneapolis Institute of Arts: 223, 262; Plate 37
Courtesy, Museum of Fine Arts, Boston: 33 (© 1978), 41 (© 1979), 61 (© 1978), 73, 98, 101 (© 1979), 131 (© 1979), 167 (© 1979), 186 (© 1979), 191 (© 1979), 227, 247 (© 1979), 248 (© 1979), 257, 258; Plates 9, 10, 14, 15 (© 1979), 46 (© 1979), 50
Museum of Fine Arts, Houston, Bayou Bend Collection: 189, 235; Plate 34
Museum of the City of New York: 93, 221
National Galley of Art: Plate 2
National Portrait Gallery, Smithsonian Institution: 128
O. E. Nelson: 190
The Newark Museum: Plate 42
New York Public Library: 69 (© Title 17, U.S. Code)
Pennsylvania Academy of the Fine Arts: 90, 282, 283
Philadelphia Museum of Art: 70, 220, 224, 225, 277; Plate 43
Mike Posey: Plate 38
Bradford Rauschenberg: 115, 135, 185, 222, 230, 242, 272, 273; Plate 45
Reynolda House, Inc.: Plate 33
Museum of Art, Rhode Island School of Design: 201, 218
Courtesy of Israel Sack, Inc.: 16, 17, 19, 20, 22, 23, 35, 36, 79, 87, 162, 181, 210, 214, 229, 231, 232, 238, 249, 252, 268, 269, 294, 303
Courtesy of the Shelburne Museum: Plate 23
Courtesy of Sotheby Parke Bernet, Inc.: 64(© 1978), 175
William F. Stickle, courtesy of the Franklin Delano Roosevelt Library: Plate 16
Joseph Szaszfai, courtesy of Yale University Galley of Art: 154
Robert Hinds for the U.S. Army Engineer Museum: 45
Virginia Museum: 158, 265
White House Collection: Plate 20
Courtesy, The Henry Francis Du Pont Wintherthur Museum: 11, 13 (© 1979), 18, 31, 38, 39 (© 1977), 40, 42, 43, 46, 47, 49 (© 1979), 50, 51, 54 (Decorative Arts Photographic Collection), 55, 56, 57, 71, 78, 117, 118, 143, 148, 151 (© 1957), 152 (©1979), 160, 171, 176, 177 (© 1979), 184, 208 (© 1979), 255, 266, 271, 281, 285 (© 1979), 289 (© 1979), 291 (© 1979), 297 (© 1979), 299, 300, 306 (© 1979), 308 (© 1979); Plates 7, 18, 32 (© 1976), 44
Worcester Art Museum: 82
Yale University Art Gallery: 127, 183, 205, 228, 234, 254, 256

Index